A Handbook for Teacher Research

A Handbook for Teacher Research: from design to implementation

COLIN LANKSHEAR and **MICHELE KNOBEL**

Open University Press

Open University Press
McGraw-Hill Education
McGraw-Hill House
Shoppenhangers Road
Maidenhead
Berkshire
England
SL6 2QL

email: enquiries@openup.co.uk
world wide web: www.openup.co.uk

and Two Penn Plaza, New York, NY 10121-2289, USA

First published 2004

A catalogue record of this book is available from the British Library

ISBN 0335210643 (pb)   0335210651 (hb)

Library of Congress Cataloging-in-Publication Data
CIP data applied for

Typeset by YHT Ltd, London
Printed in the UK by Bell & Bain Ltd., Glasgow

We dedicate this book, in appreciation, to

Let Us Now Praise Famous Men by James Agee and Walker Evans
Landscapes of Learning by Maxine Greene
Ordinary Logic by Robert Ennis
The Literacy Myth by Harvey Graff
Participant Observation by James Spradley
'Sharing Time' by Sarah Michaels
The Psychology of Literacy by Silvia Scribner and Michael Cole
Ways with Words by Shirley Brice Heath
Literacy in Theory and Practice by Brian Street
Linguistic Processes in Sociocultural Practice by Gunther Kress
Ethnography and Language in Educational Settings by Judith Green
and Cynthia Wallat
Schooling as a Ritual Performance by Peter McLaren
Classroom Discourse: The Language of Teaching and Learning by
Courtney Cazden
Ethnography: Step by Step by David Fetterman
The Social Mind: Language, Ideology and Social Practice by James Paul Gee
Getting Smart by Patti Lather
Ethnography and Qualitative Design in Educational Research by
Margaret LeCompte and Judith Preissle
Critical Ethnography in Educational Research by Phil Carspecken
Qualitative Research and Case Study Applications in Education by Sharan Merriam
Research Methods in Education: An Introduction by William Wiersma
Case Study Research: Design and Methods by Robert Yin
Education and Knowledge by Kevin Harris
and
The Practice of Everyday Life by Michel de Certeau

Contents

Acknowledgements

This book owes much to the support of friends, colleagues and organizations in different parts of the world. We want to acknowledge their contributions here, while recognizing that they bear no responsibility for any of the book's limitations.

Our first thanks go to the Primary English Teaching Association (PETA) in Australia for encouraging us initially to think about writing for teacher researchers. In 1998 PETA invited us to write a short monograph for teachers interested in researching literacy. The Association published *Ways of Knowing* in 1999, and it was largely due to the positive reception the book received from diverse individuals and groups that we continued our inquiries further when we moved to Mexico in 1999.

Mexican educationists and researchers have been highly supportive of our attempts to write accessible and practically-oriented introductions to teacher research. The Michoacan Institute for Educational Sciences has published three of our texts in this area and encouraged us to think our ideas through within conference and workshop settings as well as on screen and paper. The National Pedagogical University in Morelia has recently published a greatly expanded version of the kind of text we produced for PETA. In these endeavours we are especially indebted to the roles played by Manuel Medina Carballo, Guadalupe Duarte Ramírez, Jorge Manuel Sierra Ayil, José H. Jesús Ávalos Carranza and Miguel de la Torre Gamboa.

During the period in which we have worked on this book we have been supported economically by a range of institutions and academic grantees while working primarily as freelance educational researchers and writers. We want to acknowledge the generous support of Mexico's National Council for Science and Technology, the Centre for University Studies and the Postgraduate Seminar in Pedagogy at the National Autonomous University of Mexico, Mark Warschauer, Hank Becker and Rodolfo

Torres of the Department of Education at the University of California in Irvine, the School of Education at the University of Ballarat and, most recently, Montclair State University, where Michele is now employed.

We owe a particular debt of thanks to Alina Reznitskaya for collaborating in writing the chapters on quantitative research. Alina made time and space in the midst of her exacting workload to generate and respond to copy rapidly, at short notice, and always with good humour and utmost dedication.

Rodolfo Torres introduced us to excellent research texts in human geography, which provided an invaluable perspective on a range of methodological matters. Christina Davidson and Martha Forero-Wayne generously provided recent examples of consent forms and information provided in the act of seeking consent from student participants and their caregivers. Neil Anderson and Barbara Comber have, in diverse ways, helped open the world of teacher research to us and have been unstinting in their support of our efforts.

As always, our experience of working with Open University Press has been outstanding. Shona Mullen was enthusiastic from the outset about this project, and even after taking up a new role within the Press has provided encouragement at points when it was sorely needed. Since taking over Shona's role, Fiona Richman has played a crucial role in bringing the book to fruition. Fiona has been generous beyond the call of duty in accommodating our failure to produce the manuscript to schedule. Even when we fell several months behind time Fiona kept her faith in us to eventually come through. She maintained contact and kept us accountable, but always in the most understanding and supportive ways. We hope the final product will go some way toward justifying Fiona's patience and goodwill. We are also very grateful to Melanie Smith, Jonathan Ingoldby, James Bishop and Malie Kluever for the ways they managed the copy-editing, proofing and wider production aspects over the Christmas-New Year period and to tight deadlines.

'We wish to acknowledge formal permissions to reproduce here material that has already been published or that is otherwise the intellectual property of other people. We need to thank Matthew B. Miles and A. Michael Huberman, *Qualitative Data Analysis: An Expanded Sourcebook*, second edition, p. 55, copyright © 1994 by Matthew B. Miles and A. Michael Huberman. Reprinted by Permission of Sage Publications, Inc. We want also to thank Debra Myhill from the University of Exeter for permission to use a classroom observation schedule she developed that appears on page 223 below, and Michael Doneman for the image we have reproduced on page 240. In addition, we want to acknowledge our debt to Ivan Snook with respect to the structure of material presented in the second part of Chapter 8.'

Finally, we thank the many teachers, students and research participants who have in many ways and over many years now helped us to understand better the processes of researching classrooms and other dimensions of educational work and contexts. This book will testify to the fact that we still have a great deal to learn. Nonetheless, that great deal would have been a lot more were it not for the patience, goodwill and generosity of countless people along the way. We are particularly indebted to Francesca Crowther for her generous comments on the text which she has made available to us as our cover endorsement and we hope the book will work for many other teacher researchers in the way it has for Francesca.

Colin Lankshear, Mexico City
Michele Knobel, Upper Montclair, NJ
January 2004

PART 1

A general background to teacher research as practice

CHAPTER 1

An introduction to teacher research

Introduction

This book aims to provide a comprehensive resource for practitioners wanting to conduct good quality teacher research. It builds on the view that several features must be present in any investigation – whether primarily academic or practitioner in orientation – for it to count as being bona fide research. This chapter works toward identifying these necessary generic features of research by considering some trends and issues evident in teacher research over the past 30 years. These make it timely and important to assert a strong 'bottom line' for teacher research.

'Teacher research' is a strongly contested idea. Key issues exist on which different people take competing positions. We consider a range of these here. At the same time, there are some important points on which advocates of teacher research are generally agreed. We will begin by looking at three points of broad agreement about teacher research.

Three points of general agreement about teacher research

Three points of broad consensus among those who write about teacher research can be noted here.

Teacher research is non-quantitative (non psychometric; non positivist; non experimental) research

During the past 30 years much teacher research activity has been undertaken to counter the long-standing domination of educational research by quantitative, 'scientistic' research. As an identifiable *movement*, teacher research has been conceived and 'grown' as intentional oppositional practice to the fact that classroom life and practice is driven by research based on narrow experimental, psychometric ('rats and stats') approaches to social science (see Fishman and McCarthy 2000: Ch. 1).

Who teacher researchers are

It is widely agreed that teacher research involves teachers researching their own classrooms – with or without collaborative support from other teachers. As Stephen Fishman and Lucille McCarthy note with reference to Susan Lytle's (1997) analysis of how teacher researchers understand their own activity, it seems that 'there is agreement about the "who" of [teacher research] ... [T]eacher research means, at the least, teachers researching their own classrooms' (Fishman and McCarthy 2000: 9). There are two aspects here. First, teacher research is confined to direct or immediate research of classrooms. Second, the chief researcher in any piece of teacher research is the teacher whose classroom is under investigation.

The goals and purposes of teacher research

Several authors (e.g. Cochran-Smith and Lytle 1993; Hopkins 1993; Fishman and McCarthy 2000) have clustered a range of widely shared views of the purposes and ideals of teacher research around two key concepts. One is about enhancing teachers' sense of professional role and identity. The other is the idea that engaging in teacher research can contribute to better quality teaching and learning in classrooms.

David Hopkins (1993: 34) refers to Lawrence Stenhouse's idea that involvement in research can help contribute to teachers' experiences of dignity and self-worth by supporting their capacity to make informed professional judgements. The main idea here is that teaching should be recognized and lived as a *professional* engagement. As professionals, teachers do not merely follow prescriptions and formulae laid down for them from on high. Rather, they draw on their expertise and specialist knowledge as educators to pursue educational goals that have been established democratically.

From this perspective, teachers should not be treated like or thought of as 'functionaries' or 'operatives' who carry out closely specified routine tasks. Instead, like doctors, lawyers and architects, they draw on a shared fund of professional knowledge and accumulated experience to take them as far as possible in specific situations. When they need to go beyond that shared 'professional wisdom' they draw on specialist educational knowledge, experience, networks, and their capacity for informed autonomous judgement to make decisions about how best to promote learning objectives. They do this case by case. Doing this successfully, having this success recognized and accorded the respect due to it, and seeing the fruits of their professional expertise and autonomy manifested in objective growth and learning on the part of students, provide the major sources of teacher satisfaction (see Stenhouse 1975; Hopkins 1993; Fishman and McCarthy 2000: Ch. 1).

Teacher research is seen as an important means by which teachers can develop their capacity for making the kinds of sound autonomous professional judgements and decisions appropriate to their status as professionals. More specific benefits often associated with recognition of professional status include 'increased power for teachers', 'respect for teachers', 'greater justice for teachers', 'greater confidence and motivation on the part of teachers', 'empowerment' and 'greater voice' for teachers (see Fishman and McCarthy 2000: 13–14).

The second generally shared end or purpose of teacher research is that it can contribute demonstrably to improving teaching or instruction. This can happen in different ways. Through their own research teachers may become aware of things they do in their teaching that might result in students learning less than they otherwise could. With this awareness they can make informed changes to try and enhance learning outcomes. Conversely, existing research might identify interventions or approaches that work positively under certain conditions. Teachers in similar contexts to those where research has shown success might then be able to adapt these approaches productively in their own settings. Alternatively, teacher research provides opportunities for teachers to test the effectiveness of interventions they believe could enhance learning outcomes for some or all of their students. Where interventions are successful the teachers who conducted the original research, and others who become aware of it, may be able to implement and adapt these interventions to obtain improved outcomes beyond the original settings.

Joe Kincheloe (2003: Ch. 1) advocates a further ideal for teacher research. This is as a means by which teachers can resist the current trend towards the domination of curriculum and pedagogy by 'technical standards' based on 'expert research' and imposed in a 'top-down' manner by educational administrators and policy makers. In the grip of this trend, curriculum has become highly standardized. The diversity of school communities, school settings, and student needs and backgrounds are disregarded. Teachers of the same grades within the same subject areas are required to 'cover the same content, assign the same importance to the content they cover, and evaluate it in the same way' (Marzano and Kendall 1997; Kincheloe 2003: 4).

According to Kincheloe, this 'standards-based' approach to educational reform subverts democratic education on several levels. It negates the principle of respect for diversity at the level of communities, schools and students alike, pitting 'likes' against 'unlikes' on the myth of a 'level playing field'. It also marginalizes teachers in the process of curriculum development and goal-setting based on professional knowledge and interpretation of learning goals for local needs and conditions. Moreover, domination of curriculum and pedagogy by technical standards subverts the proper critical and evaluative purposes of education by confining activity to 'mastering' predetermined content and subverting the development of analytic and interpretive capacities during the important early and middle years of schooling. Invoking work by

Madison (1988) and Capra (1996), Kincheloe argues that the 'reductionist ways of seeing, teaching and learning' inherent in current education reform directions 'pose a direct threat to education as a practice of democracy' (2003: 9).

Kincheloe argues that in this context embracing the ideal of teachers as researchers becomes an important facet of challenging the 'oppressive culture created by positivistic standards' (2003: 18). He observes that teachers 'do not live in the same professional culture as researchers', and that the knowledge base informing educational directions and emphases is 'still ... produced far away from the school by experts in a rarefied domain' (p. 18). This, he says, must change 'if democratic reform of education is to take place ... and a new level of educational rigor and quality [is] ever to be achieved'. By joining researcher culture teachers will:

- 'begin to understand the power implications of technical standards';
- 'appreciate the benefits of research', particularly in relation to 'understanding the forces shaping education that fall outside [teachers'] immediate experience and perception';
- 'begin to understand [in deeper and richer ways] what they know from experience';
- become more aware of how they can contribute to educational research;
- be seen as 'learners' rather than 'functionaries who follow top-down orders without question';
- be seen as 'knowledge workers who reflect on their professional needs and current understandings';
- become more aware of how complex the schooling process is and how it cannot be understood apart from 'the social, historical, philosophical, cultural, economic, political, and psychological contexts that shape it';
- 'research their own professional practice';
- explore the learning processes occurring in their classrooms and attempt to interpret them;
- 'analyze and contemplate the power of each other's ideas';
- constitute a 'new critical culture of school' in the manner of 'a think tank that teaches students';
- reverse the trend toward the deskilling of teachers and stupidification of students (Kincheloe 2003: 18–19; see also Norris 1998; Kraft 2001; Bereiter 2002).

A different point of view

Our view of teacher research disputes some of these widely agreed opinions. In particular, we disagree with the mainstream view that teacher research is inherently *non-quantitative*, and with the mainstream view of who teacher researchers *are*. We will state our position on these two points before commenting on the commonly identified goals and purposes of teacher research.

Against the inherently 'non-quantitative' view of teacher research

We appreciate the concern of teacher research to redress a balance with respect to the long-standing domination of educational discourse by quantitative forms of research. Our own personal research interests and experiences are grounded in qualitative and document-based approaches. We reject key assumptions about the possibility and prospects of objective, neutral, 'proof- and truth-centred' research championed by many quantitative researchers, and we accept critiques of such assumptions that have been advanced by leading qualitative educational researchers (e.g. Lincoln and Guba 1985; Delamont 1992; Marshall and Rossman 1999).

By the same token, we do not consider it wise or useful to confront a perceived domination with a crude policy of blanket exclusion. Rather, we believe that there is a viable place in educational research generally, and teacher research in particular, for well-conceived and well-executed quantitative research that does not overplay its hand so far as 'proof' and 'truth' are concerned, and does not forget that the social world cannot be reduced to numerical abstractions – even though some very useful and interesting educational trends and patterns can be identified using numbers, and by means of experimental forms of inquiry. To our chagrin, we often find that the 'feel for' and emphasis on design we believe lies at the very heart of research as a process of systematic inquiry is often much better understood and respected by people working in quantitative research than by people undertaking qualitative and document-based projects.

It seems to us neither desirable nor sensible to simply exclude quantitative research being done by teachers from the domain of teacher research by fiat or by definition. On the contrary, when we read studies reported in collections and projects of teacher research we often find ourselves yearning for some of the rigour and tough-mindedness that often occurs *par excellence* in quantitative educational investigations (Knobel and Lankshear 1999). Consequently, we include a general chapter in this book on quantitative approaches to teacher research. Without at least this degree of recognition we would have felt uncomfortable regarding this text as a *handbook* for teacher research.

Against the prevailing view of who teacher researchers are

Our view of teacher research rejects both aspects of teacher researcher identity associated with the mainstream view.

First, we do not believe that teacher research must be confined to *direct* or *immediate research of classrooms*. Although the ultimate point of impact sought from teacher research is on what occurs *in* classrooms, it does not follow that this end is best served solely through direct empirical study *of* classrooms. Teachers may learn much of value for informing and guiding their current practice by investigating historical, anthropological, sociological or psychological studies and theoretical work conducted in other places and/or at other times. These could be studies of policy, communities, social class, the work world, non-standard language varieties and so on. Teachers with an interest in relating or interpreting documentary data with a view to forming hypotheses or provisional explanations of practice might gain a great deal from purely philosophical and theoretical discussions of educational issues they consider pertinent to their work. Alternatively, they might generate their own analyses of secondary (other people's) data that have been collected in contexts similar in important ways to their own, in order to get perspectives for thinking about their own work prior to researching their own settings. (Such data might reflect patterns of educational attainment associated with variables like ethnic or linguistic background, social class, gender, forms of disability, etc.) To confine teacher research to immediate investigation of classroom settings may cut teachers off from opportunities to gain important insights and knowledge they might miss by simply doing one more classroom study.

Second, we disagree that teacher research should be defined in terms of teachers *researching their own classrooms*. This is not the same concept as that of conducting research pertinent to one's own professional practice. While the two are related, they are quite distinct. We often get clearer understandings of ourselves and our own practices, beliefs, assumptions, values, opinions, worldviews and the like by encountering ones that are quite different from our own, and that throw our own into relief and provide us with a perspective on them. Indeed, obtaining critical and evaluative distance can be extremely difficult if we stay within the bounds of our familiar discursive contexts and experiences.

Jim Gee's (1996) idea that 'bi- (or multi-) discoursal' people are often the most likely agents of innovation and change has important parallels for teacher investigations of teaching and learning in context. Even if we have access to the ideas and perspectives of others – such as where one invites colleagues to assist in investigating one's own classroom – there is no guarantee that variations in available perspectives, attitudes and experiences will be sufficient to help us recognize and question our existing standpoints, or to understand our own practice more fully in ways that can enhance it. On the contrary, confining teacher research to the study of our own classrooms in the company of our peers might actually be a powerful conservative force within what is widely identified as being a very conservative professional domain. As Stephen Hodas (1993: 1, citing David Cohen 1987) observes in relation to the culture of technology refusal in schools, 'the structure of schools and the nature of teaching have remained substantially unchanged for seven hundred years, and there exists in the popular mind a definite, conservative conception of what schools should be like, a template from which schools stray only at their peril'.

Furthermore, we do not think teacher research must be conducted independently of formal academic involvement. We see no reason why teachers might not enrol in formal academic programmes to conduct research relevant to their own teaching needs and interests. The crucial point is that the purposes or objects of teacher research must flow from the *authentic* (or felt) questions, issues and concerns of *teachers themselves* (see Berthoff 1987; Bissex 1987). This is, perhaps, the key point that demarcates teacher research from academic research, contract research and non-practitioner research in general. In *teacher* research the ways these issues and concerns are addressed must be answerable and responsive to teachers' own decisions and ideas about what is helpful and relevant.

This is perfectly compatible with formal suggestions, inputs, collaboration and guidance on the part of academic and professional researchers, offered within or outside of formal programme settings. Everything depends on the facts of particular cases about how the relations and obligations of teacher researchers and academics running formal programmes are contracted. Under current conditions academic educationists are increasingly expected to be responsive to 'client' demand and to pursue flexibility that is consistent with individual preferences. Hence, the institutional climate is in principle, and very often in practice, perfectly compatible with the ideal of teacher research building on teachers' own questions, wonderings, hypotheses and concerns.

From this standpoint we identify teacher researchers as 'classroom practitioners at any level, from preschool to tertiary, who are involved individually or collaboratively in self-motivated and self-generated systematic and informed inquiry undertaken with a view to enhancing their vocation as professional educators'. The idea of enhancing one's vocation as a professional educator covers 'internal' aspects like achieving greater personal satisfaction and a heightened sense of worth, purpose, direction and fulfilment, as well as 'external' aspects like improving the effectiveness of one's teaching practice in significant areas.

Hence, teacher research can be done in classrooms, libraries, homes, communities and anywhere else where one can obtain, analyse and interpret information pertinent to one's vocation as a teacher. It can be undertaken within formal academic programmes, or as an entirely self-directed individual undertaking, or under any number of semi-formal arrangements that exist in between these two extremes. Teacher research may involve empirical observation of classrooms (one's own or other people's), systematic reflection upon one's own documented experiences, or close engagement with theoretical or conceptual texts and issues. It can use people, policy texts, web-based materials, secondary data sets and so on as sources of information. Finally, it can be grounded in data coming from the present or the past, and even in data concerned with the future. Its potential scope and variety are enormous.

Teacher research and professional enhancement

The approach to teacher research we will develop in this book reflects our view of the relationship between teacher involvement in research activity and professional enhancement. What is it about participating in teacher research that supports the capacity of teachers to make the kinds of informed professional judgements that are conducive to generating improvements in teaching and learning? How does researching contribute to teachers experiencing dignity and self-worth as teachers, and to countering policies and practices that undermine a democratic ideal of education? We think the relationship is best understood as follows.

The process of engaging with well-informed sources through processes of reading relevant literature and talking with people who have thought about and investigated issues and concerns similar to our own is a potent source of obtaining ideas and insights that can produce results and bestow the kind of confidence that come with being reliably informed. This involves more than just chatting with people and skimming over surfaces of experience. It is about 'getting in deeply enough' to find plausible viewpoints, perspectives and explanations pertaining to our concerns and questions. These are viewpoints and perspectives that require us to make serious evaluative judgements and decisions about which of them are worth trying out, and which it may be best to start with in trying to address our own concerns. It certainly involves looking for approaches that challenge us to question some of our own assumptions and to do more than just go along with the crowd or with what other people we know are doing. There is often a temptation in education to hope for 'magic bullets' and 'quick fixes', at the level of theory and practice alike. The current fetish for 'constructivism', which has come to mean all things to all people, is a case in point. The serious professional will take the time to check out what is said by both the supporters and critics of 'constructivism', and will strive to sort out better and more robust accounts from 'pop' and 'bandwagon' versions, as well as to consider plausible alternative concepts and theories.

The kind of reading and discussion involved here aims at trying to understand and explain the sorts of things with which one is concerned as a teacher. It is not simply a matter of 'looking for something that works' but of aiming to understand why it works and how it works, and to think about where it might not work, and why. This is to have an interest in theory, although not in a 'highbrow' or abstract academic sense. We mean here 'theory' in the sense of seriously looking for patterns, relationships, principles and 'regularities' associated with situations, experiences, and phenomena that help us to understand and explain why something might be the case and how far it might apply beyond our immediate contexts. In this sense a serious teacher researcher is not interested merely in 'something that works', but in understanding how and why it works and/or how it might need to be adapted in order to work in other circumstances or to apply to other cases. This is about wanting to understand 'what makes things tick' in education. It involves more than just information and ideas *per se*. Moreover, it is about seeing our understandings and explanations as provisional and corrigible so that we are open to understanding issues, problems and challenges more fully and deeply, and from different perspectives.

Of course there is much more to professional enhancement and doing research than reading and reflecting alone. The potential value for professional enhancement of involvement in (teacher) research has a lot to do with thinking and proceeding in ways that are imaginative and creative *and*, at the same time, methodical, systematic and 'logical'. This is what we do in research when we 'nut out' how to construct a tool or instrument for collecting data (e.g. a survey, an interview schedule or an approach to observing classroom interactions) that is consistent with a concept, belief or theory we want to apply or test out. To develop one's own data collection tools in this manner involves creativity and imagination. At the same time it requires being methodical and rigorous in the sense of trying to 'translate' the original concept or theory into tools that are consistent with it. In other words, our data collection tool must be a faithful practical or applied interpretation of the original concept, belief or theory. In the first place, this means being very clear about the concept and understanding what it involves in ways that allow us to ask the kinds of questions or develop the kinds of observation routines that really do 'tap into' what the concept (or theory) is about. This is a demanding form of higher order thinking: it involves careful interpretation and creative appropriation based on clarity and understanding. Even if we decide not to develop our *own* data collection tool but, rather, to use one that someone has already developed, we need to engage in the same degree of interpretation to know which available option 'fits' best with the concept or theory or, indeed, if one that we are thinking of using actually fits at all.

The same applies to deciding how we will analyse our data – whether this is 'fresh' data we collect in the course of our research, extant (secondary) data collected by others or data we already have available to us through personal and collegial experience (Berthoff 1987). Knowing how to make sense of one's data – to sort it into appropriate categories, or to identify within it the kinds of patterns or regularities that may help us understand and explain something relevant – is a demanding interpretative and reflective act. We have to devise approaches to analysis that cohere with the concepts and theories that are informing our research and that will throw light on the question or problem we are investigating. Beyond this, we need to know how to interpret our data analysis in ways that are consistent with our problem and our research approach.

These and other qualities and processes add up to being a particular kind of 'thinker', 'designer', 'creator', 'troubleshooter' and 'practitioner' in one's capacity as a teacher. It is this, we believe, that contributes to our professional enhancement. This is what carries a teacher beyond being a 'routine operative' to a person who thinks and acts and reflects in ways that have become associated with being a professional.

The ideal of 'professional enhancement' and teacher research in theory and in practice

In *Unplayed Tapes: A Personal History of Collaborative Teacher Research*, Fishman and McCarthy (2000) distinguish between 'two charter concepts' of teacher research. They identify one with the work of the English educationist Lawrence Stenhouse, and the other with the position taken by the US rhetoric and composition specialist Ann Berthoff. To carry our discussion further we will briefly describe the two charter concepts. We will then consider some issues arising at the level of teacher research in practice that we think may have emerged from interpretations of differences between these charter concepts.

Lawrence Stenhouse: rigorous case studies to illuminate classroom teaching and learning

Stenhouse (1975, 1985) argues that rigorous forms of case study inquiry have the potential to provide illuminating and fruitful insights into classroom-based teaching and learning that offer teachers and other educators a sound basis for making professional decisions and judgements. His idea is for teachers to develop illuminating case studies that they can then compare with illuminating cases produced by other teacher researchers. This involves teacher researchers systematically collecting and analysing well-conceptualized data from which they can generate rich case studies based on high quality and trustworthy data that stand up to tests of 'triangulation'. Stenhouse puts a high premium on careful and detailed documentation of observed and oral data, in the best manner of historical and social science fieldwork. He insists on reference to multiple perspectives – e.g. by enlisting colleagues and other observers to witness practice in action and advance interpretations for the teacher researcher to take into account. Indeed, Stenhouse goes so far as to recommend publication of teacher research in peer-viewed forums in order to attract critical responses that will provide yet further bases from which teacher researchers can understand, evaluate and build on their own researched practice.

Stenhouse (1975: Ch. 10) sees teacher research as part of larger processes of curriculum research and development that are grounded in the study of classrooms. He views teacher research as an integral part of curriculum development. Teacher research specifically refers to that component of curriculum research and development where teachers themselves study their work, rather than (simply) having it studied by others. The research contributing to curriculum development can be done by all kinds of researchers working from and between different institutional settings. According to Stenhouse, well-founded curriculum development that is supported and mediated by teacher research involves what he calls 'extended professionalism' (p. 144). This is an *expansive* and demanding concept of professionalism. It has three key characteristics, presupposing that teachers have:

- the commitment to systematically question their own teaching as a basis for development;
- the commitment and skills to study their own teaching;
- a concern to question and test theory in practice by using those skills.

Within this framework of ideas and practices involved in curriculum research, Stenhouse emphasizes the importance of a systematic and methodical approach to collecting and analysing classroom data.

In his celebrated chapter on the teacher as researcher (1975: 142–65) Stenhouse discusses a range of methodological approaches to observational case study that were available at the time he was writing. While some of these may seem rather dated now, the important point is that Stenhouse discusses each of them in terms of how they involve rigorous forms of analysis to make sense of data in ways that generate categories, distinctions, taxonomies and typologies, themes, patterns of sequences and the like. Such products of careful analysis provide the basis for illuminating and organized descriptions of cases. These enable teacher researchers themselves, and the readers of their reports, to understand and evaluate what has been observed, and to think methodically about how and where changes could be made that might lead to improved teaching and learning.

Analytic concepts and categories that name (or conceptualize) tendencies, regularities, trends and patterns evident in the data obtained about practice in the study sites are the main fruits of the kinds of observational case studies Stenhouse advocates. They offer 'materials' from which teacher researchers can develop concepts and theories that expand teachers' understanding and explanation of classroom-based teaching and learning. In so doing, they support principled, informed and strategic responses to curricular and pedagogical challenges. Research findings based on the careful analysis of good quality data provide a base from which to envisage, implement and evaluate changes and innovations in ways that are not merely random or based on 'one-off' instances.

The kind of case studies Stenhouse advocates seek to make systematic sense of what goes on in a given site. This 'sense' can then be added to other 'senseful' accounts of practice. Eventually, a body of reported observational case studies can accumulate. These become a growing store of sense-making accounts of typical everyday classroom practices that can help teachers see larger trends or patterns. They can then situate their own cases in relation to other cases and see them as more or less similar to some and anomalous to others. Similarly, they can locate their own cases in relation to reported understandings, explanations, hypotheses, concepts and lines of theory. This provides a basis for comparing their own experiences and understandings with others reported in the store of cases. On this basis they can consider how far they want to refine or modify their ideas about their own practice, consider different possibilities for further development of their practice and so on. They can 'look again' (and again and again) at their own practice, seeking to understand more fully, deeply and from different angles what it *is* or *might be* as a practice. From this basis informed curriculum development can proceed.

In other words, when you have access to a bank of well-analysed and theorized cases it is possible to see that what you thought was a situation more or less peculiar to you might actually be far more widespread. What you thought was a problem that could best be addressed by doing X may suddenly be seen as one that can actually be understood in quite different ways and from different perspectives, and how it is tackled may depend on the kind of understanding you think is most plausible.

Ann Berthoff: writing already-existing experience into knowledge

Berthoff (1987) emphasizes an approach to research (what she calls research as *re-search*) in which teachers draw on their *already-existing* and rich funds of teaching experience and write these into *knowledge*. From this perspective, research as a way of knowing is about transforming classroom experience into knowledge by subjecting one's existing experience-as-data to the kinds of disciplined reflection and analysis involved in serious composition (see also Fishman and McCarthy 2000: Ch. 1).

This is a model of writing-based research that does not simply 'communicate' or tell a story. Rather, it actually *creates* new knowledge by transforming what was previously something like 'unprocessed experience' into meaningful or 'senseful' experience. This is done by sifting, organizing, rearranging, analysing and interpreting prior experience through the practice of reflective, serious *writing* that composes knowledge by putting pieces of experience together in ways that add up to a coherent representation of what has happened. Such composition does not superficially tell a story, or simply put on paper some ideas about what one has 'been through'. Instead, it is more like the serious musician who, in order to 'write' the notation on a manuscript, has to pay careful analytic attention to musical conventions, genres, conceits, intertextual materials, form, musical theory and so on.

Berthoff stresses the importance of *theory* in teacher research. She refers to 'theory' as standing in a 'dialectical relationship' to practice in the way that 'knowing' and 'hearing' are related within the composition process. In composition, says Berthoff (1987: 30):

> You can't really know what you mean until you hear what you say. In my opinion, theory and practice should stand in this same relationship to one another, a dialectical relationship: theory and practice need one another ... The primary role of theory is to guide us in defining our purposes and thus in evaluating our efforts, in realizing them.

The clarity and apparent simplicity of Berthoff's claims here may belie the importance and sophistication of the ideas they express and the challenge they present to researchers. For example, Berthoff's claims require us to focus on what counts as a *realization*. Likewise, the 'need' that is inherent in the dialectical relationship between theory and practice is a very particular *kind* of need.

Berthoff elaborates her view of the importance of theory in teacher research by advancing further ideas and claims, of which the following are typical:

- 'Theory can help us judge what's going on, and it can also explain why something works. Suppose you look at a particular exercise that has been very successful and you say, "Terrific! Now I'll do this." And you follow X with Y, which seems appropriate, and it doesn't work. If you don't have a theory about why X worked, you won't have any way of defining the real relationship of X to Y, logically or psychologically' (Berthoff 1987: 31).
- 'Theory can help us figure out why something works so we can repeat it, inventing variations ... The centrally important question in all teaching is, "What comes next?" ... Of course, we follow something with something else like it, but we can't do that authentically unless we can identify that first something: what is really going on? Theory can help us see what act we are trying to follow' (1987: 32).
- 'Teachers have to be pragmatic; they have to be down to earth, but being down to earth without knowing the theoretical coordinates for the landscape is a good way to lose your sense of direction' (1987: 32).
- '[R]ecipe swapping can be hazardous ... [I]n my ideal commonwealth ... the NCTE [National Council for the Teaching of English] would not be allowed to operate [its Exercise Exchange] unless they instituted a Theory Exchange. And you couldn't get a recipe unless you also went there. I have a friend ... who does just that. When her colleagues say, "Oh that sounds wonderful! Can I have that exercise?" she says,

"Sure – but you have to take the theory too." And the exercise comes typed up with a little theoretical statement at the top, an explanation of whatever aspect or function of learning the assignment is meant to exercise' (1987: 32).

This kind of theorizing gives *shape* – meaning and form – to what goes on in the worlds of teaching and learning. Such shape, says Berthoff, does not come out of thin air. What is needed, she believes, is the kind of theory that is generated in *dialogue* among teachers. This dialogue is more than talk, however. It involves much more than simply generating storylines. It is close to what Paulo Freire (1972, 1974) means by dialogue as action and reflection on the world in order to know the world through transforming it by *informed* action. Without a clear conception and definition of our purposes and a basis for evaluating them rigorously and appropriately we cannot, in Berthoff's view, even begin to think in terms of teacher research – re-search – as *searching again*; of thinking about the information we have; of interpreting what goes on in learning situations and then interpreting our interpretations. All of this calls for theory and theorizing, which involves taking account of what others have said and thought and what others say and think.

Comparing the two charter concepts of teacher research

Fishman and McCarthy (2000: 14–15, 22) note that while Berthoff and Stenhouse share some important ideas in common they also differ on some important points.

They share a deep antagonism toward traditional conceptions and practices of educational research as quantitative inquiry that often seems to be more concerned with upholding positivist norms of science and shaping classroom practice in this image than with addressing teacher concerns and classroom challenges on their own terms. Accordingly, Berthoff and Stenhouse share in common the view that teacher research must be based on *teachers' questions*. They also recognize the importance of theory, and insist that theory and practice need each other. Both believe that practitioner inquiry involves teachers 'dialoguing' together. And both eschew quantitative approaches.

Despite these important points of similarity, at least two deep lines of difference divide the respective 'charter concepts'. These concern the origins, nature and role of data in research and the role of academic professional researchers in relation to teacher research.

Berthoff does not believe the teacher researcher must engage in the kind of data collection advocated by Stenhouse. Whereas Stenhouse advocates systematic and rigorous collection of empirical data in naturalistic settings, Berthoff thinks that the task of the teacher researcher is to breathe new life into extant data in the form of personal knowledge through composition in the full sense of the term.

The second difference concerns the role of academic professional researchers. Berthoff states categorically that for teachers to become researchers it is necessary to keep academic researchers out of classrooms (Berthoff 1987: 30; Fishman and

McCarthy 2000: 15). Berthoff sees the interests of researcher-academic-outsiders from universities and the interests of practitioner-researcher-insiders as inimical. Stenhouse, by contrast, suggests that their interests are complementary and mutually necessary: each kind of researcher needs the other in order to progress their own work.

We think these points of difference have subsequently been interpreted by many teacher research advocates and teacher researchers in ways that encourage considerable teacher research activity in which core research values endorsed by Stenhouse and Berthoff alike have been seriously diluted.

Disputes within the teacher research ranks

Fishman and McCarthy (2000: 3) claim that 'internal clashes have plagued the teacher-research field'. They distinguish two 'sides' within the overall 'community' of teacher researchers. One side favours 'teacher story and retrospective', while the other advocates 'systematic methods of data collection and analysis'. The former side criticizes the latter for promoting research approaches that are 'too narrowly academic'. The latter counter charges that their opponents promote research that is 'too narrowly personal' (Fishman and McCarthy 2000: 3). The first side emphasizes narrative, personal voice and classroom experience; the second emphasizes analysis, academic voice and theory:

> Carefully triangulated data collection, presented in an academic voice, has been criticized by some teacher-researchers as too removed from the everyday concerns of practitioners. Their objection is that such work is inaccessible because of its technical language and because the personal histories and motives of the researchers are hidden ... By contrast, university-based researchers see teacher stories as insufficiently systematic, too local, and too little connected to broader academic and social issues.
>
> (Fishman and McCarthy 2000: 6)

Fishman and McCarthy's work is very helpful from a historical standpoint. It identifies and clarifies some important issues by describing and explaining disputes among teacher researchers in terms of followers of Berthoff drifting from a tight academic concept of *composition* – with its commitment to reflective theorizing and analysis – toward teacher tales of classroom life. At the same time we wonder if passages like the one quoted above associate university-based researchers a little too closely with commitment to 'systematic methods of data collection and analysis' and opposition to narrative and retrospective. Within teacher education faculties we find large and increasing amounts of teacher research guided and supported by university-based researchers that fall into the 'narrative and retrospective' bag. Furthermore, it is quite common to find academics supporting teacher research projects based on versions of qualitative inquiry as case study and action research that fall short of serious engagement with theorizing, systematic data collection and rigorous analysis.

Ultimately, the fundamental division within teacher researcher ranks is between those who continue to insist on the importance of theory, analysis and rigour that are nonetheless appropriately conceived and balanced to serve practitioner needs and interests rather than to bolster academic regimes of truth, and those who do not. This division cuts across the distinction between 'research as social science/case study' and 'research as composition/writing experience into knowledge'. The matter that most concerns us here is that many teacher research projects fail to display the core research values endorsed in the original charter concepts of teacher research represented in their distinctive ways by Berthoff and Stenhouse.

Teacher inquiry without system, theory or analysis

Two brief anonymous examples may serve to illustrate here what is a much larger phenomenon. They come from a recent edited collection of chapters reporting teacher research projects from a range of English-speaking countries, in which the authors use narrative styles of reporting. From the collection we selected two chapters dealing with similar themes: open and autonomous learning. These chapters aimed to report interventions made by the teachers that were aimed at promoting more open and autonomous forms of learning. Readers will immediately recognize this, and the comments that follow, as a description that applies to a large corpus of contemporary teacher research publications.

The first thing we noted about the chapters is that they address topics that have very large and diverse literatures. These literatures are by no means exclusively theoretical and academic in nature. Open learning and autonomous learning have been popular themes for an educational 'lay' audience since at least the late 1960s. Despite the size of the available literature and the ready physical and intellectual accessibility of much of it, the authors of one chapter provide no references whatsoever to other work, and the author of the other chapter provides just one reference. This was a text on autonomous learning written by a person the teacher researcher had heard at a conference. The original presentation had appealed to the teacher researcher because of similarities between what the presenter was saying and what the researcher was interested in and felt about the area.

In place of any review whatsoever of relevant ideas and accounts available beyond the immediate context, we read of the teacher researchers 'brainstorming ideas', 'producing semantic maps' and 'talking through ideas'. There is no indication of the investigators looking beyond their own preferences and predilections to engage in open critical ways with different viewpoints. There is, in short, no sign of any critical engagement, no calling of one's own ideas into question or account and no evidence of openness to new ideas or the challenge of reading fresh and different points of view. This is a dangerous and uncritical rendition of Berthoff's idea that teachers already have all the experience they need to be able to draw on. It is not what she meant, since the whole point of writing experience into knowledge is to foster dialogue. For dialogue to support the production of theory (in Berthoff's sense) that will be useful for teachers, the dialogue must go beyond immediate local personal preferences, ideas, opinions and 'brainstormings'.

On the basis of 'brainstorming', 'talking through ideas' and 'producing semantic maps' the teacher researchers describe enacting their interventions and what they see as the general effects and outcomes of these interventions. In neither case is there anything resembling a description of data collection approaches or of the data collected. The nearest either chapter comes to this is where the authors jot down some recalled snippets of interaction between themselves and the students during a short impromptu classroom conversation where the teachers asked the students why they thought they were at school and what they were there to do. Apart from that, readers are presented with general claims that are unsupported by evidence. In a typical example, readers are informed in one of the chapters that our 'colleagues were growing'. No detail or evidence is provided as to how these colleagues were growing, or by what criteria and by what means the growth had been measured.

Neither study provided an account of how data that may have been collected more or less systematically was analysed, or of what kind of analysis might be appropriate in order to move toward conclusions and interpretations. In the study that drew on student comments recalled from a classroom conversation, the authors move directly from student statements like 'because it's the law', 'my parents work', and 'so teachers can get paid' to conclusions about how they believe these students view school. These conclusions (e.g. 'kids attend school so that teachers can be paid') had been used to inform and support a learning intervention approach.

It is easy to see how such cases of teacher story and retrospective might be judged as 'insufficiently systematic, too local, and too little connected to broader academic and social issues' (Fishman and McCarthy 2000: 6) by critics who operate from conventional academic and scholarly assumptions about educational research. We would go further, however, and say that such cases should not be thought of as research *at all*. Certainly, it is difficult to see how the kind of inquiries reported in these studies, and the ways they are reported, might contribute to substantial ideals of professional enhancement. They might even provide grist for the mills of those who would discount teaching as a profession or would seek to further reduce teachers' domains of autonomous decision making with respect to curriculum and pedagogy.

Understanding such examples

We think some of the differences between the charter concepts of teacher research identified and described by Fishman and McCarthy have subsequently been widely interpreted in ways that encourage forms of teacher inquiry that severely dilute core research values. We will elaborate this claim in two brief steps.

First, we think the idea that for teacher research to flourish academic researchers must be kept out of the arena has encouraged the accommodation of teacher research to 'school ways of doing things'. For example, describing *research* in terms of collecting and collating information and presenting a report reflects a view of 'research' as 'the classroom project'. In the venerable classroom project, students collect information (including illustrations) and organize it as collages of text and images. Projects, however, do not work with concepts of collecting and analysing data in a research sense. Indeed, they do not work with the notion of *data* at all, but with 'gathering information on a topic'. Projects do not involve framing tight and manageable *questions* based on authentic *problems*. The 'classroom project' is a classic example of a 'school way'. When teacher 'research' becomes like school projects, one consequence is that the ideal of collecting and analysing data systematically is lost.

Accommodation to 'school ways' is also evident in 'research (as) writing'. When Berthoff speaks of teacher research as *writing* experience into knowledge she invokes a rigorous sense of composition. At the elementary school level, however, where much – if not most – teacher research is done, the 'writing' paradigm is 'narrating stories'. Much teacher 'research' is self-consciously constructed as 'telling stories'. Thus, the activity of two teacher researchers gets framed as a 'journey' that becomes a 'fable' featuring flowers in the role of people (researchers). When 'research' goes to school in such ways we personally can no longer seriously regard it as *research*.

The kind of understanding, relating, comparing and evaluating advocated by Berthoff *cannot be done* if one has access only to surface-level 'tellings' that merely string together stories about what seems to the teacher researcher to be going on. Unless the accounts provided of one's study actually generate some analytical outcomes it is difficult to make effective 'relatings' and comparisons between other cases and one's own. Moreover, it has to be clear *how* and *why* other teacher researchers have derived the concepts, categories, patterns and so on that they have from their data. It needs to be clear why they have analysed it one way rather than another, and what ideas and prior experiences or theories have made them decide to approach the data in the way they have. Readers need to know why something was interpreted in a particular way before they can decide whether to accept that interpretation.

Even if we agree that teacher research is better off without (much) involvement by academic researchers, it does not follow that research activities should be accommodated to classroom culture and school ways. On the contrary, Berthoff wants teachers to engage in theorized and reflective activity that is *appropriate* for addressing teacher questions and concerns in rigorous and expansive ways. This means drawing from discourses of research in ways that keep teacher concerns in the foreground, but *not* at the expense of robbing 'research' of its substance and integrity.

Second, with respect to the other key difference between the charter concepts, we think the idea that teachers' experience constitutes data has often been interpreted in ways that have generated poor quality data sets in teacher research. There are two aspects here.

First, teacher experiences may be *rendered* as poor quality data. When Berthoff says teachers already have in their experience all they need by way of data she does not mean that this data is simply 'there' waiting to be 'played with'. She means that through theorizing, categorizing and reflecting on experience teacher researchers will *bring data into existence* in systematic ways, and through informed analytic procedures derive from it the kinds of meanings researchers seek when they try to describe, understand and explain aspects of the world. Unfortunately, where teacher researchers 'narrate' their prior experience they often do not deal with it in such ways.

Second, where teacher researchers *do* engage in 'collecting data' it is often done in ways that simulate processes of acquiring experience. These are frequently beyond our control, unforeseen, ad hoc and random. We think that associating 'data' with 'experience' can be interpreted in ways that work against teacher researchers investing data collection with the kind of 'systematicity' necessary for maximizing the *quality and trustworthiness* of data that is essential for valid research

General features of research

As discursive practice, *research* has a number of necessary and inalienable features. In other words, for something to count as a piece of *research* in the first place it must reflect those qualities that constitute 'research' (of whatever kind) as a recognizable discourse. If a piece of work that claims to be research does not reflect these qualities then, so far as we are concerned, it is not *research*.

The 'bottom line' requirement for research is that our inquiry be *systematic*. For inquiry to be systematic means that it is neither random nor arbitrary. This applies as much to 'professional' or 'practitioner' research as it does to 'academic' research. Academic research defines systematic investigation in terms of recognized academic disciplines and their associated theories. For example, a discipline like 'psychology' or 'sociology' or 'history' is not just a body of literature or content. It also has recognized ways of setting about building up and critiquing knowledge and theory in that area. Members of these discipline communities may disagree a bit on details. For an area of academic inquiry to survive, however, there must be sufficient agreement about what counts as appropriate practice. What counts as systematic procedure for a field of inquiry is at the heart of what counts as appropriate practice.

When we think of professional-practitioner research we are still thinking in terms of systematic and methodical approaches to investigation. Many of these will be derived more or less directly from *academic discipline* areas. A key difference between academic and practitioner research is that practitioner researchers aim to tackle practical problems or issues as efficiently as possible. They are not concerned with demonstrating a sophisticated knowledge of the theory and methodology of an academic discipline area (or a particular 'paradigm') *as an end in itself*.

Hence, professional-practitioner researchers will spend less time dabbling with the niceties of theory and the theoretical and conceptual disputes in the discipline area, and more time making a wise selection of systematic methods and tools for addressing the practical issue. But in doing so they must still honour and act upon appropriate standards for 'being systematic'. At a general level, these standards are pretty well exactly the same for professional-practitioner research as for academic research. The difference will be in emphasis and in detail, but the commitment to being systematic will be the same. And in many cases the kinds of 'tools' used to collect and analyse data and advance interpretations will be similar in kind and, often, in detail.

We identify six generic features of research as systematic investigation that apply as much to *teacher* research as to any other research category.

1 A research question or issue that has been carefully and clearly framed, and that is manageable

This means a question that is well-focused, that is not too general and that is certainly not too 'cluttered'. Most importantly, it is a question that we understand in terms of what will count as addressing it in an appropriate way. This is not as easy as it sounds. We will address research questions in the following chapter.

2 An appropriate research design that matches our research question

A research design is a broad strategic approach or 'logic' for conducting the research. It must match the kind of question being tackled. An acceptable research design provides a 'way of going at the question or problem' that is *coherent* or *appropriate* given the kind of question or problem being addressed. This is why it is so important to know the kind of question being asked. Different kinds of question or problem will require different kinds of research design. We may consider an analogy here. Suppose we want to build a house. Different kinds of conditions and terrains might indicate the need for a different kind of house design. Steep, slippery, unstable terrain might be better addressed by means of a design that builds on poles sunk deep into the ground rather than conventional concrete foundations. Flat solid land will support a wider range of designs.

Many different kinds of design can be used to investigate issues and problems of interest to teachers. These include quasi-experimental designs (e.g. using control groups to measure the operation of variables), survey-based designs, case study designs and action research designs, as well as a host of non-empirical sorts of design. For teacher research to be *research* the design we choose must be one that allows us to investigate our question in a coherent way. Research designs do not have to be complex sorts of things. Other things being equal, so long as it is adequate for the job, the less complicated or more elegant one's research design is, the better it is. The aim of choosing a design is to get the greatest amount of good quality information and knowledge from minimum clutter and resource inputs.

3 Something that informs the research question and how to tackle it

All kinds of data and information gathering go on that do not qualify as research. For example, teachers can assess their students and keep records of their scores/results. This on its own, however, is not seen as research. Likewise, teachers can get students to 'look up' and gather information on animals, or landforms, or weather etc. without it being research. For acts of data gathering and information retrieval to be part of research activity they must meet two conditions. First, they must be conducted in relation to something that has been framed as a problem, issue, or as a purposeful question. Second, they must be intended to contribute to understanding some phenomenon and, typically, to supporting some kind of explanation or interpretation – not simply to provide us with information.

Issues or problems, and the questions designed to 'get at them', do not arise simply out of thin air. They arise when something occurs that is unexpected, bothersome, unusual or discrepant, and where we believe there is something to be discovered and understood in order to explain what has occurred (or else, to show that it is not really unusual or problematic at all) and, perhaps, to be able to 'fix' or 'resolve' or change the situation. To take the example of classroom assessment, if the teacher merely sets 'tests' and keeps score, that is nothing more than measuring performance and maintaining records. If, however, student scores differ significantly from what the teacher expects, or if some unusual change in the pattern or distribution of scores occurs, the teacher might see this as problematic or anomalous and set about doing some research to discover what has happened and why.

The point here is that for the scores to appear unusual, problematic or unexpected to the teacher, the teacher has to have some kind of 'theory' or 'idea' in mind in the first place. Whether it is some kind of formal theory or elaborate and theoretically informed idea is not so important. It could well be based on previous experience, collective teacher wisdom, something picked up in a professional development (PD) course, etc. It might even be an intuition, a hunch, a 'feeling'. But whatever it is, it provides a stimulus for framing something to be known more deeply, understood and explained by means of systematic inquiry. The moment our teacher begins to frame a question to get at that problem concerning the assessment scores or patterns, and to wonder how to translate that question into a systematic kind of inquiry, we have the beginnings of research. At this point the teacher researcher will start looking for clues as to how the inquiry could proceed. This will typically lead into some relevant literature, and/or to people who are reputed to know something about such matters.

4 A suitable approach to gathering data

Tackling a problem or question as a research exercise means gathering relevant information in a methodical way. This doesn't *necessarily* mean gathering extra empirical data (e.g. more scores, or observations of students). It could mean using one's records as a 'data set' and then reading some research literature and theory in order to try and explain what is going on, or to see if other people have found similar things and how they have tried to explain them. On the other hand, it could mean framing a data-gathering exercise and going after more data. If this is the option taken, we need to have ways of ensuring that the data we collect is relevant, that it is of good quality, that it is trustworthy and so on. This means building into our data collection various techniques and procedures that vouch for the quality of our data and, perhaps, that can be repeated by other people as a way of enlarging the research and improving the information base on which to frame understandings and explanations. We will have a lot to say later about good quality data collection and how data gets turned into information and knowledge.

5 Some kind of analysis and interpretation components

Since research is done in response to something we want to understand, explain and be able to act on or change in the light of our findings, we need to have ways of analysing the data we gather, and ways of translating or interpreting our analysis into findings. This is where a lot of activity that people might think of or describe as 'research' actually falls short of being research. For example, we often find people thinking they are *analysing* data when they are really only *re-describing* it. Alternatively, we hear of people doing classroom interventions which aim to change things, and which *do* change things, and calling it research. In many cases it will not be research at all – simply a change intervention. For a change intervention to count as research it must involve an attempt to provide a coherent account of how and why the changes occurred, and why we might reasonably expect changes to occur (or not to occur) under different circumstances or in different settings. When we interpret findings we appeal to concepts, ideas, theories, arguments, models of explanation and the like to move from our analysis of the data to judgements which we can defend as being reasonable accounts of how and why the things revealed in our analysis have occurred.

6 Some statement or artefact that exemplifies and elucidates the five features above, conveys the conclusions drawn from the study, and identifies their implications for our work

To the extent that research makes claims to knowledge and to fostering understanding it is necessarily a public act. There must be some public record that can be accessed by other people in order for the research to be validated. Knowledge and understanding, by definition, are not private matters. The public record can take many forms, however for a study's claims to be assessed in relation to its purposes, the artefact or statement must provide its audience with the opportunity to see and evaluate the relationships between the study's purposes, its informing sources, the approaches taken to data collection and so on. Without such a statement or artefact the study exists only as *private experience* without any basis for asserting its claims.

Looking ahead

The rest of this book presents an extended discussion of how to realize these generic features in teacher research. Chapter 2 looks at the way researchers strive for systematic inquiry by ensuring coherence between their research purposes, the theoretical and conceptual frameworks that inform the research project, and their approaches to data collection and data analysis.

Teacher research as systematic inquiry

This chapter explores in greater detail the first four generic features of research and the relationships between them from the standpoint of research as *systematic* investigation.

Research questions and research purposes

Questions

A good-quality and well-framed research question is a key component of a successful research project. The more clearly and precisely a research question signals what *kind* of inquiry will be involved and what sorts of data or information will need to be gathered, the better it is as a research question. Well-framed research questions usually provide important clues about *how* and *from whom* or *from where* data will be gathered. A good question may also indicate some of the things one is assuming about the world and about the problem area being addressed.

Thus, a good-quality well-framed research question:

- is clear, concise and focused;
- is informed;
- is motivating, or personally meaningful (to sustain us through the hard slog);
- is manageable and doable;
- is significant, in the sense that the value of the answer obtained is likely to justify the effort and resources that go into addressing it;
- does not already have readily accessible answers.

The research question constructed for an investigation directly informs decisions regarding which research designs are best suited for the study, along with which data collection tools and techniques, and data analysis strategies, will be most useful in the study.

Purposes

It is helpful to explore research questions in relation to research *purposes* more generally. Moreover, it is useful to think in terms of close links existing between the task of framing clear and manageable research processes, and the tasks of consulting sources that will inform our study and of deciding how to collect and analyse our data. We think of research purposes in terms of four related ideas:

- our research *problem*;
- our research *question*;
- our research *aim*;
- our research *objectives*.

These four ideas are all closely related, but quite distinct. The relationships between them are not always well understood, and this may help to explain why beginning researchers often find it difficult to frame a clear and succinct focus for their projects. In our own work we think of the research question very much as an *angle* or a *perspective* on a problem. We see it in terms of how addressing the question will help to resolve or throw additional light on the problem or meet a challenge. We also think of the research question in terms of a focus that reflects an *aim* to be implemented in the research project by pursuing a series of *objectives* that collectively tackle and cover (or 'exhaust') the question.

As we will describe in depth in the next chapter, we believe that understanding the relationships between 'problems', 'questions', 'aims' and 'objectives' in research helps the task of generating good-quality well-framed research questions. On the basis of this understanding researchers can move through a reflexive process where they try to clarify each dimension (aim, objectives, problem, question) of their overall research purpose by considering the other dimensions. At an 'internal' level we clarify our question in 'dialogue' by clarifying our aim, objectives and problem, and vice versa.

At the same time there is a larger 'external' process involved in clarifying research purposes and our research question. In this wider process, which is also 'reflexive', we move between clarifying our purposes, consulting relevant literature and other sources of helpful information, designing and planning our approach to data collection, and designing and planning our approach to analysing our data.

To the extent that we take these reflexive processes seriously, take the time to do them well and understand the relationships between them and their components, our research question will be better and the likelihood of a successful project enhanced. We enlarge on this idea in Chapter 3.

Having an *informed* research concern

Since practitioner research is intended to contribute to improving practice, teacher researchers need some concepts and theories about what 'better' education might be like and, therefore, what sorts of things might lead to 'enhanced practice'. Without these, we have no framework for glimpsing opportunities for research or for seeing things that happen in classrooms or other sites as unexpected, or problematic, and that might be usefully explored (Heath 1983; Latour 1993; Carspecken 1996; Lankshear *et al.* 1997).

Good ways to get into viable 'spaces' for seeing and seizing worthwhile research opportunities include making connections between our various everyday resources of stimulation; for example, informed peers, professional reading, professional development policies and so on.

There are at least three 'moments' that inform the development of research concerns (as distinct from mere information gathering). The initial 'moment' is that which enables us to see something as a possible seed for research. This may result from:

- something we have read;
- an idea in a professional development programme;
- a colleague's experience;
- an unexpected outcome in our environment;
- another person's concern or surprise, and so on.

This 'moment' helps teacher researchers frame the initial kernel of a research activity.

The second 'moment' is where we deliberately and systematically try to further inform this kernel in ways that turn it into a good-quality question and into ideas about possible options for researching it. This is where we begin doing some systematic reading and inquiring about different ways in which this 'kernel' might be understood and tackled. For example:

- What are some of the different concepts of 'X' (e.g. effective literacy) that we are investigating?
- What are some of the different theories that underlie approaches to teaching reading and writing, or that explain difficulties and successes?
- What sort of research studies have been done in this area already?
- How do they differ from each other in terms of their underlying theories and concepts?
- What reasons might there be for building my own research on one kind of approach taken in these studies rather than another?

This 'moment' may be ongoing during our research – as we read and hear about things that suggest to us ways in which we might refine our research process as we go along.

The third 'moment' comes after we have done our research, as we reflect on it in the light of feedback or of other things we encounter that stimulate us to take our work further. This might become the first 'moment' in another research cycle. The thing about doing research is that it should become an aspect of the way we 'do' our professional lives; a way of 'going about our practice'; not just some one-off thing we do because we think we should, or to get a qualification. Good research practice involves us in finding ways of keeping ourselves informed so that this actually saves us time, makes teaching more energizing and attractive and gets us better results, rather than being an additional burden.

Framing an appropriate research design

Research mobilizes evidence that is relevant to a question or a problem. This evidence has been collected, organized and analysed in ways that allow us to accept that the findings are reasonable inferences – they can be inferred reasonably from the data and the analysis involved in the research. Moreover, the data and analysis themselves are appropriate in terms of the kind of problem involved and the kinds of question(s) being asked.

Our concept of research is based on the idea that we try to understand aspects of the world more clearly, accurately and predictably by assuming that:

- there is some kind of order to things; and
- this can be revealed by approaching the world in systematic and reasonable ways.

The key concept involved here is the idea of a *design*. A design can be thought of as an appropriate procedure or guideline for doing something under certain conditions. Under arctic conditions, for example, an igloo is an excellent design for a house. It would be a terrible design, however, for tropical areas. Similarly, a building design that may be very acceptable for areas where there are never earthquakes might not be acceptable for areas where earthquakes are common. The ultimate success of a research study depends crucially on its being well designed – which means we need to be alert to the importance of design from the outset. Launching into an investigation without first having thought about what sorts of concepts, theories, methods, instruments and the like might best fit the question asked, and how these can be arranged in a systematic way, is like waking up one morning and suddenly deciding to build a house and starting right then and there without having given any thought to the kind of house, the plan, the materials, the tools and the options available.

We think of developing a research design in terms of five main ideas.

First, the design for *a bona fide* research investigation will *build on clearly and concisely framed problems and questions* and a clear sense of our research *purposes* – that is, what we hope to achieve through our research. Our research purposes might be identified as a set of aims and objectives that relate to our research focus in the form of our research question(s) and/or our research problem. A clear and concise statement of our research purposes is absolutely essential for doing good-quality research. The type of research question we ask will usually circumscribe our range of design options. Some kinds of designs are not compatible with some kinds of questions, and vice versa.

Second, the research design is guided by *theoretical and conceptual frameworks* that help clarify the questions, problems and purposes we are concerned with, tell us what is already known about these matters, and help us understand how particular concepts and elements of theory might be useful for our own inquiry.

Third, our research design contains a *strategy for collecting and organizing data* that is relevant to our research problem(s) and/or question(s). This will be a strategy that enables us to collect the right kind of data for addressing our research focus, for collecting good-quality data of an appropriate kind, and for collecting an appropriate amount of data for investigating our research problem in a rigorous and illuminating way. To be more precise, our research design will contain as one of its key components a *data collection (sub)design*. On the basis of this data collection design, and in accord with the various resources of time, money, energy and so on available to us, we will eventually develop a *data collection plan*. Decisions about our data collection strategy are guided by careful analysis of our research questions and problems, by our conceptual and theoretical frameworks and by our reading of the research literature.

Fourth, in addition to a strategy for collecting and organizing our data, we also need a *strategy for analysing our data*. This may be thought of as a *data analysis (sub) design*. The most important thing about our data analysis strategy or design is that it must cohere with (or be consistent with) our research *purposes* (our research question/ problem and our aims and objectives), as well as with our theoretical and conceptual framework and the kinds and amount of data we collect. For example, if we want to collect and analyse a large amount of data we will need to use forms of data analysis that can handle large amounts of data *and* give us the kinds of findings we seek. Otherwise we will not be able to complete the research. On the other hand, if we want to concentrate on less data but analyse it in great depth, we need to use forms of data analysis that will give us the kind of depth and detail we seek.

Finally, our research design must contain a *strategy for interpreting the analysis of our data* in order to provide us with *findings* and *conclusions* from our research, and which may allow us to advance *recommendations* or *implications* based on our investigation.

These key research components are illustrated in Figure 2.1.

The important point to note here about the idea of a research design is that all of its components must 'fit' with each other or 'go together' with each other in a coherent manner. Our theoretical and conceptual framework must 'fit' with our research goals and purposes. Likewise, our data collection strategy must 'fit' with our research purposes, our conceptual and theoretical framework and our approach to data analysis. Our data analysis strategy must fit with our data collection strategy, our conceptual and theoretical framework and our research purposes. And our interpretive strategy must allow us to relate what emerges from our data analysis back to our research purposes, and forward to whatever recommendations and implications we want to suggest that pertain to our purposes.

To repeat: unless one has a research design in this sense one is not really doing research at all. When we have a viable research design in this sense, the quality of our research will be a function of how competently we develop and implement the individual components of our design.

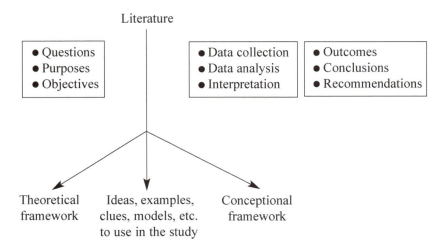

Literature

- Questions
- Purposes
- Objectives

- Data collection
- Data analysis
- Interpretation

- Outcomes
- Conclusions
- Recommendations

Theoretical framework

Ideas, examples, clues, models, etc. to use in the study

Conceptional framework

Figure 2.1   Diagram of research design components

Research designs and research paradigms

Although drawing distinctions between qualitative research and quantitative research often oversimplifies the characteristics of each paradigm, we find it useful when discussing research designs to emphasize particular – and defining – characteristic differences between these two paradigms. Perhaps the most important difference (always keeping in mind that they are not the only way of categorizing research 'types'; see Knobel and Lankshear 1999: 32) is the assumptions that underpin them. Quantitative research assumes that the world can be *measured* and that numbers accurately capture the 'probability of truth' about something. Qualitative research on the other hand assumes that in order to understand the world we need to focus on *contexts* – which variously involves paying attention to history, to politics, to language use, to the participants in a particular event, to other events happening at the same time and so on.

That being said, however, there are important points of similarity between the key features or expectations of these two research paradigms. For instance, qualitative researchers may work with hypotheses just as quantitative researchers do (see Yin 1994). They may work with samples (although typically not with representative samples). They may work with numbers and keep counts and look for numerical patterns and relationships (see May 1997; Mayol 1998). They will employ techniques to check the validity of their data – although these techniques will differ from the kinds employed by quantitative researchers and will include, for example, taking their interpretations back to the study participants to have them 'check' or verify the meanings that the researcher has made – this is known as *participant checking*. Another verification process is *triangulation*, which has a number of meanings for different researchers. We use the term to describe the process in which a piece of information is 'backed up' by other sources of information (e.g. something you observe about a child's writing habits is verified by the teacher's unsolicited comments the next day and in a conversation with the child's mother at the school gate).

On the other hand, qualitative research need *not* employ hypotheses or samples or numbers. It might involve watching what people do, talking to them about it, asking other people about it and trying to understand and explain what is going on, without any recourse to numbers or statistics or variables whatsoever. Instead, forms of coding might be employed, categories, domains and taxonomies established, patterns and similarities identified and descriptions, interpretations and provisional explanations advanced on the basis of such procedures.

Six key points about research design

There are six important things to stress about research design and developing an appropriate design for a qualitative (or quantitative) study.

1　The various kinds of research designs that exist are variations around a more or less common set of components. Every viable research design will contain a set of key concepts or constructs around which the study is organized and 'conceptualized'. Without a carefully constructed conceptual framework there is nothing to hold the study together as a coherent 'whole'. Likewise, a research design necessarily builds around some theoretical position or other. This theoretical position must 'go with' the key concepts, and both must 'fit' the research question. Next, every 'mature' research design contains methods, techniques, procedures and criteria for collecting data, checking the quality of data, organizing and managing data and for analysing data. These methods must cohere with all the previous elements mentioned. Finally, every research design must contain an element that interprets what comes out of the analysis of data into findings and conclusions. This is why it is appropriate to think of research design as a kind of logic; as the shape of an argument which starts with a question, organizes a response, mobilizes evidence, justifies points that are made and derives a conclusion which 'follows from' the previous steps.

2　Research designs should be seen as broad *types*, not as ready-made, painting-by-numbers blueprints. Any given type of research design is compatible with a range of conceptual, theoretical, methodological, analytic and interpretive options – as well as being incompatible with some others. For example, there is nothing in ethnographic design to say that an ethnography *must* include participant journals. Whether or not a particular ethnography employs participant journals must be decided in relation to the specific study and the research question being asked. Likewise, a case study may or may not involve surveys. If it involves interviews there is plenty of scope for researchers to choose different types (e.g. closed, open, projective, semi-structured), depending on the details of the research.

3　Therefore, while particular research questions will circumscribe the kinds of research design that can be used, they will often not limit the 'choice' to a single design option. And even when they do, they will by no means stipulate the precise concepts to be used, the theory to be employed, or the kinds of data collection and analysis techniques to be employed.

4   Hence, in every case, the researcher has serious work to do in designing his or her study. Apart from what are called replication studies, where the researcher aims to stick as exactly as possible to the design and approach employed by some other researcher(s), but with a different set of research participants or subjects, research designs don't come ready-made. They have to be carved out, refined, moulded, adapted and monitored by reference to the research question that is being asked, to the resources available and to criteria of coherence, clarity, sound reasoning and so on.

5   Researchers need to avoid the trap of generating good-quality research questions and then opting for a design type (e.g. because it is popular or trendy, or one has heard about it) without considering the issue of coherence between research question and research design. While this may sound like an odd thing to happen, it happens very often – not least because new researchers (as well as some not so new) often lack a well informed understanding of research design types and the sorts of questions they are good for and those they are not.

6   Having a good-quality research design is also part of a researcher's *ethical* commitment to and duties within research. Having a study 'fall over' because of poor design decisions impinges directly on the time and generosity of our research participants.

Planning tools for research design

There are any number of ways of approaching research design. One way we find particularly helpful comprises a matrix and a series of guiding questions (see Figure 2.2) (see also LeCompte and Priessle 1993). By placing the data collection column next to the research purposes column we are reminded that we have to collect data that are pertinent or relevant to our research question. The data have to fit the question. Similarly, by placing the data analysis column next to the data collection column we are reminded to select methods and techniques of data analysis that cohere with our data. Finally, we have a column called 'Guiding and informing sources'. This refers to literature (particularly, *published* literature) and other sources of information (e.g. persons with relevant experience and knowledge) that are relevant to our own research.

Research purposes	Data to collect	Data analysis approach	Guiding and informing sources

Figure 2.2   Research design matrix

Through their writing, other researchers can present us with options for the kind of framework we will use to shape and guide our research. We will need ideas, definitions, criteria and so on to help us decide how to make our data collection and data analysis approaches 'fit' (or cohere with) our research question. In more 'hard core' academic educational research this is the idea of developing conceptual and theoretical frameworks for the study. In less academically oriented forms of practitioner research, the focus may be less 'highbrow' in terms of theory. Nonetheless, the framework must still contain ideas that allow us to organize our research in ways that will promote understanding and levels of explanation adequate for using as a base to respond intelligently in our practice to the issue or problem we are investigating.

This raises an important issue. There is a tendency in much teacher research to shy away from talk of 'theory'. At one level we can understand this, because a lot of academic 'theory' is so dense, unhelpful, abstract and convoluted. At times it is almost as if something can't be theory if it is understandable and useful. This is not a problem with theory *per se*. It is a problem with unclear or unhelpful theory. Practitioner research should front up to theory confidently and with great expectations. We should 'own' theory, but insist that it be clear and helpful. Teachers need theoretical as well as practical competence. The trick is to locate and develop sound theory that is adequate to our needs.

Consequently, we do not back off in this book from talking about the need for conceptual and theoretical frameworks in practitioner research. The point is that we simply cannot collect and analyse data in a way that counts as research unless we have some ideas, definitions, concepts and the like that allow us to do this in *systematic* and *coherent* ways. What counts as relevant data for addressing a problem from the standpoint of one kind of theory may not count as data from the standpoint of another. Some kinds of data can only be analysed by using certain kinds of analytic methods – once again, for reasons related to theories and concepts.

Often we will find there is more than one kind of theoretical approach and more than one conceptual framework that we could use to produce a coherent research design. When that occurs we have a choice. We might choose a theory and a framework that we find more attractive for personal and professional reasons. Or we might choose a framework that has been used successfully by other researchers whose work we find interesting and useful for addressing questions and problems similar to our own. But whatever theory and conceptual framework we develop for our study, it must cohere with our problem and question, and it must be capable of informing us how to collect appropriate data and analyse it in appropriate ways.

We have placed the 'Guiding and informing sources' column at the opposite end of the matrix from the 'Research purposes' column. This is to remind us that we need to use our reading of the literature to ensure that *all* the components cohere with each other. We need to keep reading relevant literature and talking to people with appropriate knowledge and experience until we are confident that we understand what our question really is and what kinds of theory and concepts 'fit' our question. We also need to use that information to help us make coherent and justifiable decisions about what kinds of data to collect and how to analyse it. We are aware that we have repeated this point many times, but we do not think it can be repeated too often. Unless the components of the research design are all coherent with one another the 'research' will be either poor-quality research or, alternatively, not really research at all.

The 'Research purposes' and 'Guiding and informing sources' columns are necessary reference points (at different ends of a cycle) for keeping the data collection and data analysis components 'together' in a proper manner. We cannot determine what data to collect and how to analyse it without taking fully into account the kind of research problem and question we have. But at the same time, we cannot know what the options are and what the most effective choices will be without referring to guidance from sources in the literature and from other people who have relevant knowledge and expertise. So we 'cycle' through the process of getting the components of the research design in synch with each other. When we have a coherent 'set' – where each component 'fits' with every other – we have a genuine research design.

To understand and use the simple research design matrix to guide our research, it is useful to think in terms of a number of key questions we can put into each column. The questions we find especially useful are shown in Table 2.1. These questions act as a guide to help us structure our research project coherently. To conduct our research rigorously we need to produce answers to each of these questions. Our research unfolds as we answer these questions, implement the tasks and follow the leads provided by our answers.

A suitable approach to collecting data

Teacher researchers must collect good-quality data that are relevant to their research question and problem and that they can analyse using methods that are consistent with the overall design of the study and with which they are proficient (or will be proficient by the time they come to analyse their data). Decisions and selections regarding data collection tools and techniques need to be made during the planning phase of the study, and well before any data is collected, in order to ensure that the researcher collects sufficient data of the kind needed for the study. Some key tools and techniques characteristic of *qualitative* research are summarized in Table 2.2. This listing is not exhaustive. Neither is it meant to suggest that every item needs to appear in every qualitative investigation. Learning how to pick and choose what is most needed for a study in terms of data and data collection is a large part of what it means to become an effective researcher.

The analysis and interpretation component of research

Analysis is about finding what is 'in' the data we collect that seems to us to be significant, and *interpretation* is about saying what this 'implies' or 'means' for the question or problem underpinning our study. It involves looking for trends and tendencies, patterns and regularities in the data, as well as for what seem to be interesting

Table 2.1 Questions to be addressed when developing a research design

Research purposes	Data to collect	Data analysis approach	Guiding and informing sources
• What is my research problem?	• What kinds of research data must I collect?	• What forms of data analysis will I use?	• Who helps me understand how to frame and refine my research purposes?
• What are its key dimensions?	• How will these data help me address my purposes?	• What justifies these forms of analysis?	• What are some relevant books, articles and chapters here?
• What specific questions does it generate?	• How will I collect these data?	• How will they help me achieve my research purposes?	
• Which of these questions can I hope to address well?	• How much data will I collect?	• How are these forms of analysis conducted?	• Who provides theories and concepts relevant to my research problem and questions?
• How can I identify the key elements of my research problem and questions in order to specify a succinct set of research aims and objectives, and a finite set of research questions?	• How will I validate these data or establish that they are of good quality?	• What do I need to know, be able to do and have access to in order to use these forms of analysis in an expert way?	• How do these guide me in deciding what kinds of data to collect and how to analyse it?
	• How will I organize these data so they will be in good shape for being analysed?	• What will these forms of analysis let me 'say' about the data (and not say)?	• Who provides good advice on how to collect, validate and organize data?
			• Who provides good information about how to analyse data?

Table 2.2 Summary of common data collection tools and techniques in qualitative research

Technique	Tools	Kinds of data collected	Examples of research designs that utilize the technique
Observation	Emphasizes collecting data in real life, everyday contexts. Tools and methods include: fieldnotes and journalistic notes of events; audio recording; video recording; time and motion studies; priority observation etc. Fieldnotes are those notes written in the 'heat of the moment' during observations of events, interactions, activities and so on. Journalistic or *post facto* notes are those notes written after observations when it was not possible to make fieldnotes	Detailed and often complex slabs of written descriptions and interpretations of an event, process, phenomenon etc. are constructed	Case study, action research, ethnography
Interviews	Emphasis is on eliciting desired information from someone. Tools and methods include: interview schedules (i.e. lists of questions) which range from closed or structured (e.g. verbal questionnaires) to semi-structured (where there is room to move away from preset questions), through to open-ended (more like conversations with a purpose with no preset questions); audio recording; video recording	Structured interviews (often commercially produced) can be used to assess a trait or a person's articulation of ability; semi-structured and open-ended interviews can be used to collect a range of data (e.g. life histories, perspectives on issues, background to a development)	Case study, action research, ethnography, discourse analysis
Document collection	Documents inform present and future decisions about teaching, learning strategies, school policies, and so on. Documents may provide a range of perspectives on an event or issue. They can enable the researcher to reconstruct an account of a past event, phenomenon or practice.	Documents can provide historical background to an issue, problem or event; they can be used to examine parallel event information (e.g. the possible effects of the 1968 student	Historical studies in particular, case studies, ethnographies, qualitative surveys, action research and so on

Technique	Tools	Kinds of data collected	Examples of research designs that utilize the technique
	Documents can be classified in terms of: *primary sources*, which are original texts written by participants in the event being studied; *secondary sources* which are original texts (or fragments of original texts) reproduced in another document or paraphrasings of original documents or events generally not written by eye-witnesses; *tertiary sources* which are references that help us locate pertinent documents (e.g. bibliographies; reading lists in university courses)	protests in Mexico and their outcome) that helps contextualize a study. Similar or divergent studies that help set the scene for a new study	
Open-ended questionnaires/ surveys	Emphasis is on gathering a range of responses to set items from a range of people. Useful for identifying trends or preferences across a large number of people. Tools and methods include oral or written questions or statements to respond to. Questions are open-ended (how, what, why questions with unlimited space for response)	Large sets of data can be generated by surveys. Data are usually collected in categories (e.g. personal data, literacy practices)	Action research, case study
Journals	At least two types available: participant journals and researcher journals. Participant journals are data that participants are asked to write in order to collect their personal insights into and reflections on an event, practice, concepts, phenomenon, and so on. A researcher journal is kept by the researcher and is used to record hunches, feelings, assumptions about people or processes and	Data are often intensely personal and written from a particular perspective. Can provide important insights for the teacher researcher by providing an alternative perspective on an event, process, programme and so on (participant journals), or by making explicit personal understandings and	Case study, action research, ethnography, narrative inquiry

Technique	Tools	Kinds of data collected	Examples of research designs that utilize the technique
	the like as part of the reflective and verification process	stances on an event, issue or person (researcher journal)	
Projective techniques	An object (an eliciting device) is used to 'elicit' cultural or psychological/cognitive information from participants. Eliciting devices can be anything from dreams to photographs to everyday objects. The Rorschach Ink Blot Test is a classic example of an eliciting device	Projective techniques can collect information about a person's needs, wants, fears, worldview and so on. Asking community members to rank concepts, issues or other people can also give insights into the culture of a community	Ethnography, case study, narrative inquiry
Artefact collection	Emphasis on collecting pertinent 'traces', 'props' or 'products' used by research participants, or that are relevant to the problem area being studied. Artefacts come in many different forms, including texts, lists of objects, photographs, drawings and the like	Helps construct contextualizing data for a study. Fills in additional details (e.g. noting the magazines on someone's coffee table can tell you something about that person's interests)	Case study, action research, ethnography, narrative inquiry
Think-alouds	Process of having study participants 'talk' the researcher through a problem-solving process, other mental activity or a literacy task (e.g. completing a test, sequencing pictures, playing a video game)	Provides insights into a participant's thinking strategies and processes. Enables the researcher to collect a verbal report of an activity-in-process while observing that activity for subsequent comparative analysis between what was said and what was observed	Case study, action research, ethnography

or significant exceptions and variations to these trends or patterns. Researchers use analytic tools and techniques to 'work on' the data in order to find what is 'in there'. Analysis is always more than description or re-description. It tells us more than what is simply 'on the surface' of the data.

For example, James Spradley (1980) talks about an ethnographer making fieldnotes based on observations of a social situation, such as a lesson in a classroom or a group of students interacting in the playground. Spradley explains that the ethnographer's fieldnotes will describe what she or he sees going on there but they are unlikely to contain any or much content about cultural meaning – which is what the ethnographer wants to discover. To move from descriptions of activity in social situations as contained, say, in observational data recorded as fieldnotes to an account of cultural meanings occurring in a cultural scene, the ethnographer needs to analyse the fieldnotes. This might involve using a technique like (cultural) domain analysis (Spradley 1980) to discover patterns in fieldnote descriptions that add up to cultural meanings. Domain analysis involves searching through the data to identify 'cultural domains'. This means looking for regularities in which an 'included term' is linked to a 'cover term' through a 'semantic relationship'. The details need not concern us here (see Chapter 14 for more on domain analysis). Rather, it is sufficient to say that using domain analysis is a typical example of what is involved in analysing data – which is always more than merely re-describing it.

The point can be made by reference to a very popular analytic technique in qualitative research called *open coding* (see also Chapter 14). As described by authors like Strauss and Corbin (1990), Miles and Huberman (1994), and Marshall and Rossman (1999), open coding involves three sequential steps:

1   Breaking down data into discrete parts and applying conceptual codes to it.
2   Comparing and contrasting codes, and grouping sets of similar codes into conceptual categories.
3   Identifying the properties of each category by means of analytic questions, and locating each instance of a phenomenon belonging to this category along a continuum (i.e. 'dimensionalizing' the data).

In the first step the researcher examines data closely and develops codes to identify elements that may be significant at a conceptual level. For example, in their description of a researcher watching work going on in a restaurant, Strauss and Corbin (1990: 64–5) distinguish between applying a conceptual code to data and merely 'summarizing data' by repeating the 'gist' of fieldnotes or interview transcripts 'but still in a descriptive way'. For example, 'talks to waiter', or 'asks waiter a question' or 'reads schedule' would be descriptive whereas 'information gathering' would be conceptual. In their example, Strauss and Corbin are focusing on a woman dressed in red who is obviously performing some role in a restaurant kitchen. They see her *doing certain things* (e.g. things they code as 'information gathering', 'monitoring' etc.), doing them in *certain ways* (coded as 'attentiveness', 'unintrusiveness', 'efficiency') and so on. On the basis of the various conceptual codes they assign to the fieldnotes that recorded the activity of the lady in red, Strauss and Corbin assign her to a category of restaurant worker, which they label 'food orchestrator'. This is *their* term. Nevertheless, it almost certainly will not be the woman's official title. It captures the notion of a worker whose role it is to 'keep the flow of work going in a restaurant', and allows Strauss and Corbin to categorize this type of work and worker in contrast and in relation to other categories.

From their initial conceptual codes, Strauss and Corbin also identify two sub-categories for the food orchestrator work category. They call one 'Types of work for assessing and maintaining work flow'. This will include data coded as 'information gathering', 'monitoring' and the like. The second they call 'Conditions for being a good food orchestrator'. This will include qualities like 'unintrusiveness', 'attentiveness', and so on. We can easily see here how *conceptual coding* 'gets at stuff' in the data that summary descriptions like 'talks to waiter' does not, and makes it possible to arrive at an *analytic category* like 'food orchestrator'.

In the third step, 'dimensions and properties' can be assigned to the activities of the food orchestrator. Hence, 'watching' can be analysed in terms of dimensions and properties like 'frequency', 'duration', 'intensity' and 'extent'. This provides a basis for developing relationships between categories and subcategories on the basis of which we can make sense of what is going on, and use this as a basis for advancing explanations, understandings and so on. This is the kind of work that mere descriptions can never do, since they only state things in parallel ways rather than try to get at 'what these things are made of' and 'what makes them tick'. To extend the metaphor, we could look at and describe the surface appearance and behaviour of a mechanical clock forever without knowing anything relevant to fixing it if it broke down. The latter requires analysis of what makes up the clock. The same is true with respect to the social phenomena that make up educational situations.

When researchers have completed analysing the data they have still to perform the task of *interpreting* the analysis. Although the researcher's approach to analysing the data should have been guided throughout by his or her research purposes, relevant literature and participant feedback on preliminary analyses, the completed data analysis on its own is *not* an answer to the research question or a solution to the original problem. The nature and complexity of interpretation is illustrated and discussed in the final chapter. (Readers who wish to clarify the distinction and relationship between analysis and interpretation at this time can find the relevant section at pages 369–371 in Chapter 16.)

Having established the concept of research as a *systematic* form of inquiry grounded in an appropriate research design, we turn our attention in the following chapter to a discussion of research purposes, focusing on research problems, questions, aims and objectives.

CHAPTER 3

Formulating our research purposes: problems, questions, aims and objectives

Introduction: 'internal' and 'external' dimensions of clarifying research purposes

In Chapter 2 we introduced the idea of clarifying our research purposes in terms of 'internal' and 'external' dimensions. The internal dimension – which is the subject of this chapter – involves a reflexive process of moving between considering our research problem, question, aim and objectives respectively.

The 'external' dimension involves moving between considering our overall research purposes and engaging in the tasks of consulting relevant guiding and informing sources, conceptualizing and planning our approach to data collection and deciding how we will analyse our data. This, too, is a reflexive process, rather than one that is linear and sequential. We do not see it as a matter of *first* determining our research purposes, and *then* reading the literature to inform our study, and *then* deciding on an approach for collecting and analysing data. Rather, we might begin with a preliminary sense of a research problem or question and read some literature to help us clarify and refine our problem or question. At the same time we will be developing ideas about what kind of data (and how much) to collect, and how it might be best to analyse it. As we are thinking about these things we may decide to try out some of our emerging data collection ideas to see how they will look in practice. For instance, we might decide to write and test some interview questions or some other kind of data collection instrument (e.g. a brief survey or questionnaire, or some observations) to see how well they work, how much data they yield, how much time they involve and whether the data they provide looks like it will be relevant and useful for addressing our research concerns. At this point we might even do some reading and thinking about what will be involved in analysing this data – what kinds of data analysis options we have, how much time and effort these different options will require respectively given the kind of data we are collecting, and so on.

This kind of activity can give us a sense of how manageable the study is likely to be if we do it a certain way. In the light of this activity and our deliberations we may come to think that our question is too large or too general, or that we are only going to be able to deal with one or two aspects of a problem rather than several aspects, or the problem as a whole. So we might then do some more reading and do some more thinking about the original research problem area, the nature and scope of our research question(s), and the aim and objectives for our study.

This *reflexive cycle* may go on for some time; until we are satisfied we have the right kind of relationship and balance between research purposes, our key concepts and theoretical angle, and our approach to collecting and analysing data. When we, the authors, are doing our own research we do not worry if this process seems to be taking some time. We believe that doing it properly saves us time and worry in the long run. At the same time, we do not want it to take *too* long.

Like educational and social science researchers generally, teacher researchers will find themselves in a better position to engage in this reflexive cycle efficiently if they first understand what the cycle is like, why it is a cycle, and how experienced researchers undertake the process. In this chapter we describe our own view of these things.

The concept of research purposes

Unless its research purposes are clear, concise and manageable, a study is unlikely to succeed. Researchers can develop a strong base from which to make decisions about sound and efficient data collection and data analysis by establishing a very clear view of what their research *question* is. When we say, 'what their research question *is*', however, we do not simply mean the form of the question as a series of words, or as a selection of words. We mean also what the research question is as an *angle*, a *slant*, or a *perspective* on a problem. In other words, we see it in terms of how answering the question will help to tackle the problem or meet a challenge. We also think of 'what the research question is' in terms of a *focus* that constitutes a succinct research *aim* to be implemented in the research project through a series of *objectives* that collectively 'cover' the question.

The research problem

The idea of a problem can be approached from two different viewpoints. One is what we might call an 'existential' viewpoint. In this sense, a problem is something (e.g. a situation) that puzzles us, concerns us, troubles us or causes us 'hassles'. A problem, in other words, is 'a situation that presents perplexity or difficulty' (Pritchard 1994: 659). We have a problem in this sense when our car won't start, or our child falls ill, or we cannot seem to balance our household budget – and, of course, when pupils behave badly in class or fail to learn what we are trying to teach them. Such things affect us, 'get under our skin' and cause us some degree of 'angst'.

The second viewpoint might be called 'epistemological'. In this sense a problem is something to be solved or addressed by means of trying to understand or know about the situation. When we begin to think about why the bothersome car will not start and what we might have to do to get it going, our problem becomes an epistemological as well as an existential concern. When, as teachers, we have to decide which is the better method for teaching reading or spelling to a group of unsuccessful learners, and want to make our decision on the basis of evidence and information, we have a problem to resolve in the epistemological sense of 'problem' – although it may initially have arisen from our (existential) perplexity about the students who could not or would not learn. At this point perhaps we discover that different methods are available for teaching poor readers and writers, but we do not know which might be best for our particular students.

Teacher research can be seen as emerging at the point where problems in the first (existential) sense emerge as problems in the second (epistemological) sense. The problems that concern teacher researchers are of different kinds. These include *theoretical, conceptual* and *informational* problems, *practical* problems, and *ethical* or *valuative* problems. Many educational problems, of course, have elements of all these types. It is common to think of teacher research almost entirely in terms of practical problems. But this is by no means necessarily the case. We can see this by looking at some reasonably 'pure' typical examples of these various kinds of problems.

Consider, for example, a context of developing a policy to guide the purchase and uses of new technologies within literacy education at the school level. The problem is about having to develop a sound and workable policy in terms of cost effectiveness, teacher development etc., and of really not knowing whether the policy development team is following a feasible line. Might it be a bad move to enact the ideas currently on the table? If the policy proves mistaken its effects would live on for several years. In this case we might undertake research simply to find out whether other people have pursued this kind of policy under similar conditions to those we are encountering ourselves, and what the results were. In addition, if there are such examples we might try to understand and explain why they had the results they did. The problem in this case is one of discovering what happened, and why, in similar cases to our own. This is a *theoretical* and/or *informational* problem, even though our findings could contribute to addressing, for example, some practical problem in the area of school technology policy.

In a different case, it is possible that the school technology-literacy policy (once established) is not being implemented successfully, and we want to know how to solve this problem. This may involve experimenting with different approaches to see which one works best, and then trying to use it more widely in order to achieve successful implementation. This would be an example of a *practical* problem.

As an example of an *ethical* problem we may consider the same scenario at the level of developing the school technology-literacy policy. In this case the group focuses specifically on whether the policy being contemplated will be just and fair across the school population, or whether it might harm certain students' interests to enact the policy in its present form. Alternatively, an ethical problem might arise around a policy about using resources to enhance the learning performance of a particular group because this involves diverting resources away from other groups who are also seen to have legitimate needs and claims.

Task

Which of the following problems seems to you to be practical? Which appears to be theoretical and which appears to be ethical? What are the reasons for your selections?

- Different theorists define 'reading' in very different ways. It is difficult to know which view is best for structuring learning activities in the classroom.

- Some of my students who enjoy reading many different kinds of texts outside of school are performing badly in classroom reading. It has been suggested that their classroom work might improve if more of the kinds of texts they read in their everyday lives are incorporated into their learning activities in class.

- The literacy curriculum and resources we have in our school do not seem to relate well to the cultural heritages and life experiences of all of my students.

Of course, as noted at the end of Chapter 1, teacher research problems do not necessarily 'arrive' or present themselves immediately or as 'fully formed' problems. They may not be like the car that does not start – where we are immediately aware that a problem exists and where the problem is already 'complete'. Often we may only gradually come to see the existence of a research problem – for example, when something draws our attention to some aspect of a situation that we were not aware of at first. In other words, sometimes the elements of a research problem may already exist, but without our being aware of them. A problem starts to emerge, however, when something about the situation appears to be unusual, unexpected or discrepant, and where we come to think that there is something to be understood or discovered in order to explain this discrepancy or unexpected state of affairs. The emergence of a problem may occur because, for example, we become aware of some relevant information or theory that suddenly alerts us to something unusual in a situation that we had not previously noticed.

For example, imagine the case of a teacher who is assessing student work over the duration of an intervention by giving them a recommended task (a test or essay) at regular intervals. When the teacher looks at the results of the students over a period of time she notices unexpected or anomalous trends or patterns in the students' results. Research reports on the intervention show that individual student results normally improve equally for girls and boys. But she notices that the results in her classroom assessment show a consistent trend at variance from what the research reports say. At this point she has a stimulus for framing something to be known more deeply, to be understood, and to be explained by means of systematic inquiry. The moment she begins to *frame* a problem and a question to probe that problem concerning the assessment scores and patterns, and to wonder how to address it through systematic inquiry, we have the beginnings of research. She will start looking for clues about how her inquiry might proceed. This will lead to examining some relevant literature and, perhaps, trying to obtain information from people who know something about the kind of situation that has occurred within similar sorts of learning contexts.

The research question

Often one's initial idea of a research problem is only provisional. It may be necessary to refine the nature and scope of the problem several times during the process of clarifying one's research purposes. The process of refining research purposes involves more than simply clarifying the research *problem*. It also involves formulating a research *question* (or questions) that can be managed successfully, and specifying the research aim and objectives. Researchers may have to move through a number of 'iterations' before their research purposes are fully established.

Nonetheless, once we have identified a research problem – even if only provisionally – we can set about trying to make it as clear and specific as possible. This involves taking the problem as a situation or circumstance that can be defined in terms of something to be *resolved*, or as something for which we seek a solution or an *answer*. In other words, we begin to pose our problem in terms of questions: questions whose answers provide us with a solution or a strategy (whether full or partial) for addressing the problem.

We cannot set about addressing problems systematically unless we have some questions to guide and structure our responses. We have to re-present the research problem as a research question (or question sequence) that provides us with a focus and a strategy for addressing the problem. For illustrative purpose, consider the case of a vehicle that will not start. The fact that it will not start constitutes the problem situation; the situation to be investigated. This situation can easily be posed – or re-presented – as a question to be investigated: 'What is preventing the engine from starting?' Addressing this very general question may be necessary for answering the practical question of what needs to be done to correct the fault so the engine will start.

While this is a good start, it is too simple in and of itself. The situation with the engine is actually quite complex. The example is useful, however, because a car engine is complex in ways similar to educational research situations. Let's consider the case of the engine a little further, recognizing nonetheless that the problem-posing/question-generating activity of the mechanic is not really a research activity in our full sense.

Let us then imagine a conventional vehicle engine that won't start, and a mechanic setting about trying to find out what is preventing it. The mechanic will make use of theoretical and practical knowledge and expertise about the engine. They will know that the engine involves more than one 'system'. The engine's failure to start may be the result of something being wrong in any one or more of these systems. The problem may lie in the fuel system. There may be a blockage that needs to be cleared, or there may be no petrol, or there might be something wrong with the petrol. Alternatively, the problem may lie in the electrical or electronic system. For instance, perhaps there is no spark. The problem may exist in the mechanical system: the pistons could be seized, or the starter motor could be jammed. In this very simple example, the original question – 'What is preventing the engine from starting?' – can be made more specific by framing it as a series of questions.

Original question		'What is preventing the engine from starting?'
Refined questions	1(a)	'Is there a fault in the fuel system (and if so, what is it)?'
	1(b)	'Is there a fault in the electrical system (and if so, what is it)?'
	1(c)	'Is there a fault in the mechanical system (and if so, what is it)?'
	1(d)	'Are there faults in more than one system (and if so, which)?'
	1(e)	'Is there more than one fault in one system?'
	1(f)	'Is there more than one fault in more than one system?'

Experienced mechanics will, of course, 'ask' such questions automatically, and not even think of this activity as research. They will not write them down or even consciously *frame* them. But their activity will nonetheless take the form of addressing such questions. In the context of a particular engine there may be certain clues which encourage the mechanic to begin with one question rather than another. For instance, perhaps the model of car is one that is well-known to have electrical problems. Or maybe the mechanic can smell petrol getting to the engine and assumes that the problem is not with the fuel system etc. This is a logical procedure based on relevant prior knowledge and experience. The mechanic might not initially identify the correct system (or subsystem) where the problem is located, but by following the questions logically they maximize the chances of finding the fault by investigating in a systematic manner.

In many ways this is similar to the teacher research situation, in that teachers accumulate a lot of experience that enables them to recognize different dimensions of problems and to distinguish different aspects or dimensions of problems in a similar way to mechanics. On the other hand, unlike the experienced mechanic who has lots of prior knowledge of engines and engine systems and can generalize quite effectively to cover a wide range of cases, teacher researchers very often have to acquire relevant information or 'experience' by trawling a large literature base dealing with research and theory – simply because social processes, like education, are more complicated and diverse than mechanical processes.

We might consider here the case of a pupil who is having difficulty with reading in class. The problem situation is one of poor reading performance in school. The most general question to be researched in relation to the problem is: 'Why is this pupil performing badly in school reading tasks?' This question is not very helpful, however, because there are so many possible sources of difficulty that simply do not compare with the relatively self-contained case of a car engine. Moreover, whereas the job of the mechanic is mainly about 'fixing things that get broke', the teacher's job is mainly about enabling learners to make positive advances on the assumption that being able to do so is the norm rather than the exception. Teaching is oriented much more to 'unleashing' and to 'actualizing' or 'realizing' than to 'fixing up'. In order to begin generating some more specific research questions in a manner parallel to that of the mechanic described above, it may be necessary for the researcher to obtain some 'vicarious experience' beyond the range they already have by looking at theory and research about reading difficulties, learning failure in reading, poor performance in school work and so on.

After exploring some literature and, perhaps, talking to experienced reading specialists, researchers and so on, our teacher researcher may be in a position to frame some more specific questions (or, depending on the kind of research being done, some hypotheses to be tested). These might include questions like the following:

- Does this pupil have a history of learning difficulties and low achievement within formal education?
- Is reading difficulty a pattern within the pupil's family history?
- What is the child's self-perception as a reader (do they see themselves as a good reader, an average reader, a poor reader etc?). How do the caregivers (parents, guardians etc.) perceive the pupil as a reader?
- Does the child read efficiently outside of the school context?
- What are the pupil's attitudes toward reading as an activity?
- Do (many) other students in the class perform badly in reading within the classroom?
- How do the pupil's closest friends perform in classroom reading tasks?

The questions the researcher asks might not be 'single shot' questions – that is, questions whose answers resolve or explain the problem as a whole on their own. Rather, they may be preliminary questions designed simply to *begin* a research process that might have to pose many questions and involve a lot of data collection and analysis over several phases or projects before answers, solutions and strategies emerge. For example, the researcher may decide that, to begin with, the question they can best deal with under present circumstances is one like: 'What kind of family history in reading does this pupil have?' or, 'What kind of attitudes does this pupil (or the pupil's "significant" others – friends, peer group members, family members) have toward reading?'

Specific preliminary questions like these will often emerge from the theory or research literature interrogated by the researcher. This might include literature based on research and a particular perspective about, say, peer-group pressure, or the effects of perceptions on performance, or aversion/resistance to reading, or about the nature of classroom measures of reading in comparison to measures of successful reading in non-school settings etc.

The questions researchers eventually decide to ask will reflect a range of influences. These may include what they read, what their theoretical preferences or interests are, what their 'hunches' or prior experiences are, their relevant knowledge about a particular pupil or the pupil's circumstances and so on. We might imagine a teacher becoming interested in a corpus of studies that suggest school constructions of reading failure often label as failures pupils who nonetheless read effectively outside of school. The teacher's initial interest in the poor literacy achievements of two students resulted in some preliminary information gathering via prearranged informal conversations with a caregiver of each child. In the case of one student in particular the conversation indicated that the child participated enthusiastically in a range of activities outside of school that would seemingly involve intensive use and production of different kinds of texts. This resonated with the teacher's reading about children's out of school literacy practices. The teacher thinks it could be useful to 'map' this child's involvement with texts over a more or less typical span of his out of school activities. The child and the parent are both happy for the teacher to observe, as unobtrusively as possible, the child's activities in home and neighbourhood settings during several afternoons/evenings over a term. In the light of this opportunity the teacher decides to gather (and subsequently analyse) data relevant to three related questions.

- *What* specific texts does the child actively engage with during the periods of observation?
- *How* does he engage with them?
- What does he *do with them* or *use them for*?

Two brief digressions

Against this background of the ideas of problems and questions and the relationship between them it is useful to briefly consider two aspects of research questions that relate directly to the quality and value of the teacher research we undertake.

The first has to do with the relationship between developing good-quality research questions and having a genuine problem focus – something one really wants to find out about and respond to effectively – in the first place. One of the things supervisors or advisers of postgraduate research often encounter is the difficulty many students experience in formulating good research questions. There are many reasons for this, but one of them is that in degree-conferring research programmes it is possible to want to conduct research without already having an authentic existential or epistemological 'hassle' or 'puzzle' that motivates the wish to do research in the first place. Without some concern or circumstance one 'feels the grip of' it is difficult to formulate good researchable questions. To have a question means having a question *about* something, and the more tangible and motivating that 'something' is, the easier it is – other things being equal – to think of questions to ask about it.

Of course, not all 'somethings' are problems in the fruitful sense we are trying to describe here. For instance, there is a difference between having a problem, issue or puzzle and, say, being interested in something in a general kind of way. One popular way of asking what someone wants to research is to ask what they are interested in. But this often produces responses like 'well, I'm interested in critical literacy (or science education, or higher order skills, etc)'. This is better than nothing so far as having a 'something' goes, but it may not be *much* better. It is possible to be generally interested in some area or topic – even to be *genuinely* interested in it – but to not have the kind of focused and motivated grounding required to ask questions about it and think of angles from which to get at aspects of it.

As practitioners, teachers are in a very good position to generate genuine educational problems, or to identify focused issues and concerns that provide tangible 'targets' for *interrogating* – which is a useful way of thinking about the process of generating research questions. In paradigm situations where interrogation occurs, there is a clear focus, an object of concern and a point of view. These help us to frame the questions we ask, and to see the subject of interrogation as someone from whom we can find out some of the things we want to know. In research, the presence of a problem in the sense we are concerned with here will often provide us with the kind of 'object of interrogation' that makes it easier to generate questions.

To the same extent, teacher researchers are well placed to be able to generate high-quality research questions, precisely because they are in situations and circumstances on a moment by moment basis that can present authentic or genuine problems and puzzles. These are problems and puzzles that lend themselves to the kinds of interrogation that can quickly have us generating questions from all sorts of angles. This is especially so when we set out to enhance our sense of the problem or puzzle by considering what other people's ideas, perspectives and inquiries might contribute to our own investigation.

The second digression – which will become clearer following our discussion in Chapter 4 – concerns the way we understand and formulate our research questions in relation to the different kinds of research we might undertake as teachers. These might be broadly understood as documentary, quantitative, qualitative and 'mixed methods' research. The point here is that different kinds of research purposes tend to be best investigated by means of one kind of research rather than the others. Conversely, different kinds of research tend to lend themselves more effectively to certain kinds of purposes rather than others. The knack is to know which, and why.

For example, we might think about different kinds of research purposes concerning young people's uses of computing and communications technologies (CCTs) outside of school in relation to the different kinds of research teachers might do. In one case a teacher (or group of teachers) might be interested (for whatever reason) in how the profile of uses of CCTs of the 800 students in their secondary school compares with that of a county or national sample. In this case they might obtain a survey questionnaire used in a national or county-wide survey, administer it to the entire student population and then analyse it using the same statistical techniques employed in the original study. This would be to engage in a form of *quantitative* research. Alternatively, a teacher might be interested in typical popular cultural forms within which young people in her country use CCTs. She might decide that this is best done by reading as many published reports of research relevant to this topic as possible and then analysing the findings into a range of categories that seem appropriate to her interests as a teacher. In this case, the research purpose will be addressed by means of document-based inquiry. In a different case, a teacher might be interested in understanding the significance of some typical social practices involving CCTs in which her students are involved. This might call for looking at a small number of cases in depth. In this case the idea of 'uses' would be understood in terms of the quality and meanings of the experiences and understandings, practices and purposes, goals and values, beliefs and wishes, and so on of those people who are selected as research subjects. Here, the teacher undertakes a *qualitative* research study. Finally, a group of teachers might be interested in understanding in-depth a selection of 'typical' and 'atypical' uses of CCTs among their students. In this case they might administer a simple survey to the students at large and analyse the responses into different numerical categories. The categories that correspond to large numbers of students being involved could stand for 'typical' uses, and those corresponding to very few students being involved would represent 'atypical' uses. On the basis of this very simple quantitative survey the researchers could then select a small number of individuals who represent 'typical' and 'atypical' uses respectively, and look at these cases in depth by means of a qualitative research approach. This study would be a 'mixed methods' investigation.

Task

Take each of the four research 'scenarios' described in the previous paragraph. For each:

- Think of a *problem* at the school level that the study might have been intended to address.

- Formulate a *question* the study might have been intended to address.

The research aim

In the process of becoming clearer about our research problem and our overarching research question, we simultaneously become clearer about our research aim. This is because the two are intimately connected. A clear and useful way of thinking about the *aim* of any research we do is to see it in terms of a relationship between the research problem we are trying to address and the research question we have formulated in order to address (some significant aspect or aspects of) that problem. In other words, we can think of our research aim as being 'to contribute to understanding and resolving the problem of X [our research problem] by addressing the question Y [our research question]'.

This is a general concept of 'research aim' that can apply to *any* research study. It is, perhaps, the most straightforward way possible to think about research aims. As such, the research aim of any study can be expressed in the following form (with the kinds of variations noted).

Research aim:

> This research project aims to advance/enhance/contribute to our understanding of/knowledge of/capacity to address/ability to resolve or deal with the problem/issue/challenge/difficulty of X by addressing the question: 'How/why/what _____?

We can return here to our earlier example of the teacher who negotiates to observe a student's involvement with texts in home and neighbourhood settings of social practice. The aim of such a study might simply be to contribute something to the knowledge base for improving literacy achievement within classroom learning through identifying, describing, and understanding involvement with texts outside of school in ways that might inform potential pedagogical strategies within formal literacy education. This recalls a point raised in the section on the research problem. Such a research aim would be a *partial* aim. It is not an aim to *solve* or *overcome* a problem by means of a single study. Rather, it is an aim to make a realistic contribution toward tackling a problem: a problem that is large. In fact, many individual research projects might be necessary in order to obtain the knowledge and information required to successfully address such cases of low achievement as represented by the student in question.

The important thing for the researcher is to arrive at a realistic and worthwhile aim, and to be clear about what part of the overall contribution to addressing a problem one's own research project will make. If we manage to get this kind of clarity, we will also be helping to clarify what other useful contributions could be made to resolving the problem as a whole. Unfortunately, researchers often aim for too much, and cannot hope to achieve their aim. While it is also undesirable to aim for too little, it is usually easier to make an aim larger or more ambitious if we find we are pitching too low than it is to make an aim smaller if we have set it unrealistically high at the beginning of a study.

Once again, it is worth noting here that we are *not* saying that *first* we have to identify our problem and *then* frame our question, and *then* state our aim. Rather, researchers will usually find themselves moving backwards and forwards between problem, question, aim and objectives (see next section). It is almost certain that we will find it difficult to state our research aim clearly if we do not have a clear sense of our research problem and question. Hence, a researcher will probably arrive at a clear statement of a research aim *after* having arrived at a clear picture of the research problem and question. But this is not to imply a linear sequence of problem → question → aim. Instead, the process may be more like a spiral in which we become progressively clear about each element, albeit with the final statement of the research aim *following* closure on the problem and the question.

Research objectives

When we turn to the concept of our research *objectives* we see once again that the process of identifying and defining our research purposes is truly 'cyclical', 'iterative' and 'reflexive'. In order to develop a coherent set of objectives for a research study we need to have a clear sense of our research aim. As we have seen, this presupposes moving backwards and forwards between our research problem, question and aim. As we will now see, however, we also need to factor the research objectives into this dynamic process.

Just as we described the research aim in terms of the research problem and question, so we think of the research objectives in terms of the research aim. Our concept of research 'objectives' is of the more or less specific *tasks* or *components* researchers will undertake in order to fulfil their research aims. While this is not how everybody would define research objectives it is nonetheless a concept we find useful in our own work. A full set of research objectives in this sense would comprise tasks to be undertaken such that if we completed all of them successfully we would indeed have addressed the research question satisfactorily.

Specific research objectives will often have value in their own right as well as in terms of their contribution to achieving an overall research aim. Sometimes researchers fall short of achieving their overall research aim yet nonetheless make a significant contribution to an area of inquiry by having successfully completed one or more of their objectives. For instance, we might imagine a teacher researcher who wanted to implement and evaluate (and write up) a unit of work on critical media literacy, using a set of activities she had developed on the basis of her particular concept of *critical literacy in relation to media*. Let us suppose that for one reason or another she was unable to implement and evaluate the unit of work with the students in the time available, and only got part way through. Nonetheless, she had documented her concept of critical media literacy, compared and contrasted it with other people's accounts, and had produced documents showing how she had set about developing a set of activities based on the concepts and theories of critical media literacy she had used to inform her work – as specific objectives within her overall research purpose. The very act of completing these components (objectives) of the overall study would, on its own, represent a valuable research contribution, notwithstanding her inability to complete the study as a whole.

The process of developing a succinct statement of research objectives is not a matter of arriving at the *definitive statement* of the objectives involved. Often there will be no single definitive set of objectives for a given aim, since the aim might be satisfied by various sets of objectives. Also, what one person might see as an objective in its own right might be seen by someone else as part of a larger objective. Rather than agonizing over a definitive statement we should see the process of developing our research objectives as an opportunity for thinking about the study *holistically*: thinking about the different elements involved in the overall design and how they will cohere with each other. For this reason, our statement of objectives might include such items as clarifying or defining key concepts relevant to the study, developing appropriate data collection instruments and techniques, deciding on suitable data analysis tools and procedures, and so on. On the other hand, more confident and experienced researchers might take these objectives for granted and not include them in their statement of research objectives.

Here again we can return to the example of the teacher who intends to observe a child's involvement with texts in various home and neighbourhood contexts. The study aims to make a contribution to a knowledge base by identifying, describing, and understanding the child's active involvement with texts in such settings. The research questions posed by the teacher ask *what* specific texts the child actively engages with in these settings, *how* he engages with them and what he *does* with them and/or *uses* them for. Taking into account the different levels of specificity with which objectives could be framed, the following might qualify as typical examples of objectives for such a study:

- to develop criteria for what count as *texts*;
- to develop criteria for what counts as *active involvement with texts*;
- to 'operationalize' (i.e. to develop criteria that capture the sense of what is meant by) '*how* the child engages with a text';
- to design data collection tools based on this operationalization/these criteria to get information about how the child engages with a particular text;
- to develop criteria and data collection tools based on these criteria, for getting information about the child's 'doings with' and/or 'uses for' particular texts;
- to identify a range of texts with which the child is actively involved in home and neighbourhood contexts of social practice.

Task

Using this same research 'scenario':

1 Develop other possible research objectives at different levels of specificity.

2 Add them to the set provided above.

3 Reduce the total to a set of no more than six objectives you think would be adequate.

4 Consider the extent to which these adequately 'capture' the aim of the study.

5 Make any changes you think necessary and present your final set of objectives.

Now devise your own modification of the research scenario in which a teacher is going to observe a child's 'engagement with texts' in home and school settings. In doing this:

1 Develop your own research questions for this imagined scenario.

2 Identify a problem that warrants the research.

3 Formulate an aim for the study.

4 Formulate a set of objectives for the study.

Concluding comments

The account we have provided in this chapter of research purposes is by no means the only one possible. Other researchers might provide quite different accounts. At the same time we find that thinking of *research purposes* in terms of the relationships between the research problem, research question, research aim and research objectives provides a useful structure for clarifying what we are really trying to achieve in a given research project.

Task

1   Can you think of other concepts besides 'aim', objectives', 'problem' and 'question' that you think provide a viable alternative view of 'research purposes', or one that is preferable to the account we have provided here? If so, what are these concepts? How do they constitute *purposes*?

2   What other accounts of 'research purposes' can you find in the literature? How do they differ from our account here? What are the pros and cons of the various accounts?

3   How would you describe the process of moving from an initial idea or sense of a research *problem* to a first attempt at formulating a research *question*?

4   Do you think that a researcher needs to have a research *problem* in order to generate a research *question*? Always? Mostly? Sometimes? Occasionally? If you think they do not, what other ways might there be of obtaining a research question?

5   Locate a report of a research project (this could be an article, book, monograph, thesis, formal report etc.). What can you say about the *purposes* of the piece of research in question on the basis of the written account? Does the report specify the problem to which the research has responded? Does it specify a research *question*? Does it specify *aim* and *objectives*? If so, what are these? How well are they stated? Do they help you to evaluate the usefulness of the research?

6   Locate a report of research in which there is no elaborate account of the research purposes. On the basis of your reading, what kinds of research purposes can you think of that would be consistent with the description of the research that you have read? Try and think of purposes for each category you think are useful (e.g. aim, question, problem, objectives, etc.).

The next chapter outlines three general approaches to teacher research.

CHAPTER 4

General approaches to teacher research
With Alina Reznitskaya

Introduction

This chapter will introduce some key features of three broad research options available to teacher researchers: namely, *document-based research*, *quantitative research* and *qualitative research*. (It will also briefly mention 'mixed methods research' as a research hybrid comprising elements of quantitative and qualitative approaches.) In subsequent chapters we will discuss each of these three types in greater detail – particularly qualitative research – in terms of common approaches to data collection and data analysis. This chapter is designed to provide readers with a basic sense of the 'look and feel' of each research type.

Teacher research as document-based inquiry

In document-based research the data to be collected, organized and analysed in order to address a research question, and to be used as evidence for ideas and positions the researcher will argue for, *already exists* within available documents. The sorts of texts used in documentary research include theoretical works, accounts of concepts, commentaries, position papers, exegetic texts, policy documents, syllabus documents, historical archives, newspaper files, previously published quantitative or qualitative research studies, correspondence and so on. The image that springs to mind here is of researchers collecting their data in libraries and other public archives. These days, of course, much of this can also be done using online resources. Hence, the kinds of research questions and problems involved in documentary research are ones that do not call for generating new data but, rather, for drawing on existing formal texts to *reconstitute* (some of) their contents as data for new studies.

Documentary data versus transcripts, journal entries, and fieldnotes

The kinds of texts that provide data for documentary research are 'finished' works. They present viewpoints and substantive positions. Their authors intend them to be read as statements about some matter or another. To this extent, whatever data they are based on have already been 'processed' as much as they are ever going to be by their authors.

By contrast, documents or artefacts such as transcripts of recorded interviews or of recorded slices of natural life settings, entries made in participant or researcher journals/diaries/logs and the like, and fieldnotes of observations of real life settings are not 'finished' in this way. Rather, they are materials from which 'finished' works may ultimately be produced.

There are, of course, some blurred or fuzzy cases to be considered. For example, sometimes the fieldnotes, logs and diaries of people get catalogued or published (often posthumously) when they were not originally produced or regarded by their authors as 'finished' or 'considered' works. They might look much more like secondary data than the kinds of primary texts integral to documentary research, and yet be accessible online or in libraries in much the same way that we access works presenting formal, substantive, argued positions aimed at a public audience. We may then need to think of them and treat them differently from the kinds of works we mainly draw on in document-based research.

Typical examples of document-based research

Document-based research can take different forms. These are known by various names, such as 'research synthesis', 'conceptual-theoretical research' and the like. In the realm of academic education research a very significant proportion of the total research output falls into this broad category. For example, practically everything done in philosophy of education can be regarded as documentary research. A lot of work in education policy studies falls into this category as well, along with considerable amounts of research in theoretical sociology of education, history of education (and specialized fields like curriculum history, history of literacy, historical studies of women in education and so on), cultural studies of education, politics of education etc. Sometimes such academic research work is referred to as 'educational scholarship' to distinguish it from more directly *empirical* forms of educational research where researchers are collecting data in settings where research subjects are doing things that are being counted, measured, observed, recorded and so on.

Contemporary examples of document-based research within the academic research tradition include work like Deborah Britzman's (1998, 2003) account of 'practice making practice' and Michael Apple's (1979, 1996) writings on official knowledge, ideology and the curriculum. Similarly, Linda Brodkey's (1996) critique of 'writing permitted in designated areas only', Henry Giroux's (1983) account of theory and resistance in education, Ivor Goodson's (1994) work on curriculum history and Maxine Greene's (1978, 1995a, 1995b) writings on releasing the imagination, the dialectic of freedom and teacher as stranger are further and diverse examples. So are bell hooks' (1994) account of teaching to transgress, Joe Kincheloe and Shirley Steinberg's (1997) work on changing multiculturalism, Peter McLaren's (1995, 1997) studies of critical pedagogy, Erica McWilliam's (1995) work on feminist orientations for change and Tom Popkewitz's (1993) writings on the political sociology of educational reform.

Documentary research is especially well suited to certain kinds of questions and researcher circumstances. Indeed, some kinds of research questions can *only* be tackled by way of such research: for example, the question, 'Where does the current weight of evidence lie with respect to successful approaches to teaching English language spelling to Grade 3 ESL students from Vietnam?' Similarly, an investigation of the different meanings of 'literacy' within education policy documents is a matter for documentary research. Often, the *circumstances* of the researcher might call for a documentary research approach, such as when the researcher has no easy access to research subjects and/or lacks the resources needed for collecting and analysing fresh data. In addition, documentary research is a cost-effective and responsible option to take in areas where there is already abundant research and where one's research needs might be met equally well (if not better) by appealing to existing research rather than generating further data.

A study by Alan Pikulski (1994) provides an example of using documentary research with a view to informing classroom practice in the area of literacy education. Pikulski was interested in factors that might be associated with greater likelihood of successful implementation of early intervention programmes in reading. To this end he surveyed journals with national (USA) distribution where articles were reviewed by an editorial board prior to being published. He aimed at locating examples of early intervention programmes described in reasonable detail. He identified five programmes used in the USA at the time for which data existed that suggested they were 'effective'. These data indicated that 'student participation in the programs led to substantially better reading achievement than that of similar students who had not participated in the programs' (Pikulski 1994: 32). The study had two related aims. The first was to compare the programmes on multiple dimensions like length of intervention, kinds of materials used, assessment procedures, amount of instruction time and so on. The second was to see whether any common features could be identified on the basis of this comparison that appeared to be related to preventing reading problems. Pikulski's research logic was that identifying features 'common to successful early intervention programs' as proxies for features that are seemingly related to preventing reading problems could be useful for teachers who are planning intervention programmes or who are working with learners requiring early intervention. On the basis of this document-based study –

which refers readers to supporting data provided in original sources rather than trying to 'prove' the programmes' effectiveness or determine their relative merits Pikulski identified 11 issues corresponding to common features in the five programmes on the dimensions he used for comparing them. He concluded that attention to these issues might reasonably be expected to enhance the likelihood of making successful interventions against early reading problems.

At this point, it is worth considering a concrete (and topical) instance where teacher researchers could employ documentary research to address questions that concern them.

Clarifying 'constructivism'

For some years now 'constructivism' has been promoted at seemingly endless numbers of conferences, at professional development initiatives and within teacher education programmes as providing the best approach to planning and implementing teaching and learning activities. At the same time, the ideas teachers and educationists have about constructivism and constructivist approaches to learning vary widely and often seem unclear. In much educational talk, constructivism seems to mean little more than providing learners with opportunities to make their own sense of things in their own way – to actively construct their own versions of knowledge of the world.

This might provide some teachers with strong incentives for thinking 'there must surely be more to it than this', and for deciding to investigate what is involved in constructivist approaches to learning. They might ask questions like, 'What is encapsulated in the concept "Constructivism"?'. This kind of question lends itself to document-based research. Indeed, teacher researchers who set out to clarify 'constructivism' to their satisfaction will find very large conventional and online literatures on the topic. These literatures cover theoretical and conceptual variations associated with the work of major figures like Bruner, Piaget and Vygotsky and, in turn, with distinctions between cognitive constructivism, social constructivism, constructionism and so on. The literatures within teacher research and academic research describing research projects designed to implement and evaluate constructivist approaches are equally diverse and complex.

Teacher researchers will find here many different positions and arguments that need to be identified, distinguished and categorized in order to make any headway whatsoever toward arriving at a personal understanding of what it might mean to ground teaching on 'constructivism'. They will have decisions to make about which version of constructivism they prefer, and on what basis they prefer it.

Documentary research versus reviewing the literature (as a component of research projects)

When thinking about document-based research as a general approach to undertaking research it is useful to compare it with the kind of work done in reviewing literature as a component of research projects generally. We will look at the process of reviewing literature in greater detail in Chapter 5. Meanwhile, we can note here that a restricted form of 'documentary research' is involved in writing the literature review for any kind of study – whether it is document-based, quantitative or qualitative research.

The main difference between doing a literature review as a vital component of an overall piece of research and conducting a full-scale piece of documentary research is that the latter usually involves a range of specialized techniques of analysis, interpretation and data handling that are not typically used in literature reviews.

Researchers begin reviewing relevant literature once they have identified a problem area or issue that provides an *incentive* (Silverman 1985: 9) to undertake research on it. The point of reviewing relevant literature is to inform our research so that it will be as useful and of as high a quality as possible. It does this in two complementary ways, one of which can be seen as 'positive', while the other is more 'negative'.

From a negative perspective, the literature in a field can help us to avoid weaknesses, shortcomings, blind alleys and wasted effort when doing our research. For example, literature relevant to our inquiries does not merely report or describe things: much of it also engages in critique. Authors will point out what they regard as errors, shoddy work, irrelevance and so on, in the work of others (and, sometimes, in their own earlier work). By reviewing the literature we can become aware of things to try and avoid in our research. By looking and seeing the kind of work that has already been done we can also avoid needlessly 'reinventing the wheel': doing what has already been done to death, or coming up with what other people have previously done, and that we could have built upon productively rather than merely repeating.

From a positive standpoint, reviewing the literature can help us identify genuine gaps in the area of our research interest. It can thereby alert us to aspects we can focus on that will genuinely make a contribution to understanding more about the area or problem. In addition, it is by reviewing the literature that we develop an overall framework for designing and implementing our study. We collect a body of relevant information (i.e. content germane to framing the study); we organize this information (e.g. papers and books that draw on this theory and these assumptions, versus papers and books drawing on other theories and assumptions; material pertaining to this aspect versus material pertaining to other aspects; arguments for a given viewpoint versus arguments against it etc.); we sort out the aspects that are most relevant to our own work and identify the different positions and perspectives that other people have taken up or developed on these aspects. These will be things like the kinds of ideas and theories they have drawn upon, or the particular definition of a concept they have adopted (as distinct from other ones that are available). We produce succinct expositions of elements of the literature that are most important to our own work, and use them as a basis for discussing their respective strengths and weaknesses. We develop this into statements that help us justify the approach we will take. When all these parts are in place we assemble and integrate them into a statement that provides a rationale for what we are going to do and why we are going to do it that way. The statement will present a framework of concepts and theories to be used in implementing the study as a whole.

This background provides a basis for looking at how reviewing literature compares with and differs from common forms of fully-fledged document-based research. It is helpful here first to distinguish different types of activity that can be regarded as fully-fledged document-based research; that is, to differentiate between *general* forms of documentary research and what we call more *specialized* forms. For example, we think of 'state of the art' document-based studies as falling within the 'general' category. So do studies that take the form of 'identifying the implications that a corpus of research has for a particular question'. Examples of 'specialized' forms of document-based research include particular kinds of policy analysis, textual analysis, historical analysis and so on.

General forms of document-based research

In 'state of the art' documentary studies the point is to find out the current state of knowledge and to identify the 'leading edge' on a given problem, issue or question. An earlier example can serve as a typical instance of state of the art documentary research: namely, 'Where does the current weight of evidence lie with respect to successful approaches to teaching English language spelling to Grade 3 ESL students from Vietnam?'

The kind of study undertaken by Pikulski (1994) can serve as an example of document-based research of the 'implications of a research corpus for a particular question' variety. Pikulski is interested in a question like: 'What kinds of procedures might be associated with successful approaches to addressing reading problems in the early years?' His investigation of the literature yielded implications that might be seen as at least partial responses to such a question.

These two forms of inquiry tend to call on more or less *generic skills* and procedures for dealing with the data that is assembled from documents. These involve processes like providing fair and succinct summaries and expositions of viewpoints, assembling and synthesizing viewpoints, comparing and contrasting positions, organizing and categorizing positions, viewpoints, conclusions, findings, perspectives and the like. They also include procedures like evaluating arguments, weighing the comparative evidence for different positions, deriving implications from conclusions and sets of findings and so on. In some cases, basic forms of thematic analysis, content analysis and the like will be involved as well. These, however, are usually quite straightforward extensions of the ability to classify and build typologies, or to identify similarities and differences among elements, and to sort them and provide labels.

These, of course, are the kinds of processes that are involved in doing a standard review of literature that is relevant to a research question or problem. To put it the other way: unless one is doing these kinds of things one is not really *reviewing* literature but, perhaps, only collecting, organizing and summarizing literature. If a literature review is to explain and justify the approach one is going to take in a larger research project, there is no escape from procedures like weighing evidence, evaluating arguments and so on. To this extent, then, there is no substantial difference between the tasks and procedures involved in doing a literature review and those involved in undertaking a self-contained documentary research project of the kind reported by

Pikulski. The difference is that a literature review is part of a larger project that it is intended to inform. General forms of stand-alone document-based research, by contrast, are studies in their own right. They have their particular research problem and question, and the 'review and synthesis' they provide constitutes the study as a piece of document-based research. These are bona fide forms of documentary research, and generic literature reviewing techniques and procedures are sufficient for the job. Anyone who can review literature competently has the requisite skills, techniques and understandings for undertaking fully-fledged documentary research of (what we have called) the *general* variety.

Specialized forms of document-based research

On the other hand, there are some kinds of documentary research where the literature review component takes the researcher to a point where more specialized kinds of data analysis and modes of inquiry are required for implementing the study. For example, a researcher may be interested in understanding aspects of literacy policy and their implications for classroom work. The literature review may have raised issues about policy development she or he was previously unaware of, including the way policy impacts politically – in terms of relations and processes of power – on the life and work of schools. As a result, the teacher researcher sees a need to collect a wider range of policy literature than previously envisaged, and decides that *critical discourse analysis* is the most appropriate procedure to use for making sense of the policy data. Critical discourse analysis takes a number of forms, but all of them are more specific and specialized than the kinds of analytic procedures employed in a standard literature review. The same will be true if a teacher researcher with, say, an interest in literature wants to enhance her classroom practice by researching approaches to literary criticism and/or text analysis. This may very quickly lead to forms of documentary research analysis that are far from the routine requirements of reviewing literature germane to a study.

Hence, in many cases of document-based research one will need to use certain specialized skills and techniques in addition to the general skills and techniques involved in the literature review component. These will be specialized skills and techniques appropriate to the specific *field* (e.g. policy analysis applied to school reform initiatives), *paradigm* (e.g. critical policy analysis applied to school reform documents) and *theoretical approach* (e.g. feminist critical policy analysis) that one chooses to work in. We will further clarify these matters in subsequent chapters.

Many scholars agree that document-based research is growing as a preferred research approach on account of better access to published texts via the internet and its enhanced search functions (Cooper 1998; Hoggart *et al.* 2002). Nevertheless, despite this increasingly easier access to documentary evidence online and the fact that one does not conduct experiments or interviews, or observe children in classrooms, documentary research is no less demanding and rigorous than quantitative and qualitative research. The teacher researcher doing documentary or formal text-based research still has to develop well-framed questions, generate a sound and suitable research design and demonstrate awareness of and competence with a range of suitable techniques for and skills of data collection and analysis. In Chapters 12 and 14 we will discuss some common designs and explore a number of primary tools and methods used in documentary research in areas of concern to teachers.

The role and place of theory in document-based research projects

As with quantitative and qualitative research, documentary research must always be informed by some theory or other (otherwise it is not research in the sense we are advocating here). The theories we draw on influence how we use the data that exist in documents to address our research questions and what we see as relevant data in the first place.

We might consider as an example here a deputy principal or head of a department who is interested in what the literature has to say about how educational leadership is best developed within a school milieu. If he or she is working with a theory that defines leadership in terms of holding a formal role or position within an administration he or she will be 'tuned out' from concepts of leadership that encourage the development of capacity to lead from positions outside the official power hierarchy of the school. That will in turn preclude from the potential database a lot of literature that would be relevant if 'leadership' were construed in wider and less formal terms.

Similarly, we might think of a teacher researcher interested in how education policy documents construct the relative priority of literacy in relation to other subject areas and forms of learning during the early and middle school years. If the researcher is working from a theoretical position that sees literacy in terms of handling alphabetic print, she or he will be 'tuned out' from concepts of literacy that have to do with reading and composing images or handling numbers, as well as from notions of 'oral literacy'. Likewise, if his or her theoretical assumptions only recognize as policy documents such statements as are officially released as policy by state or federal governments, she or he will not consider as relevant texts that have been issued by professional associations, schools, political parties or (other) works produced as attempts to influence policy. Instead, he or she will only try to uncover concepts of literacy in official government policy proclamations. Other theories, however, take a much wider view of the policy arena and accept a much wider range of statements as being policy or policy-related documents.

We find the same kind of thing if we consider our example of investigating what the research evidence tells us about successful approaches to teaching spelling to newly arrived Vietnamese ESL learners. Different theories will shape different views of what counts as being a good speller. Is a good speller one who can recall accurately (long) lists of words, or one who has developed effective strategies for attacking new words, or a combination of both, and so on? Depending on theory here we may look at very different types of studies. We may not accept as being a successful approach to teaching spelling a whole range of research findings that other people (coming from different theories) see as being highly relevant. The situation is exactly the same when we are looking at existing research findings contained in the literature (which constitutes the data for library research) as it would be if we were setting out to conduct an empirical investigation of the relative success of different approaches to teaching spelling to the learners in question.

In a useful reference on this theme, Harris Cooper (1998: 80) discusses the ways researchers engaging in synthesizing already-published research will always bring particular orientations to the study that will affect the criteria used to select texts for analysis and the rating of various factors within each study. In addition, examples can be found in resources like the *Educational Researcher* journal. This journal regularly publishes position papers and comments on these positions by others where the response comments are usually written from a theoretical framing or view of the world that is quite different to the framing of the original article.

There is a second side to the role and place of theory in documentary research. In addition to drawing on theory to guide our library research, we may also undertake documentary research with a view to enriching, refining, or critiquing existing theory. That is, instead of taking the existing state of theory as a basis for doing more empirical research, a literacy scholar might look at the existing body of research pertaining to literacy and use that as a basis for seeking to modify the theory in some way. This would be to engage in library research in order to provide a new basis from which literacy researchers could conduct further research.

A good example of this is provided by James Gee's (1991) essay 'What is literacy?' The essay may be seen as a brief report of Gee's document-based research (as well as some of his field-based research) undertaken over several years as it bears on literacy theory. Obviously, one crucial component of literacy theory will be the way literacy itself is defined and understood. In his essay Gee distils some key findings and implications of the vast research literature relevant to the question, 'What is literacy?' He draws these findings and implications together and shapes them into an argument. One of the conclusions to his argument, based on his reading and interpretation of the body of data he has collected and analysed as an exercise in library research, is that literacy does not *necessarily* have anything to do with encoding and decoding printed text! Gee argues that 'literacy' should be understood as the language uses involved in what he calls 'secondary discourses'. These language uses may or may not involve print. The important issue for us here is not so much whether Gee is right or wrong on this point but rather that he undertook library research over a lengthy period with a view to making a contribution to literacy theory itself. He did not simply accept and adopt existing literacy theory in order to do more research based on that theory.

This is an important thing for teacher researchers to consider. We cannot do research without drawing on theory. This does not mean, however, that we must simply find and use some line of theory in order to research something we are interested in – although that is legitimate. Ideally, however, our research will also contribute something to enhancing the theory it has drawn on.

Task

- Documentary research has sometimes been called 'library research'. Discuss the extent to which documentary research might be regarded as library research.

- What would you count as a *document* in relation to documentary or document-based research? What kinds of texts would you *not* count as documents, and why would you exclude them?

- If you could think of a different or better name for 'document-based research' what would it be?

- Identify two education journals that report research studies and that are likely to be read by teachers. Survey the volumes of these journals for the past five years and identify the articles in those issues that you regard as reporting documentary research. What are your reasons for classifying these articles as document-based research articles?

- What *proportion* of the total number of articles in the issues identified in Question 4 is accounted for by *documentary* research? What comments would you make about this proportion? How would you try to explain this proportion?

- Identify two books published since 1998 that you believe would be of interest to teachers and that you believe are examples of documentary research. Why do you regard them as examples of documentary research? What value do you think they have for teachers, and why?

Teacher research as quantitative inquiry

Describing quantitative research in relation to education, Nat Gage (1994: 372) explains that:

> The ideals of quantitative research call for procedures that ... use precise definitions, that use objectivity-seeking methods for data collection and analysis, that are replicable so that findings can be confirmed or disconfirmed, and that are systematic and cumulative – all resulting in knowledge useful for explaining, predicting, and controlling the effects of teaching on student outcomes.

We would add that quantitative educational research is grounded on two further ideas. First, it is based on the idea that anything of interest to social researchers can and should be measured. According to a strong proponent of this position, Edward Thorndike, 'whatever exists at all exists in some amount. To know it thoroughly involves knowing its quantity as well as its quality' (1918: 16). Second, useful knowledge about the regularities that exist in the world can be generated by collecting quantifiable information from carefully selected samples and drawing inferences from such samples about the unknown characteristics of broader populations.

In general, quantitative research depends on three conditions existing in a research situation:

- it is possible to measure variables in ways that can be represented as numbers (i.e. *quantified*);
- it is possible to have theories or hypotheses prior to implementing the study and, subsequently, to test these;
- sufficiently large samples can be obtained to make it possible to arrive at measurements from these samples and draw inferences from them that can be generalized to larger populations (note that a sample size of about 30 participants is 'sufficiently large' for many quantitative studies).

Quantitative research refers to a variety of numerically oriented tools and methods. It often includes the use of probabilistic sampling strategies, carefully planned investigations and statistical modelling.

Five key concepts in quantitative research

Vogt (1999: 152) explains that quantitative research designs involve a process of *controlling variables* with a view to testing in an objective manner some theory or set of hypotheses about a process or relationship in ways that are deemed to be internally and externally valid.

Five concepts are especially important with respect to quantitative research approaches:

- variables;
- objectivity;
- testing of theory or hypotheses;
- statistics and statistical significance;
- validity of the study.

We will briefly describe these in turn.

Variables

In quantitative research the term 'variable' is used to describe those things that can change or vary within the context or scope of the research. Things that do not vary are labelled *constants*. A hypothetical example will clarify this distinction.

Mr Bryant teaches a Grade 7 class. He has a hunch based on his teaching experience that he wants to investigate. It concerns the effects of his students' attitudes toward reading on their reading performance as measured by mandated Grade 7 reading achievement tests.

He designs a study that involves collecting two sets of numerical data – one on attitudes to reading and the other on the performance scores on the mandatory test – and examining the relationship between students' attitudes to reading and their reading achievement. He decides to employ two different tests to collect data. The first will measure reading attitudes. After considering various characteristics of this measure (e.g. reliability and validity), Mr Bryant selects the Elementary Reading Attitude Survey (McKenna and Kear 1990). Second, he uses the government mandated Grade 7 reading achievement test to evaluate his hunch, or hypothesis.

In this example, reading instruction in Mr Bryant's class is a *constant*, since all the students have been exposed to the same instructional approach. On the other hand, the students' reading achievement and their attitudes to reading are *variables* – they differ among the students from lower to higher rankings.

In quantitative research, there is also a distinction between dependent and independent variables. Tim May (1997: 101) explains the difference very clearly: 'A dependent variable is one that is affected directly by another variable (usually an independent one). For example, the clothes you wear each day are dependent variables affected by independent variables such as the weather, whether you've done your washing, or what you have to do that day'.

In Mr Bryant's case, reading performance is the dependent variable. Students' attitude to reading – measured through Elementary Reading Attitude Survey – is the independent variable.

In general, the quality of conclusions in quantitative research is contingent on how well the researcher is able to measure the variables of interest. Researchers use a variety of data collection tools (e.g. tests, observations, scales) to obtain measurements that are both reliable and valid.

Reliability refers to 'the consistency or stability of a measure or test from one use to another' (Vogt 1999: 245). In other words, the teacher researcher needs to be confident that the obtained results do not excessively fluctuate over different administrations of the test, alternative forms, and scorers of the tests or other measures. Vogt's analogy for this is weighing yourself – if you weigh yourself on the same scales three times in quick succession and get three quite different readings (say, 68, 72 and 75 kilograms), your scales are not reliable.

Reliability is a necessary, but not a sufficient condition to produce results that are valid or meaningful. *Validity* here is concerned with the *inferred meaning* from the results obtained through tests, questionnaires, observations and the like. Take, for example, a test that is designed to measure a student's reading ability based on reading a passage of text aloud. Does this test measure the comprehension of the material or the ability to read aloud? The answers to such questions are gathered through validity studies, where the function of a measure is evaluated empirically.

Objectivity

Within quantitative inquiry 'researcher objectivity' refers to practices aimed at trying so far as possible to distance one's 'personal self' from the research processes and findings. Objectivity has to do with suspending values and assumptions about possible causes and outcomes, and eliminating 'passions' (feelings, wishes, personal investment and the like) that might render research findings invalid. Various research practices, such as having a researcher assign test scores without knowing the identity and other characteristics of participants, are designed to minimize subjectivity and bias by distancing the researcher from the research situation.

Testing of theory or hypotheses
Quantitative approaches call for researchers to test theories or hypotheses. Within quantitative methodologies theory is generally concerned with finding the *truth* about a phenomenon or relationship in ways that also help to explain it. A theory can be defined as a statement or group of statements about how some part of the world works (Vogt 1999: 290–1). A theory can be one already in use by other researchers, or it can be generated out of reading and reflection. It is important at this point to distinguish between the research hypothesis and the null hypothesis. The *research hypothesis* (also known as the alternative or alternate hypothesis) corresponds to the researcher's scientific hunches about causes, relationships, processes and so on. This hypothesis is a statement of what the researcher believes to be true about a particular phenomenon. In other words, the research hypothesis states the expected result of the research study based on theory and on the researcher's review of the academic literature. The *null hypothesis* is a hypothesis that posits 'no relationship' between items, processes, and so on. It is a hypothesis the researcher 'puts to the test' and hopes to reject.

In the fictional example of Mr Bryant, a possible research hypothesis he might formulate prior to data collection, based on his review of the theoretical and research literature, could be:

- There is a positive relationship between attitudes towards reading and reading performance.

The null hypothesis corresponding to this research hypothesis is:

- There is no relationship between attitudes towards reading and reading performance.

Mr Bryant will tailor his research design to test the *probability of truth* of the proposed theory and hypotheses. This testing is not so much about *proving* the truth of a theory once and for all – rather, it aims more at finding support for a research hypothesis by *rejecting* the null hypothesis.

Testing the probability of truth in any quantitative research study is based on the statistical significance of results, or the likelihood of finding an observed result strictly by chance. Finding statistically significant results does not necessarily imply that (1) the results are practically important, (2) the results are meaningful, or (3) the underlying scientific theory is correct.

Statistics and statistical significance
Statistics are a useful way of mathematically classifying, organizing and summarizing information. By statistical analysis we mean the process of making sense of, or interpreting, the data. The role of 'statistical significance' is a distinctive element in quantitative research approaches. 'Statistical significance' is the term used to describe situations where a calculated result (e.g. the obtained average value, the difference

between two groups) is significantly smaller than would be expected on the basis of *chance alone* (Vogt 1999: 278). In other words, the obtained result had a low probability of occurring by chance, and should be attributed to other factors (e.g. the effects of an independent variable).

The following are some of the more basic statistics to compute:

- minimum (lowest score);
- maximum (highest score);
- mean (the average of a set of scores);
- mode (the raw score appearing most in a set of scores);
- median (the number that signals the middle score in a range of scores);
- range (the difference between the lowest and the highest score);
- sum (total of combined scores);
- count (number of scores gathered).

Validity of the study
In addition to the validity of data collection tools used in the study, quantitative researchers are concerned with the validity of the studies themselves. There are two types of study validity: internal and external. *Internal validity* refers to the extent to which the study and its findings are 'accurate' and 'truthful'. In a study with high internal validity, it is hard to suggest a plausible alternative explanation to account for the obtained result.

One way to increase internal validity in a quantitative study is through 'controlling variables'. This refers to the process by which researchers identify key elements of the 'problem' under study, work at isolating each one and develop a research design that enables them to 'test' effects on certain elements ('dependent variables') by other elements ('independent variables').

Another way to increase internal validity is through careful assignment of participants to groups or conditions. For example, when a researcher is comparing the performance of two groups after one has been exposed to a particular treatment (e.g. instruction in mnemonic strategies), the concern is to have groups acceptably similar on important characteristics at the outset of the study. Researchers use specifically designed sampling methods to increase the likelihood of group comparability prior to the intervention.

External validity involves judging the extent to which findings can be extended to other similar populations, conditions and settings (i.e. generalized). Most teacher research investigations of their own class of students cannot be labelled 'externally valid' in a strict sense, although this clearly does not diminish the value of such studies. It simply means that the findings may not be applied to all students everywhere.

The following sources offer good accessible coverage of method and data-analytic procedures in quantitative research:

- Cooper, H. (1998) *Synthesizing Research: A Guide for Literature Reviews.* Thousand Oaks, CA: Sage.

- Creswell, J. (2001) *Educational Research: Planning, Conducting, and Evaluating Quantitative and Qualitative Research.* Upper Saddle River, NJ: Prentice Hall.
- Minium, E., King, B. and Bear, G. (1993) *Statistical Reasoning in Psychology and Education.* New York: John Wiley.
- Sax, G. (1997) *Principles of Educational and Psychological Measurement and Evaluation*, 4th edn. Belmont, CA: Wadsworth.
- Wiersma, W. (1999) *Research Methods in Education: An Introduction*, 7th edn. Boston, MA: Allyn & Bacon.

Task

- Locate a report of any quantitative research study you find interesting and identify the main ways it exemplifies the five concepts characteristic of quantitative approaches to research.

Teacher research as qualitative inquiry

Qualitative research refers to a complex array of perspectives and techniques that have grown out of diverse theories and disciplines (Mason 1996: 3). Many roots of 'qualitative ways of knowing' originate in the tradition of 'interpretive sociology' which includes approaches like interactive sociology and ethnomethodology. Qualitative research has also emerged partly out of social and cultural anthropology (e.g. ethnographic approaches to understanding the world), and strands within linguistics, philosophy (e.g. hermeneutics and phenomenology) and non-quantitative forms of psychology.

By comparison with quantitative research, qualitative inquiry makes relatively little use of statistical forms of analysis and refuses to restrict data collection to the use of highly structured, replicable and standardized instruments within decontextualized settings. However, such data collection instruments as well as statistical approaches to analysis *are* used on occasions when it is appropriate. Qualitative research does not presuppose large samples or, in many cases, samples at all – let alone samples designed to be representative of larger populations. And while qualitative researchers sometimes use hypotheses, very often (and, perhaps, typically) they do not. Whereas quantitative research is strongly concerned with identifying causal, correlative or other kinds of close *associations* between events, processes and consequences occurring in the mental and social lives of humans, qualitative research is centrally concerned with how people experience, understand, interpret and participate in their social and cultural worlds.

Qualitative researchers place much importance on data being gathered in natural or real-life settings as the 'action' happens – for instance, in playgrounds, classrooms, at a work area out on the school veranda, in communities and the like. Data collection methods primarily comprise observations of 'real practices' (e.g. bedtime story reading), or of 'real life' events (e.g. teacher talk in classrooms compared with adult talk in the home), or recordings of recounts of real life (e.g. recording oral histories, interviewing people about a practice), and stories. Qualitative researchers aim to collect data that is *contextualized*. Such data take into account the kind of school and community in which the research study takes place, the socioeconomic status of the community in which the school is located and the history of the community. Very often the data will also take into account other things happening at the time locally, in the state or province, nationally or around the world. Of course, qualitative researchers also collect data in social contexts different from those with which the study is primarily concerned. This is especially so with interviews where, for instance, a teacher or student might be interviewed in the staffroom or at home about aspects of activity in the classroom. The point here, however, is that the quality and trustworthiness of the data is not diminished (and may be enhanced) by collecting it outside of the immediate context under inquiry.

Against this background we will discuss briefly what we see as the key features of qualitative research under three broad headings:

- inquiry within and/or about real-life contexts;
- the emphasis on interpretation and meaning-making;
- the role of the researcher in qualitative research.

Inquiry within real-life contexts

Qualitative research is differentiated most easily from documentary and quantitative research approaches by its strong reliance on gathering information about events, processes, programmes, issues, activities and the like *as they occur* within real-life contexts by interviewing eye-witnesses. A major reason for the development of this approach is that researchers often want to try and understand the world from the perspective of other people (a person or a group). Qualitative research provides rich and detailed descriptions (rather than 'counts' or statistical relationships) of people in action (e.g. a teacher, a student, a school policy or curriculum writer), specific programmes or social practices. A typical example comes from a study focusing on disadvantage, literacy and technology (Rowan *et al.* 2002: 147; see also Bigum *et al.* 2000), where words are used to evoke the setting and to orient the reader towards what is to follow:

> According to Lucy, all four Year 9 boys – Stuart, Jarrod, Benjamin and Kyle – have an interesting history in terms of being thrown regularly out of most of the classes they attended each week. Indeed, the label 'troublemakers' seemed to pop up regularly in conversations about these boys with the principal and other teachers at the school. Aside from behavioural 'problems' at least three of the boys were seen by their teachers to have a learning difficulty with English.
>
> Stuart is chatty, friendly and engaging. He has a smallish build for his age. He is given to wearing over-sized, slightly tatty shirts and shorts, occasionally he would be in school uniform, but even when he was, he managed to look far more casual than other, similarly-attired students. His blonde hair is shoulder-length, and shaved close to his scalp high above his ears. He regards himself as being about Year 6 level in most things at school. He openly declares that he hates writing, and

there is general agreement with that from the others. Indeed, on many occasions Ben has actually done Stuart's writing for him at the teacher's request. Stuart also recalled – with a kind of pride – how much trouble [his teacher] had in Year 5 getting Stuart to write.

At home, he is able to strip down his motorbike and put it back together again in working order. He tells us that he learned to do this by first watching his dad work on Stuart's bike, then from being left to his own devices to figure out a problem or to tune the engine or to rebuild it once his father had taken it apart. When asked what he does when he encounters a problem that he's having trouble with when fixing his bike, he replied without hesitation that 'I read the manual when I get stuck'.

This kind of descriptive work (which also inevitably involves some interpretation prior to the formal analysis of data) provides readers with a mental image of Stuart. It also signals that the data may reveal some discrepancies between how Stuart is perceived as a literacy user at school and his actual literacy uses outside school. These data tell us much more about Stuart than would, say, a table showing his reading age score, or a chi-square statistic of probability for the relationship between his attitude to writing and his performance in class.

The importance of context in qualitative approaches to investigating literacy needs to be emphasized. 'Context' here means something much wider than the mere physical setting of an event (i.e. the site). Contexts can be seen as the sum total of meaning-making, social practices, social negotiations, interactions and references to other contexts and events that shape the *sense* to be made of a given event or idea. Quantitative research cannot access or produce these kinds of data.

Susan Tancock's case study of Catie is a good example of this (1997). Standardized test results indicated that Catie's participation in a 'pull out' remedial reading programme – where Catie was taken out of class for special instruction – was enhancing her reading scores on tests. On the other hand, Tancock's observations of Catie in class, her conversations with Catie's classmates and her strategy of having each child identify the three best readers in the class and the three worst readers showed that, *socially*, Catie was seen as 'different' by all of her classmates. Moreover, she was excluded from many of their formal and informal interactions to the extent that she often felt lonely and was not able to call on her peers for help with in-class reading and writing. Although quantitative measures of Catie's reading performance showed a marked improvement over time, Tancock's qualitative study of Catie showed that the increased scores came at an enormous social cost for Catie.

All descriptive work in qualitative research reports emerges from and reflects researcher interpretations of 'what went on'. We discuss this in more detail in the following section.

Meaning-making and interpretation

The detailed descriptions distinctive of qualitative research are often complex, and data analysis is a process of making sense of, or meaning from, these descriptions.

These meanings can then be used to help explain and to help us understand such things about our educational world as the following:

- How something comes to be (e.g. documenting the first days of school in order to see how this establishes shared understandings of certain literacy concepts and practices – see Putney 1996).
- The effects of a thing on something or someone (e.g. the social status effects of pull-out literacy remediation programmes on individual students – see Tancock 1997; the effects of siblings on young children's preparation for school – see Gregory 2001).
- Variations in practice across different contexts (e.g. a comparison of students' literacy practices in school and prior to school or out of school – see Finders 1997; Moje 2000; Volk and de Acosta 2001; Sarroub 2002).
- The social construction of learning practices in general and literacy practices in particular (see Comber 2000; Kress 2002; Gee 2003).
- The effects of teacher talk on literacy practices in classrooms (see Baker and Freebody 1989; Westgate and Edwards 1994; Cazden 2001).
- The efficacy of a specific learning programme, curriculum or policy in a particular setting (see Barton 1997; Anderson 1999, forthcoming; Jones 2001).
- The effects of location, class, ethnicity, first language and/or gender on academic performance or school experiences (e.g. how white, middle-class forms of literacy are valued most in 'mainstream' classrooms – see Heath 1983; Millard 1997; Hicks 2002; ethnicity, language and education – see Kenner 2000; Reese and Gallimore 2000; Williams and Gregory 2001; location – see Cushman 1998; Tett 2000).

Descriptions in qualitative research are always interpreted from some theoretical or normative/ideological stance. For example, an event or transcript of teacher-student interactions can be read (i.e. interpreted) in any number of ways. Different interpretations can be equally 'valid' and meaningful, depending on the theoretical orientation of the reading and the degree to which the settled-upon interpretation is accepted or rejected by readers of the research report.

Consider, for example, the following transcript from a Grade 1 class:

Making candles

Mindy: When I was in day camp, we made these candles.
Teacher: You made them?
Mindy: And I – I tried it with different colours with both of them but, one just came out, this one just came out blue, and I don't know, what this colour is.
Teacher: That's neat-o. Tell the kids how you do it right from the very start. Pretend we don't know anything about candles. Okay, what did you do first? What did you use? Flour?
Mindy: There's some hot wax, some real hot wax, that you, just take a string and tie a knot in it and dip the string in the wax.
Teacher: What makes it have a shape?

Mindy: But you have – first you have to stick it into the wax and then water and then keep doing that until it gets to the size you want it.

Teacher: Okay, who knows what the string is for?

(Closely adapted from Cazden 1988: 14–16. Transcripts originally collected by Michaels 1981.)

A researcher using one kind of theoretical lens (e.g. by drawing on ideas derived from the work of Vygotsky) might see what is going on here as an example of a teacher working to support and effectively scaffold a student's ability to speak to an audience. By contrast, a researcher who reads the transcript from the standpoint of critical discourse analysis might see it quite differently. It might appear to be an example of how a teacher 'schools' or 'regulates' the spoken narratives of students in ways that lead them to conform to expected school norms regarding the 'appropriate' (valued) structure and subject matter of 'morning talks' (i.e. topic-centred and factual, rather than narrative or episodic).

Exactly the same kinds of variation might arise in relation to the following transcript. Deena is African American and from a working-class family. In the previous transcript Mindy is white and middle class. In the following transcript, square brackets indicate overlapping speech.

Deena's day

Deena: I went to the beach Sunday
and to McDonalds and to the park
and I got this for my birthday (holds up purse)
my mother bought this for me
and I had two dollars for my birthday
and I put it in here
and I went to where my friend named Gigi
I went over to my grandmother's house with her
and she was on my back
and I – and we was walking around by my house
and she was HEAVY
She
[was in the sixth or seventh grade

Teacher: [okay I'm going to stop you. I want you to talk about things that are really really very important, that's important to you but can you tell us things that are sort of different. Can you do that? And tell us what beach you went to over the weekend.

Deena: I went to uhm –

Teacher: Alameda Beach?

Deena: Yeah.

Teacher: That's
[nice there huh?

Deena: [I went there two times.

Teacher: That's very nice. I like it there. Thank you, Deena.

(Closely adapted from Cazden 1988: 14–16. Transcripts originally collected by Michaels 1981.)

Task

1   Examine both the transcripts again, and identify where the kind of 'schooling' work referred to above could be seen to occur.

2   Suggest reasons why it might occur where it does and identify the specific ways in which this normalizing work is done by the teacher.

3   Suggest possible reasons why the teacher acts in this way, and consider the implications your findings from this analysis might have for early literacy education.

4   What effects did the different theoretical orientations (and accompanying assumptions) have on the ways in which you interpreted these transcripts?

5   What role does theory play in interpreting data?

6   What effects might these insights on interpreting data have on the way in which you will now read reports of qualitative research?

The interpretive nature of qualitative approaches to investigating aspects of the social worlds of education leads many researchers to acknowledge that research actually *constructs* realities. Research does not simply 'reflect' a reality in the way a mirror does, or as if the truth about a phenomenon is simply waiting to be discovered. Rather, qualitative researchers can be seen in an important sense as producing or constructing the reality presented – or, as it is increasingly common to say, *represented* – in their reports. In other words, just as the two very different but equally valid interpretations of the transcripts reproduced above are possible – despite it being the same data – so too does each interpretation construct a different version of reality. In one, the teacher is construed as engaging in a deliberate pedagogical strategy and in the other the teacher is seen to be reinforcing the normalizing nature of schooling.

For more on the 'effects' of theory and values in qualitative research, see:

- Gerstl-Pepin, C. and Gunzenhauser, M. (2002) Collaborative team ethnography and the paradoxes of interpretation, *Qualitative Studies in Education*, 15(2): 137–54.
- Hoggart, K., Lees, L. and Davies, A. (2002) *Researching Human Geography*. London: Arnold.
- Honan, E., Knobel, M., Davies, B. and Baker, C. (2000) Producing possible Hannahs: theory and the subject of research, *Qualitative Inquiry*, 6(1): 9–32.
- May, R. and Patillo-McCoy, M. (2000) Do you see what I see? Examining a collaborative ethnography, *Qualitative Inquiry*, 6(1): 65–87.
- Reid, J., Kamler, B., Simpson, A. and Maclean, R. (1996) 'Do you see what I see?' Reading a different classroom scene, *International Journal of Qualitative Studies in Education*, 9(1): 87–108.

The role of the researcher

Qualitative researchers pay overt attention to the role of the researcher. This is because the researcher is seen to have direct effects on the research design, findings and interpretations of a study. This stance contrasts markedly with that of quantitative approaches to research that insist on researcher objectivity, which is seen to require that studies be replicable (i.e. can be repeated by objective others who will arrive at the same findings) in order for them to be valid.

'The researcher' is regarded as a data collection *instrument* by many researchers using qualitative approaches to data collection. This is on account of the researcher's values, assumptions, beliefs and knowledge about a topic directly informing what kinds of data are collected and how they are reported. Thus, in a qualitative study it is important to acknowledge that the study has been conducted from the particular orientation or stance of the researcher, and therefore the study will always be partial and incomplete. The people participating in the study (known in qualitative research discourse as 'participants' rather than 'subjects') are also seen to be involved directly in constructing the data for the researcher. In particular, participants' comments, interview responses and the like are regarded as 'constructed' data.

For more on the researcher's role, read:

- Coffey, A. (1996) The power of accounts: authority and authorship in ethnography, *Qualitative Studies in Education*, 9(1): 61–74.
- Delamont, S. (2001) *Fieldwork in Educational Settings: Methods, Pitfalls and Perspectives*, 2nd edn. London: Routledge.
- Fetterman, D. (1998) *Ethnography: Step by Step*, 2nd edn. Newbury Park, CA: Sage.
- Hoggart, K., Lees, L. and Davies, A. (2002) *Researching Human Geography*. London: Arnold.

Mixed methodology research

Documentary, quantitative and qualitative forms of research are distinct from one another. Researchers often specialize in one or other of them, and even when they are proficient with multiple approaches they will often employ only one type within a particular study – despite the fact that the question or problem might be amenable to different forms of investigation. By the same token, we are not necessarily confined to a single option within a given research project. While many questions/problems *are* of a type that presupposes one form of research rather than another, not all problems preclude multiple approaches, and some positively lend themselves to studies that employ a mix. And, of course, as we have already seen, every quantitative and qualitative study involves some degree of documentary inquiry.

'Mixed methodology' (or 'mixed methods') research usually refers to studies that include elements of qualitative *and* quantitative methods in their designs. For example, a case study based on qualitative research may employ pre- and post-testing procedures from quasi-experimental research in order to be able to make claims about learning that took place during the course of an intervention study. Likewise, an action research project might use a closed-ended, quantitative survey as part of its pilot study to help gauge people's feelings about an issue, their knowledge about a topic and so on. Alternatively, some approaches to linguistic analysis include statistical content analysis in their designs in order to quickly analyse how many words of this and that type appear in a given text.

Not all research designs or theoretical framings permit mixed methodology. For example, qualitative research based on critical discourse analysis would rarely make use of mixed methodologies because of its focus on *discourse* rather than *measures* of discourse. Indeed, mixed methodologies appear to be used most commonly in psychology and the behavioural sciences (Tashakkori and Teddlie 1998, 2002).

Readers interested in exploring the topic of mixed methodologies further can refer to the following sources and the useful bibliographies they offer:

- Creswell, J. (2002) *Research Design: Qualitative, Quantitative, and Mixed Method Approaches*, 2nd edn. Newbury Park, CA: Sage.
- Tashakkori, A. and Teddlie, C. (1998) *Mixed Methodology: Combining Qualitative and Quantitative Approaches*. Newbury Park, CA: Sage.
- Tashakkori, A. and Teddlie, C. (eds) (2002) *Handbook of Mixed Methods in Social and Behavioral Research*. Thousand Oaks, CA: Sage.

An interesting example of teacher research involving a mixed methods approach is found in the work of Neil Anderson (1994, 1996, 1999, forthcoming). This research responded to education policy changes in Queensland (Australia) during the 1990s. One change involved 'mainstreaming' intellectually impaired students instead of locating them in 'special' classrooms or units, as was previous practice. Anderson's study involved a 10-year-old student, Belinda, who had been formally assessed as having moderate intellectual disabilities. A cognitive abilities test (using Stanford-Binet) the previous year had located Belinda in an IQ range of 56–7. By Grade 5, the time of the study, Belinda remained socially withdrawn, and steadfastly avoided anything to do with reading and writing in class other than directly copying text from books into her notepad.

Noticing Belinda's fascination with the computers in the classroom and that she would ask others from time to time how a function was executed, Anderson drew on some of his understandings of social constructivist theory to integrate computing into a purposefully designed learning programme for Belinda. This involved using desktop publishing features (e.g. graphics, fonts, text boxes) to present concepts as images, posters, fliers and the like to assist in Belinda's literacy education by drawing on something she was already interested in (computing) to carry her to areas she currently resisted (reading and writing).

The study involved developing and implementing the purpose-built learning programme and documenting and tracking Belinda's progress in literacy development during a term. The mixed methods approach combined statistical measures of Belinda's literacy performance with observations of her work with the computer. The following data were collected:

- Belinda's scores on standardized reading and writing tests before and after the programme;
- written records of formal observations made during Belinda's sessions at the computer and of her interactions with other students;
- records of conversations with Belinda;
- desktop published artefacts produced by Belinda in draft or finished form.

The purpose-built learning programme was central to the research design. This was partly developed in a trial prior to the study, and partly once the study was in process. The sequencing of the research study and the learning programme integral to it is summarized in Figure 4.1.

Phase 1: Pre-testing and trialling

Conduct standardized reading and writing pre-tests on the whole class, and ascertain Belinda's standardized scores for reading and writing. Introduce Belinda to the computer via non-threatening game-type activities.

Phase 2: Introducing non-textual features of desktop publishing

Using the theme or content being studied by the whole class (e.g. amphibians), gradually introduce Belinda to a range of non-textual features of the desktop publishing program that can be used to present an idea (e.g. having her select a page border that 'fits' appropriately with an idea or concept about frogs) without requiring her to write actual text. Implement and maintain observation records and artefact collection strategies throughout the programme.

Phase 3: Gradually introducing text

Focus on exploring and experimenting with different fonts, font sizes and font shapes by means of using the WordArt feature; gradually introduce text into Belinda's desktop published documents in a non-threatening way. Text kept to a minimum, with emphasis on expressing *ideas* rather than on the number of words keyed in (e.g. instead of writing a paragraph about frogs, Belinda keys in the word 'frog', selects a rounded font, then uses WordArt to manipulate the shape of the word so that it sits plumply on the screen).

Phase 4: Peer tutoring (developed while the programme was in operation)

Anderson noticed that as Belinda became more and more familiar and fluent with desktop publishing, her classmates would turn to her for help with or advice on their own desktop publishing. Again, he decided to capitalize on this increased communication between Belinda and the other students by formalizing such interactions in peer tutoring sessions. He carefully coached Belinda in a number of peer tutoring strategies drawn from social constructivist theory (e.g. teaching via questioning, rather than always telling), and showed her how to organize and conduct her tutorial sessions at the computer. Enhancing Belinda's self-esteem was also a key objective for Anderson.

Phase 5: Experimenting with multimedia

Introduce Belinda to a range of additional multimedia features (e.g. colour, sounds, graphics) that can be used to add even more meaning to her documents (e.g. producing a document that has a frog-related border, a frog graphic, a title/label and frog sounds inserted into it).

Phase 6: Increasing amount of text

Increase the amount of text in each document as Belinda's confidence in herself and in her ability to use desktop publishing to express her ideas and understanding increases.

Phase 7: Post-testing and evaluating programme

Conduct standardized reading and writing post-tests on the whole class and ascertain whether improvements in Belinda's standardized scores for reading and writing can be measured. Analyse collected data.

Figure 4.1 Learning programme and data collection procedures

Concluding comments

In this chapter we have tried to produce a general impression of the 'kinds of things' documentary, quantitative and qualitative research are respectively. We have tried to describe their overall 'flavours' in ways that show how they differ from each other as well as to identify some of their key characteristics. In subsequent chapters we will look more specifically at what these features and differences involve at the level of *doing* teacher research. Before turning to the details of these three approaches to research, however, there are other important elements involved in educational research of whatever kind that need to be considered.

The next chapter looks at some of the things involved in reviewing relevant literature as a necessary component of good-quality research projects.

CHAPTER 5

Informing the study: some key aspects of reviewing literature

Introduction: discussion and reading as informing modes

Whatever kind of research we are doing – whether practitioner or academic – there is usually more involved in informing our work than (just) reading. Literature is often the most convenient thing to document, and the easiest to justify in terms of authoritative support. It is by no means, however, the only source of information that really informs our research work, notably in teacher research. Before looking at the reading aspects of informing teacher research projects, then, we will briefly mention some other useful ways and modes of informing our research as teachers.

Discussion as a mode for informing the study

Among the various discussion options teacher researchers may adopt for informing their inquiries, the following are reasonably common.
  Discussion via the internet:

- internet discussion lists;
- email interchanges with identified others (colleagues with shared interests, experts, authors/researchers etc.);
- personal interest websites.

Discussion in local exchanges:

- collegial interchanges, occasional study groups;
- relevant lectures, workshops etc. that can be 'audited' by arrangement;
- school-based professional development/inservice events.

Discussion at conferences:

- dedicated teacher research seminars and conferences (e.g. such as the 'Doing Teacher Research: Documenting, Disseminating and Connecting' programme headed by Barbara Comber at the University of South Australia, or meetings connected with the Edmonton Teacher Research Project in Canada);
- general education seminars and conferences (such as the Teacher as Researcher special interest group within the American Education Research Association).

We will briefly consider the internet and conference options in the remainder of this section.

Internet-based options for informing the study

A convenient way for teacher researchers with internet access to elicit inspiration and feedback for projects is via email discussion lists. A simple internet search using google.com or some similar search engine and appropriate key words (e.g. 'teacher + research + email discussion list') returns information on scores of sites that point users to email discussion lists on teacher research generally, or on specific areas of teacher research (e.g. in science education). At 'Teacher's Research Forum' (www.jiscmail.ac.uk/lists/teachers-research-forum.html), for example, one finds extensive archives of online discussions of topics in teacher research. Even novice internet users with little experience in using search engines can quickly locate chains of hyperlinks to potentially useful discussion lists.

It is also useful to conduct an internet search to see if someone whose expertise on which you hope to draw has a personal website. David Fetterman's website (www.stanford.edu/~davidf) is a good example of an online 'clearing house' or portal that is particularly useful for beginning teacher researchers interested in ethnographic approaches to investigating a problem. Alternatively, at the National Teacher Research Panel website (www.standards.gov.uk/ntrp) information is provided about members of a national teacher research panel in Britain established 'to provide an expert teacher perspective on teachers' involvement in, and use of, educational research and other evidence'. Of course, particular care is needed with sites established by or on behalf of government education departments since it is highly likely that these will be influenced by extant policy directions and associated values – including who is regarded as 'expert'.

Personal interest websites include sites by individual teacher researchers as well as hub sites that provide links to numerous other sites concerned with teacher research generally or with particular facets of teacher research. Here again, an elementary search with a powerful search engine like google.com using a key word cluster like 'teacher + research + network' will produce links to:

- online indices to and archives of teacher research resources (e.g. http://gse.gmu.edu/research/tr/; http://www.alliance.brown.edu/pubs/voices/3qrt1999/actref.shtml; http://www.oise.utoronto.ca/~ctd/networks/links.html);
- websites showcasing teacher research projects (e.g. http://gse.gmu.edu/research/tr/TRprojects.shtml; http://www.alliance.brown.edu/pubs/voices/3qrt1999/actref.shtml; http://www.standards.dfes.gov.uk/ntrp);
- how to start one's own teacher research discussion group, using the hosting facilities of services such as yahoo.com (see e.g. http://groups.yahoo.com);
- web-based archives of materials that can be helpful in informing a study or potential study.

Where individual teacher researchers access and archive such resources and identify ones that have been fruitful in their own work they have a valuable resource to make more generally available to their colleagues and fellow researchers by forwarding such information to whatever networks they belong to.

Conference and seminar-based options for informing a study

The home page for the American Educational Research Association's (AERA) special interest groups (SIGs) (www.aera.net/sigs) has a link leading to the 'teacher as researcher' SIG (www.teacherasresearcher.org). This site provides information about international teacher researcher conferences and the teacher researcher SIG sessions at the annual conference of the AERA. It also provides archived materials and a page of links to relevant sites, including an internet-based teachers' network. Attending such conferences will be prohibitive for some teachers and intimidating for many others. For teacher researchers who can attend it is possible to generate many valuable contacts with enduring potential to inform their ongoing research efforts. While the AERA annual conference is, naturally, 'northamerocentric' in perspective, members and delegates come from all over the world and can put individual teacher researchers in contact with organizations and networks in their own countries.

The home page of the Teacher Inquiry Communities Network of the National Writing Project (www.writingproject.org/Programs/tic/resources.html) provides further information on conferences and events (including online events) of interest to teacher researchers. It also provides a helpful page of teacher research resource websites.

Task

Conduct a web search to locate websites for teacher research organizations, networks, resource pages or conferences for your own country, or for a country of your choice.

1   Using google.com key in: 'teacher researcher network'.

2   Read through the short summaries provided by Google, selecting those that seem most relevant. Pay attention to the web address of each site to see whether it is commercial (e.g. it will have the domain .com), or government sponsored (it will have the domain .gov or .edu), which country it comes from (e.g. domains that include .au are hosted on computers in Australia and are likely to contain Australian content).

3   Repeat Step 1, this time using the search terms 'teacher research "discussion list"' (be sure to include the double quotation marks exactly as indicated here). Again, read through the summaries and explore those websites that seem most relevant.

4   Repeat Step 1, this time using the search terms 'teacher research methods'.

5   Compare the results of your three different searches in order to see the difference keywords make in relation to search returns.

- Which keywords might be suited best to a search interested in locating conferences that either focus on or make special provision for reporting teacher research?

- How might you refine this search to target a particular country, region or month?

Using texts to inform the study

In the remainder of this chapter we consider the use of conventional and online texts as resources for informing teacher research projects. The discussion is organized in several sections concerned with what to read, how much to read, how to locate sources, how to read them and how to organize and manage the information we obtain by reading.

What should be read to inform a study?

The reading teachers do as researchers to inform their projects should address several important aspects or dimensions of inquiry.

Reading for awareness of relevant other research in the area
It is important to read *reports* of at least some other studies that have been conducted in our area of interest and/or *reviews* of relevant studies in the area. This will show what other researchers claim to know already about a question or problem, and opens up choices. For example, should we:

- accept what is already thought to be known about the matter we are interested in and save our time for doing something else; or
- replicate an existing study or studies to check out whether our own situation produces similar results or whether matters tend to be context-specific; or
- try an approach to researching the problem that differs from those we know have been tried so far?

It is optimal to try and survey a range or variety of types of relevant studies if they exist. These are studies that have addressed a problem or question from different angles or perspectives; for example, from qualitative and quantitative approaches, psychological as well as sociological (historical etc.) angles, or from different theoretical perspectives within the same broad field (individual cognition, social cognition, constructivist, situated cognition etc.). This helps us identify different kinds of studies we could potentially conduct, and to think about what might count as good reasons for adopting one kind of approach rather than others in our circumstances. Alternatively, we could identify different kinds of 'programmatic' approaches to addressing an issue (e.g. approaches to addressing reading comprehension), and compare their relative potential (see Pikulski's 1994 study described in Chapter 4).

Reading various accounts of key concepts for our study
Reading is indispensable to helping inform the *concepts* on which our study will be based. For example, if we are wanting to investigate factors associated with different levels of reading comprehension of narratives in a class of Year 4 primary education students it will be necessary to develop a concept of '(reading) comprehension' and, perhaps, of 'narratives' and 'reading' as well, that can guide our approaches to collecting and analysing data.

Although 'comprehension' may look like a straightforward concept, we find very different accounts provided in the literature. Important variations occur between accounts based on one kind of theory of mental functioning and accounts based on other theories. Similarly, the question may arise as to whether reading comprehension should be measured by using text narratives only, or whether illustrated narratives and multimedia narratives are permitted. This will depend on how we conceptualize 'reading'. Moreover, the concept of narrative can vary from one theoretical perspective to another. Genre theorists, whose accounts of literary genres derive from work done in functional systemic linguistics, may employ a more tightly and technically defined concept of 'narrative' than do researchers and writers who operate from some more literary theoretical standpoint.

The tools and procedures to be used in data collection must be in accordance with how we conceptualize what is to count as data, and how data are to be measured and analysed. It is crucial, then, that we construct clear concepts, use them consistently throughout the research project and can defend the way we have constructed them. To even know some of the issues and points at stake around concepts like 'comprehension', 'reading' and 'narrative', it is practically inevitable that we will have to do some 'reading around' – even if we can't read as much as we might ideally want, let alone everything that might be relevant.

Reading relevant work done from different theoretical perspectives
Reading relevant work from different perspectives can make at least two crucial contributions to informing teacher researchers' theoretical orientation to their projects. The first is to open teachers up to research options they were previously unaware of, and to give them a chance to compare the merits of their current 'default' or preferred positions with the merits of these alternatives. The second is to provide teachers with an opportunity to deepen their understandings and appreciation of a theoretical position toward which they justifiably feel committed, and of the kind of research approaches to an educational problem this theoretical position supports.

Task

Consider the concept 'bullying' (or 'leadership', 'access', 'equity', 'learning (dis)-advantage').

1   Describe your present understanding of this concept.

2   Identify any theorists and elements of theory you associate with it.

3   Locate and read any two relevant references.

4   Briefly describe what you see as any important differences between your response to 1 above and ideas about X that occur in the references you have read.

5   Describe any differences between how you previously thought of X and how you might think of it now as a result of reading these references.

Repeat the same activity for one of the other identified concepts.

Reading accounts of research designs and methods, tools and procedures of data collection, data analysis and interpretation
Let us imagine that the reading a teacher researcher does around her area of interest leads her to think that it would be appropriate to tackle her research question by doing a critical discourse analysis of recorded classroom talk. This on its own might not tell her much about how to actually *do* the kind of data collection and analysis required. At this point she will have to turn to literature specifically concerned with concrete research designs and methods. This addresses such matters as how to do particular kinds of analysis – in the present case, critical discourse analysis. It is often the easiest

and most obvious literature for researchers to recognize and locate – university library shelves are full of texts on research methods.

Methods literature is highly pragmatic and addresses the 'how to' dimensions of a research project. Hence, in the case of document-based research the methods literature includes resources on how to do effective and valid forms of document analysis, categorical coding, various kinds of feminist textual analysis, postmodern social analysis, postcolonial forms of analysis, philosophical analysis and so on. It also includes resources on how to use computer programs to assist with the analysis of written data (such as the use of concordancers or databases).

Within qualitative research the methods literature includes texts about established research designs (e.g. case study, ethnography, action research). It also includes texts about data collection techniques (e.g. observation, interviewing) and tools (e.g. making fieldnotes, constructing interview questions), as well as descriptions of data analysis techniques. The latter range from open coding and pattern matching to specific forms of cultural analysis such as domain and taxonomic analysis, thematic analysis and the like. It is important to read about data analysis options and to make informed decisions about the data analysis approaches to be used *prior* to data collection (this holds even for grounded theory and phenomenological approaches to education research). Consulting the literature on data analysis options early on in the study alerts the researcher to additional skills she or he may need to learn in order to analyse data effectively (e.g. a particular type of discourse analysis, domain analysis or thematic analysis).

The methods literature in quantitative research includes reading and writing about sampling techniques and 'rules', how to control for a range of variables (e.g. age, gender, academic ability), and how to construct and administer certain tests and measures. Data analysis literature covers such things as how to calculate and interpret a range of statistical measures and comparisons, how to maximize interpretive reliability (both internally and externally to the study) and so on.

When we come to reporting our reading of and reflection upon the methods literature germane to our study we must be able to defend our 'suite' of data collection and analysis tools and procedures in terms of our research question and the design we have chosen for addressing it. In some cases the choice of methods will be clear-cut, and the researcher may have begun the study knowing appropriate methods to be used. In other cases, however, it will be proper to be guided by the methods literature in search of the particular tools, techniques, procedures etc. that are most effective for one's research question and purposes, and to be able to document the decisions made and the grounds for making them.

How much should you read in order to inform a study?

How much teacher researchers should read in order to inform and implement their research projects depends largely on the specifics of individual cases, including the extent of prior knowledge and experience of literature relevant to the research problem or question. If the project is part of a formal academic degree programme the amount of reading to be done will be influenced by the norms of the institution and its external examiners for degrees at that level. If the research is contracted, reference groups or the funders themselves might provide criteria. Outside of such circumstances, however, no formal criteria operate. In such cases we think the amount of reading teacher researchers do to inform their study should take account of three main considerations.

First, researchers have an *ethical and professional responsibility* to those who participate in the research to produce a study that is worthy of their time, goodwill, inconvenience and trust. Enough reading should be done to ensure that the design and conduct of the study is coherent and sound. This means reading enough to understand how, in the case of one's chosen problem area, one can conduct a study that will genuinely count as research by pursuing appropriate standards of validity, reliability, interpretation and rigour. When one can defend the coherence and rigour of the study relative to its purposes one has read enough.

Second, researchers have an 'ecological' responsibility to ensure that the results and benefits accruing from a study are sufficient to justify having done it. A well-constructed study that provides information that can support a teaching innovation or curriculum initiative at the level of a single classroom in ways that enhance the likelihood of its success is, in our view, ecologically responsible. For the information from a study to be worth acting on, however, the study must be credible. Besides being methodologically sound and making sense conceptually, this requires that the study be coherent and appropriate at the level of pedagogically relevant ideas and theory. The theory does not need to be 'rocket science'. It should, however, be something that is recognizable as *educationally pertinent and useful*, in the sense of making genuine connections to ideas, issues, explanations and knowledge circulating among educators.

Third, researchers have a personal investment in *growing in vocational terms* as a result of doing research. It is not uncommon for the reading one does around a research interest to be as valuable, if not more so, to personal advances in professionally relevant knowledge and understanding, as the outcomes of one's study. In some cases, reading will make the research originally envisaged unnecessary and, in its place, open up richer and more fruitful alternatives for potential investigation.

To hazard a very crude quantification, we would be surprised if teacher researchers generally found that they could complete a worthwhile study without 'actively' reading (see below) the equivalent of at least two or three books and 10 to 15 articles or chapters germane to their topic with which they were not previously familiar.

Locating relevant literature

This section briefly describes the following strategies for locating relevant resources to inform teacher research projects:

- searching computerized library catalogues;
- doing online searches using (powerful) search engines;
- searching specific online databases;
- using citation indexes to identify key authors in a field.

Other strategies not dealt with here but that are reasonably self-evident and that parallel the above strategies include:

- searching the lists of large online bookstores;
- browsing library shelves in the vicinity of texts already located;
- trawling bibliographies of useful resources one has already located;
- using book review indexes and book review sections of publications to identify well-regarded resources.

Library catalogue searches using keywords
These days the old cataloguing systems in libraries based on author, title and subject cards have almost entirely been superseded by computerized catalogues that use, in addition to the long-standing author, title and subject search options, search strategies based on key words. Since all readers will be familiar with the use of author, title and subject options we will mainly focus on doing searches of computerized catalogues using key words.

If the researcher already knows the name of the author or title, locating the resource and its current availability is simple. One selects from the menu the search category one wants to use – author or title or author/title – and keys the author name or title into the appropriate window before pressing the enter key or clicking on the 'submit search' button. It is important to observe the protocols of the particular catalogue one is using (e.g. surname first if using an author search). After submitting the search it is normally a matter simply of clicking on the returned blue hyperlink for the author or title. This leads to a page with hyperlinks for each work that is in the library's holdings, and which displays the call number and availability status of the text (including an auto-mated 'request' option if the book is held but currently borrowed by someone else).

Sometimes a researcher's project topic or question will lend itself to a subject search. One selects the 'subject' option from the menu and keys in the name of a subject area (often based on a formal list, such as the list of Library of Congress subjects). Usually, however, the subject areas will be much more general than one's particular research focus. A subject search will throw up whatever is listed under that category as being available in the library, and from then on it will be a matter of scrolling through the resulting titles to look for ones that seem closest to the kinds of resources one needs. Often, however, the term chosen as a subject name will simply not appear on the list of options. This will require thinking of other terms for the subject – perhaps asking the librarian if there is a full list of the subjects used to organize the catalogue, so that one can try to identify from the list options that might be close. This, of course, is not easy if one is working online at a distance from the library.

The procedure we have described here applies equally for terminals in the physical library one is in and for searching online catalogues of remote libraries from one's home or office computer. The latter option, of course, presupposes having a web address (i.e. URL) for a remote library and rights to access it. We often use the Library of Congress and British Library catalogues – easily accessed via a google.com search (see below) or similar.

Task

Identify your research question or problem. Then, using a computerized catalogue:

1 Think of a possible subject term for your topic.

2 Run a subject search of the catalogue.

3 Record whether the subject term you used appears on the list.

4 If it does not, make a record of the term and try another one.

5 Keep going until you get a term that appears on the list. Record each attempt and its outcome. Then follow Steps 6 to 12.

6 If it does appear on the list, record the number of works listed for that subject.

7 Work through the list of titles and record those that seem most relevant.

8 From those references that are currently available, identify those you believe would actually be useful by locating the works and browsing them.

9 Calculate your 'strike rate' of 'actually useful works' for the subject term you chose.

10 Repeat the process for two more subject terms of your choice (keep going until you get two that are listed).

11 Calculate your overall 'strike rate' of likely useful resources from the subject search strategy. You might also calculate the amount of time used and build this into a measure of your 'subject search efficiency'.

12 Do this exercise three more times over a six-week period using different research questions or problems, and see if your 'efficiency' improves.

Often the most productive kind of search when no author or title names are available will involve using key words that seem most appropriate to one's research problem or question. Key words are words that are 'key' or central to the contents of a resource. It is common practice for authors to be asked to provide a short list of four to six key words for their journal articles and books. These are supposed to be words the author thinks best capture what the work is about. However, a further factor often comes into play here, which has important consequences for conducting key word searches. From the *searcher's* point of view a good key word is one that gives maximum accurate information about what a reader is likely to find in a given text and that will provide a fast track to a relevant resource. From the *author's* point of view, however, a good key word may be one that runs the existence of their work in front of as many eyes as possible. Therefore, for example, an author who has written a report of a study of young children using CD-ROM storybooks might use 'technology' rather than 'CD-ROM' as a key word to cash in on the large numbers of people who search for resources under that heading.

One way to get a better idea of how authors use key words and how their choices of key words relate to the topics they have written about is to look at the key words authors have actually used for their work. We might also compare the key words the authors have used with those we think we would have used for the work in question had we written it ourselves.

Task

Locate a journal that lists the key words chosen by authors for their articles. Then select an article for the following activity. Try to avoid noting the key words the author has chosen. Read the article carefully and list up to six words you would use to represent the article as accurately as possible.

- Compare your list with the key words actually used by the author.

- What proportion of the words you used appeared in the author's list?

- What are the main differences between your key words and the author's?

- How important are these differences?

- How would you describe the differences between the lists and how do you think these differences arose?

- To what extent do you agree with the author's choice of key words?

Repeat the activity with two more articles.

- Does your own list closely agree with the author's list in any of the articles?

- Has doing this activity altered your understanding of key words and/or made you rethink how you would choose key words? If so, how and why?

Doing online searching using a powerful search engine

Search engines are online programs that operate in a range of ways to search the internet for terms keyed into the program by the searcher. Some, known as meta search engines, are extremely powerful because they return searches conducted by a range of other engines. Dogpile, for example, searches across Google, Ask, LookSmart, Sprinks, and FindWhat, among others. Whereas online library catalogue searches deal with texts that are held in libraries (including virtual or electronic versions of texts), using a search engine to locate resources relevant to a research question or problem can lead to many types of resources that do not appear in library catalogues.

When conducting searches online, it is useful to know at least two things:

- the web addresses to a range of search engines, because different engines will pull up different results based on the search engine programs driving the search service, on paid subscriptions, on meta-tags used in websites, and so on;
- search engine logic.

For example, google.com is a useful general purpose search engine that includes academic-type websites in its reach. Dogpile.com, on the other hand, is especially useful for locating images and video clips online. Other search engines and subject directories useful to teacher researchers include:

- http://www.alltheweb.com;
- http://www.profusion.com;
- http://www.wisenut.com;
- http://www.teoma.com;
- http://www.allsearchengines.com;
- http://lii.org;
- http://infomine.ucr.edu.

Some search engines charge fees, but also specialize in providing academic-type texts in return. These include, for example:

- http://www.northernlight.com;
- http://www.oclc.org/firstsearch

There are also numerous guides to effective online searching. Some of the better resources can be found at:

- http://www.allsearchengines.com;
- http://www.infopeople.org/search/chart.html;
- http://www.searchenginewatch.com;
- http://library.albany.edu/internet/choose.html.

Search engines generally use Boolean logic to conduct key word searches. This is a system of 'logical operators' describing relationships between words or items such as 'AND', 'NOT', 'OR'. Some search engines make use of full Boolean logic and require the search command to include the Boolean operators. In such cases a teacher researcher interested in finding demographic statistics for her local community might type something like the following: 'peterborough AND statistics AND demographics' (Boolean operators usually need to be keyed in capital letters).

Most search engines rely on *implied* Boolean logic. The logical operators are either symbols (NOT becomes a minus sign, AND becomes a plus sign) or, increasingly, are not required at all. In the latter case, our teacher researcher interested in demographic statistics for Peterborough would simply key: 'peterborough statistics demographics'. Some search engines (e.g. ixquick.com) assume that an absence of operators signifies an 'OR' relationship. Keying in 'peterborough statistics demographics' would bring up all the pages that mention at least one of these key terms. A few simple checks of returned websites will alert the researcher to what is being assumed by a given search engine. For a useful source on search engines, Boolean logic and search strategies, see http://library.albany.edu/internet/boolean.html.

These days most search engines will also search for phrases. Phrase searches require the phrase to be enclosed by double quotation marks; for example, "teacher research network" or 'teacher AND research AND "discussion list"'.

Key words used in searches are also important. The more specific and exact the term, the more fruitful searches are likely to be. For example, compare what happens when you key the term 'research' into a search engine with what happens when you key in 'teacher research'.

Task

1   Experiment with two different search engines such as Google and Alltheweb.com to see which is best suited to your needs by entering the same search terms in both and comparing the returns.

2   Experiment with Boolean operators to see what difference their application makes to refining search results on your topic.

Searching specific databases

Using electronic databases that list bibliographic details for journal articles and books, or that access full-text articles, provides a further form of access to resources for informing teacher research. Databases can be online or contained within a CD-ROM. A full-text database archives complete digital copies of journal articles. Online full-text databases are generally fee-based, with most university libraries (and increasingly schools) subscribing to them.

Databases take different forms. Some of the most common and widely used forms of database in education studies include CD-ROM databases such as ERIC, Wilsondiscs and WebSPIRS. These are updated every three to six months. Increasingly, these databases are being placed online. Some (especially recent) databases have been developed *only* to be accessed online. These include databases like Proquest, Ingenta and Infotrac. Some databases have provision for access to full-text articles as well as abstracts and bibliographic information. This typically requires paying a subscription or paying per downloaded article.

The following will be useful starting places for teacher researchers.

ERIC database. ERIC, or the Educational Resources Information Center, is an international catalogue and text archive sponsored by the US Department of Education and provides access to a wide range of education literature. Details held in this database largely take the form of bibliographic data and accompanying abstracts and methods for obtaining the full text of the citation. The literature indexed by ERIC includes journal articles, research reports, curriculum and teaching guides, conference papers and books. Specific areas covered by ERIC include urban education, adult and vocational education, assessment and evaluation, educational management, early childhood and primary (elementary) education, information and technology, language and linguistics, rural education and small schools, and so on. For more on the ERIC database, see www.eduref.org.

Wilsondiscs. The Wilsondiscs are a series of CD-ROM databases (many of which are now also available in an online format). Each database indexes bibliographic details for journal articles and books, with some CD-ROMs including abstracts as well. Areas covered by the series include education, social sciences, business, literature, law, general science, art, biography and the like. For more on Wilsondiscs, see www.hwwilson.com/Databases/d_avail_wweb.htm.

Proquest. This is an international, multidisciplinary text database offering bibliographic details and abstracts, as well as some full-text journal articles. It covers biomedical science, business and marketing, computing, education, health, nursing, religion, social sciences and telecommunications. For more on Proquest see: www.proquest.com.

Ingenta provides full-text access to more than 5400 journal articles and 26,000 citation entries spanning almost 200 publishers. Areas covered include science and technology, education, arts, social sciences, the sciences, law, chemistry, engineering, medicine, human resource management and so on. Journal articles held on the Ingenta database can be purchased individually by non-subscribers to the service, but do not come cheap. For more on Ingenta see www.ingenta.com.

Infotrac. This academic index comprises mostly full-text articles and other documents (e.g. newspaper articles) from areas including the humanities, current events reporting, sociology and communications studies.

Web addresses for a range of free or mostly free online databases and clearing houses are listed below. For more on specific content within databases, OVID offers a comparative search of commercial databases on education (see http://www.ovid.com; click on 'products and services', then select 'content' from the centre menu). Free full-text article databases include:

- EdResearchOnline (Australia): http://cunningham.acer.edu.au/dbtw-wpd/sample/edresearch.htm.
- Education-line (UK): http://www.leeds.ac.uk/educol.

Bibliographic databases include:

- ERIC: http://www.eduref.org.
- Library of Congress (multilingual): http://www.loc.gov/z3950/gateway.html.
- Psychology-related list of journals and their contents pages: http://psych.hanover.edu/Krantz/journal.html.

Digests and research clearing houses (state-of-the-art summaries and archives of research in a particular area) include:

- ERIC Digests: http://www.ericfacility.net/ericdigests/index.
- Clearinghouse for National Literacy and Numeracy Research (Australia): http://www.griffith.edu.au/schools/cls/clearinghouse/.
- National Grid for Learning (UK): http://www.ngfl.gov.uk.
- Technology-Assisted Education Clearinghouse (Canada): http://www.utoronto.ca/cat/clearinghouse/index.html.
- Distance Education Clearinghouse (USA): http://www.uwex.edu/disted/journals.html.
- What Works Clearinghouse (USA): http://www.w-w-c.org/index.html.

- Joint Center for Poverty Research (USA): http://www.jcpr.org/index.html.
- National Clearinghouse for English Language Acquisition and Language Instruction Educational Programs (USA): http://www.ncela.gwu.edu.

Journals, education magazines and books can be found at:

- *Networks: An Online Journal for Teacher Research*: http://www.oise.utoronto.ca/~ctd/networks.
- *Educational Action Research*: http://www.triangle.co.uk/ear/index.htm.
- *Action Research International*: http://www.scu.edu.au/schools/gcm/ar/ari/arihome.html.
- *Education Policy Analysis Archives*: http://epaa.asu.edu.
- *Rethinking Schools Online*: http://www.rethinkingschools.org.
- *National Association for Bilingual Education Bilingual Research Journal*: http://www.ncela.gwu.edu/miscpubs/nabe/brj/index.htm.
- *Journal of Literacy & Technology*: http://www.literacyandtechnology.org.
- *Contemporary Issues in Early Childhood*: http://www.triangle.co.uk/ciec.
- *Journal of Computer-Mediated Communication*: http://www.ascusc.org/jcmc.
- *THE (Technological Horizons in Education) Journal*: http://www.thejournal.com.
- *Language, Learning and Technology*: http://llt.msu.edu.
- National Academies Press online books on education: http://books.nap.edu/v3/makepage.phtml?val1=subject&val2=ed.
- *Teacher's College Record*: http://www.tcrecord.org.
- Indices to education journals online:
  - http://aera-cr.ed.asu.edu/links.html (research focus).
  - http://www.scre.ac.uk/is/webjournals.html.
  - http://www.ecewebguide.com/online_ece_journals.htm (early childhood focus).
  - www.csu.edu.au/education/library.html.

Many publishers also have sample copies of their journals available free on their websites. These publishers include Triangle, Sage, Routledge, Blackwell and Kluwer.

Using citation indexes

Citation indexes are resources designed to provide a guide to reputable authors and published works. Basically, citation indexes target a range of leading/well-reputed journals where the works selected for publication have been through a rigorous peer review process. An index like the *Social Sciences Citation Index* sources scores of publications, which are listed at the front. All publications that appear in the targeted journals in the period preceding the current issue of the *Index* are identified, including articles, book reviews and comments. So are their authors, and so are the works that have been used (have been cited) in all the various texts published in the pool of targeted journals. The logic is simple: the targeted journals are reputable ones, have credible review processes and therefore the works published in them are likely to be of good quality and the authors of these works are likely to be competent. Furthermore, the myriad of works cited by these authors are likely to be credible, since they have been taken seriously by credible authors/researchers.

If a teacher researcher locates a resource and wants to know how its author 'stacks up' in the field, they can go to a citation index and see if the author has been cited in preceding years, how often and by whom. Some of the works in which this author has been cited can then be tracked down to see whether the citations are agreeable/positive, or whether they criticize the author. This in turn provides grounds for the teacher researcher to make judgements – including what they think about the works in which the author has been cited.

Such procedures can help a teacher researcher get a sense of where different authors are positioned in a field: whether they are more or less leaders in a field or more or less marginal or newcomers; whether their work is mainly regarded favourably or unfavourably, and by whom; which other authors they are 'like' and 'unlike'. These procedures also provide the researcher with clues as to the structure and intensity of debate in a field, what the key issues are, what the competing perspectives and approaches are and so on. This can be very useful as a systematic way of organizing one's reading and shaping up a research design and selection of methods.

Besides the *Social Sciences Citation Index* typical examples of relevant citation indexes for teacher researchers include the *Arts and Humanities Citation Index*, the *Science Citation Index*, the *Web of Science*, the *ISI Web of Knowledge* and the *Australian Education Index*.

How to read the resources we locate

Informing our study means providing a basis for making *informed decisions* that we can support with good reasons. These are decisions about *what* we are going to do in our research, *how* we are going to do it, *why* we are doing this rather than that, in this way rather than that, and so on. Accordingly, the kind of reading involved in good-quality research is reading that is:

- active;
- critical;
- discriminating;
- evaluative;
- methodical.

Reading actively

Active reading means actually *acting on the text in the process of reading it*. This involves engaging with the text (as well as making notes elsewhere) with pencil, pen, highlighter, coloured font, digital highlighter and so on. There is more to this than just underlining or shading words and sentences we think are relevant to our project – although it does include this. It also involves writing questions and comments as we think about what is being said in relation to our work – even things like 'what does this mean?' where something is not clear. It will include things like marking in comments like 'This differs from what S says', or 'This provides a reason for using semi-structured interviews'. It might mean sorting out parts of the text where the author is making statements or claims from parts where she or he is providing reasons or evidence for these claims. It may involve cross-referencing one part of the text to another or one point to another (e.g. by using a post-it sticker that says 'Compare this with what she says on p.74').

Reading critically
This involves subjecting texts to appropriate forms of critique or interrogation. When we think something is unclear or ambiguous we will note that as a criticism – one that we can use in developing our own position or argument in our project report. Likewise, when a significant claim is made that is open to doubt but no supporting evidence is provided for it we should note that as a criticism for further comment and use as appropriate. Or if the author says something on page X and something else on page Y that seems to contradict it or undermine it we may note that as well. These are all forms of negative criticism. Conversely, however, if a point is made well and is relevant to our study we can (positively) note and affirm it – possibly using this point in our own study to support a claim or interpretation. Alternatively, when we find a point or argument and know that other authors have competing views we should note that. 'X disagrees' counts as a critical comment, although it is neither a negative nor positive evaluation as it stands, and does not imply that X is correct. Rather, it draws attention to the fact that an issue exists here that we subsequently may need to follow up and try to resolve.

Reading to discriminate and compare
One of the most important functions of reading within the conduct of research is to discriminate (or distinguish) different categories, concepts, positions, viewpoints, designs, procedures, outcomes, interpretations and so on, and to know what is at stake between the differences. If we are reading a range of studies relevant to our area of interest we will want to know how they compare and differ in terms of their main constructs/concepts, their approaches to data collection and analysis and their results. We will also want to know their respective reasons for being more like some studies and less like others.

Task

1   Locate and read *three* articles that report research involving young children using CD-ROM stories.

2   Compile a table or matrix that summarizes your responses to the following questions.

- Was a research question explicitly stated in each study?
- If so, are the questions significantly different, and how?

- How do the research problems underpinning the three studies compare with or differ from one another?

- To what extent do the studies draw on different kinds of theories?

- To what extent do the studies employ different (or similar) kinds of research design?

- What are the most important *concepts* involved in the three studies?

- To what extent are these studies ultimately concerned with similar or different educational issues or concerns?

Some sources of pertinent articles include the *Journal of Research on Computing in Education*, *Reading Research Quarterly*, the *Journal of Literacy Research* and ERIC documents.

Reading from an evaluative point of view

Reading in order to inform a research project with the intention of doing the best quality and most useful piece of research we can involves learning from existing work, and selecting from ideas and approaches that seem better, clearer, more economical or effective, and more relevant to our needs. When we read material relevant to our research purposes and questions it is important that we *evaluate* it, so that we can build on the strengths of other people's work and improve on some of its weaknesses.

Reading with a view to evaluating elements of the literature involves asking questions like the following, and providing reasons for our responses.

- Which of these different accounts of 'literacy', 'technology', 'gender relations', 'bullying', 'constructivism', 'scaffolding', 'behaviour management' (or whatever) seems most applicable to my project? Which is most clear? Which is most useful? Which seems most plausible?
- Does the evidence contained in the data that is presented in this study adequately support the findings its author reports?
- Does this article provide reasons for thinking that the kind of sample or selection of participants used in the study is actually the most appropriate for the research problem it addresses?
- Which of these three studies (of truancy, effective learning, pedagogical innovation, or whatever) uses the kind of research design most appropriate to my own research context and purposes?
- Which of these different types of data collection methods and tools would be most appropriate for my own study, and why?
- Does the author of this study provide me with good grounds for thinking their data is of good quality and is trustworthy?

Reading methodically

It is important to apportion the time we have available for reading appropriately across the different aspects of the research process. One way to do this is to draw up headings

Table 5.1 Headings and questions to guide reading

Question	Concepts	Theory	Data	Analysis
In what ways do my first grade students help each other in small group reading and writing activities?	Who writes about 'helping' in the context of literacy work? What accounts do they provide of 'helping'? What other concepts may be relevant here, who writes about them and how are these concepts defined?	What theories do these writers draw on? Who are some of the theorists they refer to? Which of these writers and positions seem most relevant to my study, and why? Whose work can help me decide what is most relevant?	What kind of data have the researchers in similar studies collected? Who writes about collecting such data? What do they say? What issues are involved in collecting such data, and who can help me address these?	How have other researchers analysed their data? Which approaches seem best for my study and who can help me decide this? What more do I need to learn about analysis and who can show me what I need to know?

of areas or aspects to cover in our reading and keep a record of what we have read and whether it is enough. The kind of matrices developed by LeCompte and Preissle (1993: 52–3, 128–33) are very useful in this context. One can fill in the cells of a matrix as one reads and keep track of where the gaps are (see also Hedrick *et al.* 1993: 90–1). Having identified our research question we might then develop headings and questions for our reading such as those shown in Table 5.1.

It is possible, of course, to use different headings and questions altogether. The important point, however, is that something like this approach provides a means for reading methodically, covering pertinent ground, allocating time appropriately and recording who we have read, why, with what 'answers' and with what 'gaps' remaining so far as informing our own project adequately is concerned.

Organizing and managing the information we generate from our reading

Reading systematically as part of our 'systematicity' in conducting research involves *keeping track of what we read*. In the remainder of this chapter we describe our own preferred approach to doing this.

Constructing a record system for the material we read

There are multiple ways to construct a record system for one's reading. Some people prefer to use software programs like Endnote (www.endnote.com) or Papyrus

| Keywords, methodology or relevant project (e.g. sociocognition, data collection methods, case study, rapport) | **Detailed bibliographic entry here** |

Details about the text, including:

- Synopsis of the main argument
- Identification of theoretical perspective(s)
- Definitions used/constructed by the author(s)
- Assumptions made about the world by the author
- Cross-reference to similar, opposing etc. views, interpretations, research
- A photocopy of the contents pages if a book or whole journal
- Your comments, critique etc.

Figure 5.1   Front face of a standard reading record

(www.researchsoftwaredesign.com) to record bibliographic details, and perhaps some notes about each text they want to keep track of. The advantages of using this kind of system include being able to construct bibliographies for one's articles and final research reports at the tap of a keyboard button. For us, a possible minus in using this kind of approach is that it can encourage a focus on bibliographic details, rather than encouraging extended documentation of arguments proposed in the text and one's critique of them.

Our own preference is to use a system involving file cards, for several reasons:

- We can use them as a bookmark and copy important/useful quotes and write comments as we read.
- File cards easily enable us to list authors we have read who have something to say about a particular theory or topic, a concept, a research method and so on, according to our needs.
- File cards enable us to lay a number of them on the table as reference sources while we are constructing an argument in our writing.
- They are extremely portable.
- They are extremely easy to manage.
- They can be used to record all manner of information that makes retrieval of the whole text or ideas, claims, insights from the text as efficient as possible (e.g. we record whether we have a photocopy of the text, whether we own the book or

journal or borrowed it – and if from a library then the name of the library and the book or journal's call number, in order to keep track of where all this stuff *is*).

The downside to this approach is that it is time consuming and still leaves the bibliography to be keyed at the end. In any event, *some* kind of system is necessary. Ultimately, individual researchers need to develop a system that works for *them* in terms of ease of management, ease of construction and ease of use. The following sections describe our own preferred approach, using file cards.

Size and 'look'
The size of file card we prefer to work with measures approximately 20 cm by 12.5 cm. We prefer this larger size because it lets us write more. Nevertheless, students we have worked with have used much smaller cards very effectively.

Layout
Having a standard layout for your file cards is crucial for two reasons: (a) you know where to look for certain information, and (b) you have more of a chance of writing

---

Research methodology: ETHNOGRAPHY

History:
LeCompte & Preissle (1994) – Chap. 1

General guides to classical ethnography:
Fetterman (1998)
LeCompte and Schensual (1999) – methods & procedures
Spradley (1980)

Critical ethnography:
Simon and Dippo (1986)
Carspecken (1996)

Interpretive ethnography:
Denzin (1997)

Ethnography & discourse:
Hymes (1996)

Autoethnography:
Brodkey (1996)

Writing ethnographies:
Zeller (1995)
Coffey & Atkinson (1996)
Clifford & Marcus (1986)
Brodkey (1996)

Figure 5.2 Cross-reference subject or topic card

down all of the details you need (publication details, page numbers etc.). Figure 5.1 sets out the general layout we use.

We use the format shown in Figure 5.2 for our 'cross-reference' cards. These cross-reference cards are always 'in process' as we continue to add references and categories that are found in or emerge from our reading.

Compilation
We hand write our file cards using a standard colour (e.g. black pen) for the synopsis of the argument, quotes from the text and other summary-type data. This is important because it allows for annotating the card using other colours. This way our comments and cross-references to other texts are identified easily. Our preference is to write the card in black pen first and then add criticisms and comments in pencil. This allows us to revisit early comments and change them in line with subsequent insights and understandings. We use another colour to cross-reference arguments, claims and assumptions among theorists, researchers and commentators. At other times, we use yet another colour to mark in the top left-hand corner of the front face of the card other projects this particular text might be useful for. This is handy if one is juggling multiple writing and research projects at once (e.g. writing an article from work done

---

| Social cognition & learning | Göncu, Artin & Rogoff, Barbara (1998) Children's categorization with varying adult support. *American Educational Research Journal*, Vol. 35, no. 2, pp. 333–349. CQU library: S370.78 44 |

Aim: To investigate how "varying roles of adult leadership in decision-making yielded differences in children's learning of a categorization system" (p. 334).
→ research population: 5 y.o. chn, mid class, US ← **narrow research pop., but compare with Rogoff (1995 & esp. 1984).**

General focus on shared thinking & intersubjectivity, in which participants in an activity engage in thinking processes together – critiques "democratically-organized collaborations" (p. 334) by pointing to problems in previous studies re. asymmetries re. "who is responsible for what" (p. 334) cf. Studies in Cole, Engeström & Vasquez (1998).

"Asymmetries between partners in responsibility for decision-making may be unimportant as long as the learner participates in the thinking process – perhaps making some or all of decisions or perhaps following another's thought processes" (p. 335).

Key finding: Chn learn better when thinking is shared in some way with an expert. **V. interesting addition to Rogoff's model of cultural apprenticeship.** Shared thinking: see also Heath 1983, consider Vygotsky's zone of proximal development in light of these findings.

Words in: black = summary of text; **Bold** = reader's comments; underlining = cross-references to other texts

Figure 5.3   A sample reading record file card

as part of obtaining a higher degree, research assistant work for a lecturer and your own research project).

Symbols or codes also help us to quickly identify particular elements – for example, writing 'def' inside a circle at the beginning of a quote or paraphrase to indicate a definition, or circled or bracketed page reference numbers after a quote or point. We also use idiosyncratic shorthand symbols for writing notes quickly (e.g. a capital 'K' for 'knowledge', a capital 'R' for research, 'R.qq' for 'research questions' etc.).

In general our reading record cards look something like the example presented in Figure 5.3.

We also use the back of each card and, where necessary, staple a number of cards together when more than one is needed for a given record of a text (such as when including a summary of the structure of the argument provided in the text, or copying out the contents page of a book or edited collection).

Hints for constructing effective reading records and for managing cards

- Enter the author(s) first name in full. Some publishers or journals require this for the bibliography, and some publishing conventions use an author's first name the first time their work is cited directly within the text.
- Include the state where a text was published as well as the city in the bibliographic details. Again, some publishers and journals require this information in the bibliography.
- Take care with maintaining correct Australian, UK and American English spellings when copying quotes and titles.
- Clearly indicate where you are paraphrasing something closely or quoting directly from a text. On our cards we use a system of quotation marks – double quote marks for direct quotes and single quote marks for close paraphrasing – to help avoid plagiarism in our writing.
- Include page numbers for journals and chapters.
- Keep all completed cards in the one place – some sort of box where you can arrange your cards alphabetically is ideal.

Task

Identify an alternative approach to keeping a record of your reading from that we have provided here. What do you see as the relative pros and cons of the respective approaches?

The next chapter, which deals with ethics and teacher research, will conclude the first part of this book.

CHAPTER 6

Ethics and teacher research

Introduction

Within educational research, ethics is concerned with ensuring that the interests and well-being of people are not harmed as a result of the research being done. The extent to which people's interests can be harmed directly and indirectly as a consequence of research in which they have participated is now well-known. Harm can range from people experiencing affronts to their dignity and being hurt by conclusions that are drawn about them all the way through to having their reputations or credibility undermined publicly. Sometimes it is individuals who are hurt or whose interests are otherwise harmed. Sometimes it is a group, a school, a school community, or even an entire social group (e.g. a racial or ethnic group who experience generalized attribution to them of conditions, traits or dispositions associated with individuals in the research). The harm can be direct, as when a particular individual is identifiable by others in a research report and negative consequences result from aspects of the research becoming public. It can also be indirect, as when a family has to pay more money to support the education of its children at the local school because school resourcing has been cut by policies rationalized by findings of a research study.

As recently as 15 years ago it was possible for educational researchers to conduct research in classrooms and on individual children with weak, negligible or non-existent ethical protection mechanisms in place. Recognition of demonstrable harm resulting from research activity has led to criteria and codes for 'ethical research practice' being widely established and implemented within the education sector in places like Australasia, Britain and North America. These assert moral principles and obligations that are binding on researchers undertaking any investigation within their jurisdiction. Universities and other research institutions routinely require researchers conducting studies under their auspices to obtain approval from an ethics committee or its equivalent.

Whereas postgraduate students and academics have clear guidelines and processes to follow in the conduct of research – laid down by formal university ethical clearance committees – the existence and operation of codes of ethical practice for research by teacher researchers in their own classrooms is uncertain and easily overlooked. The matter is often downplayed or absent in teacher research literature. This chapter will provide an elementary introduction to the topic and suggest some resources that may be useful for teacher researchers unfamiliar with research ethics issues and procedures. (We also address some ethical issues with specific reference to data collection in Chapter 9. Readers are referred to the sub-section on ethical principles on p. 184.)

Institutional contingencies

Whereas universities and other research institutions routinely have their own ethical codes and procedures governing research, schools often do not. And even where state or regional departments of education have formal procedures and requirements governing the conduct of research in their schools, teacher researchers may not be aware of these or may think they do not apply to their particular research. The line we recommend here is that teacher researchers assume any research they intend to conduct that uses human subjects (even if only for interview and observation) is subject to formal ethical codes and procedures, and set about looking for them. If the school does not have them, teacher researchers will need to go to the next level in the administrative chain, until the codes are found or the 'end of the line' is reached.

Our view is that even if one reaches the end of the line without locating formal mandatory ethical requirements pertaining to one's project, this does not absolve the researcher from ethical obligations. In such cases we recommend action on two levels. First, actively pursue the development of formal arrangements within one's own school. This, simply, is good practice. Second, locate an appropriate ethical code and operate it on one's own behalf as though it were a formal requirement in one's own circumstances.

Literature on research ethics

Karen Halasa (1998) provides a very useful annotated bibliography on *Ethics in Educational Research*. An online version can be found at: www.aare.edu.au/ indexx.htm. Click on the 'Code of ethics' button under 'Publications' and then click on the 'Annotated bibliography' link. The resources available in this bibliography provide teacher researchers with an excellent coverage of the major issues relevant to their activities.

Codes of research

Many education associations have their own codes of ethics to guide members' research activity. The Australian Association for Research in Education provides an ethics code on the site where Halasa's annotated bibliography appears (see www.aare.edu.au/indexx.htm and go to 'Code of ethics' under 'Publications'). Similarly, the AERA provides its code of ethics online at www.aera.net/about/policy/ethics.htm. It also documents the initiatives it is involved in as a professional educators association with respect to human research protections. This is available at www.aera.net/humansubjects/HRP-AERA.htm.

While there is no fixed, general code for teacher researchers, *ethical research* considerations largely overlap with *ethical teaching* practices. Halasa (1998: 3) suggests that 'teacher researchers see themselves as doubly bound to ethical behaviour both as teachers and researchers'. She cites the Fairfax County Public Schools Teacher Network statement of ethics as a useful set of guidelines:

> They are teachers first. They respect those with whom they work, openly sharing information about their research; consult with teaching colleagues and supervisors to review the plans for their studies, explain research questions and methods of data collection and update their plans as the research progresses; use data from observations, discussions, interviews and writing that is collected during the normal process of teaching and learning, secure principal's permission for broader surveys or letters and permission to use data already gathered by the school; may present the results of their research to colleagues in their school districts, are honest in their conclusions and sensitive to the effects of their research findings on others. Before publishing written releases must be obtained from the individuals involved in the research including parental permission for those under 18. The confidentiality of the people involved in the research is protected.

Some ethical principles for good research practice

Taken in conjunction with typical codes of research ethics, linking teaching and research ethics is helpful in identifying criteria and principles to be met by teacher researchers when conducting formal investigations in their classroom or school. These include:

- have a valid research design;
- obtain informed consent;
- avoid deception;
- minimize intrusion;
- ensure confidentiality;
- minimize risk of harm;
- demonstrate respect;
- avoid coercion or manipulation;
- reciprocate.

Have a valid research design

Poorly designed research wastes participants' time and often leads to their refusal to participate in any other research studies. Mertens (1998: 24) reminds us that 'faulty' research 'is not only a waste of time and money but cannot be conceived of as being ethical because it does not contribute to the well-being of the participants'. Related to this criterion of validity is the need for the researcher to be able to 'do' the proposed research. She or he must have – or be able to develop within the time frame of the study – the requisite skills for completing the study effectively. The discussion in Chapter 2 earlier applies directly to this ethical requirement (see pp. 30–31).

Obtain informed consent

The participants in qualitative or quantitative research projects – often the teacher's students – need to give their informed consent with regard to their participation in the project. Research differs from assessment. Teachers are expected to collect information about students' learning in order to monitor progress. Formal research usually goes beyond this kind of data to study, in depth, students' attitudes, practices, self-perceptions and so on. This can potentially be intrusive. It is particularly important that the consent be *informed*. Participants must be aware of the general aims of the study and what it will involve. Consent should extend to include publications that may grow out of the study.

Depending on the age of the student it may be appropriate for parents or caregivers/guardians to provide informed consent on the student's behalf. Our personal preference is to seek each student's informed consent wherever possible in addition to parental/caregiver permission. Extending as far down the age range as one can automatically forces one to get as clear as possible exactly what it is one plans to do in the study. Unless one is clear an explanatory statement is unlikely to inform a younger participant.

Since consent must be *informed*, the researcher must develop at least two types of statement for seeking consent. One is the form signed by the participants (or participant proxies). The other is a statement – an information letter – that explains what the research is doing, what risks may be involved, what the participants will be protected from and so on. Both need to be produced in language that the signatories can understand and relate to. These statements are then binding on the researcher.

Depending on the particular teacher researcher's circumstances, consent may have to be obtained from (one or more of) the school principal, the local and/or state department of education, a university ethics committee and so on.

A classic example of what *not* to do occurred in Australia in June 1999, when Grade 7 students in a school were surveyed by two university academics about highly intimate and personal topics without parental permission having been sought for the survey (Busfield 1999). Parents were outraged, and the university involved was asked to explain the lack of formal consent to the public and to Education New South Wales, the state education department. Although in this case academics were involved, the example forewarns teachers to seek written consent from students and parents when conducting research of whatever type in their classroom.

There are other more subtle issues around consent. For example, one might be focusing on just a small number of case study participants within a much larger class. To the extent that the research nonetheless impinges on other class members it may be necessary to gain their informed consent as well (and that of their parents) – albeit at a different 'level' from that of the primary participants. It is also important to assure those from whom consent is sought that in no way will any disadvantage accrue from withholding consent and from choosing not to participate in the study.

Figures 6.1–6.5 are typical examples of documents used to seek informed consent.

Dear Parent/Guardian

I am seeking your consent for your child to be involved in a study related to writing that I am going to carry out at [name of school].

The study is titled [name of proposed study]. It focuses on understanding more about how children learn to write. It will involve video and audio recording of writing lessons in your child's classroom (approximately ten hours). The teacher and children will be recorded as they talk and interact during their daily writing activities. Children will not be asked to do any special activities or to do anything differently. Recording will occur during the mornings for an hour each day.

Copies of children's writing may also be taken. Names of children will be removed from copies and the writing will only be used if it relates to the talk and interaction that has been recorded on video.

As part of an ethical approach to this study I assure you that:

- children will be completing their everyday learning activities in the usual way

- the study will not interfere with children's learning

- individual children will not be identified or named

- your child will not be assessed or tested or graded

- you may withdraw your child at any time from the study

If you decide to withdraw your child from the project, then recordings that show your child will not be used.

To ensure confidentiality and protection for your child I promise that:

- tapes will only be used for research or educational purposes

- you may ask to see and view any tapes that record your child

- you may request that parts of tapes that show your child not be shown to any others

- you may request that your child's writing not be used in the study

Your child's classroom teacher has agreed to be involved in the study. Permission from the school principal and the department of education has also been given. I am grateful for this support.

Thank you for considering this. If you wish to speak to me further about this project, please contact me at [telephone number], or speak to me when I am visiting your child's school.

Would you please complete the attached form and return it to your child's class teacher by [date].

Yours sincerely

[researcher's name].

Figure 6.1 Sample information letter for parents/guardians (adapted from Davidson, in preparation)

Parent/caregiver consent form

I am willing/I am not willing (please cross out the one that does not apply) for my child [child's name] to participate in the study being conducted by [researcher's name] at [name of school].

I understand that the identity of my child will remain confidential and that I may withdraw my child from the study at any time.

Signed:_____

Printed name:_____

Relationship to child:_____

Date:_____

Figure 6.2 Sample consent form for parents/guardians (adapted from Davidson, in preparation)

Teacher consent form

I am willing/I am not willing (please cross out the one that does not apply) to participate in the study being conducted by [researcher's name] at [name of school].

I understand that the research study will include video-taping my students and my classroom teaching. I also understand that my identity will not be revealed and that I can withdraw at any time from the project should I choose to.

Signed:_____

Printed name:_____

Date:_____

Figure 6.3 Sample consent form for teacher (adapted from Davidson, in preparation)

Student consent form

FOR QUESTIONS ABOUT THE STUDY, CONTACT:

[Researcher's name]

[Phone contact details]

DESCRIPTION: You are invited to participate in a research study, the purpose of which is to better understand if the use of computers in schools contributes to educational achievement. You will be asked to fill out two brief questionnaires: the questionnaires will ask for simple responses, such as rating things related to schoolwork. You may also be asked to participate in interviews, which are basically casual discussions about computer use. Your names and responses will be kept strictly confidential. The data will be collected and analysed for research purposes to study the link between computer use and educational outcomes.

RISKS AND BENEFITS: Occasionally, students do not like to answer questionnaires. This is the only risk associated with this study. The benefits, which may reasonably be expected to result from this study, are that you may be helping to improve under- standing of how students use computers.

SUBJECT'S RIGHTS: If you have read this form and have decided to participate in this study, please understand your participation is voluntary and you have the right to withdraw your consent or discontinue participation at any time without penalty. You have the right to refuse to answer particular questions. Your individual privacy will be maintained in all published and written data resulting from the study.

If you have any questions about your rights as a participant in this study, or are dis- satisfied at any time with any aspect of this study, you may contact – anonymously, if you wish – the [name and contact details of institutional body under whose auspices the study will be conducted].

The extra copy of this consent form is for you to keep.

Student name:_____

Student's signature:_____ Date:_____

Figure 6.4 Sample student consent form containing information about the project (adapted from Forero 2001: 125–6)

Parent/guardian consent form

Your child has been invited to participate in a research study [period of study] that is being conducted by [description of researcher]. The purpose of the study is to better understand if the use of computers in schools contributes to educational achievement. It will be conducted at your child's school as part of his or her regular classwork. Your child will be asked to fill out two brief questionnaires; the questionnaires will ask for simple responses, such as rating things related to schoolwork. She/he may also be asked to participate in interviews, which are basically casual discussions about computer use.

Participation is voluntary and you have the right to withdraw your consent or dis- continue your child's participation at any time without penalty. The individual privacy of students will be maintained in all published and written data resulting from the study. All students will be informed that they are under no obligation to participate in the study if they do not wish to and that even if they do choose to participate they have the right to refuse to answer particular questions. Student names and responses will be kept strictly confidential. The data will be collected and analysed for research purposes to study the link between computer use and educational achievement.

If you have any questions about your rights as a parent or guardian of a participant in this study, or are dissatisfied at any time with any aspect of this study, you may contact – anonymously, if you wish – the [name and contact details of institutional body under whose auspices the study will be conducted].

IF YOU OBJECT to your child's participation in this study, please sign and return one copy of this form to school with your child or contact [researcher's name and phone number]. If you do not object to your child's participation in this study, you do not need to send the form back. If I do not receive this form from you, I will assume your permission is granted.

The extra copy of this form is for you to keep.

☐ I do not give permission to my child to participate in this study.

Parent/guardian's signature:_____   Date:_____

Student's name:_____

FOR QUESTIONS ABOUT THE STUDY, CONTACT:

[Researcher name and contact details]

Figure 6.5 Sample parent/guardian consent form containing information about the project (adapted from Forero 2001: 127–8)

Avoid deception

Obtaining informed consent is closely linked to the ethical principle of avoiding deception in the life of a research study. It is crucial that research does not 'trick' students into participating in a study, or into thinking that the research will focus on one thing when it actually focuses on another. For example, students should never be led to believe they are simply completing an exercise when it is actually a 'test' of some dimension of their literacy ability. Students must consent to the 'real' project. Quite apart from offending against a general moral principle not to deceive others, researchers also risk damaging their relationships of trust and confidence with students (and parents/caregivers) if they attempt deception. The practice of obtaining informed consent and providing clear and comprehensive information about the study and the guarantees extended to participants helps safeguard against unwitting corner-cutting. It makes the fact of the research public and, to that extent, invites scrutiny. This in turn can heighten a researcher's sense of accountability and responsibility towards participants.

Some commentators (e.g. Cohen *et al.* 2000: 63–6) note that the issue of deception is more complex than the 'blanket' approach adopted in the previous paragraph. They acknowledge that in areas of social research a degree of deception might sometimes be necessary in order to address an important problem or issue. They distinguish between first and second order deception. First order deception involves withholding the whole truth from subjects about 'the true purpose and conditions of the research' or 'positively misinforming them' (Cohen *et al.* 2000: 63). Second order deception is where researchers allow individuals to believe 'they are acting as researchers or researchers' accomplices when they are in fact serving as subjects' (2000: 63–4). Cohen and colleagues suggest that from the social researcher's point of view the problem of deception involves a question of balance: 'What is the proper balance between the interests of science and the thoughtful, humane treatment of people who, innocently, provide the data?' (2000: 63).

This is similar to ideas in the following section about judging when a marginal increase in intrusion will bring a quantum increase in significant findings. The territory is dangerous, and our personal preference is not to go there – although we recognize that some degree of (unwitting) deception is likely to occur in any research involving human subjects, if only because it is impossible to give participants an exhaustive understanding of what is involved. Moreover, there are historical instances of untold human benefit resulting from research involving first and second order deception. For researchers who will be 'sailing close to the wind' with respect to deception, Cohen and colleagues refer to Kelman's (1967) suggestions for addressing the problem of deception. The first is to become as aware as possible that it exists as a research problem, and of the dimensions on which it exists. The second is to try to minimize and counteract any negative consequences of deception for participants. The third is to try and develop creative approaches that 'displace' deception with something less unpalatable – such as using role play or 'as-if' experiments (Kelman 1967: 65).

In the end we believe that teacher researchers constitute a special case, and we opt for our initial position. Teacher researchers stand in relation to their main participants (students) in a different way from 'outside' researchers. They stand to betray trust and cause damage that 'outside' researchers can avoid. In the end, our view is 'don't go there'.

Minimize intrusion

All research that involves participation by human subjects is, by definition, intrusive to a greater or lesser extent. Whenever research involving human subjects occurs, the lives of participants are different to some degree from what they otherwise would have been because of the researcher's intrusion into their routines. Giving informed consent does not obviate intrusion; it simply gives the researcher permission to intrude. The intrusion in question may be minimal, as when a sensitive and 'skilled' researcher conducts observations almost unnoticed in a classroom. Even here, however, social dynamics are impacted to some extent. The degree and kind of intrusion are amplified when interviewing, surveying, measuring, artefact collection and the like are involved. Intrusion is amplified and compounded still further if data collection goes beyond a single setting (like the classroom) into playgrounds, community spaces and homes.

While it is impossible to eliminate intrusion altogether, researchers should aim to minimize intrusion by avoiding impositions that do not contribute productively to their research purposes. 'Minimizing' needs to be understood carefully in this context. It involves a balancing of costs and benefits, and does not equate with 'the least possible amount'. For example, too little intrusion may result in a genuine subtraction of value from the project. This would be the case when a marginal increase in intrusion would have generated a considerable increase in significant findings. Making such judgements in the field is difficult and the concept can easily become interest serving. The capacity to make good judgements generally improves with research experience. At all times, however, it is better to err on the side of 'under-intruding'.

Intrusion has several dimensions. It is not just the physical 'taking up of space' or 'being in the way'. It can be 'non-spatial', as when data collection pries into areas it does not need, or has no right, to go. Researchers need to keep their data collection purposes very clear and be vigilantly honest about the information they *need* for addressing their question well. Our own preference for a rule of thumb here is 'If in doubt, don't ask (gather, observe, etc.) it' – especially if the data in question are in a recognized area of sensitivity (e.g. religious, political, sexual, cultural, ethnic areas and so on).

Intrusion can also be 'temporal', in the sense that whether or not 'being there' is experienced as an (undue/unwanted) intrusion may be a function of the researcher's 'timing' – such as, 'now is not good, but the same thing later would be fine'. This is why it is important to establish agreed times and places with participants and stick to them punctually unless participants initiate changes. Even then, however, an agreed time and place could turn out to be intrusive because of contingencies. It is important that participants genuinely feel comfortable about negotiating changes. Often they will not. Hence, it is important that researchers strive to be as alert as possible to signals of inconvenience or unease and, if in doubt, ask participants whether they are uncomfortable about where things are going and/or whether another time/place would suit them better.

Anybody who is reasonably sensitive in interpersonal exchanges and who remains open to the possibility that research activities may at times be experienced as unduly intrusive is likely to pick up on signals that they are close to crossing a line. Of course, it is possible to sense a signal and disregard it. Acting on a possible signal can be as easy as asking participants if they are feeling put upon, and being prepared to act appropriately on the response provided.

Ensure confidentiality and anonymity

Participants should be assured in writing that their identities will be masked as much as possible in any report of the project outcomes and processes. This is a traditional criterion of ethics, and aims at minimizing negative repercussions for participants in light of the outcomes of the study. Nevertheless, assuring confidentiality and anonymity is actually quite difficult to put into practice as some schools are readily identifiable because they are unique or easily recognized in the region. Focusing on a student with literacy difficulties means that many of the teachers in the school will know who the child is despite a pseudonym being used (see Frankfort-Nachmias and Nachmias 1992).

Preserving anonymity is not absolutely binding. Some teacher researchers decide, for one reason or another, to use the real first names of the students they studied. Neil Anderson (1994), for example, obtained written permission from Belinda's parents to use her first name in articles about her. This was a way of celebrating her personal achievements during (and following) the study.

Minimize risk of harm

Teacher researchers must always ensure that 'duty of care' responsibilities are enacted throughout a research study. This includes doing all one can in advance to foresee any possible harm that could come to participants as a result of a study. In the example mentioned previously of university academics surveying Grade 7 students, questions were asked about body image. These questions severely depressed at least one young female participant. Other items instructed students to describe their pubic hair development. The school subsequently banned all further university research on its site.

Harm can occur at a number of recognized points in research. For example, there is a potential for the interests of certain students to be harmed through 'omission' when control groups are used in a quasi-experimental research design. This can occur when members of a control group are disadvantaged by not receiving an intervention that enhances some aspect of learning available to other students in the experimental group. One way to circumvent this is to ensure that control groups (will) receive the same intervention at a later date. The point here is that such matters have to be anticipated as far as possible at the time a study is conceptualized and designed. Likewise, harm to students may occur when an intervention has not been thoroughly planned and prepared and the outcomes of participation lead to exclusion, teasing or depression.

There is no way that all potential risks of harm can be pre-empted in research. By the same token, teacher researchers can forewarn themselves by reading accounts of ethical issues and dilemmas arising for researchers within educational settings. Besides the annotated bibliography provided by Halasa (1998), an excellent overview with extensive references is provided by Cohen *et al.* (2000: Ch. 2).

Demonstrate respect for research participants at all times

Although demonstrating respect for students is part and parcel of being a teacher, it is especially important to demonstrate this attribute during formal research. This helps maintain one's trusting relationship with students during a formal study so that they feel free to answer honestly, knowing that this will not adversely affect their academic performance evaluations on school reports and the like. In our experience, students involved in a research study that includes some sort of intervention often provide incisive and extraordinarily helpful evaluations at the end of the programme; respecting their input enhances the results of the study. Demonstrating respect includes respecting the privacy of participants and not asking them to discuss aspects of their lives that have nothing significantly to do with the research question. It also includes refusing to engage students in research that intrudes unnecessarily into their religious or moral lives. Demonstrating respect for students means that the research in which they are asked to participate is genuinely useful to the class and/or students like themselves, and is not a form of exploitation that will only significantly advantage the researcher.

Often the point at which harm in general, and failure to respect participants specifically, most occurs is in reporting research. The practice of participant checking can play an important role as an ethical guide or 'touchstone' at this stage (see also Chapter 16). For instance, if a researcher feels uneasy about participants reading (part of) a report this may well signal a potential breach of the researcher's duty of care responsibility – and troubling elements of the report may need to be rewritten.

Avoid coercion or manipulation

Teacher researchers must be aware of the unequal relationships between themselves and student research subjects in relation to power and the effects that this might have on interview and observation results. These effects include children producing the kinds of opinions that they feel will please the teacher as researcher, to 'acting up', through to acting in ways that they think the teacher wants them to act (e.g. self-fulfilling prophecies). At worst, student subjects may feel coerced into providing their consent to participate in a project, or manipulated to respond or act in certain ways during the course of the study. From the standpoint of the research itself, lack of careful attention to the effects of the teacher – a person of authority in the classroom – on any study can render it invalid.

Reciprocate

Research is best practised as a 'two-way street'. The goodwill and generosity of research participants can be met by some returning of 'favours and commitments' on the part of the researcher. This can help build 'sense of mutual identification' (Glazer 1982 cited in Glesne and Peshkin 1992: 122). More importantly, it demonstrates the researcher honouring the contribution of participants rather than taking it for granted, and actively seeking to put something back in return for what has been requested (see also Chapter 8). Specific examples on the part of teacher researchers with respect to student and parent participants might involve running some after-hours parent-and-child computing activities, or giving some time to a sports team or club in which students/parents are involved, or organizing an event that benefits participants. The case of Neil Anderson and Belinda (Chapter 4) provides an exceptional example of reciprocity in teacher research. The educational benefits for Belinda were enormous and enduring, as were the benefits to the researcher and his community. The rule of thumb here is for researchers to be aware of the extent to which they are receiving goodwill and generosity from their research subjects and to think of manageable ways to recognize this in action.

From the outset

Teacher researchers need to build awareness of ethical issues into the research design and take account of them from the very start of a project. Ethics are not something that can simply be tacked on to the end of a project as an afterthought.

Ethical considerations in teacher research are complex. We have provided only a brief outline of key criteria to be met in any formal research study conducted by teacher researchers. These, however, should be enough to get beginning researchers started in ethically acceptable ways. As always, however, we recommend reading more widely on the topic. A good starting point are the following:

- Cohen, L., Manion, L. and Morrison, K. (2000) *Research Methods in Education*, 5th edn. London: RoutledgeFalmer.
- Frankfort-Nachmias, C. and Nachmias, D. (1992) *Research Methods in the Social Sciences*. London: Edward Arnold.
- Knobel, M. (2003) Rants, ratings and representations: issues of validity, reliability and ethics in researching online social practices, *Education, Communication and Information*, 3(2): 187–210.
- Lankshear, C. and Knobel, M. (1997c) *The Moral Consequences of what we Construct Through Qualitative Research*, www.geocities.com/c.lankshear/moral.html (accessed 9 September 2003).

Looking ahead

This concludes the first part of this book, which has been concerned with a general background to teacher research as practice. In Part 2 we introduce teacher research as document-based and quantitative investigation, beginning in the next chapter with an account of teacher research as documentary inquiry.

Introduction to teacher research as document-based and quantitative investigation

CHAPTER 7

An introduction to teacher research as document-based investigation

Introduction

In this chapter we use examples from a range of theoretical and discipline perspectives within educational investigation to discuss aspects of research design, data collection, data analysis and critical assessment of the quality and validity of data in document-based research.

Research purposes in document-based research: three kinds of questions and problems

Document-based researchers address different kinds of problems and questions. We have organized this chapter around three broad kinds of educational research purposes that can be served by document-based studies.

1   *Research that undertakes 'readings' to identify 'meanings'.* Researchers often engage in document-based research in order to investigate the kinds of *meanings* constructed through texts. This reveals the kind of *ideological work* texts may do and how they may 'position' and encourage us as readers to view and approach the world – or 'bits' of it – in some ways rather than others. This purpose is addressed by gathering texts relevant to the researcher's area of interest and then subjecting

them to some kind of reading through textual analysis. This involves a process of arguing that the text – or text corpus – generates certain kinds of meanings and meaning effects.

2 *Document-based research undertaken to develop a 'normative' stance on an educational issue.* A second purpose involves mobilizing and scrutinizing a corpus of texts in order to produce an argument for what one thinks is a preferable, proper, worthwhile/desirable stance to take on some educational matter. This category spans a very wide range, from research intended to inform a stand on ethical issues in education (respect for difference and diversity, fairness, children's rights) and the politics of education (power relations in schooling, dis/advantage etc.), to research concerned with how best to understand and address issues of assessment, 'at risk' learners, literacy education, educational outcomes, research priorities and so on.

3 *Research that uses texts to advance substantive findings about the world.* Our third category of document-based research purposes aims to use extant texts to describe, understand and explain things going on in the world. It is one thing to use texts to identify or construct meanings of, say 'literacy'. It is another to draw on textual content to describe distributions of different literacies among populations and to explain these distributions. Analysing documentary data to produce *substantive findings* about the world operates at this latter level.

Research that undertakes 'readings' to identify or construct 'meanings'

Here the teacher researcher focuses on a text or body of texts and subjects them to some form of textual analysis. For areas of interest like gender reform in education, literacy education, curriculum policy and change etc. the corpus could include policy documents, curriculum and syllabus statements, published speeches, legislation, literary works, classroom textbooks and the like. The kind of textual analysis employed will depend on the theoretical perspective adopted by the researcher. The analytic approach they adopt must cohere with their conceptual and theoretical framing of the research problem. Applying textual analysis yields a *reading* of the text(s) that responds to the original research question.

For instance, a research question might be concerned with the political or ideological character of a policy document, or with the 'possible worlds' constructed by a textbook, or with what a deconstructed reading of a novel might look like. Or it might simply ask how literacy is represented in a national statement on English, a national plan for literacy and numeracy education, or in some wider range of education policy documents and directions.

Examples of making readings for meanings: research design, data collection, analysis and interpretation

Meanings of 'literacy' in education policy documents
Some of our own recent work has involved investigating documents to identify meanings of 'literacy' in contemporary education policy discourse (Lankshear 1997, 1998; Knobel 1999). The design and procedures employed in this work were straightforward. The aim was simply to 'map' more or less distinguishable *categories* of meanings of 'literacy'. The study addressed the question: 'What are the main meanings of literacy in contemporary education reform texts?'

Research design
The design for this research had three main components. First we surveyed print and online resources from Australia, Britain and the USA to identify and assemble a corpus of typical types of texts falling within education reform policy discourse, where there was a significant focus on literacy. Text types included: policy legislation; official curriculum and syllabus statements and frameworks, mandatory tests and achievement profiles developed in response to legislation; formal reports of research projects, working parties, task forces, discussion/position papers and the like commissioned by governments/administrations; policy discussion and draft policy documents, official media reports of and commentaries on policy directions, policy related speeches released by or on behalf of government and administration officials; and texts identified by scholarly commentators on educational reform as having been influential in shaping reform policy outcomes (Lankshear 1998: 352–3). Second, we analysed the corpus using basic coding and elementary forms of content and category analysis. Third, we interpreted the range of meanings in relation to the wider sociohistorical context within which the policies had been developed.

Data collection: surveying relevant sources and assembling a corpus
Initial searches were conducted on the web using different search engines, the key words 'education reform', 'education policy', 'literacy' and the country names. Online searches of major library catalogues were also employed. Our searches yielded scores of texts of the types we sought. They also yielded a range of commentaries on education reform policy and texts about education policy theory and analysis, which in turn generated additional education reform policy texts through their bibliographies. They also generated further key words and concepts, some of which we used to search for further resources and, later, to analyse the data.

Our aim was to sample a typical range of reform documents. Our concept of 'typicality' was guided by texts written by education reform scholars representing different theoretical and political perspectives. These provided a sense of the dimensions of education reform beyond 'language and literacy education' itself in which literacy was a significant focus – such as 'technology initiatives', 'outcomes-based assessment' and the like. While gathering our corpus we began looking for patterns and repetitions in the texts that suggested they contained a range of meanings of 'literacy'. When little or nothing new and different was coming through in the most recently identified sources, we stopped collecting data/texts. (For examples of the corpus texts, see the bibliographies in Lankshear 1998 and Knobel 1999.)

Data analysis

We read each policy text several times, marking [with a highlighter] passages containing content that could reasonably be said to be concerned with literacy. These passages did not always refer explicitly to the term 'literacy'. Related terms like 'communication skills', 'computer programming', 'analysing and synthesizing', 'problem solving', 'symbol manipulation' and the like were also taken as markers of literacy whenever the context involved text-mediated practices. These choices were guided by our prior knowledge of the 'literacy' field and of the range of concepts often associated with literacy, as well as by ideas conveyed in the commentaries and other secondary source materials previously mentioned.

When we had identified and highlighted all the text 'bits' we could find pertaining to literacy, we assembled and organized them into clusters of similar ideas using different colour codes for identifying 'likes' and 'unlikes'. Policy commentaries and theoretical works often guided us here, sometimes providing 'pre-formed categories', like 'basics' or 'basic skills', which we could use initially as headings under which to organize some of the data. Besides obvious concepts like 'basics' they also provided important organizing ideas like 'symbolic analysis' (Reich 1992), which capture important textual practices within daily routines (especially work) in the 'information age' and 'postindustrial economy'. Documents relating textual practices to 'globalization' and the 'changing world economy' were especially helpful guides for data analysis since these concerns dominate so much contemporary education policy.

Following preliminary organization of the data under various headings we used a form of category analysis. We wanted a succinct 'set' of meanings that were each genuinely significant in their own right (not just minor variations on other meanings). So we reduced the categories to the smallest number possible without sacrificing important details and distinctions.

Results, findings, interpretation

We arrived at five conceptual categories we thought accounted for the most significant meanings of literacy in our sample of contemporary education reform policy texts. We called them 'lingering basics', 'new basics', 'elite literacies', 'foreign language literacy' and 'information literacy' respectively.

In the final step in the analysis we identified the extent to which these different meanings of literacy are often associated with different target populations, with different positions within the 'new work order' (Gee et al. 1996) and with different corresponding levels of social opportunity and reward. This led us to posit the idea of a 'new word order' and the possibility that education policy texts dealing with literacy might actually contribute to generating highly unequal and stratified educational outcomes.

Reading the 'literacy crisis': what the data 'means'
One of the most protracted debates in education during the past 50 years has been over how best to teach reading and writing. Although the 'reading wars' are much more complex than a struggle between whole-language and phonics 'sides', these may serve as convenient shorthands for present purposes.

A central point in the struggle concerns how research data on reading achievement is to be interpreted, and which data should be appealed to. This has practically become an 'art form' in the USA. The antagonists interpret key data differently and, in many cases, have their preferred 'funds' of data that they believe are most worthy of attention. Readers less familiar with this debate can get a quick gloss via the following recent sources.

- Coles, G. (2000) *Misreading Reading: The Bad Science that Hurts Children*. Portsmouth, NH: Heinemann.
- Krashen, S. (2002) Another urban legend, *Rethinking Schools*, 16(4). http://www.rethinkingschools.org/archive/16_04/Urb164.shtml.
- Lyon, G.R. (1997) *Report on Learning Disabilities Research: From Testimony of G. Reid Lyon on Children's Literacy*. Washington, DC: Committee on Education and the Workforce, US House of Representatives.
- McGuinness, D. (1997) *Why Our Children Can't Read and What We Can Do About It: A Scientific Revolution in Reading*. New York: The Free Press.
- McQuillan, J. (1998) *The Literacy Crisis: False Claims, Real Solutions*. Portsmouth, NH: Heinemann.
- National Center for Education Statistics (NCES)(1994) *Data Compendium for the NAEP 1992 Reading Assessment of the Nation and the States*. Washington, DC: US Department of Education.
- Spear-Swerling, L. (n.d.) Straw men and very misleading reading: A review of *Misreading Reading. Learning Disabilities Online*, http://www.ldonline.org/ld_store/reviews/swerling_coles.html.
- Stewart, J. (1996) The blackboard bungle: California's failed reading experiment, *LA Weekly*, 18(14): 22–9.

The specific 'case' of California illustrates succinctly how different readings are made of the same data in the form of test scores and reported research findings such that they come to *mean different things*. California became a key focus of attention among opponents of whole-language approaches to literacy pedagogy during the mid-1990s (McQuillan 1998: Ch. 1). In 1987 California officially adopted a reading curriculum that 'emphasized reading books and decreasing (but not eliminating) phonics and skills instruction' (McQuillan 1998: 8). In 1992 California performed in the bottom third of the US states in the National Assessment of Educational Progress (NAEP) tests, and its fourth-graders ranked last (Krashen 2002). In 1994 it performed in the bottom 25 per cent. Some writers (e.g. Stewart 1996) read these results to mean that the state's reading test scores had 'plummeted' and that the decline was due to the curriculum approach adopted in 1987 (Levine 1996).

McQuillan (1998) argues that the test results *cannot* be read in these ways.

Acknowledging that the state's students 'clearly performed poorly compared to the rest of the nation', the scores nonetheless cannot be used to show a decline unless figures are available at both the beginning (1987) and the end of the time period in question. State level NAEP scores are not available before 1992. No other standardized reading measures equivalent to the NAEP tests exist. Hence, there is no way of knowing whether scores went up or down following implementation of the new curriculum approach. The sole data available before and after the change (California Achievement Program scores) show no indication of dramatic changes in either direction. Moreover, McQuillan claims the NAEP scores data cannot even be used to argue that the curriculum approach may be associated statistically with the low scores of Californian students, let alone a decline in performance.

Task

Locate the references noted above for Krashen and Spear-Swerling, and address the following questions:

- What do you think may be some of the main reasons for researchers and commentators reading literacy test scores and research findings so differently?

- Do you think such differences could be avoided?

- If so, how and to what extent? If not, why not?

- Krashen and other researchers went beyond the data on test scores to consider other kinds of data. What were these other kinds of data, and why do you think they referred to them?

- Do you think that Spear-Swerling and the researchers she considers most plausible would refer to these other kinds of data? If so, why and to what extent? If not, why not?

Document-based research undertaken to develop a normative stance on an educational issue

Many different kinds of research take existing documents as a database from which arguments are developed for views about 'what should be', 'how things could be better', 'how it is best to understand or view something' and so on. We provide brief examples here from document-based research on literacy.

How best to understand 'literacy'? 'Autonomous' and 'ideological' models

In 1984, Brian Street introduced into literacy research and scholarship an important distinction between two models of literacy. He called these the 'autonomous' and 'ideological' models respectively. Although the 'common sense' of many, if not most, people would support the 'autonomous' model, Street argues that the 'ideological' model is superior.

According to Street (1984, 2001), the autonomous model of literacy is based on three beliefs. First, that literacy is the same thing wherever it occurs. In Street's words (2001: 7), literacy is 'universal', in the sense of being a unitary thing, the same for everyone. Second, literacy is seen as a neutral *tool* or *skill*. It does not 'side' with some ways of being and certain ways of doing things. Rather, from the autonomous standpoint, literacy is just about encoding and decoding a system of signs. It represents, prefers or privileges nothing on its own. It does not 'tell' people how to use it, it does not affect them in any inherent ways. Rather, once people 'get' literacy they can then go about using it any way they like and for any purpose whatsoever. The choices they make are seen as having nothing to do with literacy but, rather, everything to do with how individuals pick up the tool and work with it. Third, proponents of the autonomous model believe that literacy in and of itself 'will have effects on other social and cognitive practices': in other words, it will have causal efficacy and act as an independent variable. Since it is universal, other phenomena don't affect it. But it has effects on other social phenomena and processes. Hence, it is an independent variable. It can be applied to the world by people in ways that make them more productive, more efficient, more developed, more able to take control of their lives and prosper, and so on.

Obviously, this is an intuitively plausible and widely held view of literacy. Within educational theory and research it is most closely associated with cognitive psychology, psychometrics and allied fields. Street, however, argues that the autonomous model is seriously flawed. He draws on a burgeoning body of evidence from various fields of sociocultural theory and research like social psychology, ethnographic studies of literacy and communication, anthropology and social linguistics, and development studies, to criticize what he sees as its weaknesses and to advance an alternative model of literacy. Such research suggests that there is no such thing as a universal literacy 'essence' but, rather, myriad diverse social practices of reading and writing. Rather than trying to reduce literacy to a universal essence, which Street (2001: 7) sees as nothing less than an imposition of a particular western conception onto cultures at large, it is better to think of the nature and meaning of literacy in terms of the forms literacy practices actually take within given social contexts. What literacy 'is' and 'means' *here* may be quite different from what it 'is' and 'means' *there*.

In preference to the autonomous model, Street proposes his 'ideological' model of literacy, according to which, literacy is 'a social practice, not simply a technical and neutral skill' (Street 2001: 7). To adopt the ideological model is to 'concentrate on the specific social practices of reading and writing' (1984: 2), rather than on some abstracted tool, skill or technology. It is to recognize that literacy is really *literacies*, and that whatever form a given literacy might take it is 'always embedded in socially constructed epistemological principles' (2001: 7). Street means by this that the ways in which particular groups of people address reading and writing are always already grounded 'in conceptions of knowledge, identity, being' (2001: 7). For example: 'The ways in which teachers or facilitators and their students interact is already a social practice that affects the nature of the literacy being learned and the ideas about literacy held by the participants ... It is not valid to suggest that "literacy" can be "given" neutrally and then its "social" effects only experienced afterwards' (2001: 8). Rather, argues Street, every particular form that literacy takes is deeply infused with social and cultural 'ways' – and the values, purposes, omissions, commitments and so on that these 'ways' involve.

These are not simply a matter of cultural 'differences' and 'varieties' however. If they were, this model could be referred to as the *cultural* or *culture-dependent* model of literacy. Street, however, calls it the *ideological* model because of the inescapable ways that literacy is related to matters of *power*. The practices and conceptions of reading and writing that constitute literacy from Street's perspective evolve and exist within power structures and relations, and they reflect contests between competing interest groups and their worldviews. The varying views people have of what counts as literacy and being literate; what they see as 'real' or appropriate modes and manners of reading and writing; the ways people actually read and write in the course of their daily lives – these all reflect and promote values, assumptions, beliefs and practices that help to shape how life is lived within a particular cultural setting and, in turn, influence which interests are promoted or undermined as a consequence of how life is lived there. Street claims that literacy is 'always contested' (2001: 7–8). It is contested in terms of 'both its meanings and its practices'. Hence, particular versions of literacy are always grounded in some particular worldview or other, and 'in a desire for that view of literacy to dominate and to marginalize others' (Street 2001: 7; see also Gee 1991).

Since literacy should be seen as an integral dimension of social practices more widely – as simultaneously reflecting and promoting certain beliefs, values and processes – it actually *mediates* the consequences for people's lives of living under these social practices and arrangements, rather than *causing them* in the manner of an independent variable. Far from being *autonomous*, literacy is really integral to social and cultural 'ways' and deeply implicated in their politics. Understanding literacy from the perspective of the ideological model, Street believes, is better than understanding it from the perspective of the autonomous model.

A typical example of the kind of documentary data Street uses to support his view comes from work by Kulick and Stroud (1993), who are anthropologists and social linguists. Street describes how Kulick and Stroud, doing anthropological research in New Guinea villages, started by asking the question: 'What is the impact of literacy?' This, of course, is to ask a question from the standpoint of the autonomous model of literacy. Kulick and Stroud soon ran into problems with this approach. For example, in New Guinea the missionaries had brought literacy to many villages with particular purposes in mind. However, when Kulick and Stroud looked at concrete literacy practices in these settings they found that not only were the people reading and writing for very different purposes than those the missionaries envisaged, but that the very *ways* they were reading and writing were distinctive, idiosyncratic. Kulick and Stroud found that

> People were using literacy in the way they had used oral interaction. There were precise conventions for making a speech, the dominant one being that you must not appear to put anyone else down when you make it. It is ... inappropriate to

put someone down and inappropriate to speak in a braggardly way about your-self, and yet at the same time you want to get your own way. So a variety of clever political discourses and conventions emerged. Kulick and Stroud discovered, when they looked at the texts being written, that people were using the same social linguistic conventions, the same discourse strategies as in this speech making ... So instead of talking about impact [Kulick and Stroud] talk about *taking hold* ... There are now many such examples from around the world which indicate how the communicative repertoire varies, from people simply taking literacy and doing with it what they had already done, to people discovering new functions for it which may be quite different from what the school teachers or the missionaries had in mind.

(Street 2001: 8–9, emphasis added)

On the basis of research findings and other information generated by researchers (e.g., Kulick and Stroud) being made available in publications and databases it is possible for *other* researchers (like Street, in the present example) to undertake document-based research and engage in analysis, critique, development of arguments and so on in order to advance normative viewpoints about educational issues, practices and processes.

Research that uses texts to advance substantive findings about the world

Much social science research falls into the category of document-based research that aims to establish substantive findings about the world. This draws on empirical work that has already been published, as well as upon other kinds of extant texts that comprise part of the social and historical record. A classic recent example is provided by work undertaken over the past 15 years by Manuel Castells (1996, 1997, 2000, 2001) on patterns of contemporary change. Castells mobilized a huge literature reporting empirical investigation of contemporary change trends and systematically weighed its evidence in accordance with his theoretical perspective. On this basis he has advanced an account of major current trends on a global scale, explained why these trends are occurring and identified likely patterns during the years ahead. Only very rarely does Castells refer to any field-based research of his own. His research is almost entirely 'documentary'.

Castells' work addresses the current and foreseeable future scenes by examining reports of contemporary trends. Document-based research, however, can also be used to advance substantive findings about the past. Historians do this all the time. Sometimes such historical work can be used to provide a perspective on the present. An interesting educational example that is highly relevant to teachers is provided by Harvey Graff's (1979) study of literacy and social structure in the nineteenth-century city.

Researching the 'literacy myth': Harvey Graff on literacy as an independent variable

Graff, however, was interested in our everyday beliefs about the 'power' or 'causal efficacy' of literacy and the extent to which we take these beliefs for granted and rarely question them. One such belief is that literacy is a key source of personal benefits to individuals. Graff saw it as an open question whether literacy brings advantages to individuals in such terms as personal development, happiness and equal opportunity to pursue such ends as economic advantage, social mobility, job satisfaction and personal enrichment.

He framed this as a question about whether literacy is an independent variable that can compensate for 'ascribed characteristics … stemming from ethnic origins, family and class backgrounds … sex and race' (1979: 71), and enable individuals to achieve social mobility and a better quality of life. This is a question that requires a considerable time span to investigate, since the kinds of benefits claimed for literacy are only evident over time. If the question is to be researched we either have to begin now and collect data longitudinally over an appropriate length of time, or we have to look at cases retrospectively, comparing where people began and where they have ended up, and at how literacy has figured in this.

Design
Graff decided to conduct a historical or retrospective inquiry. His design had four main requirements. First, he needed research sites where there were good records about individuals over a period of time. Second, there had to be a mix of literate and illiterate people. Third, there had to be data about 'proxies' that could serve as indicators of mobility, personal quality of life/benefits, etc. Fourth, there had to be adequate data pertaining to ascribed characteristics like class, race and ethnicity, and the like. Basically, Graff's research design involved identifying the literacy status (literate or illiterate) of individuals with different ascribed characteristics and seeing whether literacy had an impact on the benefits and mobility of these individuals over time by holding the other variables (the ascribed characteristics) constant.

Data collection
Graff identified three Canadian cities meeting his design requirements for data collection. The three cities of London, Hamilton and Kingston in Ontario all had census data for literacy status, a significant illiterate population and good documented records pertaining to ascribed social characteristics. The sources of data for Graff's study were as good as a historian could possibly hope for. Each town had a high proportion of migrant citizens. These were mainly Irish, English and US born. Many of the US born were black. The ascribed characteristics most closely associated with being illiterate were Irish birth, Catholicism, colour/race and being female. Older persons with these characteristics were more likely to be illiterate than were younger people. Graff drew a sample of literate and illiterate persons across his key ascribed characteristics.

To test for the alleged 'personal benefit' consequences of literacy, Graff compared the literate and illiterate populations in his sample in terms of occupation type and level, and income level: the most readily measurable forms of personal 'benefit'. He made an initial comparison for the year 1861. In addition, Graff identified those illiterate adults in his population who were still in the same town in 1871 and collected data on their occupation and income level. He also identified the literate sons of these illiterate adult males and collected data about their occupational status and income levels.

Data analysis
Graff used some basic statistical analysis to identify correlations between literacy status and types of work, income level and changes in occupational and income status over time and across generations for each of the ascribed characteristics and different combinations of ascribed characteristics. Analytic categories used for occupational status included 'unemployed', 'unskilled', 'semi-skilled', 'artisan/skilled', 'commercial', 'clerical' and 'professional'.

Results and findings
Graff's data analysis revealed that many literate workers had the same occupational status as illiterate workers. For example, 75 per cent of unskilled labourers and 93 per cent of semi-skilled workers were literate. At the same time, almost 20 per cent of the illiterate males were working in artisan or skilled work across a wide range of occupations. Moreover, some illiterate adults were employed in clerical, commercial and professional occupations. More than 50 per cent of the illiterate English-born Protestant males were employed in skilled or non-manual work. Illiterate male workers who stayed in the same town achieved modest improvements over the ten years from 1861–71 in occupational status, wealth and property ownership. By 1871, no illiterate English-born Protestant males remained poor; all were within Graff's category of the 'middle class'. The population of literate sons of illiterate fathers achieved a measurable degree of advantage over their fathers (e.g. semi-skilled over unskilled; skilled over semi-skilled), but nonetheless remained in working-class occupations.

Contrary to our everyday assumptions, for many adults being literate provided no advantage at all over others who were illiterate. For the great majority of Irish Catholics, women in general, and African-American migrants, 'the achievement of education brought no occupational rewards at all; [ascribed or] inherited factors cancelled the potential of advancement through literacy' (Graff 1979: 75–7). There was only one scenario where being illiterate was clearly a disadvantage and being literate an advantage in terms of occupation: where one *already had* the 'right' ascribed characteristics. Illiteracy seems to have imposed an important barrier against an English-born Protestant moving upward into skilled labour, but it had no measurable significance for those who were Irish-born and Catholic. Moreover, where being literate correlated with higher levels of income (e.g. literate skilled workers earning more than illiterate skilled workers) the main factor operating seemed to be ascribed characteristics.

On the basis of analysing documentary data, Graff found no basis for the view that literacy functions as an independent variable to bring about personal benefits in occupational and economic terms. He concluded that 'literacy's role [here] was neither as simple nor as direct as contemporary opinion would predict' (1979: 56). Far from operating as a causal factor in its own right, let alone a major determining factor of personal well-being and mobility, 'literacy interacted with ethnicity, age, occupation, wealth, adjustment, and family organization, reinforcing and mediating the primary social processes that ordered the population, rather than determining their influences' (Graff 1979: 56).

Means for critically assessing the quality and validity of data in document-based research

In the remainder of this chapter we outline some elementary concepts, tools and techniques that can be used to assess and filter documentary data for the purposes of deciding what to count as good evidence for advancing a conclusion or asserting a position on the basis of one's research.

These concepts, tools and techniques apply to two different 'levels' of documentary sources as data or evidence. The first is where *specific* claims or points advanced in a document are treated as data or taken as evidence for some position or belief. At this level one could, for example, use Graff's claim that more than 50 per cent of illiterate English Protestant males obtained skilled or non-manual work as evidence for the claim that in cities like Hamilton Ontario in the 1860s there was no need for skilled workers to be literate. But is this *good* data that one can count on to support one's view about the language requirements for skilled work in a given time and place? To decide this one would scrutinize Graff's sources and ask whether the kinds of records he used to assess individuals' 'literate' status are appropriate for one's own purposes.

The second level is where we take the *overall conclusions or findings* advanced in a document as a piece of data or as evidence for a position we wish to advance. At this second level, for example, we could use Graff's conclusion that 'literacy does not function as an independent variable' as a unit of evidence against (what Street calls) the 'autonomous' model of literacy. This, obviously, is a much 'larger' unit of 'data' than the specific 'bits' of data that constitute our first level. If we want to use such 'second level' data we need to evaluate it to decide whether it is good enough for us to use. To assess the quality of data at this second level we must scrutinize both the 'first level' data used by the original researchers to argue for their conclusions/findings *and* the 'argument' they have developed on the basis of their data.

The procedures we describe below cover both levels of documentary data. Many other tools and techniques exist besides those we mention. The ones we describe, however, are ones we have found especially useful in our own work. They are generic tools that can be adapted in different ways to use with different kinds of data and research. Moreover, they are key tools and techniques used in reviewing literature as a core component of all kinds of research project. An important aspect of reviewing literature involves deciding which texts to take most seriously and use to support our inquiry, which to take less seriously, and why.

Identifying, analysing and evaluating key statements made in texts

One of the most basic and effective things we can do as researchers working with documentary data is to *scrutinize* key claims that are relevant to our study. This involves asking questions like: 'Is this claim clear?'; 'Is it ambiguous?'; 'What kind of claim is it?'; 'What kind of evidence would warrant accepting this claim?'; 'Has enough of that kind of evidence been provided, or is it otherwise available?'

We can't, and needn't, scrutinize *all* claims in a document. The idea is to identify through close reading of the text what the most important claims are so far as treating the text as data for our own research is concerned. Having identified such claims we can ask whether the author has provided enough of the right kind of data for us to take them seriously. There are two matters to consider:

- What is the right *kind* of evidence/support for a particular claim?
- How *much* of such evidence is needed to warrant accepting it?

'The right kind of evidence' depends on the kind of claim being made. For present purposes we can work with three kinds of claims: 'empirical', 'conceptual' and 'normative/value' claims respectively.

Empirical claims

These are claims asserting something about how the world is (or was). They are supported by evidence based ultimately on observation and, in many cases, on measurement of what can be observed. This includes reference to documented reports of observation and measurement of phenomena and processes. For example, Graff's argument about literacy in three Ontario cities during the 1860s–70s is based on evidence derived from documented reports of which individuals were and were not literate at the time. For argument's sake, whether or not we decide to accept such figures might depend on what we can find out about how the original data were collected. If the data came from self-reporting by people in response to census questions asked orally we could have reservations about the data in ways we might not if the original data had been based on records of school achievements in turn based on tests of reading and writing conducted by education authorities. Empirical claims are what we often call 'factual claims' or statements of fact.

Classifying claims is not always straightforward. Becoming adept at allocating claims to one or another category requires practice.

Task

Which of the following would you classify as being empirical claims, and what are your reasons?

- Literacy standards have risen in the past two decades.

- Australia is a more literate society than Spain.

- Most people learn more effectively if they are motivated.

- Darwin is north of Brisbane.

- Humans are innately rational.

- Current policies for administering schools are going in the right direction.

- Corporal punishment is a more effective strategy for managing boys' behaviour than positive reinforcement or detentions.

How much evidence is appropriate for accepting a claim will vary from claim to claim. If it is a contentious claim, or in an area most people know little about, we should expect the researcher to provide more evidence rather than less. If the claim is reasonably well established the researcher may get away with providing little direct evidence for it and, instead, provide references to some authoritative sources. This is a recognized strategy researchers can use to support a claim.

Good judgement on the part of authors and readers alike comes into play here. Sometimes authors can mobilize a lot of evidence/support for a claim simply by referring to authoritative studies where evidence is provided. They can cite studies and thereby direct readers to them, rather than having to spell out the evidence themselves. This strategy is most plausible when the studies or authors cited are already recognized as authoritative. Often, if we are not experienced as researchers or are not familiar with an area of research, we may not be in a good position to know immediately whether a cited author is regarded as authoritative or not. If we are not sure, because we are not familiar with the original research in question, and if the claim is very important to the argument or to our immediate purposes, we will probably need to go back to the original source and satisfy ourselves that it does the work it needs to do in order for us to be warranted in accepting the claim as data.

In our own work with documentary data involving empirical claims we try to follow the following kind of sequence:

1   Identify the empirical claims in a document that are most significant for our own research – that we need to have as much confidence in as possible because they are important data for us.

2   Identify the support provided in the document for each such claim (e.g. by highlighting it).

3   Determine what kind of support strategy has been used (e.g. the author cites data from her own research as evidence; the author cites the research of another person as authoritative support).

4   Consider how contentious or questionable the claim might be (e.g. in the light of contrary positions and evidence one is aware of; how novel or unusual the claim seems to be; how well established the theoretical or methodological approach being employed is etc).

5   Depending on the degree of contentiousness, consider how much evidence and/or what degree of 'authoritativeness' of support we would need to accept the claim as plausible or warranted.

6   If we are unfamiliar with the authorities or works cited, decide whether we need to check out their standing in the field and/or whether we should go back to the original sources to see what they say and whether they have been used/cited appropriately.

7   Consider whether we should check to see if there is contrary evidence. If the author does not report contrary evidence and if we think it is likely that there could be such evidence, it is best to check.

8   Weigh up our deliberations and decide whether we will accept the claim and, if so, at what general level of confidence: from a high level of confidence to provisional acceptance.

Many of these steps involve substeps. For example, even if we know a person is a recognized authority in an area, does that mean the piece of research cited in a given context is good research? How would we decide whether we should check that out? And if we decide that we should, how would we set about evaluating the research?

Conceptual (or analytic) claims

These are claims whose acceptability or plausibility depends upon the *meaning of terms*. If we know that John is a bachelor we know that John does not have a wife. If we accept the information that John is a bachelor it makes no sense to then ask if he has a wife. We might ask if he has a partner or even if he has what used to be known as a 'common law wife'. But if we trust the information we get that John is a bachelor it makes no more sense to wonder if he has a wife than it does to wonder how many triangles we could find in 30 minutes that had more than three sides.

While such examples seem trite and far from any serious research matters, the point is that if we assume certain meanings are operating in a given context we will not expect or provide certain kinds of evidence for claims that invoke these meanings. If we have ascertained by questionnaire that less than 5 per cent of people in a community have ever had any contact with a computer we might feel justified in describing the community as having a low level of 'information literacy' or as being 'information poor', without providing any further evidence. In other words, we may think the truth of the claim that the community has a low level of information literacy follows (by definition, by dint of meaning) from the fact that less than 5 per cent of its members have had any contact with computers. In this case we would be assuming that part of what it means to be information literate is to know how to use a computer.

When we use documentary data we need to make sure we do not simply ride along on the top of other researchers' assumptions about meanings. It is one thing for another researcher to *advance* a claim about a community being information illiterate based on a particular meaning of information literacy. It is another thing for users of that research to be warranted in *accepting* that claim without some supporting argument. While it might follow for someone who either stipulates or assumes a definition of 'information literacy' tied to 'computer use' that a community with 5 per cent computer use is 'information illiterate', it certainly will *not* follow for anyone who does not assume such a definition or accept such a stipulation. In such cases we need to know what we are buying into by accepting claims that assume certain meanings for concepts.

Take 'literacy', for example. A study about literacy levels might use a concept of 'literacy' defined as the ability to read and write at a ninth-grade level. For the researcher conducting this study it follows that all adults who read at or below an eighth-grade level are illiterate, and all who read at or above a ninth-grade level are literate. And they will analyse their data and advance their findings accordingly. But whether or not it follows for us that all adults reading at or below eighth-grade level are illiterate depends on our meaning of literacy. When reading and conducting research we need to be very careful with conceptual claims.

An obvious problem with concepts in the area of educational research is that they are often contested. It may be odd to think of someone wanting to dispute the truth of the conceptual claim that all square figures have four sides. It is not at all odd for someone to want to dispute the 'truth' of the claim that 'literacy' means being able to decode printed text (see Gee 1991). It is even less odd to imagine someone disputing the claim that adults who cannot read at an eighth-grade level are illiterate or, conversely, that people who can read at an eighth-grade level *are* literate. Being able to identify conceptual/analytic claims is a useful ability. In addition, however, we need to know how to assess such claims: how to decide whether to accept them or not, and on what grounds.

Task

Which of the following claims seem to you to be conceptual, and why?

- Triangles have three sides.

- Spanish speakers use the word *triangulo* to refer to a type of three-sided figure.

- Literacy is a basic skill.

- Literacy includes numerate skills as well as conventional print skills.

- Literacy is the 'core business' of primary education.

- Literacy needs are becoming more and more sophisticated in the information age.

- If you do not have adequate literacy skills you will not be able to get a job.

All concepts, even those seemingly least beyond dispute – like 'square' or 'triangle' – are cultural productions. As such they are ultimately *contingent*. Yet, they assume the character of being necessary and beyond question, and of providing us with sure knowledge. For some people it is simply indisputable that someone who cannot read a basic text is illiterate, just as it is indisputable that if something is a square it has four sides. But in the end all such meanings are just conventions. There is always space for questioning conceptual claims – the question is how much point is served by doing so?

This will vary from case to case. For most of us there may be very little point in challenging the conceptual link we all assume between 'square' and 'having four sides'. By contrast, however, there might be a great deal of point in challenging conventional links between the concept of 'literacy' and the 'capacity to read printed texts', or between 'achievement' and 'performance on certain kinds of tasks', or between 'competence' and 'having certain credentials'. When we use documents as data we should look carefully at what their conceptual claims do so far as shoring up particular meaning systems and the various beliefs and practices based on these is concerned. And we should ask whether we want to go along with these conceptual claims and their entailments. If we don't, we should *not* accept them.

Within education there often exist multiple accounts of key concepts. This is because educational researchers and theorists work to influence meanings as a part of their projects to enhance educational practices. Of course, whether or not we want to go along with a particular alternative construction of a concept to one we are already not happy with is something we need to consider. In the end we may have to advance our own distinctive meaning for a concept and defend it. When there is room and reason for questioning the particular meaning assigned to a concept – for questioning a conceptual claim – we have different options. We can argue that there are better ways to understand the concept, or good reasons not to accept the definition provided, and advance our alternative. Equally, we can look for existing accounts of the concept we think are better than the one we are disputing and provide our reasons for thinking they are better.

Normative or value claims

These are claims that deal with matters of good or bad, right or wrong, things that ought or oughtn't to be the case, and so on. They cover objects (e.g. that is a superb painting; what an ugly building; that is a very good essay) as well as actions (e.g. that was the wrong thing to do; behaving like that is immoral); processes (e.g. that's the right/best way to proceed) and products (e.g. that's the best cake).

Consequently, there are different kinds of normative/value claims. They can be statements of moral value, aesthetic value, political acceptability, pedagogical quality, economic efficiency etc. What vary are the criteria used for making and defending normative judgements. For example, the criteria for judging in the domain of morals are likely to be different from those used for making aesthetic value judgements. Likewise, judgements about good pedagogy may be based on very different criteria and grounds from judgements about good economic performance.

Normative claims cannot be advanced, justified or defended by simply providing straightforward empirical evidence. In most cases, providing some direct empirical evidence will be part of the process for supporting a normative claim. For example, we might provide evidence of John's loyalty in support of the claim that he is a good person. But this means we accept loyalty as a criterion for being judged a good person. This, however, is not a straightforward empirical matter. Behind the empirical considerations lurk other sorts of 'things' – like worldviews, principles, axioms, metaphysics and so on. And these have to be identified and argued for. When someone makes a significant value claim we should be looking for more than evidence that certain criteria have been met. We should also be looking to see if there are good grounds for accepting the criteria themselves.

This can be hazardous terrain. Take the claim 'John is loyal'. Is this a value claim? Loyalty usually carries connotations of positive value: being loyal is usually seen as a good thing. However, it is possible that when someone claims that John is loyal she might simply mean that John demonstrates the kind of behaviour that usually qualifies as being loyal. In such cases the claim is a (descriptive) empirical one. (The person may not in fact value loyalty especially highly. She might just be responding to a question from a selection panel – is John loyal?) In other contexts when someone says that John is loyal they may be intending to convey that this is a good thing and John is a worthwhile person. With normative claims, as with all sorts of claims, we need to remember to look closely at the context to decide whether the kind of claim being made is normative or something else.

Task

It is very important not to make hasty judgements about claims just by looking at the words. Take 'should', for example. In many cases, to use 'should' is indeed to make a normative judgement and to express a value. But not always. Consider:

1   You should speak more respectfully to your father.

2   If you don't stop too often you should make it inside four hours.

3   'Should' implies 'can'.

- Which of these claims is/are normative?

- How do you know? What are your reasons?

- If any of these claims is not a normative claim what is it/are they, and what are the reasons for your judgement?

Now, consider the following claim:

4   A leader who works towards building a professional community helps staff towards realizing goals they believe in.

- What kind of a claim is this?

- Can it operate as more than one kind of claim? If so, what kinds of claim and how would you make your case?

- In its particular context it was given no elaboration; no supporting evidence was advanced. If supporting evidence were to be sought, how would the evidence vary according to the type of claim being advanced?

Identifying and evaluating conceptual definitions, distinctions, categories and taxonomies that are employed in research-based documents

To the extent that we draw on documents as sources of data, the quality of the conceptual definitions, distinctions and categories developed and employed by the authors of these documents will impact significantly on the relevance, validity, quality and trustworthiness of the data we 'take' from them. Consider, for example, a teacher researcher investigating the significance of literacy for redressing social disadvantage. Perhaps she has read Graff's finding that many literate sons within his sample enjoyed some measurable mobility over their illiterate fathers, but at the same time they remained within the working class itself. Moreover, interclass mobility was 'quite exceptional ... literacy and education did not have *that* kind of impact on the social structure' (Graff 1979: 189). If she wants to use this finding as data within her own study it might be important for her to identify the way Graff defines his category of 'working class'. Perhaps another researcher using the same data but employing a different concept of 'working class' might have found that there *was* significant interclass mobility. Certainly, if the teacher researcher wanted to try and make links to her own context it will be necessary for her to consider how well the social class classification used by Graff – developed in the context of industrial capitalism – 'maps onto' a contemporary postindustrial economy.

None of this is to call Graff's classification into question. It is simply to illustrate the kind of attention that needs to be paid to concepts and categories in relation to our own research settings and purposes if we want to have confidence in documentary data.

We use *concepts* to think about and make sense of our world. We need concepts of different things (trees, people, buildings etc.) to be able, literally, to *see* what lies within our field of vision. Similarly, we need concepts to be able to function on a daily basis (e.g. without the concept of time we could not arrange to meet someone). The same holds for investigating and reporting phenomena. To do research on numeracy acquisition in classrooms presupposes concepts of 'numeracy' and 'acquisition'. Of all the things that go on inside a classroom, which are relevant to *numeracy* acquisition and numeracy *acquisition*? How could we demonstrate that X but not Y, impacts on numeracy acquisition? To do this we need workable concepts. For researchers to communicate their investigations to others they need to make sure their concepts are clear, that they use them consistently (they mean the same thing by them whenever they use them) and that they are not too *idiosyncratic*. When we read others' work we should assess their concepts in terms of their clarity, consistency, usefulness and so on. It is also valuable to check how their particular concepts relate to other people's accounts and what is at stake between different accounts.

Task

Locate and read Michael Goldhaber's online article 'The attention economy and the net', found at http://www.firstmonday.dk/issues/issue2_4/goldhaber/.

- What do you think are the key concepts in this article?

- How does Goldhaber elucidate these concepts?

- Is their meaning clear?

- Does he use them consistently throughout the article?

- Do you think his use of these concepts is useful?

- How does his use of these concepts differ from other people's accounts of them?

- Are such differences significant and, if so, how? (e.g. compare Goldhaber's notion of attention and an attention economy with that of Richard Lanham at http://www.arl.org/arl/proceedings/124/ps2econ.html and source additional references at http://www.alamut.com/subj/economics/attention/attent_economy.html.

- By what criteria might we judge the appropriateness of someone's account of a concept for research purposes?

- By what criteria might we judge the clarity with which someone uses a concept?

- When do you think it might be appropriate to reject or criticize the way someone uses a key concept in their research?

Distinctions also are invaluable in research and scholarly writing. Sometimes a useful way to clarify a concept is by *distinguishing* it from some similar concept(s). Within language and literacy research, for example, many researchers have distinguished between 'learning' and 'acquisition'. Others have tried to distinguish instances of 'explicit' teaching from instances where teaching has not been explicit. Elsewhere, researchers and theorists have tried to distinguish between different forms of literacy (e.g. cultural literacy, basic literacy, functional literacy, higher-order literacy, critical literacy and so on). Such distinctions can be useful when researching what goes on and doesn't go on in classrooms; for recommending on the basis of research findings what should go on in classrooms and so on.

The extent to which we can use the documented research of others as data in our inquiries may depend greatly on the appropriateness of particular distinctions they have drawn – and around which they have based data collection, data analysis and interpretation of results – for our own research purposes. If their distinctions, and any concepts and categories based upon them, are in fact different from ours and/or from other versions that we draw on, we may be mistaken in the use we make of their work as data in our own study. Deciding whether or not distinctions drawn by other researchers translate to our own research, and allow us to derive data unproblematically from the studies in which they are used, requires identifying, comparing and evaluating such distinctions. If a distinction is drawn in different ways by different researchers and theorists which is most pertinent to our purposes? Does the researcher sustain the distinction consistently throughout a study? How well does the distinction really work? Does it account for all the cases we need it to? Do instances fall between cracks in the distinction? Are we left with ambiguities? These are some of the things we need to address very consciously in our research.

Task

- What are some of the main distinctions Goldhaber draws in his article 'The attention economy and the net'?

- What does Goldhaber's point seem to be in drawing each of these distinctions?

- By what criteria might we judge the adequacy of such distinctions?

- How do these distinctions help Goldhaber develop his argument?

- Does Goldhaber relate his key distinctions to theory and research? How? Where?

- Can you think of a study in which one could use some of Goldhaber's distinctions? What would the study be like? Why might one do such a study?

Categories and taxonomies are closely related and are indispensable within research. *Categories* pertain to 'similar and different sorts of things'. Things that are the same belong to the same category; things that are different belong to different categories. When we do category analysis we look in the data to find 'samenesses' and then think of labels under which to categorize the instances of each 'sameness' we have found. The old classifying system (or 'taxonomy') of animal, vegetable and mineral sought to arrange all existing things under one or other of these categories. *Taxonomies* are systems of categories. For example, we might develop a taxonomy of the various different categories of 'instructional acts' that we find in our data as a basis for describing, understanding and explaining what happens (and does not happen) in a given classroom.

When we read other people's research we should read to get a clear picture of the categories they develop and compare these with those developed by other people and those that might be pertinent for our own research. If we want to use existing documents as data for our own research we may have to examine the kinds of categories and taxonomies employed in the original research in order to understand the data collected in that original research, and how it was analysed, before we can decide how and where it is appropriate to draw on the research as data. Sooner or later we will have to make judgements and decisions about what kinds of categories, distinctions and taxonomies are most useful in our research. The more practice we get in looking at how other people do this work, and the more we 'play around' with the categories and distinctions that they use, the more adept we will become at using these tools in our own work.

Questions like the following are useful for identifying and evaluating the kinds of classifications other researchers develop and employ:

- What are some important categories used in this research project?
- How does the researcher describe these categories?
- By what criteria might we judge the adequacy of such categories?
- Do the categories form a system?
- If so, what work (e.g. for describing, understanding, explaining) does the system do?
- Do other researchers working in the area employ similar or different categories? Who? What?
- How do these categories work to group the data and represent the context being investigated?
- What other kinds of categories might have been used?
- How different might the representation of the context be had other categories been used?
- How well do such categories relate to my own research purposes?

Identifying and assessing arguments in other research

In research the concept of *argument* arises in two ways. The first is at the level of the organization and presentation of the text or research report. Do the steps in the written presentation meet the criteria for a good-quality argument? The second is at the level of the design and implementation of a research project itself. This is the idea that the various components in the research design all go together in a 'logical' way, and that they are implemented in a sequence and a manner that gives us confidence that the findings and conclusions presented by the researcher actually do 'flow' out of the project in a 'proper' manner.

In this section we focus only on the *textual notion* of argument. If this is clear to readers it will be easy also to understand the point we have laboured in the opening chapters about the importance of all the components of the research design and methods 'fitting' together and cohering with one another.

An argument involves a set of premises organized and presented in a way intended to lead to a conclusion the presenter wants us to accept. Any worthwhile research article, book chapter or book contains an argument. Our job as readers is to sort out what the argument is in order to judge whether it is compelling/convincing/plausible or not.

The ideal for an argument (which is practically impossible to accomplish outside of 'pure analytic' systems like mathematics) is what philosophers call a *sound argument*.

A sound argument meets two criteria:

- Its premises are true. (In social research we usually have to settle for premises being well enough supported by evidence that we feel inclined to accept them.)
- The reasoning (sequencing of premises) is formally valid: it conforms to rules of logic.

If we want to use someone else's findings as data we need to be satisfied that the argument supporting the findings is formally valid and that individual components of the argument are acceptable. An argument fails if one or more of its premises fail. This is where analysing and scrutinizing claims and concepts is especially useful. If we find a key claim that is suspect it undermines the strength of the entire argument. Our task is to work on getting to grips with the argument in a research text, sort out its premises and key concepts and then evaluate them.

When we read (and write) research texts we should be working hard to identify their argument. This involves more than just providing a synopsis of it. We need an account that captures as economically as possible the *structure* of the argument – the way the case has been organized. If we think a document is important to our research we should read it and reread it until we can conceive of it as a short series of steps (premises) and the conclusion the author derives from these steps. Any good argument is designed so that serious readers can follow its progress.

Once we have the argument of a text sorted out as premises and conclusion, we can then:

- sort out its major claims (the premises), run tests on the evidence presented for them (scrutinize them) and identify and evaluate the key concepts used in them;
- look closely at the *logic* of the argument as a whole to see if it is coherent – in good shape – such that the conclusion *follows* from the premises.

Often we will find that a document contains a series of smaller 'contributing' arguments as well as its main overall argument. We need to identify these and see how they all 'hang together' to make the argument as a whole. This can be approached via two parallel tasks.

Task: identifying the overall argument

1   Return to Goldhaber's article about the attention economy.

2   Read it slowly and thoroughly to get a good idea of what it is saying. Make notes as you think appropriate.

3   Reread it more quickly two or three times, to get familiar with it.

4   Answer the question: what is the conclusion to this text? What is the main thing the author wants to convince us about? Write it down.

5   Now, go back through the paper and work out what you think are the four or five main steps in the argument. Try and keep these to no more than four or five, because otherwise the argument will get too cumbersome to work with. You will probably want to put these steps into your own words – to summarize them. When you have done this, put them into a sequence and call these the premises of the argument. Set them out as a numbered set of premises with the conclusion coming at the end.

Don't worry too much about 'trying to get it right' first time. Just keep experimenting with and practising the process. What you are likely to find is that the argument can be set out in a number of different ways. Keep in mind, however, that the title of the text should provide clues as to what the conclusion is likely to be about.

Task: identifying 'sub-arguments' and constructing an 'argument map'

1   Pick any one of the premises you identified in the previous task.

2   Gather together the content that applies to this premise: the 'chunk' of the article associated with the premise.

3   Think of this premise as the conclusion of a separate argument and organize its content as a set of premises, followed by its conclusion.

4   If this can be done, set out this 'sub-argument' as you did the main argument of the text: numbered premises and conclusion.

5   Repeat this activity for the other premises you identified for the main argument and assemble the whole thing as an 'argument map'.

6   The sub-arguments will provide you with closer points of focus for critiquing the overall argument. They will also increase your sense of the argument as a whole and help you to lay out the overall argument as economically as possible.

Dealing with the claims and concepts as a way of handling the argument's premises is only half the job so far as assessing arguments is concerned. There is also the matter of the *logic* of the argument. Is it *valid*? Here we will describe very briefly the concept of 'logical validity', beginning with a distinction between 'deductive' and 'inductive' reasoning.

Deductive reasoning and logical validity
In a sound deductive argument all the information contained in the conclusion is actually contained in the premises. Compare the examples in Figure 7.1.

In argument (A) all the information is contained in the premises; in (B) it isn't.

A		B	
1	All birds fly.	1	All birds fly.
2	This is a bird.	2	This flies.
THEREFORE		THEREFORE	
3	This flies.	3	This is a bird.

Figure 7.1   Two deductive arguments

Argument (A) displays valid reasoning while argument (B) doesn't; the argument is invalid. This can be conveyed diagrammatically by a system called Euler circles. In some cases the pictures help to communicate what is at issue (see Figure 7.2).

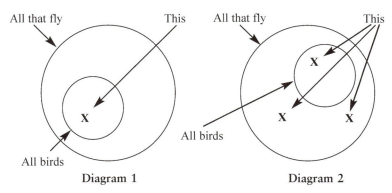

Figure 7.2 Euler circles

In Diagram 1 (representing Argument A) the **X** that signifies 'this' (particular bird) is located inside the small circle that signifies 'all birds'. The small circle containing **X** is in turn, *inside* the large circle signifying 'all the things that fly'. This portrays the fact that all the information contained within the conclusion is in fact contained within the premises. In Diagram 2 (representing Argument B), however, the **X** (signifying 'this') can be *anywhere* inside the big circle (signifying 'all the things that fly'). It does not necessarily fall within the smaller circle that signifies 'all birds'. Hence, Diagram 2 portrays the fact that *not all* of the information contained within the conclusion is contained within the premises.

If you 'get' this you understand all the logic you need to know to assess the validity of arguments. The first argument (which is a simple syllogism) presented in Diagram 1 is formally valid. The second argument is not. Note, however, that while argument (A) in Figure 7.1 is a *valid* argument, it is not a *sound* argument. This is because its first (major) premise is false. For instance, if the bird in question (the 'this') were a kiwi, the conclusion would be false. Turning to argument (B), the reasoning is invalid *and* the first premise is false. But if the 'this' referred to in the second premise and conclusion were a sparrow, the conclusion would be true. Even then, however, the argument would not be acceptable. As it stands the argument has two kinds of fault: faulty reasoning (invalid form) and a faulty premise (the false claim that all birds fly). This shows, among other things, that the relationship between 'truth' and 'logical validity' is not straightforward. We can get true conclusions from invalid arguments, and we can get false conclusions from valid arguments (although never from *sound* arguments). In research, however, we aim for the best approximation to soundness because research is not supposed to be a practice where we stumble on 'truth' by 'accident'.

Inductive reasoning and logical validity
In everyday life, including in research activities, we draw on more than deductive reasoning alone. We also use a kind of logic called *inductive logic*. In fact, we use it all

the time. By its very nature, however, inductive logic contains more information in the conclusion than in the premises. Hence it cannot ever be formally valid in the strict sense of validity involved in deductive reasoning. For example, each morning we get out of bed and expect the floor to support us. We are operating inductively in this case (albeit unconsciously). But, *it doesn't follow necessarily from the fact that the floor has always supported us in the past that it will always do so in the future and, specifically, in this case.*

The famous example shown in Figure 7.3 is a case of inductive reasoning. Clearly, it does not *follow* (in the manner of deductive reasoning) that the next crow will be black. It could conceivably (or, logically speaking) be white – or green, for that matter. What we can say, however, is that crow #10,001 will *most probably* be black – if we induce from previous cases to the likelihood of the next case. We cannot *deduce* this from the previous 10,000 examples, but we can *induce* it. What we see here is that what we induce draws upon information that is outside the information we have available to us. Deduction occurs from within a set of information, whereas induction (which is what most science draws on) involves predicting from a data set to what is likely to occur beyond that data set. It is not a formally valid logical procedure, but it is enormously powerful as a mode of reasoning.

> **Premises**
>
> Crow #1 is black
>
> Crow #2 is black
>
> Crow #3 is black
>
> Crow #4 is black
>
> Crow #5 is black
>
> ...all the way to...
>
> Crow #10,000 is black
>
> THEREFORE
>
> Crow #10,001 will be black

Figure 7.3 Inductive reasoning

The point about using inductive logic is that the best it can manage is *probability*. Since empirical educational research is based on inductive logic, its findings are always provisional. Whatever research that is based on induction entitles us to conclude now may well be disproved later.

So far as evaluating other people's arguments and developing our own arguments are concerned, the main point is to ensure that the information contained in the conclusions or findings is as close as possible to that contained in our premises. This requires (a) that the premises are carefully constructed and arranged in an appropriate (logical) sequence; and (b) that these premises are supported by the 'right' amount of evidence, and this evidence is of an appropriate kind. When the second of these conditions is met we can use *specific* information from a document as data (at what we called the 'first level of data'). When both conditions are met we can also use the findings reported in the document as data at the second level.

For further reading on reasoning, argumentation and logical validity see:

- Ennis, R. (1969) *Ordinary Logic*. Englewood Cliffs, NJ: Prentice Hall.
- Hospers, J. (1996) *An Introduction to Philosophical Analysis*, 4th edn. Englewood Cliffs, NJ: Prentice Hall.

Task

Drawing on the account of the nature of a sound argument provided in the previous pages:

1 Spell out what you think is meant by the idea that a well-designed and well-implemented research project can be seen to comprise a successful argument.

2 Describe how you think the idea of a research project as an argument relates to the idea outlined in earlier chapters that the various components of the study as a whole must cohere (or 'fit' properly) with one another.

The next chapter introduces teacher research as quantitative investigation.

CHAPTER 8

An introduction to teacher research as quantitative investigation
With Alina Reznitskaya

Introduction

In this chapter we describe some key elements involved in conducting quantitative research. In contrast to qualitative research, quantitative studies are focused on the numerical summaries of regularities that exist in the world. We begin our discussion of quantitative research by defining several important terms. Next, we describe common experimental and associative research designs, including true experiments, quasi-experiments, correlational and causal-comparative research. We then briefly review characteristic strategies for data collection and analysis. Finally, we talk about surveys, which can be considered both a research design and a data collection method.

Some common quantitative research designs

Table 8.1 overviews the five common quantitative research designs used in educational research.

Table 8.1 Some common research designs in quantitative research

Research design	Characteristics	Kinds of research questions asked
True experiments	• Participants are *randomly assigned* to two or more treatment conditions • Independent variable(s) are being *manipulated* • Best suited for investigating *causal relationships* • Data are numerical and may be collected through tests, performance assessments, observations, etc. • Especially useful in addressing questions regarding learning processes • Rarely done in classrooms by teachers	Does adding a graphical representation to accompany the text improve understanding of a concept? What are the effects of an auditory and auditory-visual method of phoneme instruction on the ability of pre-readers to decode synthetic words?
Quasi-experiments	• Participants in *already existing groups* are compared with regard to two or more treatment conditions • *No random assignment* to treatment conditions • Independent variable(s) are being *manipulated* • Often is used for evaluating some sort of intervention (e.g. a math or spelling programme) • Data often comprise test scores calculated before the intervention and again after the intervention	What effect on children's reading fluency does one-to-one instruction have? What effects does direct teaching of summarizing strategies have on the reading comprehension of learning disabled children?
Correlational	• The *association* among two or more *quantitative variables* is studied • *No attempt is made to manipulate* any of the variables • Often used to explore *already existing* relationships and make predictions • The finding of a correlation does not, in itself, imply a casual relationship • Data are numerical and usually collected through tests and scales • Useful for selection/admission purposes	Which students are likely to need additional help in reading instruction? How does vocabulary knowledge relate to reading comprehension?
Causal comparative designs	• The *association* among two or more variables is studied, where at least one of the variables is *categorical*	What differences in reading preferences are related to gender?

Research design	Characteristics	Kinds of research questions asked
Survey designs/ data collection strategy	• No *attempt is made to manipulate* any of the variables • Useful for exploring the *probable causes or effects of differences* that *already exist* in two or more groups • Data are numerical and usually collected through tests, questionnaires and school records • Information is collected to make *inferences* and/or *describe characteristics* of a group by asking questions • Often involves methodically selecting people to participate, preferably using probabilistic 'sampling methods' • Data collection tools include multiple choice questions, checklists, scales and rankings	Are students enrolled in classes that involve a heavy use of discussions better able to write a persuasive essay? What sense of different genres in terms of their social purpose and uses do children have in the Brisbane region? How often and why do my Grade 6 students watch *The Simpsons* each week?

Useful terms

Before we begin our discussion about the types of quantitative designs used in educational research, let us define some terms. We start by explaining different classifications of variables. Next, we discuss common sampling methods.

Variables

Quantitative researchers usually investigate relationships between two or more variables. A *variable* is a characteristic that may take on different values. It varies. Reading ability, age, or instructional method are examples of variables.

There are many ways to classify variables. One important distinction is between categorical and quantitative variables. *Categorical variables* differ in some qualitative respect, while *quantitative variables* exist in some degree along the continuum from 'less' to 'more'. In the example above, reading ability and age are both quantitative variables. It makes sense to think of people having less or more reading ability, or as being younger or older.

On the other hand, instructional method, such as lecture versus discussion, is a categorical variable. These two instructional methods represent mutually exclusive categories and differ in quality or kind, rather than in amount or degree. The distinction between categorical and quantitative variables is useful, as different research designs and data-analytic procedures are used with different types of variable.

Another important classification is between independent and dependent variables. An *independent variable* is the one the researcher chooses to examine in order to determine its possible effects on one or more other variables. That is, an independent variable is the one that is presumed to somehow influence another variable. As we will see, the manipulation of independent variables is a characteristic feature of experimental designs. For example, a researcher who suspects that instructional methods influence student learning will systematically vary his or her teaching methods in order to examine the effects of each method on student achievement. Note that not all variables can and/or should be manipulated. For example, if a researcher is interested in exploring the effects of gender on interest in science fiction, she or he would not be able to manipulate either variable (i.e. gender or interest). In such cases, a researcher would use non-experimental or associative designs (such as correlational or causal-comparative) in order to investigate the research question.

The variable that the independent variable is presumed to influence is called the *dependent variable*. It depends on what the independent variable does to it. In the previous example, student achievement and interest in science fiction are both dependent variables.

Sampling methods

In quantitative research, investigators often are interested in drawing inferences or *generalizing* from a sample of observations to a broader population. In other words, they hope to apply the results of their investigations to a group larger than the one selected to be in the study. For example, a researcher wants to find out about teacher attitudes towards a new state-wide reading curriculum. Instead of surveying every teacher in the state, he or she may select a sample of 300 teachers to whom the surveys will be administered. From this sample the researcher would like to generalize about typical teacher attitudes towards the reading curriculum in the entire state.

When and to what extent would such generalizations be warranted? This depends on the sampling method used in the study. *Sampling method* is the process of selecting a portion of the population. The important goal of sampling in quantitative studies is to include equivalent representations of the relevant characteristics found in that population overall (e.g. representative demographics in terms of such things as economic class, ethnicity, education levels, political allegiances, income). Selected participants should, in all important respects, be just like the ones who are not selected.

There are several sampling methods applicable to teacher research. These include:

- Random,
- Stratified random
- Purposive and
- Convenience.

Random sampling
This is not 'random' in the sense that any procedure for selecting participants will do. Rather, it requires researchers to use specific and well-tested techniques for constructing representative samples. In a random sample, each member of a population has the *same chance or probability of being selected*.

For true random sampling, researchers start by listing every member of the population. Then they will use a table of random digits or a statistical software package to select a random sample from this all-inclusive list. (Tables of random digits can be found in guides to research like Fitz-Gibbon and Morris 1987; Cooper 1998; and Wiersma 1999. The Statistical Package for the Social Sciences – SPSS – is a popular choice of software that helps generate random samples.)

In the long run (i.e. over repetitive attempts), random samples tend to be *representative* of a population in all respects, although there is no assurance that a particular random sample selected at one point in time will be representative. In random sampling, the differences between the population and the sample are due to chance or sampling error. That is, when sample characteristics differ from those of a population it is the result of random fluctuations rather than of systematic bias. The absence of systematic bias makes random sampling the best method for obtaining samples representative of a larger population in all respects.

Random selection vs. random assignment

So far we have described the random sampling procedure when it is used to *select* participants for the study. In true experiments, random sampling is also used to *assign* participants to treatment groups or conditions. When assigned to treatment conditions randomly, each participant has an equal chance to be administered a given treatment. In general, treatment groups constructed through random assignment tend to be equivalent on all characteristics. Although there is no guarantee that random assignment will result in acceptably similar groups (especially when groups are small), it is more likely to produce equivalent groups than any other method. We will discuss the use of random assignment in experimental studies later in the chapter.

Stratified random sampling

Martyn Denscombe (1998: 12) defines stratified random sampling as the process in which 'every member of the population has an equal chance of being selected *in relation to their proportion within the total population*' (original emphasis). The population is divided into subgroups or 'strata' according to the characteristics of most interest to the researcher. For example, in a study investigating reading practices in working class, middle class and upper class homes, the teacher researcher would stratify the school population according to these three categories. She or he would then determine the proportion of students in each category and match these proportions in each sample, randomly chosen from each stratum. The advantage of stratified random sampling is that it increases the likelihood of a sample being representative in terms of particular characteristics deemed important by the researcher (e.g. socioeconomic class). It may, however, make the samples less representative in other respects.

Purposive sampling

Purposive sampling involves researchers hand-picking respondents for a study. Here, a researcher uses their judgement to choose participants for the specific qualities they bring to the study. For example, a researcher may select an award-wining teacher to participate in a study of effective teaching practices. Purposive sampling can provide data that are more specific and directly relevant to a research concern or interest. However, the extent to which the findings can be generalized to a broader population is unclear.

Convenience sampling
Convenience sampling involves selecting individuals who are (conveniently) available to study. For example, a researcher may interview students coming to a university gym on Wednesday morning about the quality of sport facilities on campus. While this sampling method has the advantage of being practical, convenience samples contain unknown types and degrees of bias, in addition to random variation. For example, students who exercise on Wednesday mornings may not represent well their full-time working peers. Convenience samples are unrepresentative of a broader population (e.g. all university students) in unknown ways and to an unknown extent.

Experimental research: true and quasi-experiments

Experimental research designs include *true experiments* and *quasi-experiments*. The distinctive feature of experimental designs is that the independent variable (or variables if the researcher wants to use more than one) is being manipulated in order to examine its effects on the dependent variables. The logic of experimental designs is quite straightforward: try something and see what happens. For example, consider a researcher who is interested in examining whether explicit instruction in text structures improves reading comprehension of various types of prose (e.g. narrative, expository, persuasive etc.). In this study, the independent variable is the instructional method (e.g. whether or not students receive explicit instruction). The dependent variable is reading comprehension of texts representing different types of prose.

In an experimental design, a teacher researcher would assign participants (e.g. middle-school students) to two groups or conditions. In the *treatment condition*, students are given explicit instruction in the structural elements of prose. In the *control condition*, students do not receive explicit instruction. Note that in education research it is always good for students in the control condition to receive some kind of instructional treatment, rather than no treatment at all. It may rightly be argued that any method of instruction is likely to be more effective, compared to complete absence of instruction. In our example, students in the second condition may be given practice in silent reading of texts representing different types of prose without getting any explicit instruction. Because students in the second condition are also receiving a treatment (although not the one of direct interest to the researcher), it is more appropriate to call the second group a *comparison*, rather than a control condition. In much published research, the terms *control* and *comparison* are used interchangeably.

Following the treatment, the researcher will administer to both conditions a reading comprehension test specifically targeting different types of prose. The researcher will compare the average comprehension scores in the two conditions to determine whether or not the treatment had an effect on students' reading ability. If the average scores on the reading comprehension test do differ and one cannot find any other plausible alternative explanations for this difference, it is reasonable to conclude that the treatment is likely to cause the difference (for more on this, see p. 155).

Internal validity

In general, the extent to which a study contains plausible alternative explanations for the effect of independent variable(s) is referred to as the measure of its *internal validity*. When many plausible alternative explanations can be advanced, the study has low internal validity. Let us reflect on the previous example concerning the effects of reading instruction. Considering the short description of the study presented above, we can easily think of several alternative explanations. For example, perhaps the students in the treatment condition were better readers of the various types of prose at the outset of the study. Thus, it may not be explicit instruction that produced the difference in comprehension scores. Moreover, we need to consider whether or not students in both conditions have been given the same reading comprehension test. If students in a treatment condition received an easier test or a test that contained text passages that were more enticing to students, the conclusions regarding the effectiveness of explicit instruction may not be valid.

Researchers try to increase the internal validity of experimental studies by rigorously controlling, or keeping constant, the variables that are not being manipulated. Controlling such variables makes the interpretations of the effect of the manipulated (independent) variable(s) unambiguous. For example, in the study of reading instruction, the researcher will try to create groups that are similar in terms of reading ability at the outset of the study. Also, the researcher will administer the same test in both conditions, so that the differences in reading comprehension cannot be ascribed to the difficulty level or the appeal of the text.

External validity

In addition to internal validity, researchers in quantitative studies are concerned with external validity. *External validity* refers to the applicability or generalizability of the results of a study to broader populations, settings and conditions. Suppose a researcher is conducting a study of reading instruction with a sample of 60 middle-school students. She or he observes that a treatment group receiving explicit instruction performs significantly better than the comparison group. Can a researcher generalize these findings to other middle-school students? What about elementary-school students? Will these findings apply to situations where students read various types of prose outside of the classroom? The answers to these questions depend on the extent to which a researcher used well-established procedures to increase the external validity of the study.

There are several ways to increase external validity in quantitative research. For example, the results are more likely to be generalizable to a broader population if study participants are representative of the population of interest. Representativeness of a sample on all characteristics is best achieved through random sampling.

Generally, experimental settings and conditions should be similar in all important respects to those settings to which the researcher is interested in generalizing their findings. In our example, the researcher can increase the generalizability to other settings and conditions by, for example, having the reading comprehension test include authentic text passages, such as those used in published stories, children's magazines or school newspapers.

True experiments

The main difference between true and quasi-experiments is that in a true experiment a researcher has full control over the experimental procedures. This is especially important with regard to the decision concerning who receives which treatment. In experiments, a researcher randomly assigns participants (e.g. middle-school students) to different treatments (e.g. explicit instruction versus silent reading). As previously explained, with random assignment each participant has an equal chance to be administered a given treatment.

With random assignment, the likelihood of having equivalent groups at the outset of the study is greater than with any other sampling method. Random assignment helps us to eliminate the influences of the intervening variables (those not being manipulated) on the outcome of the study. Random assignment is a distinctive feature of true experiments that generally makes them more powerful than other quantitative designs for establishing causal relationships between two or more variables.

As researchers in true experiments have full control over the experimental procedures, they try to eliminate or minimize the effects of all variables that can influence the outcome of the study, *except* for the effect of the independent variable being manipulated (e.g. instructional method). Thus, researchers are able to isolate the influence of the independent variable from all other factors.

An example of a true experiment

William Wiersma (1999) offers a straightforward example of a true experiment. The researcher wants to test the effects of three different modes of providing instructions – verbal, written and a combination of both – on student performance in solving abstract problems involving numbers. She designs an experiment involving 60 subjects from a first-year university cohort. Twenty students are *randomly assigned* to each of three groups. One group receives verbal instructions for solving the problems. The second receives written instructions. The third receives a combination of written and verbal instructions. All receive their instructions individually and then attempt individually to solve the problems. Scores are kept and comparisons made at the end of data collection. In this experiment, the *dependent variable* is problem-solving ability. This variable is quantitative. The *independent categorical variable* is the mode in which the instructions are given.

Because subjects are randomly assigned to three groups it is highly likely that the groups will be sufficiently similar in all respects at the outset of the study. For example, the three groups will tend to have roughly similar prior experiences pertinent to solving the kinds of problems involved (which may be little or no experience at all), they will have roughly equivalent levels of aptitude for solving such problems and so on.

Following random assignment, the three groups are given different kinds of instructions. All students in the 'verbal' group receive one type of instructions, which is different from that of each of the other two groups. The same holds for the 'written' and 'verbal-written' groups. All other variables that are deemed relevant to a problem-solving performance, such as the length of instruction, the difficulty level of the problems, the lighting and the level of noise in the room are being *controlled for*, or kept constant among the three conditions.

The logic is that (1) because the groups are seen as more or less equivalent, (2) because the influences of all other variables (e.g. length of instruction, noise level in the room) are eliminated by keeping them constant, and (3) because the only difference among the groups is the kind of instructions received by students, any variation in the performances of the groups is likely to result from the mode of instructions provided. In other words, researchers control (all) other variables (such as ability, prior experience, the length of instruction, the noise level in the room etc.) so that the only variable likely to account for any differences in performance will be the independent variable being manipulated – which in this particular case is the type of instructions provided to the students.

Quasi-experiments

In contrast to true experiments, in quasi-experiments a researcher does not have full control over the study procedures. *Quasi* means 'as if' in Latin, implying that quasi-experiments are lacking some important features of true experiments. A quasi-experiment occurs when a researcher 'treats a given situation as an experiment even though it is not wholly by design'. Accordingly, the quasi-experimental researcher 'is limited in what he or she can say conclusively' (Palmquist 2003: 1).

The most fundamental difference between true and quasi-experiments is the *absence of random assignment to conditions* in a quasi-experiment. In quasi-experiments, a researcher often works with already existing groups (e.g. classes of students). As with a true experiment, the researcher manipulates the independent variable or variables in order to study their effects on some dependent variable(s). The researcher is still concerned with having treatment and comparison groups being equivalent at the beginning of the study and to address this issue, he or she tries to *match* groups on important characteristics. For example, when comparing instructional methods in a quasi-experimental study, classrooms are matched in terms of initial abilities, teacher experience, demographic characteristics, and so on.

For teacher researchers in particular, quasi-experimental designs are extremely useful for evaluating intervention programmes and treatments. The study populations usually of greatest interest and most immediate concern to teacher researchers – as well as being most readily available for research purposes – are already ordered socially or institutionally into 'intact groups', such as classrooms. Thus, quasi-experimental designs are often the only option available to researchers in educational settings. It should be emphasized, however, that lack of random assignment results in a generally lower internal validity of quasi-experiments, compared to true experiments.

An example of a quasi-experiment

A study of the use of educational computing games undertaken by Rosas and colleagues (2003) provides an example of quasi-experimental study. Briefly, the study aims to evaluate the effects of educational video games on student achievement and motivation in first- and second-grade classrooms. The independent categorical variable in this study is exposure to educational video games. The dependent quantitative variables are student achievement and motivation.

In the treatment condition, students played the video games for 20–40 minutes daily during class time over 12 weeks, alternating between games with language and mathematics content. Classrooms assigned to the treatment condition were carefully matched with comparison classrooms who engaged in their regular classwork. The matching variables included general academic achievement level (measured on a national achievement test), socioeconomic status, location and officially measured level of 'vulnerability' (Rosas *et al.* 2003: 80).

All participants were subjected to pre-tests and post-tests on reading, writing and mathematics using the same test instruments. To identify any (intervening) variables other than the game playing that might explain differences in outcomes, the researchers conducted several pre- and post-intervention surveys. These sought to gauge teacher characterization of the students, teacher expectations of any relevant changes that might occur as a result of introducing games into classrooms and student motivation with respect to the games.

The data were analysed using two common statistical procedures: analyses of variance (ANOVA) and analyses of covariance (ANCOVA).

Task

Activity:

An example of a study where researchers manipulated the independent variable is provided by Grejda and Hannafin (1992). They evaluated the effects of using word processing on the quality and revision patterns of young writers. Locate and read the article:

Grejda, G. and Hannafin, M. (1992) Effects of word processing on sixth graders' holistic writing and revisions, *Journal of Educational Research*, 85 (3): 144–9.

1   In your own words, describe the design of the study, including independent and dependent variables, sampling and assignment procedures, etc.

2   Do you think the authors were neutral, disposed toward or disposed against the use of word processing before they conducted their study? What evidence can you provide from the article for your judgment?

3   Does the report of the research in their article tell you all you need to know about the conduct of the experiment? If not, what is missing?

4   Are there any ambiguities or confusions in the article that you think are relevant to evaluating the quality of the study?

5   Comment on the following sentence from page 146 of the article: 'Each composition was evaluated "blind" by at least two of the raters by comparing the works to a rubric consisting of six competency levels ranging from lowest (1) to highest (6)'. Do you agree with the authors' choice of scoring procedures? Why or why not?

6   Do you think the researchers provide sufficient information about their data analysis? If so, what are your reasons? If not, why not?

7   Do you think the researchers are justified on the basis of their investigation in concluding that 'in the present study, face evidence for improving editing via word processing is strong'? What are the reasons for your judgment?

8   Comment on the scope and adequacy of the references provided by the researchers.

9   If you were conducting and/or reporting this research what changes would you make, and why?

Types of experimental design

The specific designs of experiments and quasi-experiments can take on a variety of forms, with some being better than others. A design is more effective when it adequately controls for various alternative explanations and when the finding can be confidently applied to larger populations and settings. In other words, a better design permits higher internal and external validity. In this section, we will review two common designs in educational research: the matched pre-test/post-test comparison group design and the matched post-test only comparison group design. Note that both of these designs are quasi-experimental, as they do not include a random assignment of participants to conditions.

Matched pre-test/post-test control/comparison group design

A simple matched pre-test/post-test control group design involves two groups: a treatment group and a control/comparison group. Let us use the previously discussed example of a research study regarding the effectiveness of explicit instruction in various text genres to illustrate this type of design. The treatment group will receive the treatment of direct interest to researcher (e.g. explicit instruction in text structures). The control/comparison group is generally given some other treatment (e.g. silent reading).

Before giving the groups their respective treatments, the researcher needs to decide on group composition. In matched pre-test/post-test control group design, the two groups are matched on specific characteristics identified by the researcher as having the potential to influence the outcome of the study. In a study of reading instruction, the researcher may match classrooms in terms of grade level and general reading ability.

After groups have been constructed through matching, the researcher will administer a pre-test to measure 'baseline' performance on aspects the intervention is intended to address. This is the pre-test phase, prior to the intervention. For example, in a study concerned with improving student ability to read narrative, expository and persuasive prose, a researcher will pre-test the students to measure their initial ability to comprehend different types of texts. Teacher researchers may use standardized tests or develop their own measures of performance.

The teacher researcher then implements the intervention. After the intervention the researcher tests the members of the matched groups again (the post-test) to determine whether or not the learning change occurred. Figure 8.1 is a pictorial representation of this design.

	2 groups	Pre-test	Treatment	Post-test
10 middle-school classrooms → Matched on grade level and reading ability →	*Treatment:* classrooms # 1, 3, 4, 6, 9	Test of reading comprehension of different text genres	Explicit instruction	Test of reading comprehension of different text genres
	Comparison: classrooms # 2, 5, 7, 8, 10		Silent reading	

Figure 8.1 An example of matched pre-test/post-test control group design

Using comparison classrooms minimizes the number of alternative explanations for the occurrence of observed results. The comparison group acts as a 'baseline' for evaluating the effects of the treatment of interest (e.g. explicit instruction). The idea is that *apart from the intervention itself* the comparison and treatment groups are acceptably similar in relevant respects. They were matched on their grade level and general reading ability, they are likely to undergo similar developmental or maturation progression and experience the same teaching and learning opportunities outside of the intervention throughout the course of the research. It stands to reason that any differences between the groups measured in the post-test can be attributed (positively or negatively) to the intervention.

Note that compared to random assignment, matching has serious limitations. It may result in groups that differ in many ways not identified and/or matched by the researcher (e.g. motivation to read). Because the groups are not equivalent on all characteristics (as would be likely with random assignment) there are important limits to what can be concluded from the study.

There are other complications with the matched pre-test/post-test control group design that could affect the validity of conclusions regarding the effects of the intervention. They include:

- developmental changes irrelevant to the intervention occurring in both groups at different rates;
- practice effects of multiple testing, such as students becoming alert to what is being studied through the pre-test and performing better on the post-test;
- 'seepage' of the intervention programme into the comparison classrooms (especially if the two groups are in the same school);
- students or teachers being aware that they are part of a research study and trying harder than they usually might or vice versa as they perceive the other group to be receiving something of more value.

Such potential pitfalls need to be taken into account in any claims based on the outcomes of quantitative studies in general. They also serve as effective criteria for evaluating published studies.

Matched post-test only comparison group design

Another popular quasi-experimental design involves giving matched treatment and comparison groups a post-test only following the treatment. Here, researchers can address one of the pitfalls of the previously described design, namely the effects of multiple testing. The design is identical to the matched pre-test/post-test control group, except that groups do not receive a pre-test. Consider the pictorial representation of this design shown in Figure 8.2.

The more similar the comparison and treatment groups are, the stronger the grounds for inferring likely cause and effect relationships. However, because matching, rather than random assignment, was used in creating the groups represented in Figure 8.2, it is less clear how comparable the groups are at the outset of the study.

By eliminating the pre-test in this design, the researcher is able to remove several alternative explanations for the effect of the intervention related to multiple testing, such as practice effects or increased alertness to the content of instruction. On the other

	2 groups	Treatment	Post-test
10 middle-school classrooms — Matched on grade level and reading ability	*Treatment:* classrooms # 1, 3, 4, 6, 9	Explicit instruction	Test of reading comprehension of different text genres
	Comparison: classrooms # 2, 5, 7, 8, 10	Silent reading	

Figure 8.2 An example of matched post-test only control group design

hand, she or he no longer has information about the initial standing of study participants on the variable directly related to the research question (i.e. ability to comprehend different types of prose). As you can see, *choosing the research design is always a compromise*, where a researcher considers a particular context and problem, then selects or tailors a design that is both manageable and appropriate. The design optimally plans for the collection and analysis of data that can be interpreted meaningfully in response to the research question(s) driving the study.

There are numerous variations on the experimental and quasi-experimental designs, each trying to counter the potential pitfalls or alternative explanations for the results. These include designs such as:

- time series;
- counterbalanced designs;
- factorial designs.

For descriptions and explanations of these designs, see:

- Creswell, J. (2002) *Research Design: Qualitative, Quantitative, and Mixed Method Approaches*, 2nd edn. Newbury Park, CA: Sage.
- Fraenkel, J. and Wallen, N. (1996) *How to Design and Evaluate Research in Education*, 3rd edn. New York: McGraw-Hill.
- Wiersma, W. (1999) *Research Methods in Education: An Introduction*, 7th edn. Boston, MA: Allyn & Bacon.

Task

Locate and read the article:

Yen, S. (1998) Empowering education: teaching argumentative writing to cultural minority middle-school students, *Research in the Teaching of English*, 33: 49–83.

- What is the independent variable in the study?
- What are the dependent variables?
- What type of design is used in the study?
- What was the sampling method used?
- What conclusions would you draw from the results of the study?
- How would you rate the *internal validity* of this study?
- To what extent do you think the study would have *external validity*? What are the reasons for your judgement?

Associational research: correlational and causal-comparative designs

Correlational and casual-comparative research designs are examples of *non-experimental* or *associational research*. Here, the relationships among variables are examined *without influencing or manipulating them*.

There are several reasons for researchers choosing not to manipulate variables in their studies. For instance, they may be interested in examining the relationship between socioeconomic status and academic achievement; smoking and anxiety; nutrition and language development; or incidence of abusive relationships and self-concept. For various biological, practical and ethical considerations none of these variables can be manipulated by a researcher. For example, for ethical reasons a researcher cannot assign participants to conditions and then expose them to 'smoking' versus 'no smoking' treatment.

As variables are not being manipulated, associational research involves investigating phenomena or conditions that *already exist* independently of the study. Associational research is not a matter of creating some kind of intervention or treatment intended to produce new effects to be measured, and then measuring those effects. Rather, it investigates aspects of the world *retrospectively*. Two particular designs representative of associational research are correlational and causal-comparative. The only difference between them is the type of variables being used in the study. In correlational research all variables are quantitative; in causal-comparative research, at least one variable is categorical.

Correlational research

In correlational studies, researchers explore the relationship between two or more variables. Importantly, the variables are quantitative, or varying in the amount or degree. For example, a researcher is interested to know whether there is a relationship between students' writing and reading abilities. They select a sample of 30 students and administer a reading and a writing test to each student in the sample. By examining pairs of scores on the two tests for each student, the researcher can find out whether high scores on reading generally go together with high scores on writing (and low scores on reading generally go together with low scores on writing). The presence of such a relationship would indicate a positive correlation between the two variables. See Figure 8.3 for an example of positive correlation between two variables.

In addition to examining the direction of the relationship between the variables, the researcher can assess the strength of this relationship. Here, they will look at how tightly or consistently high scores on reading relate to high scores on writing (and low scores on reading relate to low scores on writing). Graphically, the strength of the relationship is represented by how much scatter there is among the points.

A common use of correlational studies involves assessing the direction and strength of the relationship between the variables. Another use of this research design is focused on *prediction*. If two variables are sufficiently related, the researcher can make a prediction of a student's standing on one of the variables from knowledge of the student's standing on the other. For example, if there is a strong positive correlation between reading and writing scores, knowing a student's reading score can help us predict her writing score.

When interpreting correlation, it is important to keep in mind that the presence of correlation between the two variables does not, by itself, indicate a *causal relationship*

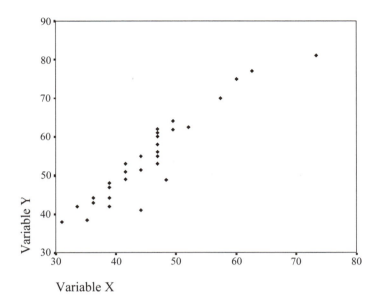

Figure 8.3 A scatter plot showing a positive correlation between two variables

between them. In other words, *correlation does not imply causation*. For example, finding a correlation between student achievement and student motivation does not establish which variable is causing the other. It may be true that high achievement is causing increase in motivation, alternatively, higher motivation may cause people to achieve more. It could also be that the relationship between the two variables is circular, or that there is some other variable (e.g. parental involvement) which causes the values on both variables to increase. Merely examining the correlation does not enable one to choose among all these possibilities. Experimental, and to a lesser extent quasi-experimental research designs are better suited for investigating causal relationships.

The fact that causality cannot be unambiguously established through correlational research does not imply that such research is of no importance. For example, discovering a relationship between achievement and motivation is informative in itself and may help to inspire more theoretical and empirical investigations.

Causal-comparative research

To recap, the main difference between correlational and causal-comparative research is the type of variables being investigated. In causal-comparative research, at least one of the variables is *categorical* (e.g. different in kind or quality). For example, in a causal-comparative study, a researcher might be interested in exploring the relationship between gender and mathematic achievement. She or he would select two samples – one comprising female students and the other male students. Next, the researcher would perform statistical analysis to find out whether or not the two groups are similar in terms of their average level of mathematic achievement.

Note that the variable 'gender' is categorical. Moreover, the researcher is not manipulating any variables, but rather is examining the relationships that already exist.

As with correlation research, great care is needed in drawing inferences in causal-comparative research. Although there is the word 'causal' in the name of this design, causal-comparative research is more concerned with *exploring* possible causes, effects and consequences than with establishing them. In the previous example, it may be societal expectations (rather than gender) that resulted in different levels of mathematic achievement in the two groups.

Because causal-comparative research tries to understand aspects of the world without manipulating variables and setting up experimental situations, the role of theory is extremely important in this type of design. When attempting to explain group differences, the choice among the possible causes (e.g. gender versus societal expectations) must rely on a sound theoretical framework.

For more on causal-comparative research see:

- Fraenkel, J. and Wallen, N. (1996) *How to Design and Evaluate Research in Education*, 3rd edn. New York: McGraw-Hill.
- Wiersma, W. (1999) *Research Methods in Education: An Introduction*, 7th edn. Boston, MA: Allyn & Bacon.

Task

- Identify some conditions or phenomena that might be amenable to causal-comparative research.

- What would the dependent variable be for your study?

- What might some independent variables be?

- What types of conclusion would be justified in this study?

Data collection in quantitative research

Investigators who use quantitative research designs draw on a pool of widely recognized data collection tools and methods. Examples of commonly used data collection tools in quantitative research include:

- standardized tests of reading and/or writing (e.g. the Torch Test);
- teacher researcher made tests addressing specific needs of the study;
- interview schedules;
- survey questionnaires;
- scales and inventories (e.g. Student's Perception of Ability Scale, Miller Motivation Scale);
- structured observation schedules.

Data collection tools (also called *measures*) may be standard 'off the shelf' instruments obtainable by researchers in ready-made form and simply administered to subjects (such as intelligence tests and standardized achievement tests). Alternatively, they may be purposefully developed instruments researchers create themselves in accordance with the particular needs and circumstances of their studies.

Data collection methods refers to procedures or processes involved in using these tools. For example:

- delivering a survey questionnaire to subjects (e.g. via mail, phone, email);
- administering and marking tests;
- observing a classroom using predetermined and quantifiable observation schedules (i.e. a preset list of things to look for).

Table 8.2 overviews some key elements of data collection in quantitative educational research.

Reliability and validity

Researchers in quantitative studies are concerned with using data collection tools that are both reliable and valid. *Reliability* here refers to the *consistency* of the scores/ results when a data collection tool (e.g. a test) is administered on different occasions, when alternative forms of the same test are used, when different scorers grade and tally tests and so on. For example, students' test scores on an algebra test should not change significantly when the test is given on two occasions close in time, or when an alternative form of the same test is administered. If the test contains open-ended items, the test results should remain similar, regardless of which scorer grades the test.

Validity here refers to the *meaningfulness* of the results. It is concerned with a judgement regarding how well a data collection tool measures what it claims to measure. For example, just because a tool is called an 'aggression scale' does not mean that the attitude being measured is actually aggression. What is actually being measured is properly defined by gathering and examining empirical evidence regarding the functioning of the test scores.

Here are some examples of validity concerns:

- Are scores on the aggressiveness test positively related to such behaviours as swearing and physical assault?
- Do scores on the test of reading ability show progressive changes with age?
- Do scores on the anxiety test increase after a stressful experience?

As mentioned before, researchers can either choose commercially available measures or develop their own. The advantage of selecting an already developed measure is that its important properties (reliability, validity) are usually described in the accompanying manual. Thus, a researcher can choose a data collection tool of high quality.

The disadvantage of using measures developed by others is that such tools may not fit the specific needs of the researcher. Note, however, that constructing a good quality measure is a time-consuming process that requires expertise. It is not enough, for example, to simply 'think up' the questions that should go on a test and hope for the best. Such unsystematic ways of test construction (although quite common) typically

Table 8.2 A selection of common data collection tools and techniques

Techniques	Tools	Kinds of data collected
Standardized testing Emphasis is usually on measuring a trait or attribute against some 'norms'. Norms represent the test performance data of a representative sample of students, whose test results become the 'baseline' for interpreting the scores of subsequent test-takers. Standardized tests have clearly defined administration and scoring criteria	Commercially produced tests (e.g. the Neale Analysis of Reading Ability Test, the GAP Tests, the Gapadol, Milton Word Test, WISC, the Torch Test, Canberra Word Test, the Burt Word Reading Test). A manual which includes (1) a set of norms to be used for evaluating individual scores; (2) a set of instructions for administering and scoring the test; and (3) information regarding psychometric properties of the test, such as validity and reliability	Data comprise test scores, generally calculated as standard scores (e.g., z-score), norm-referenced scores (e.g., national norms), ranks, percentiles, percentages.
Teacher-developed tests Emphasis is on measuring a specific trait or attribute directly relevant to the research question, for which no commercially available test exists	The test is constructed by the teacher and geared explicitly towards the research question underpinning the study. A development of a good-quality test requires following a systematic process	Test scores – usually expressed as a total number of points – can be used for comparative purposes across students and/or over time for each student
Surveys Emphasis is on gathering a range of responses to set items from a range of people (usually a sample from a designated population) and then analysing these responses statistically	Survey schedules (the list of items) can be closed (e.g. checklists, multiple choice), or scaled (e.g. Likert Scales, Osgood Semantic Differential Scale, Guttman Scale, Thurston Scale, Factorial Scales)	Data are often presented in numerical form, such as numbers on a scale. Responses are categorized and tallied up for further analysis
Systematic observation Emphasizes a carefully-planned approach to observation, usually with predefined categories or checklists of what behaviours are to be observed	Observation protocols or checklists of categories can be commercially produced or teacher-constructed. Observations are recorded on a checklist for purposes of converting observations to numerical data	Categories of observations that are ticked and then converted into numerical scores to be further analysed for rates of occurrence, patterns, interactions etc.

result in measures that are unreliable and invalid. They may contain irrelevant questions and omit important behaviours.

Constructing a good-quality measure is a carefully planned process, involving such steps as:

- identifying the purpose and target population for the measure;
- determining relevant behaviours to be measured;
- identifying relative importance of selected behaviours;
- evaluating and revising individual items;
- conducting reliability and validity studies.

Most published measures undergo the systematic development process just described. This is why researchers often choose already existing data collection tools for their studies. However, in the studies requiring custom-made measures, researchers face the additional challenge of developing data collection tools of good quality.

Data analysis in quantitative research

Once the data have been collected, quantitative researchers conduct statistical analysis to summarize and interpret their findings. There are two main branches of statistics: descriptive and inferential. With *descriptive statistics* the goal is to organize collected data so it is easier to comprehend. With *inferential statistics* the goal is to draw inferences about some population of interest based on a sample from the whole population (for more on this distinction see Minium *et al.* 1993; Wiersma 1999).

There are many statistical procedures available to handle the variety of questions being examined in quantitative studies. In general, the choice of a particular statistical procedure depends on a combination of factors, including:

- type of design (e.g. quasi-experiments, correlational);
- type of variables used in the study (e.g. categorical, quantitative);
- characteristics of the study (number of dependent/independent variables, number of groups, number of data collection sessions).

The appropriate choice and use of statistical procedures requires a fair amount of training in statistics. For an accessible, easy to read explanation of the most common statistical procedures used in educational research see:

- Minium, E., King, B. and Bear, G. (1993) *Statistical Reasoning in Psychology and Education*. New York: Wiley.

Survey research

In the remainder of this chapter we will describe survey research, as it is frequently used to address various questions in education.

Surveys in the form of 'polls' conducted by marketing consultants, newspapers, radio and television stations to interrogate a sample of the population for their views on and attitudes toward something of current interest are ubiquitous. So are questionnaires found in magazines and aeroplane seat-back pockets, or street pollsters equipped with clipboard and pen asking passers-by to answer 'just a few questions'.

The survey can be considered as both a research design and data collection method. Surveys involve obtaining information through asking questions. Three common survey types include:

- simple descriptive surveys;
- cross-sectional surveys;
- longitudinal surveys.

Simple descriptive surveys are the most common research option. Mertens (1998: 108) describes these as 'one-shot' designs used 'for the purpose of describing the characteristics of a sample at one point in time'.

Cross-sectional surveys involve description and inferences from responses collected at one point of time. Information is gathered on a sample chosen from a targeted population. The purpose of cross-sectional survey research is to generalize the responses from a sample to the broader population of interest. For example, a researcher may select a representative sample of 100 parents in a particular school district to collect data about their attitudes towards school choice. From this sample, a researcher hopes to make conclusions regarding the typical attitudes towards school choice in the entire district.

Longitudinal survey designs 'survey one group or cohort of subjects at different points in time' (Mertens 1998: 108). For example, a sample of students could be surveyed about their out-of-school computing practices in Grade 8, in Grade 10 and the year after they leave high school.

Surveys typically seek anonymous responses (apart from codes used to track survey response rates in postal and telephone surveys). It is assumed that people will answer more openly and honestly when not asked to identify themselves in traceable ways.

It is important to distinguish surveys from tests. In surveys, respondents are not given tasks to perform. Rather, they are invited to express their opinions and feelings on a given issue. Surveys are used to gather information about attitudes, preferences, habits and the like, while tests measure such characteristics as 'ability', 'aptitude' or 'intelligence'.

Unlike interviews, surveys mostly generate numerical data by asking closed questions (e.g. multiple-choice questions), and results are often presented in the form of percentages or fractions.

As a rule, surveys collect data from large numbers of people – 1000 is a common sample size. They can, however, be used effectively with as few as 30 people if the survey is focusing on a very small number of variables. Note that larger samples are not necessarily more representative of a broader population. It is the choice of sampling method (e.g. random) that makes a sample representative.

Types of survey items: questions and scales

The *survey instrument* (the total list of questions and statements for respondents to address) may contain different kinds of items. Closed questions are the most common item type. Rating scale items are also widely used. 'Closed-questions' or multiple-choice questions pose a question and offer a fixed range of answers to choose from. For example:

Many students like to do their maths homework with music or television in the background.

Which of the following do you most prefer to have in the background while you do your maths homework?

a)   the radio
b)   the television
c)   music (compact disc, cassette, midi files etc.)
d)   radio and television
e)   silence

Commonly used categories of question types in surveys include:

- Demographic or classification questions. These are questions about the respondent (e.g. occupation, languages spoken and so on).
- Attitudinal or opinion questions (e.g. 'Do you think the National Grid for Learning is: (a) a good idea, (b) a good idea but not in its current form, (c) a waste of taxpayer money, (d) never heard of it').
- Behaviour-related questions (e.g. 'How much time do you spend reading newspapers each day: (1) no time, (2) 1–10 min, (3) 11–20 min, (4) more than 20 min?').
- Factual questions (e.g. 'What is the name of the basal reading program used at your child's school?' (a) Endeavour, (b) Reading 360, (c) Mt Gravatt Reading Scheme, (d) PM Readers, (e) don't know').

Researchers must heed a range of criteria developed for judging the quality of survey questions when deciding how to word their items (see Creswell 1994; May 1997; Mertens 1998). Below are some questions to be considered in constructing survey items:

- Is the question ambiguous? (Do words used have more than one possible meaning? Does the question ask the respondent to answer more then one thing at a time? Are vague words or terms, such as 'literacy', 'reading programme' and 'benchmarks' eliminated or clearly explained?)
- Is the language used straightforward and jargon free?
- Is the language used as free of prejudice towards certain groups as far as is possible?
- Is the question concise?

When using a survey, a researcher must consider whether the respondents are (a) able to answer and (b) willing to answer the questions. For example, questions requiring memory of distant events often produce inaccurate answers (e.g. asking parents to recall their primary-school reading lessons). So do questions that are sensitive, threatening, or embarrassing for respondents. It is also wise to avoid hypothetical questions since respondents may not bother answering them.

Rating scale items ask subjects to select a response located on a scale (e.g. a five-point scale comprising of 'strongly agree' through to 'strongly disagree'). For example:

When you get home from school, you do your maths homework before you do anything else.

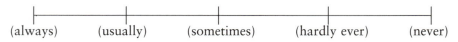

(always)   (usually)   (sometimes)   (hardly ever)   (never)

Teacher researchers may construct their own scales for survey purposes or, alternatively, they may use appropriate commercially available scales. Some common examples of the latter include: the Osgood Semantic Differential Scale, the Student's Perception of Ability Scale, and the Pictorial Scale of Perceived Competence and Acceptance for Young Children. The Likert Scale – named after its inventor – is a popular format for self-constructed scales. It uses a five-point scale ranging from 'strongly agree' to 'strongly disagree'.

As with other data collection tools, teacher researchers must follow a systematic process and invest time and effort in constructing surveys that produce reliable and valid results. This may require evaluating the quality of items by conducting pilot studies prior to the study proper.

Survey modes

Surveys can be conducted in a variety of *modes*. The chosen mode will depend on the purpose and the resources available to the teacher researcher. The following modes are common:

- postal (where the survey is mailed out to a sample of people);
- email (similar to postal mode but sent via email);
- on-the-street (where the respondent is stopped in the street and asked to answer a few questions);
- take-home (where the survey is delivered via a network of contacts; e.g. students taking a survey home to parents);
- telephone (telephone surveys usually use random direct dialing technique – a random, computerized technique – to select respondents).

Postal, email and take-home surveys require self-completion, whereas on-the-street and telephone modes do not – and generally have higher response rates. Despite this advantage, on-the-street surveys use the convenience sampling method. Thus, it is unclear whether or not and to what extent the inferences from the samples obtained through on-the-street surveys may be appropriately generalized to a broader population of interest.

Tools

The main survey research tools are the survey instrument itself and a covering letter or brief explanatory statement. Every survey conducted by mail or via networks (email or friends etc.) requires a covering letter. If conducted in person or on the street a standard explanation statement is needed. The covering letter explains the purpose of the survey (e.g. to gather your opinions about children, literacy and computers) and generally assures anonymity. Mertens (1998: 131), among others, provides useful guidelines for writing covering letters and explanatory statements.

Some pros and cons of survey research designs

Surveys are good for collecting large amounts of data about people relatively quickly. In comparison with experimental and quasi-experimental designs, surveys are usually relatively low-cost approaches. In educational research, surveys provide a useful way for assessing what people know about particular programmes or policies (e.g. the way reading instruction is approached in a school), or how they feel about particular practices (e.g. pull-out versus in-class remedial literacy tuition).

A common drawback of survey data is that they are often left to 'speak for themselves' with little or no informed interpretation about what the findings signify (May 1997; Mertens 1998). Survey researchers often leave findings as 'factoids' rather than interpreting what survey results (might) *mean*. As with any other research, surveys must have a significant point and a valid purpose.

Another hazard of survey research concerns limiting possible answers/responses by using 'close-ended' questions and 'x-point' scales. These cannot be infinitely subdivided to allow every possible shade of response. This may limit findings to the kinds of possibilities expected or identified by the researcher, when something different might be the case. Finally, researchers using surveys should be concerned about the response rate. When the response rate is low, the generalizability of the findings needs to be questioned. It may well be the case that those respondents who chose to return the survey differ in important ways from those who did not return the survey. A variety of strategies (e.g., follow-up mailings, incentives for responding, attractive survey formats) are used by researchers to increase the response rate.

Task

1 From any journals of your choice since 1990 that report educational research:

- Identify two articles that report studies using quasi-experimental designs.

- Describe these designs and how they relate to the research question(s).

- Compare and contrast the two studies in terms of the tools they use.

- Describe and comment on how they address matters of external and internal validity.

2 Repeat the same activity for articles that employ survey designs.

In this chapter we have reviewed common designs in quantitative research, described data collection and analysis techniques and discussed survey research in some detail. Part 3, which focuses on teacher research as qualitative investigation, begins in the next chapter with a background to qualitative data collection.

Teacher research as qualitative investigation

CHAPTER 9

A background to data collection in qualitative research

Introduction

In this third part of the book we address qualitative teacher research at length, in accordance with its overwhelmingly dominant standing within teacher research as a whole. Discussion is organized around the three main types of data involved in educational research: spoken, observed and written data. Individual chapters on collecting and analysing each type of data are presented.

This chapter addresses six key ideas applying to data collection in teacher research:

- the concept of data in general;
- different *kinds* of data: in particular, spoken, written and observed;
- data collected in more or less 'naturally occurring' contexts of educational activity, versus data that is generated and collected as a result of the researcher deliberately setting up contrived data collection situations and opportunities that would not otherwise have occurred;
- the distinction between (using) 'new' and 'existing' data;
- some general principles to guide data collection;
- the concepts of *designing* and *planning* data collection.

The concept of data

Data can be defined as 'bits and pieces of information found in the environment' (Merriam 1998: 70) that are collected in systematic ways to provide an evidential base from which to make interpretations and statements intended to advance knowledge and understanding concerning a research question or problem. What counts as data depends heavily on the questions or hypotheses driving a study, as determined by the researcher. Teacher researchers using theories and research methods from conversation analysis to understand how 'scientific explanation' is accomplished in a classroom may be keenly interested in data that reveals hesitations, self-corrections, pauses, hedges and the like occurring in a teacher's talk during a science lesson. By contrast, researchers interested in boys' and girls' respective participation in science lessons will have little interest in such data.

Three points are noteworthy here.

First, data are not 'out there' awaiting collection (Merriam 1998: 69). Data are always *constructed* by researchers during the research process. For example, fieldnotes written during observations of a staff meeting present a particular version of what occurred, as seen, understood and recorded by the researcher. Any two people participating in the same research study and observing the same event probably never record the same information in their fieldnotes about what occurred. Each focuses on what most interests them: aspects resonating with previous experiences; what they consider most salient for the study etc. The same applies to collecting spoken and documentary data.

The amount of data collected or recorded, the sources from which it is collected and the time span the data covers feed directly into how the researcher construes the *data set* for a particular project, and how this shapes and supports a particular 'version' of events. A researcher can argue for their 'version' and provide a justification for it. Yet, every such version is partial, and constrains what can and cannot be said about the problem being investigated. This is what research is like.

Second, data collection is always *selective*. Researchers cannot collect all potential data concerning a phenomenon (e.g. an event, programme, interpersonal exchange etc.). They must make decisions at strategic points about what to include and exclude. From the outset the research questions developed by the researcher inevitably foreground some data and background or exclude other data. Methodological decisions made in accordance with the research questions also entail selection. Consider video-recording data. It is impossible to capture with a single camera everything happening in a classroom, staffroom or playground. What comes to count as data when using video-recording is the selective account generated by the limits of the camera lens or angle or position of recording.

Third, data is never 'raw' in the sense of being *neutral* items of information. Data are constructed by means of the collection process and shaped by what is collected and what is not. Consequently, data are always already interpreted to a significant extent by the researcher, at and before the point of collection. This happens as the researcher makes procedural decisions about what is being studied (e.g. who to interview and why), as they 'read' contexts or processes through the theories that frame their study, and as data are read through their beliefs and assumptions about what is being studied.

Consider, for example, researchers investigating 'sharing time'/'morning talks' in a Grade 1 classroom. A sociolinguist will be likely to audio-record carefully children's individual presentations and their respective interactions with the teacher and other children, to understand how sharing time is constructed in this particular classroom, and/or which children are (dis)advantaged by this construction (see Michaels 1981; Heath 1983; Cazden 1988). A 'constructivist' will be likely also to collect carefully audio-recordings, but may focus on how the teacher questions individual children or rephrases their utterances to try to support and scaffold successful performance.

Different kinds of data: spoken, written and observed

Spoken data

'Spoken data' can be defined as any stretch of oral language recorded in some durable or lasting form (e.g. an audio cassette recording, a digital sound file stored on a CD-ROM, a printed transcript or written notes) that can be revisited as desired. Spoken language is constructed as data by means of the devices used to collect and store it. As language it is language; as words it is words. But as stored (or 'made durable') records of language 'captured' to serve a research purpose as evidence or relevant information, it is *data*.

Some finer points and distinctions should be noted.

First, it is important to distinguish between spoken data collected with a view to obtaining information about some matter or issue, and spoken data collected to investigate spoken language uses and language processes (and their effects) in their own right.

In the first case we might interview someone to get their ideas about something, to find out how they feel about something, or to get them to tell us what their values are. In the second case we might record a segment of talk in the classroom to see what patterns can be found (e.g. whether some people talk more than others, talk others down, use language in ways that have implications for how power is exercised in class, etc.).

Teacher researchers may be interested in one kind or the other, or both, depending on their purposes. A teacher researching bullying might talk to students to find out how much bullying they think is going on, what forms it takes and what they feel about it. This is collecting spoken data to obtain information about bullying. Another teacher might be interested in how some students bully or intimidate others by the language they use and how they use it. She might record slices of naturally occurring conversation to look at the language itself as a potential medium for bullying.

Second, this difference may in turn be associated with different ways (devices) of collecting language as data. A researcher might interview or set up a conversation with one or more research participants (e.g. students) and simply make notes of what is said, without even audio-recording the conversation. Knowing what information is relevant to her research question, the interviewer simply jots down some words (as 'word for word' as possible) to record what her subjects or informants have said in response to questions.

At the other extreme a researcher interested in the intricacies of classroom talk needs to be able to see exactly who it is that is speaking at a given moment, where they are sitting in relation to other participants and, perhaps, even to capture their gestures (seen as adjuncts to/dimensions of spoken language) as they speak. Much more might be involved than using a highly sensitive recording device with a multidirectional microphone. It might be necessary to 'wire' individual participants with a microphone and to use multiple video-recording devices.

Third, these examples raise a question about demarcating spoken and written data. Why might not the information recorded by interview and taken down as notes or subsequently transcribed be regarded as written data? This is a legitimate question. We must note here that the distinctions we draw between spoken, written and observed data are not exact, mutually exclusive or definitive. They are categories we use in our own work and find useful, but they do not definitively section off one type of data from others. Researchers need to develop categories that work for them. We think ours are useful, but they are not the only ones.

In relation to the question, the key point for us is that a researcher who is just making notes about what they are told is likely to be getting significantly different information from what would be obtained from sources that research subjects had written and that had subsequently become available to the researcher (e.g. by getting access to a diary, or by asking people to provide written responses to questions). Situations like interviews and conversations are very different from situations where people just write. In conversations or interviews there are more opportunities to 'bounce off' things, or have one's memory jogged (e.g. by a probing or follow-up question) that may not be present in a writing situation. Conversely, some people might be inclined to divulge information via writing (perhaps under cover of anonymity) that they might not divulge, or might not divulge in the same way, within face-to-face encounters.

Internet-based interactions (e.g. instant message exchanges, emails between friends, discussion lists between peers) provide a further case in point. The text usually appears in written form. However, it acts – socially and grammatically – more like spoken language than written language. There are no hard and fast rules for deciding what kind of data belong within which category. Grammatical features of a text can, however, give some clues as to the kind of data in question. Judging the lexical density of a text (i.e. the ratio of nouns to verbs) can indicate whether it is grammatically more like a spoken text or more like a written one (see Martin 1992; Martin *et al.* 1997). An informal, chatty email text written from one friend to another might reasonably be classified as spoken language, whereas a formal petition meant for public viewing and sent out over email can reasonably be classified as written language. Texts found on the internet using search engines that were not generated for the purposes of a study might be classified as written texts, whereas texts generated within chat spaces in response to questions asked by a researcher of consenting participants could be taken as spoken texts.

The main thing is to be aware of the differences within and between the categories and to know when and how to collect spoken data of the *content* variety and when and how to collect spoken data of the *process* or *quality* variety.

Observed data

Observed data are pieces of information collected by means of systematically watching (observing) people going about their daily lives, or watching events as they unfold. In education, the most common observation data are records of classroom lessons or classroom life. Observed data includes:

- written records of direct observations (e.g. fieldnotes made in the 'heat of the moment' as things are happening);
- indirect records of observations (e.g. *post facto* notes that are written from memory after the observation period has ended);
- collected artefacts (e.g. clay pots made by children in an observed art class; child-generated drawings; commercial wall charts in classrooms);
- videotapes of activity (e.g. a classroom lesson, children's play during lunch break at school);
- observed data reported in other studies or collected by other people.

To this extent, observed data will include fieldnotes of written-down spoken and written information, together with artefacts we noticed and have referred to in records of our observations. When we analyse observed data that include references to speech and written artefacts, however, we are analysing our *observations* of these, and how we saw them located in the situations we observed. This is different from analysing transcripts of speech and analyses of texts *per se*.

Written and other visually-presented data

In general, written data includes a wide range of pre-existing texts that the researcher collects as part of a study. For example:

- policy documents;
- official and unofficial records (e.g. attendance rolls, pupil records, specialists' reports);
- documents generated originally for personal purposes (e.g. letters, notes passed in class, student work);
- historical documents (e.g. letters and diaries written by people who are significant for understanding past events, as well as old newspapers, posters and magazines);
- contemporary newspaper reports, magazine articles, advertisements;
- television documentaries and advertising;
- textbooks and other text-based school resources;

- teacher-generated texts (e.g. wall charts and posters);
- textbooks and other institutional documents (e.g. commercial wall charts and books, pamphlets);
- art works;
- websites;
- archived, internet-based discussion lists;
- literature (including lyrics to popular songs, narratives etc.);
- 'functional' texts (e.g. bus tickets, food labels, menus).

Written data also include certain texts generated at the researcher's initiative during the course of the project that are recorded in printed or print-analogue form. Examples include questionnaire and survey responses and texts the researcher has asked participants to write (e.g. diaries, journals, logs, records of events, inventories, sketches, photographs, diagrams, various kind of 'exercises' or 'activities').

Similarly, written data includes artefacts in the form of printed or visual inscriptions generated by participants during a study that are relevant to the researcher's questions but have been produced independently of participation in the research *per se*. These might include things like school assignments, speech or presentation notes associated with participants' formal roles or involvements, computer-assisted designs or slide-shows made for fun etc.

We also regard transcripts of interviews that have nothing to do with the present research project among written data that may be collected as part of a study. Many transcripts of television interviews or interview transcripts available on the internet fall into this category. Likewise, we might include certain documents and artefacts that were originally forms of spoken or observed data in some other person's research. Researcher B might use researcher A's fieldnotes, or transcriptions of interviews from A's project. These were *originally* (in A's study) forms of *observed* and *spoken* data. However, by the time B uses them they *already exist* as written texts. We regard them as examples of written data because they were not generated by the study that is now making use of them. Of course B might *choose* to use some of these texts as examples of spoken or observed data rather than as written data – in which case this is what they are. Sociolinguists often use other people's transcripts of spoken data as data for conducting their own analyses of spoken data (cf. Michaels 1981; Cazden 1988; Gee *et al.* 1992).

Categorizing data in terms of different types is useful for organizing and managing our data collection and, subsequently, our data itself. We will say more about this in the chapters on data analysis. At the point where we ask what kinds of data we need to collect in order to address our questions, having some categories can be useful in helping to ensure we do not overlook types of data that are relevant. Asking 'What forms of written data may be useful in terms of my question?', or 'Do I need to collect observed data in order to answer my question?' provides prompts that help us to prepare a comprehensive design and plan for collecting data.

'Naturally occurring' and 'contrived' contexts of data collection

Two different kinds of data collection contexts apply to teacher research. One is where the researcher simply finds ways of recording what is already going on and would be going on regardless of whether a research project was underway (e.g. a teacher who is interested in aspects of her own pedagogy). Finding out potentially useful things about how she organizes and manages teaching and learning situations might be as simple as setting up a tape-recorder or a video-recorder before an already scheduled lesson, switching it on and 'conducting business' as naturally or normally as possible as if it were any other day and a recording device was not operating.

Often, however, teacher researchers want to find out things that are unlikely to be forthcoming in the normal course of events. For example, students might be unlikely to offer spontaneous or unsolicited information about how they feel or what they think about the way teaching and learning activities transpire – other, perhaps, than by yawning, or looking bored, or by showing signs of animation and interest. To find such things out the researcher is likely to have to create special or artificial data collection contexts, like interviews, to ask students to keep journals that record their thoughts and feelings about lessons and so on.

'Naturally-occurring' or contextualized approaches to collecting data

Research designs, like ethnography and many kinds of case study research, require teacher researchers to audio-record or video-record activity and talk *as it happens* in the contexts being studied. Here, teacher researchers aim to capture everyday 'slices of life' that will help them to address the questions guiding their studies.

For example, a researcher may want to record English lessons in different Grade 7 classrooms to get a sense of the extent to which the students and teacher share a metalanguage for talking about written and spoken genres. Interviews are unlikely to produce the kind of information needed to ascertain this, since what people say they do and what they actually do are often two very different things. Neither could a researcher rely solely on teachers' accounts of what they say they do in order to develop a shared language for talking *about* language with their students. The researcher will almost certainly have to audio-record multiple English language lessons within each classroom (for comparative purposes and to hedge against the effects of the presence of recording devices), as well as undertake hours of observation.

Contextualized spoken data is most often recorded by means of audio- or video-recording. This is ideal for teacher researchers because they can switch on the machine and let the tape roll while they go about teaching their classes. There are decisions to be made about recording spoken talk in classrooms and other contexts, as well as numerous things that can go wrong. In the following chapter we discuss aspects of recording contextualized spoken data effectively.

Task

Identify which of the following research questions require *contextualized spoken data*:

1 In what ways do the teachers in my school define 'disadvantaged students' and how does this compare with how 'disadvantage' is defined in school policy documents?

2 To what extent are there differences and similarities between how disadvantaged students are spoken to by the teacher, in comparison with how he or she speaks to 'advantaged' children?

3 What are the key strategies Grade 3 teachers in Xalapa report using to teach grammar?

4 In what ways do the adult students participating in this basic education programme define 'being literate'?

5 What are the key features of a successful masters thesis in education in the School of Education at the University of Rockville?

6 What cultural information is conveyed by young children's oral presentations to their peers in four Grade 1 classrooms in Abbotsdale?

7 What kinds of teaching identities do teachers X, Y and Z construct by means of their talk in the classroom?

8 In what ways do six primary-school teachers in this region establish the social rules and norms for their classrooms during the first two weeks of school?

Researcher-generated (spoken) data

While there is a sense in which recording contextualized data is a process of *generating* data – because the sound recordings would not exist independently of the study – conducting interviews is seen as 'interventionist' on the part of researchers. Interviews generate information that would not otherwise have existed. Indeed, they produce situations that would not otherwise have existed. Researchers generate interview data deliberately and systematically. Moreover, interviews are rarely contextualized in ways that recorded slice-of-life data are. Interviewer and interviewee usually locate a quiet space away from the action where they can talk without interruption. Interviews are *decontextualized* in that the interview itself is the focus of activity, rather than everyday life as it happens on a moment-by-moment basis.

'New' and 'existing' data

Collecting data with which to address a research question may involve collecting either or both 'new' data and 'existing' data. The main point about the data one collects in order to conduct a piece of research is that they need to be relevant or germane to one's research question. This will often involve collecting new or fresh data, since data that relate directly to the research question may not already exist. If, say, one is researching some specific current activity or teaching approach within a particular classroom there will be no alternative other than to collect data as the activity unfolds or proceeds.

At the same time, there may exist data collected on other sites at other times that are available and that may be useful to one's study (e.g. for making comparisons or establishing a wider context for the study). Such data may exist in archives, be presented in detail as appendices to reports and so on. Tracking these data down for possible use as a component in one's own research can be seen as part of the data collection process.

It is possible to do much educational research drawing almost entirely on data sets that already exist and are available in the public domain. All historical studies of educational phenomena are like this. They may involve digging up data that have not previously been available – such as getting access to the letters or diaries of people not previously researched. In the sense that this body of correspondence already exists, it does not constitute *new*, researcher generated data in the same sense that interviewing somebody or recording and transcribing a classroom lesson does.

A relevant consideration here concerns the use of resources in data collection. If data relevant to our research already exist and are readily available, it is more 'ecological' to use that than to generate new data. A key question to ask at the outset of collecting data concerns the extent to which one might be able to use existing items of data to address one's research question, as opposed to prevailing on people's time and goodwill in order to generate fresh data. 'Ecology' is never the only consideration when collecting data for research. Nonetheless, it never hurts to raise the question, and it is always reasonable and responsible from a research standpoint to consider how far it is possible to use existing available data.

Task

- Which of the following research questions do you think could be addressed entirely or to a large extent by using already existing data?

- Which do you think would require a researcher to generate mainly new data?

- What are the reasons for your responses?

1   What kind of student do schools in this region aim at producing as indicated by their school policy documents?

2   What are the out-of-school literacy practices of four boys who are failing English at school?

3   Over the past five years, in what ways have two national newspapers pathologized youth or presented them as increasingly dangerous to society?

4 What are the historical, theoretical and methodological antecedents of 'out of school' literacy studies, and in what ways have these contributed to the development of 'out-of-school literacy studies' as a distinct field of research?

5 What understandings of the differences and similarities between real-life violence and on-screen movie violence do my Grade 4 students appear to have?

6 In what ways has 'teacher accountability' been constructed over the past ten years in federal government press releases about education issues and initiatives?

Some general principles to guide data collection

Collecting data is resource intensive. It consumes time, energy and goodwill, as well as material resources like money and technologies of various kinds. It can be intrusive, often calls for a lot of trust to be invested on the part of research subjects and researchers alike, and when it goes wrong the costs are borne by all parties involved. Consequently, data collection cannot be taken lightly. It needs to be designed, planned and implemented carefully and thoughtfully.

We consider three main kinds of principles helpful in providing useful checks and guides for the conduct of data collection. We call these 'epistemological', 'ethical' and 'methodological' or 'procedural' principles respectively. Our account is by no means the only way to think about approaching data collection and others may prefer alternatives. The position we describe here is how we try to approach data collection in educational research and it has served us well so far.

Epistemological principles

In this context we think of epistemological principles as concerned with the quality of data collected, in terms of the confidence it gives us as evidence for our knowledge, understanding and explanatory claims about an educational problem, issue or phenomenon.

Collect the right kind and amount of data
First, and obviously, the data we collect must be *relevant* to our research question. What counts as 'relevant', however, is not necessarily straightforward. For example, teacher researchers concerned with questions about 'literacy competence' or 'effective learning' or 'appropriate uses of technologies in pedagogy' do not all mean the same thing by these concepts. In addition, they approach their research questions from the standpoint of different kinds of theories. Someone who views literacy in terms of encoding and decoding print may have a very different concept of 'literacy competence' from someone who views it in terms of language uses peculiar to particular discourses or genres. The two people might come from very different theoretical positions on literacy (e.g. from cognitivist psychological theory in the first case and sociocultural

theory in the second). What counts as the 'right kind of data' for their respective research questions is very likely to be quite different.

Hence, it is not enough for pursuing the right kind of data that it simply seems to be relevant to the area or focus of one's research question. It must also be consistent with the kind of conceptual and theoretical position one has adopted for the study. In preparing for data collection it is crucial to be as clear as one possibly can be about what kind of information one needs in order to really be addressing one's research question – which is always related to one's conceptual and theoretical commitments and preferences as well as to the topic or problem area in more general terms.

Collecting the right amount of data is much trickier than may appear at first glance. Because data collection is resource intensive it is wasteful to collect more data than we need. At the same time, collecting insufficient data to be able to arrive at useful or plausible conclusions is similarly wasteful, since we are unable to do anything satisfactory with the resources we have already used to collect the data. There is no simple right or wrong answer to 'How much is the right amount?' The point here is to be aware of the issue. When preparing for data collection we need to keep in mind the question 'How much data am I likely to need as a minimum for generating plausible claims or for having a rich enough database to produce useful and interesting categories?'

To some extent one only gets a feel for this on the basis of experience. At the same time there are things that even the most inexperienced researchers can judge from the outset. For example, if we want to explore what school principals in the state or local area authority think about a new policy on class sizes, interviews with one or two principals will almost certainly not provide enough data. Neither would collecting data from principals from a narrow range of school types. The best approach might be to think about how one is most likely to get a *range* of opinions, on the one hand, and how to maximize one's chances of getting some *patterns* in responses to emerge as quickly as possible. This may involve thinking about profiles of school types in the state or local area. There may be other kinds of studies done previously that provide clues as to profiles of schools. Decisions would need to be made about the relative usefulness of questionnaires in comparison to interviews; of open-ended questions in relation to multiple-choice items; and so on. Taking advice from experienced researchers who have done parallel or reasonably similar kinds of studies would come into the picture. The point is to be aware of the 'right kind and right amount' principle from the outset, and to have it in the forefront of one's mind throughout the entire process of preparing the data collection component of the study. One might need to think about modifying the original question on the basis of these deliberations. Maybe it is best to focus just on the principals of certain *kinds* of school; for example, schools who have difficulties recruiting teachers, schools with high proportions of students whose first language is not English etc.

Obtain valid and reliable data
Using terms like 'validity' and 'reliability' in the context of qualitative research involves some risks. Such terms are loaded with meanings and connotations from quantitative research that many qualitative researchers reject and want to avoid (Flick

1998). Nonetheless, a number of leading educational researchers have looked for ways to reconceptualize validity and reliability in ways they find acceptable for post-positivist research (see Lincoln and Guba 1985; Lather 1991; Kincheloe and McLaren 1994). We use these terms cautiously here to indicate a range of things we think it is important for qualitative researchers to aim for when planning and implementing their data collection.

It is helpful to think of valid data as data that actually does 'get at' what we aim to find out through our data collection. For example, it has become popular in educational research to talk about investigating people's *perceptions* of this or that. This raises the question of what is involved in getting data about perceptions as distinct from, say, people's *ideas* about something, or their *feelings* about something, or their *impressions* of something. In other words, 'When is a research subject actually reporting a perception?'; 'How can we know?'; 'What kind of data collection tools can genuinely "get at" perceptions?' In this example, our data will be valid in so far as our data collection methods find out things about perceptions, rather than about impressions, ideas or feelings.

This is not so much a matter of tracking down 'the truth' on perceptions, and of being among the few researchers who have really found out about perceptions. Rather, it is about developing a plausible and useful account of 'perceptions', such that finding out something about certain sets of perceptions will do useful educational work and serve some worthwhile purposes. In addition, it is a matter of developing data collection tools that we can argue *do* obtain information about the phenomenon of perceptions *as we have conceptualized it*. Finally, validity involves implementing these tools successfully in the process of collecting our data, so that they achieve their potential and obtain the information we want and that we have developed them to obtain.

This idea of validity and valid data can be applied to diverse teacher research interests. Educational researchers often want to investigate phenomena like learners' 'identities', 'self-esteem', 'beliefs', 'values', 'learning styles', 'critical awareness' and so on. Like 'perceptions', these are all phenomena that quickly blur into other things. For example, if we want to obtain information about 'beliefs' we will need to be careful to develop and successfully implement data collection tools that elicit information about beliefs rather than superficial thoughts or opinions. Concern for validity in data collection is a matter of taking care to do the best job one can to construct data collection instruments faithful to one's informed and developed concepts of the phenomenon one is investigating, and then to apply them carefully and consistently.

We think of 'reliability' in data collection also in terms of being careful in certain ways about how we develop and implement our data collection tools. If we want to collect data on a specific thing (X) from more than one person it is important that their understandings of what we are asking them are as close as possible to our own understandings, as well as being as close as possible to those of the other research participants. When different informants/participants understand the same interview question in different ways we cannot collect data *on the same matter* from these different people. Rather, we are collecting data about different things from different people. This means that we cannot *compare* their responses, because they will not be about the same thing. We won't have collected *equivalent data* from the various members of our research population. The same applies when research informants understand something different by the questions we ask from what the researcher means by those questions.

To obtain reliable data in this sense requires taking great care to ensure that our questions are as transparent and unambiguous as possible. We need to check this by testing questions with different people and checking how they understand them. Similarly, we need to take care when we address a question to different participants. For example, we need to make sure that in our attempts to make a question clear we have not inadvertently turned it into a different question from what it was when we addressed it to another informant. It is possible to transform the same question into a different question by the way we ask it of different people or by the sequence or circumstances under which we address it to them.

Some variation is inevitable. But our duty as researchers seeking reliable data is to aim to minimize the amount of variation by being as careful as we can in developing and implementing our data collection tools.

Credible and trustworthy data

Researchers want others who read their research to have confidence in their data and to have good grounds for respecting its integrity. Researchers themselves want to have reasons for believing they have good-quality data. Just as the best cook in the world will be unlikely to produce a successful cake using rotten eggs and stale, dry ingredients, so the best data analyst in the world will be unable to produce sound research from low-grade data. Teacher researchers can take some fairly elementary steps to increase their own and other people's confidence in their data.

One simple procedure involves checking with the research participants that what we (the researcher) think they have said is what they in fact intended to say. Although it is probably impossible to obtain a 'one-to-one correspondence in meaning', researchers can nonetheless increase the grounds for confidence in their data by checking with their informants. This can happen at the time of data collection or later when the researcher has assembled the data. The procedure can be very simple. It might involve asking a question like: 'I think what you have just said is X, Y and Z (putting them into one's own terms). Is that what you meant?' This gives the respondent a chance to clarify anything that needs clarifying or making more precise. It also gives researchers something they can report in their research as grounds for confidence that they have in fact entered as data what the subject provided as information. We call this process 'participant checking' and return to it shortly.

Whether or not the data researchers collect is trustworthy involves having grounds for believing that what their informants told them is as genuine as possible. The point here is not so much that respondents can deliberately give researchers false information – although this can happen – but that respondents may give information that is authentic in terms of how they see themselves, but which might be different from how other people see the situation. Alternatively, the way a respondent is thinking or feeling at the time may prompt a response that is different from how they would have responded at a different time or under different conditions, or in a different context.

Consequently, it can be very useful for qualitative researchers to think about developing and implementing their data collection tools in ways that build in opportunities to check for consistency between responses. It might be a matter of asking another person a question that provides a kind of check on what a respondent has said. For example, a 13-year-old boy might say that he does not read very much at home, and that he only spends 15 minutes a night on homework. He might genuinely believe this information is correct because it is integral to the image he has constructed for himself as a boy with a particular kind of identity. Yet, if one were to ask his mother she might say that he reads quite a lot out of school, and that he typically spends at least 45 minutes a night on homework. This is a form of 'triangulating' data. The higher the level of similarity between what an informant tells us and what someone who knows the circumstances of the informant tells us about the same thing, the stronger the researcher's grounds are for believing the data are trustworthy.

Another procedure is to ask an informant similar things at different points in time (later in the same interview, or in a subsequent interview, or casually in a conversation) and/or from slightly different angles or perspectives, and then to compare the data provided (another kind of 'triangulation' check).

Ethical principles

Important ethical issues can arise with respect to data collection, especially when researchers need to collect data from family members or community members in sites outside the classroom. Data collection is intrusive and time-consuming, and participants can easily be made to feel under pressure, inadequate, 'invaded' and so on.

Some issues that arise may not be apparent to the researcher at first glance. These include frictions between the right to privacy of potential participants/informants and the need of researchers to obtain telephone numbers or addresses to establish contact. Another example involves the anxiety people often experience when they wonder 'Why me?' after being approached to participate in a study. It is not unusual for potential research subjects or participants to feel there must be something peculiar or problematic about them if they are asked to participate in a research project.

When negotiating and conducting data collection it is important that researchers consciously try to guide their work by appealing to principles like respect for the privacy, dignity and integrity of those from whom they obtain data – whether children, adults or colleagues. Often it is not apparent before the event, or in the abstract, just what such principles might involve and when we might unwittingly infringe them. Researchers often find themselves on the 'strong' side of uneven power relations that develop in the context of research projects. The researcher will typically be seen as being backed by the authority of a school, or by university or government agencies and so on. Potential participants will often feel they have little or no right to decline requests to participate. Moreover, once they are in the context of being researched they may believe they have to accept the line or direction the researcher (the *expert*, the *teacher*) is following.

Consequently, researchers should not assume that merely obtaining the formal consent of research participants takes care of the ethical issues involved in data collection and other aspects of the research process. Obtaining written consent in no way automatically guarantees that the study will be ethical. Some researchers believe 'that consent forms have become like "rental car contracts"' (Hilts 1995), in the sense of being designed to protect the company/university/researcher without necessarily dealing with the possible moral consequences of participating in a study (Denzin 1997: 288). Seeking, obtaining, documenting and honouring informed consent are tied to issues of trust and honesty. When properly understood and respected, 'consent' establishes a stringent researcher obligation to protect the privacy and respect the dignity of every study participant. This can create difficult demands. For example, if a researcher is conducting a classroom-based case study that focuses on four students, it may not be enough just to obtain consent from these four students and the teacher. This is because all students in the classroom become part of the data collected. Hence, their interests are also implicated in the research.

Issues involving the dignity and integrity of research participants can enter from unexpected places and confront researchers when they are least prepared for it. For instance, in some of our own research we have been told of nervous breakdowns, childhood traumas, family secrets and other sensitive things. The participants have not referred to these as 'secrets' in the data collection process, perhaps because they felt comfortable in an interview and simply 'opened up'. This raises questions during and after the data collection process. What should one do when this occurs? How does one judge whether such information is relevant to the study? If it is not relevant, should the researcher try to move on to another topic as quickly as possible? But if the researcher decides to move to another topic, how are they to know whether this might deny the participant a badly needed opportunity to confide in someone they believe they can trust? To do so might destroy a valuable opportunity to practise the ethics of reciprocity – by giving back to the participant something valuable in return for their own generosity in giving the researcher precious time and trust. If the researcher does decide to listen to such things, how should they decide what to do with the information – especially if it proves to be important for interpretations and findings, and yet is sensitive and would make the informant vulnerable if it were published in a report? There are all kinds of moral implications and possible moral consequences here. To include such information in reported work may risk participants' vulnerability; to leave it out may compromise rigour; to negotiate it might risk pain or intrusiveness, or consume time participants had not anticipated having to give when they consented to be researched.

Maintaining trust involves reciprocity during and after data collection. In qualitative research, reciprocity is typically enacted through an exchange of 'favours and commitments' that 'build a sense of mutual identification' (Glazer 1982 cited in Glesne and Peshkin 1992: 122; see also Lather 1991: 60). This is not easy. There seem to be few things researchers have to offer that can match the generosity of participants who allow them to observe for hours, if not weeks, in their classrooms; who open their homes to observations and inventories; or who endure seemingly interminable questions about processes, rituals, habits and other practices. Researchers can aim to at least partially reciprocate by recording all actions and utterances diligently and meticulously, and respecting informants' views or actions. Reciprocity also includes completing seemingly mundane (but often appreciated) tasks. Examples include helping with drying the dishes, chopping vegetables, child-minding, acting as a sounding board for ideas, actively listening as a participant talks through a problem, writing character reference statements, accompanying the teacher on playground or bus duty, arranging visits to the university for students to use the computing equipment, offering and channelling obsolete university equipment into resource-deprived classrooms (which can involve much paperwork and negotiation), offering free training sessions and workshops, and so on (see also Glesne and Peshkin 1992).

Data collection should employ rigorous methods and standards for compiling meticulous notes that record events or ideas. Times, dates, contexts, participants and the like should be duly recorded, as should authors, page numbers and sources in text-based research. Detailed notes or 'thick descriptions' (Geertz 1973: 10) enable the researcher to revisit and reflect on events and ideas, to try out different interpretations and look for corroborating (or conflicting) evidence and authoritative support. This, in turn, builds a strong case for making claims about the validity and trustworthiness of interpretations. It is also the researcher's responsibility to ensure that collected field-work data is kept confidential, and any that is shared with colleagues is 'doctored' in order to maximize participants' anonymity. This involves finding reliable storage spaces for data and returning borrowed artefacts quickly and in the same state in which they were borrowed. It is difficult to explain lost or damaged data to study participants.

Researchers should take great care to respect the time commitments study participants agree to. It is important to avoid going back time after time to collect additional bits and pieces of data that were not envisaged at the start. Hence, data collection methods and timelines need to be carefully planned and matched with research goals and purposes.

Acting ethically does not mean maintaining a formal distance from participants – this is *impossible* when conducting ethnographic and certain case study variants of qualitative research. It does mean, however, that social conventions for interactions are respected, and researchers must take the necessary time and make the necessary effort to know what these involve. Interview questions and other data collection methods must respect social and cultural conventions and boundaries between what is acceptable and what is not. Researchers can minimize potential problems by designing interview schedules that are sensitive to the social conventions followed by the respondent, as well as to those followed by the researcher. This may involve deciding who can and cannot be researched. A good example here is provided by Loukia Sarroub's study of a Muslim community (Sarroub 2002). She had initially intended to include boys and girls, men and women in her study. She discovered, however, that because she was a woman it was not culturally appropriate for her to interview boys on a one-to-one basis. In addition there were various community events she could not gain access to because she was a woman. Of necessity, she changed the focus of her study to an investigation of Muslim girls only.

Methodological or procedural principles

Certain procedural principles can provide helpful guidance in preparing for and conducting data collection. We will consider three here: the principles of 'elegance and economy', 'practicality' and 'realism'.

The principle of *elegance and economy* is concerned with getting the greatest amount of high-quality data from the minimum use of resources, and with the least possible complexity in the operation. Enacting this principle involves thinking carefully about the kind of data that will be both necessary and sufficient for addressing the question, and looking for patterns and combinations that will allow 'more to be done more easily with less'. It may involve things as simple as knowing that a particular timetabling arrangement frees up several key people at the same time, which would allow for the information required to be obtained via a single focus group interview session rather than from conducting several separate interviews at different times (assuming that a focus group interview would be appropriate in this particular circumstance). Even at the earliest stages of operating as a researcher it is possible to see ways in which more can be done with less. If archives of relevant transcriptions of classroom talk or video-recorded material already exist that are appropriate for one's research purposes there is a presumption in favour of using these rather than collecting fresh data. Similarly, if a community-school network is in place and a key member is willing and able to assist in facilitating data collection, and where doing so would generate well-founded confidence among potential participants, time spent with this person might bring optimal results with minimal friction.

The principles of *practicality* and *realism* are about aligning what one plans to do in the way of data collection with the resources and opportunities that are actually available or likely to be available. Unless one has very good grounds for believing that the group one would like to investigate by means of a full ethnography will be willing to participate in an ethnographic study it is wasteful to spend a lot of time doing the necessary reading, planning and preparation for ethnographic data collection. Similarly, unless one has resources available for transcribing large amounts of audio- and video-recorded material, or for spending time with the tapes such that one can decide appropriately which parts of which tapes need to be transcribed and which can be referenced and handled in other ways in the data analysis phase, it is wasteful to collect a lot of recorded data.

It is equally bad research practice to rush into data collection without reading, discussing and finding out as comprehensively as possible from knowledgeable sources what the chances are of successfully collecting the data one envisages collecting, and whether all of it is necessary in the first place. Invariably, time spent thinking about procedural principles in the company of informed sources will prove to be time well spent.

Data collection designs and plans

Developing a data collection (sub)design is an important part of a research study's overall design. A well-conceived data collection design component includes an indication of what different types of data are to be collected, and the relationship between the data and the research questions. Such a design can be developed by addressing areas such as the four presented in Table 9.1.

Table 9.1   Areas to be considered in data collection

Kind of data to be collected	Means of data collection	Justification of the data to be collected	Sources of information and guidance
What kinds of data do I need to collect in order to answer the research question?	What kinds of data collection tools and methods will be used to collect the various types of data I need?	How does each kind of data to be collected help in answering my research question? What other kinds of data could be used? Why are the kinds I have chosen preferable for the task? Can I justify my decisions? How?	Who provides good advice or information about data collection in general? Who provides good accounts of the data collection means I will use? Who explains how to do these kinds of data collection? How do I identify and locate the best exponents of the kinds of data collection I want to do?

Table 9.2 provides an example of a data collection (sub)design produced on the basis of these four areas.

It is useful for researchers to try and divide up the time they have available in which to collect their data. An example of this is provided in Table 9.3. It shows the time to be allocated to collecting spoken data from *one* student, his teacher, his family and his fellow students in class. The student in this example was one of four participants in a multiple case study investigation.

After considering the kinds of issues raised in this chapter the researcher might produce a complete plan for data collection. This will often be provisional. Once data collection has begun the researcher may decide (on the basis of experience) that the initial plan is too ambitious. It may then be necessary to modify the original research question to one for which it is possible to collect the data required to address it competently.

Table 9.2 A sample data collection (sub)design

Research question: What linguistic and social purposes and practices are enacted in the everyday lives of four adolescents living in Bolton?			
Data to be collected	*Data collection methods*	*Relationship between data to be collected and research question*	*Sample sources of information and guidance*
Students: data concerning students' presentations of themselves as readers, writers, speakers, listeners, viewers etc.; data concerning values, beliefs, identities; student reflections on a particular lesson and their understandings of the teacher's lesson goals etc.	Semi-structured interviews and conversations with a purpose (audio-taped)	Interviewing students provides insights into/ another perspective on what kinds of things they do with literacy in school and out of school	Gee 1999

Hatch 1992

Schiffrin 1994 |
| *Teachers*: data about the goals and objectives for particular lessons; their professional assessment of the literacy capacities of the focus student; their understandings of what the focus student can 'do' with literacy outside school | | Interviewing teachers provides insight into the links they are making between what young people are doing literacy-wise outside school, and what is being done with literacy inside classrooms. | |
| *At school*: specific data concerning participation in literacy and other lessons, texts produced at school, networks of support drawn on to complete literacy tasks etc. | Observations in school and outside school contexts, to be recorded and compiled as fieldnotes etc. | Conversations with a purpose with case study participants and their families provide useful contextualizing data with regard to literacy practices out of school | |
| *At home*: specific data on literacy events (e.g. video-game playing, doing homework, attending church) and patterns of literacy use each student is observed engaging in (e.g. computer use, talk around the dinner table) | | Enables identification of key literacy practices in which participants engage during observed moments. Generates possibilities of comparing what people *do* with what people *say they do* literacy-wise in school and out of school contexts | Green and Wallat 1981

Hull and Schultz 2002 |

Research question: What linguistic and social purposes and practices are enacted in the everyday lives of four adolescents living in Bolton?			
Data to be collected	Data collection methods	Relationship between data to be collected and research question	Sample sources of information and guidance
Daily written and/or audio-taped log recorded by case study student concerning something to do with reading, writing, listening, speaking or viewing they had done that day	Journals kept by participants	The role of participant journals is to gain insights into students' understandings of the ways in which they use language in their everyday lives	Fetterman 1989 Gee 1999
Daily written log recording main events observed or heard that day, reflections on what was seen or heard, connections drawn between previous days' data collection or previous data collection for a different case study student. Record of hunches, tentative interpretations and the like. Space for recording emotional responses to the research act (e.g. nervousness during the first visit to a case study home, not understanding a look passed between a mother and son in response to something said)	Journal kept by researcher	Research log for guiding the organization of other data collected Private repository for ideas, hunches, reflections and self-evaluations, notes about emerging patterns in findings Space for interrogating, as much as possible, various roles as researcher and learner, and the biases and research expectations held	Fetterman 1989
Data in the form of physical samples of texts produced by students in a range of contexts at home and school; school policy documents concerning literacy instruction; copies of teachers' literacy unit	Artefact collection	Information about the 'props' (see Gee 1996) used by participants in fashioning their everyday literacy practices (e.g. notes passed in class, letters from friends, school	Gee 1999 Jackson 1998

Research question: What linguistic and social purposes and practices are enacted in the everyday lives of four adolescents living in Bolton?			
Data to be collected	Data collection methods	Relationship between data to be collected and research question	Sample sources of information and guidance
plans; copies of school-developed literacy resources etc.		worksheets, religious books and documents)	
		Policy information that informs the school context dimension of the study	

Table 9.3 Data collection time allocation matrix

Time frame: 2-week period	Interview	Language lesson	Journal
Case study participant	3 half-hour semi-structured interviews (audio-taped)	2 classroom lessons (audio-taped)	1 week (audio-taped)
Teacher	2 1-hour semi-structured interviews (audio-taped)	2 classroom lessons (audio-taped)	
Family, classmates and others	Informal discussion		

Preparing provisional data collection plans enables the researcher to be concise about the length of time participants will need to commit to the study. It also helps with balancing the amount of time allocated to data collection with the time required to conduct a proper data analysis that does justice to the data collected. Data collection plans and timetables also remind researchers when specialized equipment might need to be hired or borrowed. A data collection plan might be drawn up along the lines shown in Table 9.4.

Table 9.4 Example of a data collection plan

Participants	General observations (direct and post facto) outside school	General observations (direct and post facto) in the classroom	Interviews	Audio-recorded English lessons	Audio-recorded literacy diaries of participants	Artefact collection
Case study participants (details are for each of four case study participants)	8–12 hours of peripheral participant observation Fieldnotes Audio recordings Conversations	35–40 hours of peripheral participant observation Fieldnotes Audio recordings	3 × half-hour semi-structured interviews (audio-recorded)	2 English lessons	Diary during 1 week: written and/or audio-recorded Audio-recorded selection of literacy events	By case study participants from a range of contexts By the researcher from a range of contexts
Teacher (details are for each of four teachers)		35–40 hour of peripheral participant observation Informal discussion and conversation	2 × 1-hour semi-structured interviews (audio-recorded)	2 English lessons		By the researcher: lesson plans, teaching notes, resources etc.
Family, friends, others	Peripheral participant observation Fieldnotes Audio recordings Conversations		Informal discussion			By the researcher: notes, lists, newspapers and magazines, books, videos etc.

Task

Describe a study you would like to do, or that you can imagine doing. Provide a brief account of the research purposes for this study – especially the research problem and the research aim. Identify the research question. Describe the amount of time you would have available to conduct the study. Describe the kinds of data collection resources and facilities you would have available to you. Using this scenario as a background:

1 Describe the kind of data you think will have to be collected.

2 Provide a justification for this data.

3 Identify the methods and tools of data collection you will use to collect this data.

4 Develop a data collection (sub)design for this study at a similar level of detail to the example in Table 9.2.

5 Develop a provisional data collection plan.

Having considered some of the key concepts associated with data collection in general within the kinds of qualitative studies educational researchers are likely to conduct, we turn in the three following chapters to more specific aspects of collecting spoken, observed and written data respectively.

CHAPTER 10

Collecting spoken data in qualitative teacher research

Introduction

This chapter focuses on collecting spoken data for the purpose of obtaining information as well as for investigating language uses and language processes and their effects in their own right. We describe five general methods of collecting spoken data and various tools associated with the different methods. By 'data collection methods' we mean systematic ways of going about the task of collecting data. 'Data collection tools' are relatively concrete devices used in the process of collecting information, such as a set of interview questions to ask participants or a photograph used to elicit an oral narrative from someone.

The data collection methods addressed in this chapter are contextualized recording, interviewing, projective methods, 'think-alouds', and collecting extant transcripts.

Contextualized recording of spoken language

Here the researcher 'freeze-frames' part of an event or activity as it occurs by using some durable recording device (audio or video, analogue or digital) to capture speech *in situ* in order to focus on language uses and language processes relevant to their research question. 'Contextualized' spoken data occurs 'naturally' (so far as possible with recording equipment present and participants aware that they are assisting with research) within a given setting like a classroom, staffroom, school reception area, sports training session, school car park and so on. Recording contextualized spoken data requires preserving as far as is possible the complexity of and relationships between the interactions, activities and language uses that take place during the course of an event.

Within educational research much contextualized recording of spoken data occurs in classrooms. Since the early 1980s educational researchers – inspired by the emergence of sociolinguistics as a field of theory and research based on developments in anthropology, cultural psychology and linguistics – have become increasingly interested in studying classroom language use. Of particular interest has been the question of how classroom language use helps define and constitute what counts as being a successful student at school (see Michaels 1981, 1986; Baker and Freebody 1989; Cazden 2001). During the past 10–15 years many teacher researchers have recorded contextualized, 'slice of life' verbal interactions in classrooms, staff meetings and playgrounds, in order to better understand the social functions (and effects) of language within educational settings (see Kempe 1993; Knobel 1993).

At its simplest, audio-recording 'slice of life' data involves using a single micro-cassette recorder strategically placed in the room. More complex approaches involve wiring students and teachers with microphones, placing standing microphones around the room and controlling the microphones from a single receiving and recording base. The degree of sophistication in the recording set-up depends on:

- who the focus participants are (e.g. mainly the teacher, one particular student, the entire class);
- the particular lesson or event in which data are to be collected (e.g. recording a teacher reading to a class of students and then discussing the text with them is much easier than recording lessons involving small-group work);
- teacher researcher access to audio recording equipment.

There are always limitations involved in audio-recording contextualized spoken data. For example, it is impossible to collect *all* talk that occurs within a classroom, meeting, play event or other setting. The ebb and flow of spoken language within these contexts does not always relate directly to the main stream of interaction within the activity or event being focused on. A single cassette recorder placed somewhere in a large and noisy classroom cannot pick up all the talk occurring in the room. Indeed, unless a single recording device is extremely high in quality it is unlikely to provide a good-quality record of spoken language in a general setting at all. Small-sized audio recorders are most useful for such things as recording a group of three to four students working collaboratively on a task, or for taping meetings that involve only a handful of people within a closed space.

Prior to data collection the teacher researcher must decide such mundane things as whether to use a recorder that takes micro- or conventional-sized cassettes. This is not a matter simply of choosing a device on the basis of availability. It will often be important to consider the device that will be used for eventually transcribing the tapes. Transcribing machines are pedal-operated audio-tape players. They automatically backspace when the tape is stopped, so the person doing the transcribing does not miss any speech by turning the player on and off as they try to 'take down' what has been said on a stretch of tape. Making a 'bad' choice about cassette size for initial recording may impact on one's transcribing options later. Of course, many professional transcribers have machines that accept both types of cassette. But the general point is that one does not simply charge into audio-recording without taking the mechanics of transcription into account.

Some researchers have begun to use digital recording devices to capture spoken data. This requires some technical expertise in terms of deciding file types for recording data (e.g. deciding whether to record data in WAV file format that is very large but easy to edit, or to record in smaller, more difficult to edit MP3 file format). An hour-long interview will produce a WAV file that is roughly 14 *megabytes* in size. Compression applications (like StuffIt! or WinZip) and CD-ROM burning capabilities can help where file storage is concerned. The researcher needs to ensure a digital recording device has sufficient memory for his or her purposes (most digital voice recorders in the lower price range currently store less than two hours of talk). Transcribing issues also come into play when using digital devices to record spoken data. Speech-to-text conversion software is still far from accurate, and shifting on-screen between digital playback software and word processing can be awkward and cumbersome. Benefits of digital recording include ease of storage and being able to duplicate sound files easily (Davidson 2002).

To capture as much spoken language as possible during lessons it is often useful to equip the teacher with a wireless microphone – or for teachers researching their own classrooms to wire themselves. This allows the teacher's talk to be recorded regardless of whether they are speaking quietly to one or two students or addressing an entire class. Of course, wiring only the teacher with a cordless microphone means the teacher becomes the main source of spoken data. If this is not appropriate, one or more students can also be equipped with wireless microphones or, alternatively, they can be wired instead of the teacher. This again changes the sources of data, with implications for the study focus. Hence, decisions about who to wire and/or where to place microphones need to be made in the light of the study purposes.

Likewise, diverse options are available when filming an educational activity or event. These range from using a hand-held camcorder through to using television-quality film cameras and lighting. Deciding what kind of video configuration to use will depend on who and what is to be recorded, as well as on what access the teacher researcher has to video-recording equipment. Education researchers generally use a single video camera on a tripod to record spoken language in a classroom. They 'pan' regularly across the classroom, zooming in and out on items of interest as the lesson progresses. When preparing for video recording in an educational setting it is useful to carry an extension power cord, spare batteries, spare tapes and even a spare video-recorder wherever possible. Similar backup arrangements apply equally to audio recording. One should always carry spare batteries, cassettes and power cord extension leads, and carefully test the recording unit immediately prior to each data collection session.

As with audio recording, video recording can never catch everything that is taking place or being said within a given context (Bottorff 1994). Nevertheless, videos do capture useful visual information that cannot be captured by audiotapes alone, but which can greatly augment spoken data. For example, video recording can identify speakers and capture gestures accompanying speech that inflect the speech and make it possible to derive enhanced meaning from spoken data. In deciding whether to audio- or video-record (or both) to gather spoken data, teacher researchers need to consider such issues as school policies on recording students' faces, the time needed for transcribing videotapes compared with audiotapes, the quality of recording possible with either option, and so on.

When recording contextualized spoken language, one always aims to collect data that are as authentic as possible, while recognizing that the very act of recording – even in one's own classroom – interferes with regular classroom dynamics. Participants may become unsettled when they know they are being audio-recorded, or unusually self-conscious about what they are saying, or may refuse to speak at all. Teacher researchers are therefore well served by careful preparation prior to formally collecting spoken data. This preparation includes making trial-run recordings that enable participants to grow used to being recorded in the settings under investigation. Generally, after a few days of experiencing researchers and recording devices in classrooms, students appear to no longer notice the equipment (or even the researchers in most cases). Where prior preparation is impossible – for example, taping the first day of school in a particular classroom – researchers need to do their best to explain the presence of the camera and provide students with opportunities to 'ham it up' in front of the camera before settling down to their work. This helps remove much of the mystery of the camera's presence and, subsequently, much of the students' interest in it being there.

One drawback concerning sophisticated recording arrangements is that the more complex they become the more obvious or intrusive they can be. It is much easier to make audio recording a relatively inconspicuous affair when a small cassette recorder is used than when standing microphones and large receiving boxes are used. Conversely, less sophisticated recording arrangements may mean poorer recordings. When making decisions about how best to record contextualized talk within the classroom (or some other context), teacher researchers need to weigh the time available for familiarizing students with the recording equipment prior to the start of formal data collection against the quality of recording they need.

Task

Return to the questions presented in the Task on page 178 and see if you still agree with your original responses. Change any responses you now think are mistaken. Then address the following questions.

- How did you decide which questions needed contextualized spoken data?

- In what ways might this decision process help you with designing your own approaches to collecting spoken data?

- In those questions calling for contextualized spoken data, how much data do you think would be needed in order to address the question satisfactorily?

- On what do you base your estimates?

- What kind of consideration enters into making your estimates? Do you have to supply additional information in order to estimate?

- If so, what kind of information is required?

- What might this suggest for your own research planning?

For further reading in this area we suggest:

- Bottorff, J. (1994) Using videotaped recordings in qualitative research, in J. Morse (ed.) *Critical Issues in Qualitative Research Methods*, pp. 242–61. Thousand Oaks, CA: Sage.
- Cazden, C. (2001) *Classroom Discourse: The Language of Teaching and Learning*, 2nd edn. Portsmouth: Heinemann.
- Davidson, L. (2002) Digital recording advice for research interviews, davidson. cba.hawaii.edu/digitalrecording.html (accessed 12 October 2002).

Interviewing

Interviews are planned, prearranged interactions between two or more people, where one person is responsible for asking questions pertaining to a particular theme or topic of formal interest and the other (or others) are responsible for responding to these questions. Interviews are generally conducted face to face or over the telephone and, increasingly, via email. The purpose of interviews is to generate detailed and desired information about an event, programme or person that would not otherwise be possible to obtain by means of observation or artefact collection. Interviews can be used to:

- generate content about an event from an 'insider's' perspective;
- access a person's definitions and understandings of concepts and processes that are of interest to the teacher (e.g. critical literacy, mathematical reasoning);
- tap into beliefs, values, worldviews and the like on the part of the interviewee;
- study the way in which a teacher represents his or her identity by means of the words she or he chooses to use;
- collect personal oral narratives about teaching (and learning);
- collect biographies or life stories of teachers, administrators and others.

Phil Carspecken (1996: 155) notes that participants often say things in interviews they would not speak about in everyday conversation. The interviewer's intense interest in what interviewees are saying encourages the latter to 'open up'. This same intense interest, conversely, can induce interviewees to make fun of the interview process and fabricate interview responses (see Glesne and Peshkin 1992: 39; note also the famous case of Margaret Mead's 1928 research in Samoa).

Teacher researchers need to remember that what people say in interviews is always said at a particular point in time and within a contrived interaction. It will not capture everything a respondent thinks, feels, values or believes about something. It cannot be assumed that respondents are always able to articulate what they think, feel or believe. Data collected in interviews are always partial and incomplete. In short, interview data can never be used in a study as though they are direct representations of some definitive 'truth' as expressed by the respondent. Despite such limitations, interviews remain the best available means for accessing study participants' opinions, beliefs, values and situated accounts of events at a particular point in time.

Interview data are always *contrived*, since 'some conscious shaping of the verbal exchanges' by both interviewer and interviewee always takes place (Fetterman 1998: 5). Often, what is talked about is shaped directly by the kinds of questions asked and prompts given by the teacher researcher. In unstructured and semi-structured interviews particularly, *how* an interviewee responds to a question will often shape the following question asked by the researcher, just as the question itself shapes what the interviewee says in response. For example, an interviewer who is interested in a participant's values might ask a question like: 'Tell me about a time when you've had to make a really hard decision. How did you go about deciding what to do?' There is no way a researcher can know in advance what the next question will be, since they have no idea what the respondent will say. By the same token, what the respondent says with respect to their values might be very different from what it would have been if the interviewer had used a different question. Hence, interviewing can be seen as a process of interviewer and interviewee co-constructing data, and the interviewee is more a participant in the research process than just a subject on which research is done.

Collecting interview data

Interviews are recorded in three main ways: by notes, audio recording and video recording. Using handwritten notes to make a durable record of an interview necessarily focuses the teacher researcher's attention on the content of *what* the interviewee says and much less on *how* they say it. Audio and video recording enable the teacher researcher to capture a good deal of the interviewee's intonation, voice quality, hesitations, self-corrections, asides and so on. Video recording also captures many of the gestures, facial expressions, body movements and the like made during the course of the interview.

Deciding which recording tool to use requires careful thought about what data are needed to address the research question: information-oriented data or data lending themselves to analysing language use and processes. For example, a teacher researcher is readily able to jot down a list of computer uses identified and comments made by students within a small group interview format as part of a study that focuses on technology take-up in high-school classrooms. These notes can be fleshed out once the interview has been finished. The teacher researcher does not require a detailed transcript of a group interview to be able to say something about student comments on school uses of new technologies. This saves substantial time in terms of transcribing spoken data, especially with group interviews, where participants often talk over each other, interrupt and so on (Walford 2001: Ch. 6). On the other hand, videotaping group interviews may help the teacher researcher remember who said what at which point in a group interview when participants were asked to comment on a controversial issue that led to heated discussion.

Researchers also need to keep in mind that taking notes during interviews is a laborious task and is not well suited to interviews lasting more than 10 to 20 minutes. A combination of using a recording device and note-taking is often a useful approach to collecting spoken data. Notes act as a backup should the recording fail, and as useful data management information for summarizing tape content in readily accessible form. Recording enables interviewers to maintain good eye contact with speakers, to concentrate more on what is being said rather than on copying it down, and to obtain a verbatim record of what was said that can be revisited time and again.

The time frames set for a study also influence how interview data are collected. An hour of interview recording generally takes an experienced researcher three to four hours to transcribe (more if the transcription is to be verbatim). An hour of video-recorded interviews can take six to eight hours to transcribe when gestures, expressions and other non-verbal signals are included in the transcript.

Task

Which of the following interview scenarios would be served best by recording spoken interview data by means of (a) notes, (b) audio-taping and (c) video-taping? Why?

1   A student who is widely recognized by teachers and students as being a school bully is going to be interviewed about an episode in which they hurt a younger child. The teacher researcher aims at better understanding what motivates bullies to physically hurt other people in order to generate a response to the growing problem of bullying within the school.

2   A group of parents who regularly attend Parents and Citizen Association meetings at the school are going to be interviewed about what they believe the role of the Association is and what the relationship between the Association and teachers ideally should be like.

3   As part of gaining insights into Grade 1 students' experiences at school during the first month of the school year, a Grade 1 child has been asked by the teacher researcher to draw and explain a map of the school that shows the areas the child is most familiar with, those they are least familiar with and those that they actively avoid and why.

4   In a study of policy decision making at the school level, the teacher researcher needs to interview the school principal. The principal is far from keen to be interviewed; however, after some gentle persuasive pressure she has finally agreed to participate, albeit reluctantly.

Interview types and characteristics

Interviews can be as structured or as unstructured as required. Structured interviews aim to maximize comparisons across responses to interview questions. The key tool used here is a pre-set list of questions asked in a fixed order. There are no deviations from the list, regardless of the response to the question just asked. Email interviews are typically structured interviews. Structured, spoken interviews are best suited to research requiring data from many people because the format of the interview enables relatively easy comparisons to be drawn across responses to each question.

Unstructured interviews have no pre-prepared lists of questions. Researchers begin the interview with a general idea of the topic to be discussed in mind, but let interviewees determine the direction of the interview and the ground covered in the discussion. Unstructured interviews aim to solicit as much information as possible without confining respondents to particular themes or topics. For instance, they are a useful way to identify areas of concern for study participants at the outset of an action research project, to establish rapport with a participant at the beginning of a case study investigation, or to access important biographic or narrative information.

Advocates of unstructured interviews often claim that this approach actually minimizes research bias, by allowing questions to spring 'naturally' from the discussion and/or by encouraging open discussion through the disruption of 'normal' power relations between interviewers (powerful) and interviewees (less powerful). Such claims are easily overstated, however. Researchers *always* have the study aims and research questions in mind when talking with someone. These shape the questions posed and the direction in which the discussion runs. Moreover, claiming that unstructured interviews are 'more democratic' than other types may actually hide unequal power relations between the teacher researcher and the interviewee (Lather 1991; Addison and McGee 1999; Bernard 2000; Hoggart *et al.* 2002).

Unstructured interviews are usefully seen as 'conversations with a purpose': occasions when teacher researchers are chatting with students, teachers, parents or others, with one ear directed towards the goals and purposes of the study, but without turning the conversation into an interrogation (see Clandinin and Connelly 1998).

Semi-structured interviews lie halfway between structured and unstructured interviews (see Figure 10.1). Russell Bernard describes this continuum as representing the amount of *control* the researcher tries to exercise over people's responses (2000: 190). Looked at this way, structured interviews try to control responses as tightly as possible for comparative (and often statistical) purposes, while unstructured interviews try to minimize researcher control of participants' responses.

Semi-structured interviews include a list of pre-prepared questions, but the teacher researcher uses this as a guide only, and follows up on relevant comments made by the interviewee. Both semi-structured and unstructured interviews allow teacher researchers to probe interviewees' responses. They encourage elaboration of important themes emerging in the course of the interview, rather than tying interviewer and interviewee to a fixed schedule that can limit opportunities to enrich spoken data and gain insights into how interviewees 'see' and understand the world (Heyl 2001).

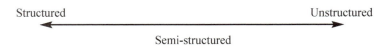

Figure 10.1 A continuum of interview approaches

Semi-structured interviews can never be repeated in exactly the same way with each interviewee. Nevertheless, they retain the 'virtues' of both structured and unstructured approaches to interviewing. Researchers can readily compare different responses to the same questions, while at the same time remaining open to important but unforeseen information or points of discussion.

Generating 'good' interview questions

Whatever the type of interview, researchers need to think carefully about what makes a good interview question before beginning interview data collection. Good-quality interview questions are:

- unambiguous;
- one-question questions;
- 'non-leading';
- culturally sensitive and ethically informed.

Unambiguous questions
Questions are ambiguous when interviewees can reasonably interpret them in multiple ways. This can generate misleading data for the researcher. The following question is ambiguous and potentially confusing:

What can you teach children now that will be useful to them as adults?

'What can you teach' is ambiguous here since the interviewee could interpret it either as asking about what she or he (or anyone) is *capable* of teaching under ideal conditions, or as asking about what she or he is actually teaching *now* that will be useful to students when they leave school. Different participants' answers will not be comparable in any useful way if some refer to what they are doing now in their classrooms and others to what they would be teaching under ideal circumstances. Moreover, the researcher will have no way of knowing which is which unless (further) clarifying questions are asked. Minimizing ambiguity highlights the importance of testing research questions with different people prior to interviewing.

One-question questions

Stringing multiple questions together is potentially confusing and can force the path responses take. For example:

> What citizenship skills are most important to teach young children and where are these skills taught best: at home or at school?

A respondent who believes that good citizenship involves much more than a set of skills has little opportunity here to express an alternative or more complex position outside a skills-only focus. The question will yield better information if it is broken into smaller, clearer and more open components. For example:

> For you, what skills – if any – need to be learned by young children in order for them each to be a 'good citizen'?

> What else, in your opinion, do they need to learn in order to be a good citizen?

> In your opinion, what ideally – in a perfect world – *should* the role of parents be in helping their children to become good citizens?

> What do you feel the current reality is at present in terms of parents in this area helping their children to be good citizens?

> What are some of the reasons for this?

> In your opinion, what ideally *should* the role of teachers be in helping their students to become good citizens?

> What do you feel the current reality is in terms of teachers in this area helping their students to be good citizens?

> What are some of your reasons for taking this position?

Closely scrutinizing interview questions encourages the researcher to evaluate them and their relevance to the study's purposes prior to interviewing participants (this is especially important in email interviews where it wastes interviewees' time to have to email interviewers for clarification).

Interview questions should be designed to minimize the extent to which they direct respondents to answer in a particular way. The following question fails badly in this respect:

> Many people find the new maths syllabus very difficult to use and think it is causing a lot of problems for everyone – what do you think of the new maths syllabus?

This, of course, is a gross example, and much more subtle challenges exist to the ideal of (maximally) unbiased questions. Compare, for instance, the effects of word choice in the following questions:

> What are some of the complexities facing educators who are concerned with issues of equitable education at present?

What are some of the difficulties facing educators who are concerned with issues of equitable education at present?

The questions are close in type and content. Yet they signal different researcher positions in relation to teachers' work contexts. 'Complexity' and 'difficulty' are very different orientations (or mindsets) with respect to pursuing equity in education.

Task

Identify different orientations that might be operating in the following pairs of questions:

1a In what ways do you establish the social rules and norms of behaviour in your classroom during the first week of school?

1b In what ways do you and your students establish the social rules and norms of behaviour in your classroom during the first week of school?

2a In what ways do students who struggle with school literacy in your class deal with reading and writing?

2b In what ways do your 'at risk' students deal with reading and writing in class?

3a In what ways have larger class sizes affected your teaching?

3b What effects have larger class sizes had on your teaching?

Teacher researchers can help minimize overt influence by reflecting carefully on the words used in each question and the effects these word choices could have on interviewee responses. It is easy to become so immersed in a study that we overlook how our word choices shepherd responses. A useful strategy for checking whether one's questions are 'leading' is to test them on colleagues.

The *order* in which questions are asked can also shape how they are 'heard' and responded to by interviewees. Consider the following sequence:

1   How much in-service training have you had in relation to using new technologies within your school subject area?
2   In terms of software purchases, how well resourced is your subject area?
3   How much input have you had personally into new technology-related decisions within this school?
4   What has been your experience in terms of positive and negative student outcomes as a result of using new digital technologies in your own teaching?

This sequence is likely to produce an emphasis on negative outcomes in relation to using new technologies, given that time for sustained professional development and inclusive decision-making practices, and money for resource acquisition, are typically in short supply. The sequencing of research questions can also cue respondents into what they think the teacher researcher is looking for or *wanting* to hear (see e.g. Mertens 1998; Bernard 2000). Teacher researchers need to be aware of the possible issues concerning question sequencing and to reflect on possible confounding effects that may interfere with the quality or trustworthiness of interview data collected in a given study.

It is impossible to construct completely bias-free interview questions. Language is not neutral, and all research interviewing occurs within studies that are influenced by particular theories, worldviews and assumptions. Nonetheless, teacher researchers should aim to identify biases in their questions and build this awareness into their interpretations (Bernard 2000: 214).

Culturally sensitive and ethically informed questions
Interview questions must be as culturally sensitive and ethically informed as possible. 'Cultural sensitivity' means paying close attention to question wording in ways that respect cultural differences in order to minimize risk of insult to others (including those not being interviewed). Such differences include cultural heritage, religious beliefs and practices, worldviews, social practices and language. Researchers often find that asking direct questions and having them answered immediately and directly is not an observed practice among members of groups they are researching (LeCompte and Schensul 1999). Other researchers warn against using 'subtly derogatory terms' such as the phrase 'those people' to refer to parents or a specific group of parents, teachers or students (Mertens 1998: 114).

'Culture' here refers to much more than ethnicity or race. It covers any recognized social group within a larger society (e.g. local groups of prisoners, parents who home-school their children, ballroom dancers, computer virus writers). Formulating culturally sensitive questions takes into account who the people are that will be participating in the interview. A key element in asking culturally informed questions is to know about the cultural group being interviewed. Strategies for enhancing culturally sensitive interviewing include reading research already conducted with same or similar cultural groups prior to generating interview questions, identifying taboo topics for the group and having a respected member of the cultural group read and comment on one's interview questions prior to interviewing.

Formulating culturally sensitive questions also involves attending to research ethics. Interview questions need to conform to basic conceptions of what counts as 'right' and 'wrong' things to ask people. Research communities generally have their own sets of what can and cannot be asked of others (see e.g. Fontana and Frey 1998; Mertens 1998; see also Chapter 6), although there are principles common to all research that uses interviews for data collection. These include:

- never ask questions that range far beyond the scope of the study outlined in the consent form signed by the participant;
- refrain from asking potentially threatening, humiliating or embarrassing questions, unless they form a significant part of the study and have been agreed to by the participant;
- do not ask questions that appear to be collecting data on one thing but are really concerned with another (e.g. asking migrant children how their parents came to the country in order to gather information about the parents' legal immigrant status);
- potentially embarrassing or controversial questions that really do need to be asked for the purpose of the study are best asked towards the end of the interview when the respondent is more likely to feel confident that his or her answers are being treated with respect by the interviewer.

The best rule of thumb with respect to constructing ethically informed interview questions is to ask of each question: 'Would I like to be asked this question and be expected to respond to it?'.

Finally, it is good interviewing practice to end one's list of interview questions with an invitation to respondents to ask questions and/or comment on the interview or study. This gives respondents an opportunity to raise any concerns they may have and, in turn, creates an opening for the researcher to attend to anything that may need resolving in the interests of sound data collection and ethical practice. Responses to these questions can often pre-empt possible misunderstandings and misinterpretations that are more difficult to amend at the end of the research. They can also help to keep researchers 'honest' in other ways, as when an interviewee asks something like: 'So tell me, what are you getting out of these interviews with me? What are you personally getting out of this study?' or asks how the study is going to be reported (e.g. a report, a book) and so on.

Question types

There are two broad categories of interview question: closed questions and open-ended questions. Closed questions provide a range of possible responses, usually in the form of multiple choice answers, yes/no answers, rating scales and so on. They also include questions requiring only readily verifiable factual responses (e.g. name, age, total years of teaching experience, number and type of university degrees held). However, interviews involving such questions are of little use when collecting spoken data. Open-ended questions, on the other hand, have no pre-set, yes-no answers and are used deliberately to encourage respondents to give their opinions on something, describe their experiences, provide insights into how they view the world around them and so on.

Task

Identify which of the following questions are closed questions and which are open-ended questions. Identify the criteria you used to distinguish between them.

1   How many years have you been teaching at this school?

2   In your opinion, what is the most effective method for achieving orderly behaviour in the classroom?

3   What are some of the most important things a beginning teacher should know?

4   How many speakers of languages other than English do you have in your class?

5   To what extent do you see your school's policies on new technology use as relevant to your own teaching?

6   What textbooks – if any – do you set for your classes?

7   What software programs do you have installed on your classroom computer?

Any given interview is likely to include both open and closed questions. An unstructured interview might begin with asking respondents some closed-type questions such as name, age, ethnic affiliation and so on. Similarly, structured interviews may end with open-ended questions that invite interviewees to discuss their experiences within a programme, a classroom or a particular school. The main consideration when devising interview questions concerns the kind of information most needed from the interview in order to address the research question guiding the study.

Interview configurations

Besides choosing from structured, semi-structured and unstructured interviews, teacher researchers can also choose between different interview configurations.

One-to-one interviews
One-to-one interviews involve just the researcher and the interviewee. Typically, the interviewer begins by asking a question to which the interviewee responds. This question-response process is repeated until the interviewer has no more questions to ask, or until the time allocated for the interview has run out. Structured, semi-structured and unstructured interviews can all use a one-to-one format.

It helps for interviewers to convey genuine interest in what an interviewee has to say and in what can be learned from the interviewee about the problem, topic or issue being investigated. This is conveyed by attentive listening (e.g. nodding and smiling in appropriate places, making encouraging or 'please go on' comments and sounds), by not interrupting or talking over the respondent and by providing them with ample time to formulate responses. Interviewers should not be afraid to say things like, 'I don't understand' or 'I'm not familiar with that, can you tell me more about it?'. In semi-structured and unstructured one-to-one interviews interviewers should commit to memory the focus or theme of the interview questions overall (rather than specific questions). This way they can remain flexible in asking questions, while ensuring that data needed for the study are generated over the course of the interview.

Small-group interviews

Small-group/focus group interviews are gaining in popularity in qualitative research studies. They can help teacher researchers maximize data collection within decreasing research time frames. They involve 'the systematic questioning of several individuals simultaneously in formal or informal settings' (Fontana and Frey 1998: 53). The goal of small-group interviews is to generate discussion rather than engage in question and response sequences. Small-group interviews are particularly useful data collection methods for accessing alternative points of view, for obtaining insights into group consensus or divergence on an issue or across accounts of an event, and for clarifying the researcher's in-process interpretations garnered or developed from already-collected data. For example, small-group interviews with school students could be used to follow up on observations of classroom lessons, where the students are asked what they thought the teacher's learning goals for them were.

Some researchers regard up to 10–12 people as a manageable interview group size (Marshall and Rossman 1999: 114). With children and adolescents, three or four interviewees may produce the most useful data (Hopkins 1993: 124). Group interviews leave less time for asking questions since more discussion usually occurs with each question than in one-to-one interviews. Developing concise and directly relevant interview questions is paramount when there may be time to ask only three or four questions.

There are risks that one participant may dominate the discussion within a group interview or that the interview itself may head off on tangents unrelated to the researcher's goals. Nonetheless, the potential benefits of small-group interviews outweigh likely drawbacks. Group interviews have 'the advantages of being inexpensive, data rich, flexible, stimulating to respondents, recall aiding, and cumulative and elaborative' (Fontana and Frey 1998: 55). They are 'relatively low cost ... provide quick results, and ... can increase the sample size of qualitative studies by interviewing more people at one time' (Marshall and Rossman 1999: 115). Group interviewing also maximizes possibilities for unanticipated but highly pertinent matters being raised as respondents 'bounce off' of each others' comments and claims (see Hopkins 1993: 124).

Conducting interviews

Interviewing begins with identifying who is to be interviewed, gaining informed written consent from them and organizing a time, date and place to meet.

Who to interview

In many cases deciding who to interview is relatively straightforward because selection criteria are explicit in the study focus. For example, a study concerned with identifying the issues of most concern to school technology coordinators within the local administrative region specifies precisely who should be interviewed. So do studies concerned with analysing the induction experiences of local teachers in their first two years of service, or with the previous schooling experiences of new arrival learners at school X.

In other cases, however, deciding who to interview might not be so easily determined. The research question, 'What conceptions of "good citizenship" are operating within this school community?' does not closely specify who needs to be interviewed. The researcher's definition of 'school community' will help provide some ideas here about who best to interview (e.g. administrators, administration staff, teachers, students, parents, school caretakers and other staff, volunteer helpers, those living near the school). Even so, it may be impossible to interview everyone in these categories. Hence the researcher will need to develop and defend particular criteria for making judicious selections that ensure a suitable cross-section of the 'school community' is interviewed.

Constructing matrices based on the kinds of considerations and characteristics most relevant to one's research purposes can be helpful in clarifying decisions here. The example shown in Table 10.1 reflects an interest in achieving a certain range of diversity within a very small number of case study participants.

Time considerations

A general rule of thumb is one hour for interviews with adults so as not to impose too much on their time and 30 minutes for children so their patience isn't taxed too heavily. Interviewing can be exhausting for everyone involved, especially one-to-one interviewing. Structured and semi-structured interviews require careful attention to what the other person is saying, and to think about what is being said in a focused manner. Conversations with a purpose, on the other hand, often range over a variety of topics over an extended period of time and seem to require much less concentrated attention. Regardless of the type of interview and its configuration, the researcher needs to pay close attention to signals from interviewees that they have had enough, and be prepared to cut an interview short if necessary. Teacher researchers also need to be alert to the possibility that interviewees may require more than the prearranged time to respond to questions as fully as they would like. This might mean scheduling interviews after school to avoid running up against timetables and other interruptions, or offering the interviewee another time to meet in which to respond to remaining interview questions.

Location

Structured and semi-structured interviews call for quiet, out of the way places, which can be difficult to find in schools. The more out of the way the room is, the better, as it

Table 10.1 Sample matrix of study participant profiles

	Nicholas	*Layla*	*Jacques*	*Hannah*
Sex	Male	Female	Male	Female
Teacher-rated literacy competence	Well above average	Average	Well below average	Above average
School community income levels	Predominantly middle to upper middle class	Middle class	Broad representation of classes	Predominantly working class
School location	Suburban	Urban	Suburban	Satellite city
School type	Lutheran	Catholic	State	State

minimizes the chances of noisy and repeated disruption, and the easier it becomes to obtain good-quality recordings.

In the case of conversations with a purpose, on the other hand, teacher researchers rarely have much control over when and where they occur. It might be while walking with a teacher on playground duty, waiting with parents for school to finish, chatting with a secretary between phone calls and administrative duties. Consequently, it is often difficult to obtain a taped record of conversations, let alone a good-quality recording. This makes it important for the teacher researcher to make detailed notes about such conversations as soon as possible after they occur (making sure to note down the date, the time, the person or people spoken with, the key content of the conversation etc.).

Characteristics of effective interviews for collecting spoken data

Interviews are more likely to be effective if researchers attend to matters like the following:

- Careful pre-planning. This involves ensuring that interview questions are well constructed and pre-tested on a sample of people; that the list of questions to be asked is printed out beforehand and ready to be used; that the interviewer knows the way to an agreed-upon meeting place and arrives punctually; that the interviewer calls that day to remind the interviewee of their arrangement to meet; and the like.
- Checking recording equipment just prior to the interview and always having spare batteries, an extension cord if using mains electricity and spare tapes close to hand. It is also a good idea to have a backup audio or video recording machine running if the interview is really important. As soon as possible after each interview, spend some time jotting down as much as possible of what can be recalled – in case the recording did not work.

- Being mindful of the effects of power (and perceptions of power) within an interview relationship. Ways of minimizing overt displays of power include establishing an easy-going but respectful rapport with the interviewee (this includes not sitting with a desk between the interviewer and the interviewee, never sitting with one's back to the sun so that facial features become difficult to see, dressing appropriately, beginning with general 'chit chat' questions or talk to help put the interviewee at ease and so on).
- Signalling regularly that one is listening to what is being said without making too many interjections that interrupt the flow of talk.
- Managing the pace of the interview effectively so that the interviewee is not imposed upon by being forced to spend more time than agreed in being interviewed, while at the same time providing the interviewee with sufficient time in which to respond as fully as he or she would like.
- Making a follow-up telephone call or sending an email message after the interview has taken place to thank the respondent for giving up her or his time to be interviewed.
- Making sure that the purpose of the study overall is explained clearly and concisely on the interviewee's consent form, as well as orally prior to the interview.
- Being genuine about one's research requiring only voluntary participants.
- Doing one's best to put interviewees at their ease prior to the commencement of an interview. This can be done by asking easily-answered questions not directly connected to the study (e.g. 'Did you find this room without any trouble?'), or commenting on something of likely shared interest to both parties (e.g. the weather, weekend sports results, a striking outfit).

For further reading in this area we suggest:

- Dunn, K. (2000) Interviewing, in I. Hay (ed.) *Qualitative Research Methods in Human Geography*, pp. 50–82. Melbourne, VIC: Oxford University Press.
- Hoggart, K., Lees, L. and Davies, A. (2002) *Researching Human Geography*. London: Arnold.
- Hopkins, D. (1993) *A Teacher's Guide to Classroom Research*, 2nd edn. Buckingham: Open University Press.
- Spradley, J. (1980) *The Ethnographic Interview*. New York: International Thomson Publishing.

Projective methods

Teacher researchers can make use of some object, activity or text to draw out information from respondents. The primary tool in a projective method approach to generating interview data is an *eliciting device*. This might take the form of a photograph, a drawing, a cartoon, a film, a piece of student-produced work, a specific memory, a computer game, a hypothetical or real problem, a curriculum document, a school policy, a short narrative, scenario or anecdote etc.

Uwe Flick (1998: 77) describes an approach to using eliciting devices in media research. Participants are shown a film, or listen to a radio broadcast, and then are asked a series of pre-prepared questions concerning the impact of the media item on the respondent. Flick explains how this method can be used to examine subjective responses to different forms of mass media. Another variation using a concrete stimulus to generate a research interview is the 'problem centred' interview (Flick 1998: 88). Here researchers focus on a particular problem relevant to interviewees. Examples in teacher research include teachers having to prepare students for standardized tests while still covering syllabus material and including additional resources such as new technologies in their pedagogical approach. The interviewer has respondents discuss their experiences, difficulties and successes in relation to this problem.

In recent education research, projective approaches and elicitation devices have been used to gather information about contexts, study participants, past events or practices, attitudes and motivations, beliefs, past and present everyday life, hopes and expectations and so on (see Harper 1998; Plummer 2001). Eliciting devices used in this approach to gathering spoken data can be anything from recalled dreams, to photographs, to work tools or teaching resources, to everyday objects. The question, 'What would you wish for if you had three wishes?' might serve as an eliciting device to obtain insights into participants' values. Carspecken suggests using 'typical day', 'significant event', or 'tour' questions to elicit information from interviewees (1996: 156). He provides three sample questions or requests that are useful guides for teacher researchers in developing their own eliciting questions and devices (1996: 156):

- 'Tell me about a typical day in the classroom. Start from when you first enter the school, then take me through all your activities, one by one. Don't be afraid of giving too much detail: I am interested in everything.'
- 'Can you think of a recent time when you had a dispute with a student about something? You can? Good! Now please tell me everything that happened. Describe it as if you were making a movie about it.'
- 'Here is a diagram of your classroom with the desks and other things draw in. I'm not a very good artist, am I? Anyway, could you give me a tour through the diagram and explain everything about each item? You can add items important to your work that I have missed.'

> **Task**
>
> - What is it that appears to distinguish projective methods or elicitation questions from general interview questions? (Compare the sample questions asked by Carspecken above with the interview questions appearing in the previous section.)
>
> - Is the difference important? Why?
>
> - What might projective methods enable you to access that more 'standard' interview questions might not? Why is this the case?
>
> - Are projective methods and more conventional interview methods mutually exclusive? Why/Why not?

Using projective methods is similar in many respects to conventional interview processes. Projective-type interviews or discussions can be one-to-one, or involve an interviewer and a group of respondents. Respondents are handed, shown, or told the eliciting device. The spoken interaction proceeds from this point along lines directed largely by the respondent, although the interviewer can play a guiding role in steering the interviewee onto terrain related to the study's research questions. Prompting the respondent for more details is very important in effective projective-type interviews. Cues like 'Tell me more about that' signal attentiveness and interest, and can greatly enhance the amount, detail and quality of the talk that is collected. We have also found projective-type interviews to be extremely useful in obtaining spoken data from very young children, who are often notoriously difficult to interview (see Rossman and Rallis 1998; Hicks 2002).

Eliciting devices in the form of physical objects – like a photograph, a map, some object produced by the interviewee – often require more response time than more conventional interview questions. Eliciting devices typically require setting aside an hour and a half for use with adults and 30–45 minutes with children. As with more conventional interviews, it is always useful to audio- or video-record projective-type interviews, to maintain a permanent record of the exchange. Indeed, the concrete nature of many eliciting devices, and the ways in which they are included or directly referred to in participants' responses, often means that video recording is the best method for collecting data generated by this approach.

> **Task**
>
> Which of the following questions are most likely to be asked in a projective-type interview? How do you know?
>
> 1 Tell me about what's happening in this photo. Is this your family?
>
> 2 Do you study best when: (a) there is complete silence; (b) the radio is playing;

(c) when the television is on; (d) when the radio and television are both turned on?

3   How old are you, if you don't mind me asking?

4   So this is your favourite computer game. What makes it your favourite?

5   When did you first start using computers?

6   Why is it, do you think, that boys don't seem to like reading novels much?

7   Which of the following best describes your approach to teaching: (a) child-centred; (b) teacher-directed; (c) guided participation oriented; (d) community of learners-based?

8   Many people talk about a digital divide that's widening between the digital technology haves and the have nots. What are your thoughts on such talk about a digital divide?

There are some potential issues associated with using projective approaches for collecting spoken data. It is important to take care that the object selected does not invoke disturbing memories for respondents, or lead them to divulge information that should be kept secret and so on. Here again it behoves teacher researchers to know something about their respondents before selecting eliciting devices and commencing interviews. One also needs to be flexible about the length of the interview and patient in relation to the themes and content covered in the course of the interview when using eliciting devices. Very often one recalled memory or explained event leads to another and then another.

For further reading in this area we suggest:

- Bernard, R. (2000) *Social Research Methods: Qualitative and Quantitative Approaches*, pp. 264–76. Thousand Oaks, CA: Sage.
- Ewing, M. *et al.* (1998) The hard work of remembering: memory work as narrative research, in J. Addison and S. McGee (eds) *Feminist Empirical Research: Emerging Perspectives on Qualitative and Teacher Research*, pp. 112–26. Portsmouth, NH: Heinemann.
- Flick, U. (1998) *An Introduction to Qualitative Research*. Thousand Oaks, CA: Sage.
- Walford, G. (2001) *Doing Qualitative Educational Research: A Personal Guide to the Research Process*. London: Continuum.

Think-alouds

The development of think-aloud techniques was a direct response to the problem of how to get at people's thinking strategies and processes as they went about completing a task. Think-alouds are also known as the 'verbal protocol analysis method' (Branch

2000). They are used to generate spoken data by engaging speakers in completing a task, solving a problem or gathering information and asking them to *talk through* the thinking and decision-making processes they are consciously bringing to bear on the task, process or problem (Branch 2000). The task or problem might be something like solving a maths equation, planning a written narrative, playing a complicated computer game or conducting an internet search. Think-alouds differ from projective approaches in that they focus explicitly on *cognitive processes* rather than on eliciting information about an event, or participants' values, feelings and beliefs.

The method involves the study participant talking the researcher through a task. Researcher prompts are important during the process. For example: 'I'm really interested in how you go about solving long-division problems. I have a problem here that I'd like you to work on while you talk me through everything that is going on in your head while you work. I know it's tricky to work and talk at the same time, so we can go as slowly as you want to. I'm very interested in every single detail you can give me about how you solve this division sum so please take as much time as you need to talk me through what you do'.

When using think-alouds with children, it is a good idea to first model the process for them and then have them practise it. A teacher researcher might talk the student through the thought processes involved in solving an addition sum before having the student talk through the processes involved in solving a division sum. This introduction to the think-aloud process may require two or more sessions if the study participants are very young children. This kind of preparatory work helps reduce the risk of confusing the student's ability to do a think-aloud activity well with information concerning their thought processes during the activity.

Think-alouds can provide interesting insights into children's thinking processes in general, although the method is usually most effective when a child is talking through the decision making required by a reasonably familiar task. If the task is too unfamiliar, the child's energies will be directed towards the task rather than towards talking about how they are thinking about the task. If the task is too difficult it may generate feelings of frustration and even failure. Conversely, if the task is too familiar, study participants may overlook important thinking processes as they complete the task almost automatically.

A potential difficulty associated with think-alouds concerns their basis in the assumption that people are able to articulate their thought processes in relation to completing a task. Think-aloud data can never be complete nor give wholly accurate representations of a person's thought processes in completing a given task. Instead, the data stand as an articulation of a process at a given point in time within a particular research-generated context. Hence, the data are always provisional.

Another snag associated with think-alouds involves the risk of over-prompting students when they appear 'lost' or unsure of themselves while undertaking the task set for them. One approach to this is to prompt occasionally, but then watch what the child does and use this data as *observational* rather than spoken data. This can then be triangulated with any spoken data collected during the think-aloud.

Task

Which of the following tasks to complete or problems to solve are suited best to the think-aloud method of collecting spoken data? How do you know? What research questions might require these activities as part of their data collection design?

1 Conducting an internet search for information on medieval times.

2 Working in a group to build the tallest tower in the class out of paper strips and sticky tape.

3 Writing an essay on the history of corporal punishment in schools.

4 Drawing and labelling a diagram of a beetle.

5 Solving a division sum in maths that involves decimal places.

6 Making a sandwich from a range of possible ingredients.

7 Dividing a cake among seven friends.

8 Creating a clay pot.

9 Writing a lesson plan.

10 Reading a book that is written in the child's emerging second language.

11 Drawing up a playground supervision roster.

For further reading in this area we suggest:

- Afferbach, P. and Johnston, P. (1984) On the use of verbal reports in reading research, *Journal of Reading Behavior*, 16(4): 307–22.
- Branch, J. (2000) The trouble with think-alouds: generating data using concurrent verbal protocols, in A. Kublik (ed.) *CAIS 2000: Dimensions of a Global Information Science*. Proceedings of the 28th Annual Conference of the Canadian Association for Information Science, Alberta. www.slis.ualberta.ca/cais2000/branch.htm (accessed 13 October 2002).
- Ericsson, K. (1988) Concurrent verbal reports on text comprehension: a review, *Text*, 8(4): 295–325.
- Kucan, L. and Beck, I. (1997) Thinking aloud and reading comprehension research: inquiry, instruction, and social interaction, *Review of Educational Research*, 67(3): 271–99.

Collecting extant transcripts

Making use of transcripts of interviews or classroom talk that were produced by someone else in the course of a different study remains an under-utilized method of collecting spoken data. Collecting extant transcripts of spoken data reduces the time needed for data collection and increases the time available for data analysis. This approach is particularly well suited to teacher researchers who typically operate without research budgets and have strictly limited time available for collecting 'fresh' spoken data. Collecting extant transcripts saves time in all directions, since the actual interview (or other spoken language event) does not have to be arranged, recorded or transcribed.

Extant transcripts can be obtained from various sources. Local university researchers are often interested in having others conduct a different or related study using spoken data collected for another purpose. Intact transcripts can also be found as appendices in published research reports (e.g. Freebody *et al.* 1996). The internet is a growing source of extant transcripts directly relevant to education research. These include verbatim interviews with politicians and other persons of note, oral histories that are the product of one or more interviews with individuals or distinct groups of people (e.g. teenage mothers) and transcripts of student interactions (e.g. within a classroom, in online chatspaces). Email and online discussion board lists are also a rich source of spoken data that is written down (again, the lexical density of these texts generally places them towards the spoken end of the written-spoken language continuum), although these texts tend to blur public and private domains and care needs to be taken in obtaining appropriate permissions to use such data (e.g. contacting the webmaster or list owner, contacting individual message writers). For more on conducting ethical investigations of language use in cyberspace, see Hine (2000).

Speech transcripts relevant to education policies can often be accessed from government websites (e.g. www.fed.gov.au, www.whitehouse.gov). Alternatively, they might be located by using a general-purpose online search engine, employing search terms such as a specific politician's name along with items such as 'speech' and 'transcript'. Various online search engines specialize in locating transcripts from television and radio broadcasts (e.g. web.lexis-nexis.com/universe). A search phrase as simple as 'classroom AND transcripts' will locate numerous spoken data transcripts online. See, for example:

- Transcript of Edenvale/San Jose, California – Idalina/Sao Paulo, Brazil Chat, www.garlic.com/~lullah/brazilus2/dpedchat.html, www.garlic.com/~lullah/brazilus2/lastchat.htm.
- Discussing the Research: Live Chat With *Reading Online* Authors, www.readingonline.org/research/explorer/chat.html.

Video and audio data are also increasingly available on the internet. These, however, generally require high-speed internet connections powerful enough to pull down large digital files. A number of search engines can be configured to search specifically for video and audio data.

The most obvious restriction imposed by using extant transcripts is that research questions will need to fall within the parameters of the available data set. Even so, when a data set is rich it is usually possible to 'tweak' one's research purposes to make them cohere with the data while keeping the study in an area of maximum personal interest and commitment. The lack of contextual data available to teacher researchers using extant transcripts presents a potentially trickier challenge. Unless transcripts are very detailed the quality of voices and modes of delivery are lost. So are gestures and other relevant contextual aspects that are present when spoken data is collected in person. This need not impact significantly on the study, and will not when appropriate research purposes have been defined. It simply means that the researcher is confined to the 'words on the page' as the data set. But this is compatible with diverse research questions and approaches. Finally, teacher researchers using extant transcripts often cannot obtain information about the extent to which transcripts have been edited grammatically and semantically, or confirm that the data have been collected in an ethical manner. Such considerations have to be weighed against the utility of using extant spoken data.

In Chapter 11 we discuss the collection of observed data.

Collecting observed data in qualitative teacher research

Introduction: types of observed data

Carefully and systematically recorded observations of 'slices of everyday life' generate richly detailed accounts of practices rarely obtained through interviews alone, and can provide deep insights into social practices, events and processes. Collecting observed data emphasizes recording 'naturally occurring' or *contextualized* data about what is happening in social settings *as it happens*. Ethnographies, case studies and action research approaches make much use of observation data to construct richly descriptive and interpreted accounts of events, practices or cultures over time.

Observed data are pieces of information collected by systematically watching people going about their daily lives; watching events as they unfold. Collecting observed data is relatively self-explanatory. Researchers carefully watch events and interactions occurring within circumscribed settings and create detailed records of what they 'see'. Types of observed data include:

- written records of direct observations (e.g. fieldnotes made in the 'heat of the moment' as things are happening);
- indirect records of observations (e.g. *post facto* notes written from memory after the observation period has ended);
- videotapes of activity (e.g. a classroom lesson, children's play during lunch at school);

- observed data reported in other studies or collected by other people.

This chapter introduces four specific methods for collecting observed data:

- direct observation;
- artefact collection;
- physical trace collection;
- indirect or secondary observation.

Direct observation

Observation involves carefully planned, deliberate and systematic examinations of what is taking place, who is involved and when and where everything is happening. James Spradley (1980) makes a useful distinction between *descriptive*, *focused* and *selective* observation (see also Flick 1998: 142).

Descriptive observation

Observations tend to be quite general to begin with – concerned with describing the setting, the people present and the activities taking place. This often includes sketching 'maps' of the physical milieu. At the early stage the researcher is trying to take in the overall scene. It is important to establish a methodical approach to collecting observation data from the outset. Phil Carspecken (1996) describes getting around the dilemma of trying generally to observe an entire class of students by shifting his observational focus every five minutes. This gave him the best chance of observing as many people as possible as they took part in an intervention programme he was studying.

Using observation prompts (e.g. questions) provides another approach to observing methodically. Spradley (1980: 82–3) offers a set of categories from which question prompts can be developed to guide observations. These include: space, object, act, activity, event, time, actor, goal and feeling. The questions Spradley identifies that are especially useful for descriptive observation data collection include:

- Can you describe in detail all the places?
- Can you describe in detail all the objects?
- Can you describe in detail all the activities?
- Can you describe in detail all of the actors?

Focused observation

Researchers begin making focused observations once they start to reflect on and analyse observation data they have collected already, and patterns or loci of interest begin to emerge. This phase concentrates on the ways things are *related*, *structured* or *organized* within a given context. Spradley (1980: 82–3) suggests the following prompts for making focused observations:

- Where are objects located?
- What are all the places activities occur?
- Where do actors place themselves?
- What are all the ways activities incorporate objects?
- What are all the ways time affects objects?

Selective observation

Drawing on successive descriptive and focused observations researchers can begin purposefully focusing during their observations on particular aspects that capture their attention. They begin following up hunches and testing ideas or hypotheses that occur to them in an attempt to get at the significance of certain events or practices. Jill Cole's (2003) multiple case study of what motivated certain students in her Grade 1 classroom to read illustrates this process nicely.

Cole's research involved detailed observations of four students. One was a young girl called Brooke. Cole focused on the students' reading practices and their interactions with others around texts. Initially, Cole assumed Brooke had little interest in reading because she regularly appeared to be disengaged from much of what was taking place during whole-class picture book reading events. After extended observations, however, Cole realized that Brooke was, in fact, much more engaged with books and reading than she had initially thought. Descriptive observations suggested that Brooke – who chose to sit at the back of the group during whole-class reading sessions – was something of a daydreamer in class. Cole reports that in one session Brooke's 'expression was blank, and she spent a lot to time looking around the room instead of concentrating on the book' (2003: 334). Focused observations of Brooke during whole-class reading sessions and independent reading times revealed, however, that she was in fact an avid reader who took great interest in stories as well as in the look and feel of books.

Cole's observations drew her attention to Brooke's practice of keeping a pile of picture books from the classroom library in her desk. Brooke treated these carefully and kept track of when another student asked to borrow them. Cole also noticed that even when she asked Brooke to return the books in her desk to the shelves for others to read she quickly accumulated a new pile. Selective observations based on these initial findings led Cole to observe that even though Brooke enjoyed working collaboratively with her classmates, she preferred to read on her own to better lose herself in the book. This in turn led Cole to observe that Brooke worked best when given additional time to complete a writing task. When accommodations for extra time were made for Brooke, it usually resulted in work that was more extensive and detailed than that of her classmates (Cole 2003: 334).

Types of observation

Researchers can select from a range of observation *types* those most appropriate for their particular research purposes. The main types of observations fall along two continua (see Figure 11.1). Observations can be more or less structured or unstructured and more or less non-participant or participant.

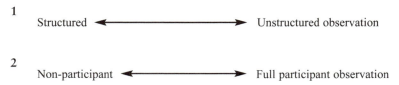

1   Structured ←————————→ Unstructured observation

2   Non-participant ←————————→ Full participant observation

Figure 11.1   Continua of observation

Structured observations
Observations can be planned tightly beforehand and organized into a detailed observation schedule: a checklist of the actions the teacher researcher expects to observe in the setting. Structured (or 'direct systematic') observation is mostly used in quantitative research, but can also be used as a component of 'mixed methods' and (predominantly) qualitative projects.

In a recent study of teacher-student interactions within the classroom researchers tailored an observation schedule that had been developed for a previous study to suit the current research project (Myhill 2002). The research team wanted to document verbal and non-verbal responses, and decided to focus on four children in each of six classrooms selected for the project. Accordingly, the schedule provided space for recording observations of four students per lesson (see Figure 11.2). Such structured approaches to observation can enhance possibilities for teacher researchers to make relatively straightforward and defensible comparisons across data sets constructed from different lessons or even from different classes altogether.

Unstructured observations
Unstructured observation involves observing a context, event or set of activities with few or no specific or tightly defined data collection goals in mind. It is the idea of going into a setting open to 'going with the flow' and trying as much as possible just to 'see' what is there to be seen.

Researchers who want to use maximally unstructured/minimally structured observations will very likely need to conduct observations over extended periods of time to be able to derive defensible patterns and explanations from the data. Because of constraints on the time they have to make observations, teacher researchers will usually find that at least some structuring will be necessary in order to obtain acceptable returns on the time and energies spent observing. The following kinds of questions can be useful prompts for making data collection decisions when preparing to conduct observations:

• Where do I watch? Why?
• Whom do I watch? Why?
• What do I watch? Why?

CLASSROOM OBSERVATION SCHEDULE

Teacher-led whole-class work

School:

Year group:

Lesson:

	High achieving girl	High achieving boy	Low achieving girl	Low achieving boy
Puts hand up				
Answers question after invitation				
Joins in collective response				
Asks question				
CHILD INITIATES TALK WITH TEACHER				
Task related				
Task unrelated				
SHOUTS OUT				
Task related				
Task unrelated				

OFF-TASK BEHAVIOURS *Record every 5 minutes*	5	10	15	20	5	10	15	20	5	10	15	20	5	10	15	20
Fiddling and fidgeting																
Not looking to the front																
Talking to neighbour																
Off Task Rate 1–4																

Off task:
1 = rarely off task
2 = occasionally off task
3 = repeatedly off task
4 = off task throughout

Note:
- 'Initiates talk' with teacher and 'shouts out' might not always be easy to distinguish. As a rule of thumb one is an attempt at conversation, the other attention seeking behaviour.
- As both 'initiates talk' and 'shouts out' could be an example of 'asks question' record as examples of both

Figure 11.2 An example of a structured observation schedule (Myhill 2002: 51)

- How long do I watch? Why?
- Over what time period (days, weeks, months etc.) do I watch? Why?

Alternatively, Spradley's (1980) categories and questions can provide a useful guide for collecting relevant and good-quality observation data in ways that are not highly structured. Researchers can select from among the prompts when planning their observations and/or while observing.

We personally find it helpful to write down in advance what we think needs to be 'looked at' during an observation session in a social context like a classroom, playground, meeting etc. This is partly because observing is exhausting. It requires high levels of sustained concentration, and fatigue can easily interfere with remembering what the *point* of the observation is. Preparing written guidelines in advance is also helpful since observing people and practices involves processing enormous amounts of information. It is easy to lose the observation 'plot' without the support of an observation prompt question (or set of questions). There is a risk of becoming so engrossed in what is taking place that one forgets one's study objectives, and begins collecting data better suited to different research objectives altogether.

To help manage the sheer amount of data collected and to help make subsequent data collection and analysis manageable, researchers using some form of unstructured observation data collection aim to be systematic in their observations. This can be done in different ways. For example, one might focus on one part of a classroom for five to ten minutes, before shifting attention to another part (see e.g. Carspecken 1996). Alternatively, one might focus on a particular student and those with whom he or she interacts (see e.g. Hicks 2002; Cole 2003). This can be circumscribed even further by specifying locations in which observations will take place, such as in the classroom (see e.g. Tancock 1997), or in the classroom and in the student's home (see e.g. Pahl 2002). A third means involves focusing on different groups of students during group work, one after the other (see e.g. Lankshear and Knobel 1997c). Finally, one might make the teacher the focus of observation (see Freebody *et al.* 1996).

It is necessary to observe 'a bottom line' when deciding how structured or unstructured an approach to take for collecting observation data. To be able to speak confidently about their observations, researchers must ensure they have sufficient data, and that they can cross-reference these with other sources. As a rule of thumb, once data begin to become overly repetitive or redundant, one has collected enough (see Fetterman 1998). Observation data gain in explanatory strength when they can be cross-referenced to interview data, artefacts and other kinds of data.

Non-participant observations

When teacher researchers are non-participant observers they remove themselves as much as possible from the context they are observing. This approach is often associated with clinical research (e.g. children are observed playing with blocks from behind a one-way mirror wall) and with using structured observation schedules. Non-participant observation can also be possible within everyday contexts, provided researchers attempt to become as invisible as possible and do not interact in any way –

directly or indirectly – with anyone around them. This is, of course, extremely difficult to achieve, especially when researchers are writing down their observations and their very presence within any context affects or contributes to the dynamics of that context.

Full participant observations
In full participant observation researchers engage directly and completely with the context being observed. At its extreme, full participation requires researchers to become as much as possible 'insiders' to the 'scene' being investigated. Full participant observers thoroughly understand and are able to participate in a practice as though they have been doing it for a long time.

Teacher researchers have an advantage when it comes to full participant research since, by default, they are full participants in the everyday life and practices of their own classrooms. They can rightly claim an insider perspective on what takes place. This lends weight to their data interpretations. The down side here, however, is that insider status can blinker a researcher's observations. This risk can be addressed by carefully documenting, reading through and reflecting upon observations, drawing on multiple sources of data and discussing the ongoing project and preliminary findings with other teachers and teacher researchers.

Types of participant observation include:

- complete but anonymous immersion in a social group (which poses serious ethical issues);
- full and explicit participation (i.e. participants know the researcher is studying them); and
- peripheral participation (which involves a fluid mix of full participation, partial participation and non-participation, depending on the events or activities being observed).

Researchers must tell people when they are being observed and studied, to ensure no deception is involved in the research (Lankshear and Knobel 1997c).

Participant observation conducted by teachers in other teachers' classrooms can be challenging for the teacher researcher as well as unnerving or unsettling for the teacher being observed. Things for the teacher researcher to keep in mind when observing others include:

- Being punctual and organized.
- Being absolutely discrete about what takes place in the classroom. This is not data to be discussed with other teachers at the school or with others who know the observed teacher.
- Working hard to put the other teacher at ease. The role of the teacher researcher is really that of a learner, one who asks: 'What can I learn about X by observing this teacher?'
- Avoiding interjections in lessons (unless the teacher actively includes you in the lesson).
- Paying attention to facial expressions – look interested and engaged at all times.

- Clarifying one's observer role with the teacher prior to observation (e.g. will you be introduced to the students and interact with them during small-group work, or will you simply sit at the back of the room and be ignored by the teacher?).
- Avoiding any criticisms of lessons, even when asked for feedback by the observed teacher.
- Making fieldnotes readily and openly available to the teacher to read whenever asked (this may put limits on what can be written about, but ethical treatment of research participants outweighs such concerns).

Task

Conducting useful and detailed observations requires practice and developing an eye for detail. Russell Bernard (2000: 331) suggests a number of specific exercises for developing observation skills, such as the following: 'Walk past a store window at a normal pace. When you get beyond it and can't see it any longer, write down all the things that were in the window. Go back and check. Do it again with another window. You'll notice an improvement in your ability to notice little things almost immediately'.

Try this exercise for yourself, and then respond to the following questions:

- Why is it important to be able to notice or recall details when conducting observations?

- Why might developing one's powers of recall be important for collecting useful observation data?

Deciding on an approach for making observations

The two continua (see Figure 11.1) yield four broad types of approach to observing. Researchers can select from these types and modify them according to degree of participation or structure required by their research question and in accordance with personal preferences (within the bounds of research coherence).

Non-participation with structured observation
Here, researchers carefully pre-plan what is to be observed and remove themselves as much as possible from any direct engagement within the observed context. For example, a teacher researcher might want to document the relative time spent on task and off task in science lessons within a particular group of students with learning difficulties in comparison to a group of students who have advanced science understanding. To this end, prior to data collection, the researcher develops a checklist of behaviours signalling forms of activity deemed to be on task and off task respectively. The researcher then uses two video cameras to record each group working collaboratively during science lessons throughout a two-week period. The videos are each viewed repeatedly and a checklist is completed per student per lesson. Entries in the

checklist are quantified as percentages and comparisons made across the groups and across activity types.

Within this broad option, a researcher might take up different positions within the 'non-participant' and 'structured' spectrums as appropriate. They might, for example, use semi-structured observations that blend pre-set checklists of behaviour to be observed with more open-ended observations and fieldnotes. Conversely, they might use multiple structured observation schedules and vary their degree of participation within the learning contexts. This could involve using a broad-based checklist during whole-class sessions and a finer-grained checklist of student behaviour that focuses on a small group of students during periods in which the researcher applies some intervention (e.g. completing a science experiment).

Non-participation with unstructured observation

Researchers may choose to observe a context or event in a completely unstructured way that does not involve them as direct participants in what unfolds before them. The most 'pure' form of this approach removes the teacher researcher altogether from the context being observed. This can be done by equipping study participants with visual recording devices (e.g. video cameras, disposable cameras) and the researcher instructing them to record certain elements in their everyday, out of school or in-school lives (Bernard 2000; Pahl 2002).

A variant within this broad option involves the researcher being present but not directly involved. For example, a teacher researcher might be interested in documenting student social interactions during lunch breaks. They could sit in a section of the playground that offers an optimal vantage point for observing a maximum number of students interacting during the break. They write down as much as possible of all they observe during the lunch hour.

Here again teacher researchers can vary the degrees to which they conduct themselves as non-participant observers and the degree to which their observations are unstructured. For example, a researcher may be investigating and documenting popular cultural dimensions of young adolescents' interactions. Their observations could include sitting with a group of female students while they have lunch, chatting with them about current favourite television shows, films, songs and bands. When lunch finishes the researcher's role might shift to one of non-participant observation, where they sit back and watch the girls play basketball against the boys.

Full-participation with unstructured observation

Conducting unstructured observations while fully participating within an event or activity generally requires a great deal of time before useful patterns pertaining to a study's guiding question begin to emerge. The researcher will typically spend much time engaged in general or descriptive observations before honing the study direction by means of more focused observations.

Alternatively, teacher researchers might find that a short period of full participation and unstructured observation provides a useful 'pilot study' or 'preparation' for a more focused approach to conducting observations in their own classrooms. This period of general observation may help them to notice the unexpected – like Brooke (see p. 221) who appeared disinterested during literacy lessons but turned out to be hoarding books in her desk.

Full participation with structured observation
Full participation and fully structured observation checklists are largely mutually exclusive. Commitment to contextualized accounts reflected in the decision to participate fully in some event or process conflicts with continuously consulting and filling in a checklist of expected behaviours. Nonetheless, researchers can modify the reach of their participation and the degree of structured observation they conduct in ways that can enhance data collection by offering important support structures to the observation process. For example, a teacher researcher may choose to participate fully in an event, but come prepared with a series of prompt questions to guide their observations during the event.

For further reading on direct observation approaches we suggest:

- Adler, P. and Adler, P. (1998) Observational techniques, in N. Denzin and Y. Lincoln (eds) *Collecting and Interpreting Qualitative Materials*, pp. 79–109. Thousand Oaks, CA: Sage.
- Schensul, S., Schensul, J. and LeCompte, M. (1999) *Essential Ethnographic Methods: Observations, Interviews, and Questionnaires (Ethnographer's Toolkit*, Vol. 2). Walnut Creek, CA: Altamira Press.
- Spradley, J. (1980) *Participant Observation*. Fort Worth, TX: Holt, Rhinehart & Winston.

Data collection tools

The four main ways of recording observations are:

- observation schedules (see Figure 11.2);
- headnotes;
- *post facto* notes;
- fieldnotes.

Headnotes
These are mental notes researchers make while systematically watching an event within a context where writing observation notes in the heat of the moment is impossible. Headnotes are stored in the researcher's memory until they can be written down in detail (as *post facto* notes). It is impossible to capture all the observed details stored in memory. Writing headnotes down at the earliest opportunity is crucial for producing observation records. Subsequent observations can interfere with memories of early observations and details can quickly get forgotten.

Post facto notes

These are written down headnotes – records of observations written as soon as possible after an observed event that was impossible to record in writing while in process. They are analogous to cases where journalists observe an event taking place, make rough notes where possible, and return to the office as soon as they can to write up the event. Some researchers refer to *post facto* notes as *journalistic notes* (Carspecken 1996). The more closely in time to the observed event that headnotes can be used to produce *post facto* notes, the more detailed the *post facto* notes are likely to be.

Fieldnotes

Fieldnotes comprise finely detailed written accounts of what was observed. James Clifford (in LeCompte and Schensul 1999: 3) describes good fieldnotes as having a 'you are there' quality. They are mainly written in the heat of the moment as events unfold before the researcher's eyes and tend to be the primary data collection tool during observation. We personally make a practice of keeping detailed fieldnotes even when we are video- or audio-recording events, in case of equipment malfunction.

Key components of fieldnotes include:

- Writing legibly: sometimes the teacher researcher may not revisit their fieldnotes for some weeks. They need to ensure that they are able to read them even after a lapse of time since the notes were first produced.
- Regular records of time that don't just mark the start and end of lessons, for example, but that act as a guide to the length of observed activity or behaviour. We make it a practice to mark down the time every ten minutes (or less) when writing fieldnotes.
- Descriptions of what is taking place as well as direct quotations of what is said wherever possible.
- Writing notes in such a way that should study participants ask to see them there would be no hesitation in handing the notes over to them.
- Using codes (e.g. pseudonyms, alphabet letters) for people's names, so that if the fieldnote book gets lost or misplaced it will not reveal the identity of study participants if the notes are read by others. We generally use the first letter of key participants' names to identify them in our notes.
- Developing a shorthand language that will help speed up the often laborious task of writing fieldnotes. For example, 'teacher' could become 'Ter', 'students' could become 'Sts'. In our own fieldnotes of classroom observations we use numbers and gender codes to distinguish different students, especially during the initial days of observation when we do not yet know students' names.
- Drawing maps and classroom layout diagrams to show where action is taking place during an observed lesson or event. For example, one might pay particular attention to student desk layout and whether or not this layout changes in different lessons, or whether students move to different desks for different lessons and so on.

Many researchers recommend writing fieldnotes up in more detail after observations have been completed (LeCompte and Schensul 1999). We certainly find that it helps to have fieldnotes as word-processed files when it comes to analysing data (e.g. fieldnotes can be printed and physically cut up during categorical analysis) and writing the final report.

Fieldnote practicalities

Relatively small spiral-bound notebooks with heavy-duty covers are good for recording notes. They can be turned back upon themselves without the spine breaking, and one can write notes comfortably with the notebook balanced on a knee or while standing upright. We strongly recommend not using letter-writing pads and a clipboard. Their obtrusiveness reminds study participants they are being observed and clipboards often intimidate.

The sheer intensity of writing fieldnotes calls for pens that minimize stress on the fingers. Medium- or fine-tip rollerball ink pens glide easily over the page, although the ink mark made can penetrate to the other side of the page. We prefer to write on only the right-hand page, and use black pens since they produce better photocopies. We use colour pens to mark where we have collected artefacts, supplemented observations with audio-taping or video-taping and so on. Black text makes these codes easy to see. We carry two backup pens and a backup fieldnote book (these fill surprisingly quickly).

Fieldnote layout

There are no hard and fast rules for laying out fieldnotes. Some researchers prefer to write in an almost stream of consciousness manner. Others divide each page up into distinct columns or sections that structure data collection and fieldnote recoding in a particular way (e.g. columns in which to record the time, teacher activities, student activities, location, resources used). A useful way to organize fieldnotes is to divide the page into two columns. One column is devoted to recording fieldnotes in the heat of the moment. The other is used for making methodological, theoretical and analytical annotations, and anecdotal or personal comments written during reflective moments – at the time or later (see Emerson *et al.* 1995; Schensul *et al.* 1999; Hoggart *et al.* 2002). Figure 11.3 provides an example.

The language of fieldnotes

It is important to be non-judgemental when writing fieldnotes. Most researchers who regularly conduct field-based observation recommend focusing on *describing* behaviour, rather than 'attributing meaning to it' (Hoggart *et al.* 2002: 280). For example:

> rather than describing [someone] as 'poor and dishevelled', it would be more accurate to describe the person as 'dressed in blue jeans with shredded edges, an army jacket with dirty spots on the back and a torn collar, no belt, a white T-shirt with red smudges around the collar, and shoes with ripped edges, carrying a bulging backpack and a paper bag full of newspapers'.
>
> (Schensul *et al.* 1999: 115)

The emphasis here is on recording 'evidence'. If inferences are made later during data analysis the researcher will have sufficient evidence to back up claims that that someone did indeed appear to be 'poor and dishevelled'. (Of course, it may transpire after further observations that the person observed was on their way home from a

Fieldnotes Recorded on Tuesday, 11 October 1994. 10:21 a.m. at school. Day 2 of observations.	
Observations	Theoretical/analytical notes
10:21 a.m.	
Ter and N talk about a report. Ter asks what's in a report.	Ter's attempt at metalanguage.
N: I don't know.	Common interaction pattern.
Ter: Don't you remember?	
N drifts off to talk to s'one, then drifts back to Ter N (to Ter): I spent 2 hours on my project & I only got this much done ((indicates with fingers)). It took <u>so</u> long.	Quantifying schoolwork again.
S appears beside teacher and the 3 discuss N's handwriting.	
N asks to do it on the computer and <u>then</u> handwrite it. Ter: No. S: But you must use the technology if it's there. They debate merits of handwriting and technology.	cf. computing at home with logic of 'most direct path'. Peer support and techno knowledge.
	Tensions between traditional and techno literacies; cf. Green and Bigum 1993; Papert 1993.

Figure 11.3 Sample fieldnote page layout

fancy dress party or a movie set and was far from being poor and dishevelled in their everyday life.)

Researchers often emphasize using verbs when writing fieldnotes and minimizing the use of adjectives. This way fieldnotes will follow the action, rather than get caught up in describing surface features. Schensul *et al.* (1999: 115) advocate describing behaviours *behaviourally* rather than trying to attribute motivations to them: 'Fidgeting with a pencil and keeping eyes downcast in a meeting may mean several things: boredom, disagreement, lack of understanding, angry, frustration, or preoccupation with another matter'.

Hence, rather than writing 'X was absorbed', the researcher will describe the specific actions taking place. It is almost impossible to attribute states of being to others during observations where we only have external indicators to go on. Any interpretations of states of being should be couched in a cautious manner, like 'X appeared to be listening avidly', and followed up with a description of behaviours supporting this interpretation (e.g. 'The student's eyes followed the teacher's every move as he filled the test tubes with water. The student did not speak to classmates when they spoke to him during the teacher's demonstration'.).

Word choices impact directly on observation records. It is impossible to be completely objective or neutral when recording observations. Researchers, however, still need to pay attention to the effects their word choices have on representations of people, places and events, and to the personal values laid bare by their word choices. For example, there is an important semantic and representational difference between the words 'giggled' and 'laughed', and between 'protested' and 'muttered'.

Task

Compare the following accounts of an event:

Account 1
A student complains grumpily about the heat, and Ms Bryant comments brusquely that it's hot every summer in Queensland. Jacques comments to no one in particular, 'Get an airconditioner!'

Emily proudly shows me a project book with neatly glued-in newspaper clippings inside it. She tells me that they have to collect seven clippings by the end of the term. Jacques looks shocked and I ask him how many he has collected. He draws '0' in the air with his finger. He tells me he was going to start last week, but will probably get to it next week.

Ms Bryant finally comes to the desk and helps Emily and Jason with some of their questions. Jacques hesitatingly explains to her that he can't think of things about area. Ms Bryant looks exasperated and reminds him of his maths lesson (earlier that day) and Jason quickly reminds him about the formulas they covered in that lesson.

Account 2
Someone complains about the heat, and Ms B. explains that it's hot every summer in Queensland. Jacques calls out, 'Get an airconditioner!'

Emily shows me a project book with glued-in newspaper clippings inside it. She tells me they have to collect seven clippings by the end of the term. Jacques opens his eyes wide in an exaggerated but comical 'shocked' expression and I ask him how many he has collected. He laughs and draws '0' in the air with his finger. He tells me he was going to start last week, but will probably get to it next week (he laughs again).

Ms B. comes to the desk and helps Emily and Jason. Jacques tells her that he can't think of things about area. Ms B. reminds him of his maths lesson (earlier that day) and Jason reminds him about the formulas they covered in that lesson.

- In what ways does each account represent Ms Bryant and Jacques differently? Do these differences matter?

- What would you need to know in order to judge which account is most accurate? Why?

- Which account is most likely to be of most use to the teacher researcher? Why?

Some further reading on fieldnote records we would recommend:

- Clifford, J. and Marcus, G. (eds) (1986) *Writing Culture: The Poetics and Politics of Ethnography.* Berkeley, CA: University of California Press.
- Emerson, R., Fretz, R. and Shaw, L. (1995) *Writing Ethnographic Fieldnotes.* Chicago: University of Chicago Press.
- Fetterman, D. (1998) *Ethnography: Step by Step,* 2nd edn. Newbury Park, CA: Sage.
- LeCompte, M. and Schensul, J. (1999) *Analyzing and Interpreting Ethnographic Data (Ethnographer's Toolkit,* Vol. 5). Walnut Creek, CA: Altamira Press.
- Spradley, J. (1980) *Participant Observation.* Fort Worth, TX: Holt, Rhinehart & Winston.

Conducting observations online

A recent development in qualitative research involves collecting observational data in publicly accessible online spaces, such as chat rooms, online games 'worlds' and other kinds of virtual worlds built by members of websites for communicating with others. While almost no reported teacher research to date has involved such sites, it is worth noting some of their advantages for research generally.

While observation-based online research is still an emerging methodological field of study, it can be characterized as follows:

- In online spaces, the 'field' of fieldnotes becomes distributed and nebulous (see Hoggart *et al.* 2002: 292). In response to this quality, online observation is defined by the reach and type of (inter)relations and relationships to be had within an online space, rather than by boundaries set in place by physical sites and locations (Leander and McKim 2003); or, as Christine Hine puts it, online observations of necessity draw on 'connection rather than location' in defining their object or focus (2000: 10).
- Much of the observation that takes place online is text-based. Characters describe their actions, rather than produce visible gestures and behaviours. This 'textuality' is beginning to change, however, with the increasing availability of three-dimensional, image-based virtual worlds.
- In observation studies conducted entirely within one or more virtual worlds, participants in online worlds need to be taken at face value in terms of the identity they choose to present within that space. Identity play and experimentation is a common occurrence online, but without interviewing and observing participants offline as they participate online, it is next to impossible to make claims about who they are in their everyday lives.

Key issues associated with conducting online observations include:

- Dealing with the often transitory or impermanent nature of online spaces. Researchers should pay attention to the 'age' and 'stability' of an online space and the likelihood of it staying online until data collection has been completed.

- Negotiating the ease with which it is possible to participate fully within an online virtual world without alerting others to one's research status and intentions (Leander and McKim 2003).
- Becoming a technologically proficient operator within a virtual world. In their discussion of online ethnographic methodology, Kevin Leander and Kelly McKim (2003) remind us that whereas in traditional settings the work of ethnographers might be supported by a lack of cultural knowledge, a knowledge of internet practices is very important for obtaining and maintaining access to online settings. Presenting oneself online as technologically proficient enhances one's credibility as a participant in the world being studied. This in turn can contribute to one's credibility as an 'authentic' and capable researcher.

For further reading in this area we suggest:

- Hine, C. (2000) *Virtual Ethnography*. London: Sage.
- Jones, S. (ed.) (1999) *Doing Internet Research: Critical Issues and Methods for Examining the Net*. Thousand Oaks, CA: Sage.
- Leander, K. and McKim, K. (2003) Tracing the everyday 'sitings' of adolescents on the internet: a strategic adaptation of ethnography across online and offline spaces, *Education, Communication and Information*, 3(2): 211–40.

Other tools for enhancing the observation record

In many studies it can be useful to augment fieldnote recordings of what was observed with other kinds of recordings, such as photography, audio recording and video recording (Hoggart *et al.* 2002: 284–5). Audio and video records can help corroborate fieldnotes as well as provide opportunities to 'revisit' scenes and 'find' more in them. Sometimes a series of single photographs can be 'conceived and constructed as records' (Prosser and Schwartz 1998: 125). Of course, photos and dynamic recordings do not speak for themselves. They are always mediated by theory – whether prior to making the recording or subsequently, when interpreting the data and/or analysing it: '[T]heory tells you when an image contains information of value, when it communicates something worth communicating. It furnishes the criteria by which worthwhile data and statements can be separated from those that contain nothing of value, that do not increase our knowledge' (Harper 1992 cited in Prosser and Schwartz 1998: 126).

Peter Loizos (2000: 106), a cinematographer turned visual anthropologist, provides a list of useful questions teacher researchers can use to help decide whether or not to supplement fieldnote records of observations with photographs or videotapes:

1 Will the use of a visual record make an important improvement to my research output?
2 Do I have the recording skills (sound and picture) to carry out the recording myself?
3 Have I calculated the time needed to process the resulting body of visual data?

4   Have I designed a friendly logging/cataloguing system for managing, storing, retrieving and analysing the visual data?
5   Have I adequately explained my intentions to the people who will be filmed, and I have their written consent? Will I be deemed intrusive? Or a 'management snooper'?
6   Will I have the copyright freedom to publish the resultant material? Have I obtained written permission from the owners of personal photographs, or videos?
7   Do I need to further inform myself about the issue of image ownership and publication?

Researchers must know what a school's (or education department's) policy is on photographing or videoing children, as well as possible cultural or religious issues associated with capturing people on film. Many schools or departments of education advise teachers not to photograph or video students in a way that shows their faces, unless the resulting image is to stay within the school. Some groups do not permit their children to be photographed or filmed. Caregivers must be well-informed about intentions to photograph or film their children.

For further reading in this area we suggest:

- Bernard, R. (2000) *Social Research Methods: Qualitative and Quantitative Approaches*. Thousand Oaks, CA: Sage.
- Schensul, S., Schensul, J. and LeCompte, M. (1999) *Essential Ethnographic Methods: Observations, Interviews, and Questionnaires* (*Ethnographer's Toolkit*, Vol. 2). Walnut Creek, CA: Altamira Press.

Artefact collection

Artefacts are physical 'props' people use to get things done within the contexts of their daily lives. Within contexts investigated in teacher research, artefacts include samples of student-produced texts, student artwork, notes passed surreptitiously in class, letters teachers send home to parents, students' homework diaries, lists of items in the school library or staffroom, school policy documents, school report cards and the like. Collecting artefacts adds important contextual details to the data available for analysis.

Artefacts like those listed above may arise 'naturally' from a particular context. They can also be purposefully generated within the research process as when, for example, a researcher asks a student to draw a map of the school to gain insight into what might be most salient on the campus to the child. Artefacts are concrete evidence and can alert researchers to useful avenues of investigation and provide additional insights into participants' everyday lives. Artefacts like texts, graphics and music can add useful contextual dimensions to other forms of collected data (Myers 1992; Finders 1997).

Task

Examine the following table summarising a study design.

Research purpose	Research question	Data to collect	Data collection methods	Data analysis approach and sources
To identify and analyse the ways in which 'literacy failure' is constructed in classrooms	Over a 2-week period, what are the in-school and out of school literacy purposes and practices of one male, a reluctant reader and writer?	Data concerning what kinds of literate activities the participant engages in and the kinds of literate knowledge he displays	Observations of activities within and outside school settings. Artefact collection Interviews with participant, teacher, participants' parents	*Pattern matching*: Fetterman (1998); Patton (2002)

From the following list, select the four artefacts you think will be of *most* use in helping the teacher researcher respond to the research question:

1 School policy on discipline.
2 Participant's maths exercise book.
3 Narrative texts written by the participant at school.
4 School's literacy curriculum document for that year.
5 Texts produced by the participant at home using the family computer.
6 Teacher's literacy curriculum for the class for that year.
7 List of books available in the school library.
8 List of books on the shelves in the participant's bedroom.
9 Information texts produced by the student during class time.
10 Notes passed by the student during lessons.
11 Teacher's lesson timetable.
12 The state's literacy education syllabus document(s).
13 Copies of song lyrics from the internet that the student has printed out at home.

- How did you go about deciding which artefacts would be of most use to this teacher researcher? Why?
- What does this tell you in relation to designing your own study?

As with all other data, the role and significance of an artefact are always a matter of researcher interpretation. A researcher committed to psychological theories of reading that focus on individual text processing within formal literacy lessons may not regard a note passed in class as a text-processing artefact. Conversely, a researcher committed to a sociocultural model that associates literacy with social interactions might regard such a note as a *key* artefact for a study of literacy practices of students identified by their teachers as resistant readers and writers.

To be most effective, artefact collection must be systematic and carefully planned prior to beginning data collection. This doesn't mean researchers will not serendipitously identify artefacts that could never have been planned for prior to the study. It means they must be tuned into artefact collection from the outset, and that artefact collection must be carefully managed. It is important to resist any urge to try and collect every single thing study participants are observed using. When deciding which artefacts to collect, researchers need to keep their research questions to the fore and continually remind themselves of their study focus and purposes.

Researchers can use various strategies to maximize the usefulness of the artefacts they collect. With reasonably long data collection periods one can use a sampling approach and, for instance, collect exemplars of student work at fixed points (e.g. at the start, quarter-way, halfway, three quarter-way and end point of the data collection period). Alternatively, teacher researchers may also choose to systematize artefact collection by confining it to a single facet of the study. For example:

- one subject area;
- one grade level within a school;
- a particular group of students or teachers;
- a particular area (the school library, the classroom science centre, the reception desk area).

Artefacts are typically collected along with other types of data. It is important to organize them carefully in ways that (a) preserve a clear sense of the context in which the artefacts were collected, and (b) make for easy and rapid retrieval of artefacts from storage during data analysis.

Linking artefacts with other collected data

One way to maintain a sense of the context in which each artefact was collected is to use one's fieldnote book as a general register, clearly marking in the notes when an artefact is collected and to what event or activity it pertains. We use a series of codes in our research to record this information in a way that can be readily cross-referenced. Figure 11.4 contains fieldnote excerpts from one day of observing a participant named Nicholas. The codes pertaining to artefacts appear in the 'time' column and were inserted at the end of each day, once copies of selected artefacts had been made. The code is also written onto the corresponding artefact, or onto the container in which the artefact is stored.

'A' signifies 'artefact' (we write in other codes, such as 'T' or 'V' to signal observations that have also been audio-taped or video-taped respectively). 'N' signifies our

Monday 10 November, 1994 **(Day 1 of observations)**

10:55   **Literacy lesson:**
       Ter instructs Sts to organize themselves into 3 groups and begin their respective activities: library lesson, grammar textbook exercises & basal reader work.
AN.1 2 girls sit at the computer.
       N takes out textbook and shares with Rajiv.
       Ter explains grammar task.
AN.2 N throws a piece of rubber at Stuart, scores a hit and makes an 'impact' noise.
       N asks Ter if he can write in pen in the textbook. Ter replies that it must be done in pencil. Two boys move to lend N a pencil and are reprimanded. N calls out to Ter asking for clarification of which exercises are to be completed.
       ((Notes for the day continue on))

Key: Ter = teacher St(s) = student(s) A = artefact N = Nicholas

Figure 11.4   Organizing fieldnotes as an artefact registry

target study participant Nicholas. The number records the order in which each artefact was collected:

- **AN.1** corresponds to photocopied pages from Nicholas' grammar activity exercise book.
- **AN.2** corresponds to pieces of the eraser Nicholas and the other boys had torn off and thrown at each other during class.

Systematic artefact storage

One can store and keep track of artefacts during data collection in numerous ways. Some researchers place all artefacts in a single box for subsequent analysis. Others file them in hanging files. Our preferred method is to place artefacts in individual transparent plastic sheet protectors and store them in ring binders. In multiple case study projects each case can be assigned an appropriately labelled folder and artefacts stored chronologically, assisting fast and easy retrieval. Each folder has a 'contents' page indexing artefact codes and briefly describing the artefact itself. Retrieving artefacts then becomes a straightforward and streamlined process.

For further reading on artefacts in research, see:

- Lancy, D. (2001) *Studying Children and Schools: Qualitative Research Traditions,* pp. 14–15. Prospect Heights, IL: Waveland Press.

- LeCompte, M. and Preissle, J. (1993) *Ethnography and Qualitative Design in Educational Research*, 2nd edn. San Diego, CA: Academic Press.

Physical trace data collection

Observations can be supplemented with various 'unobtrusive' or 'non-interactive' data collection methods. Recording physical traces (Fetterman 1998: 57) is an especially useful option for teacher research. Physical traces – or the 'material culture' of a group (Rossman and Rallis 1998) – are 'tangibles' left behind from the things people do and the ways they do them. They indicate the ways a space or place is occupied or used.

Within educational research, collecting material pieces of evidence often provides more detailed information about patterns of behaviour or activity than do interviews with participants. Consider, for example, a teacher researcher interested in child nutrition at school. They are much more likely to get a detailed and data-rich account of what children do and do not eat at school by examining playground garbage bins over a two-week period than by interviewing children (see Bernard 2000: 406).

Collectively, physical trace data can build a reliable empirical account of people's habits and practices. They include things like:

- Traffic patterns – vehicular as well as pedestrian (e.g. worn stair treads in a particular area suggesting heavy, long-term use of that area; deep skateboard scratch marks on stair banisters or railings suggesting that groups of young people frequent that place).
- Smells (e.g. musty book smells, suggesting a school library that is not always open to students or that contains a large number of old books).
- Occupancy (e.g. numbers of closed up classrooms, suggesting a shrinking student population in a school; significant numbers of students sharing chairs and desks in a classroom suggesting a rapidly growing school population).
- Found or discarded objects (e.g. syringes in a school bathroom suggesting a drug presence within the school; books, papers and pens strewn around a classroom suggesting possible lack of care with resources).
- Environmental texts or written texts that are found in the environment such as graffiti, traffic signs, billboards etc. (e.g. warmly-worded welcome signs at the main entrance to a school suggesting an open and friendly place).
- Structures and structural changes, such as those associated with building and buildings, roadways, renovations etc. (e.g. an area where a number of dilapidated houses are undergoing extensive renovations may be an area that is being gentrified).

Task

This photograph, taken inside the main administration building of a large primary school, is a physical trace record. Examine the picture closely, then answer the questions below.

© Michael Doneman 1999

- What kinds or types of physical traces do you see in this image?

- What other data would you need to collect in order to verify your initial interpretations of how this particular space is used?

- What interpretations of the culture of this school or relationships between people associated with this school do these physical traces evoke?

- What other data would you need to collect in order to verify your initial interpretations of this culture or these relationships?

Focusing on physical traces requires researchers to look for what is and is not present within the context being studied. David Fetterman notes how absence of graffiti on the walls of an inner-city school is as important as its presence (1998: 58). In a study of teacher morale the presence of a generously-filled coffee urn and a plate of biscuits in a staffroom may suggest a school's administration actively encourages staff 'conviviality' (see Rossman and Rallis 1998: 187). Conversely, absence of easy chairs, magazines and journals in the staffroom may suggest a context that does not promote teacher conviviality.

The main method for collecting physical trace data is direct observation. Researchers must keep their eyes and ears open (Fetterman 1998: 57). The most common tools for recording physical trace data include still cameras, video cameras, fieldnotes, and audio-recorded monologue or 'travelogue' (as the teacher researcher walks through an area describing aloud what they see).

Physical trace data can be very misleading. A 'house with all the modern conveniences and luxuries imaginable can signal wealth or financial overextension verging on bankruptcy' (Fetterman 1998: 58). Using physical trace data requires researchers to support interpretations by cross-checking physical trace data with interview, observation and other kinds of data, to arrive at credible and defensible interpretations of the evidence collected.

For further reading in this area we suggest:

- Fetterman, D. (1998) *Ethnography: Step by Step*, 2nd edn. Newbury Park, CA: Sage.
- Hoggart, K., Lees, L. and Davies, A. (2002) *Researching Human Geography*. London: Arnold.
- Rossman, G. and Rallis, S. (1998) *Learning in the Field: An Introduction to Qualitative Research*. Thousand Oaks, CA: Sage.

Secondary observation data

Rapid developments in digitized video applications, online digital video streaming and digital storage capabilities enhance researchers' access to extant observation data that can either serve as complete data sets in themselves or be used for comparison with in-person observations of similar or related contexts. For instance, universities are increasingly placing digitally streamed videos of 'best practice' classroom lessons online. These archives are often freely available to teacher researchers (e.g. California Learning Interchange 2003; In-Time 2003).

Secondary observation data is also available in the form of research fieldnotes created by others, or as photographs and videos produced expressly for research and other purposes. Research programmes that have been running for several years, as well as long-term studies, generate enormous amounts of video and written observation data. Graduate research students and other researchers regularly make use of such data in their own studies, without having to actually collect it themselves (see Putney 1996).

Collecting and using other people's observations as data

As with interview data, collecting and using fieldnotes compiled by other people and supplementing these with relevant artefacts and other contextualizing data (e.g. school data and policies) germane to the questions and problems one wants to investigate can save teacher researchers much time. Teacher researchers interested in using other people's data can usefully contact education faculties in universities and colleges and discuss the possibility of using fieldnote data sets compiled by experienced researchers.

It is important to recognize that using other people's observational data is rarely straightforward. Contextualizing details are often missing (e.g. information about the age of the school, the weather on a particular day, the colour of the classroom walls etc.). As Schensul *et al.* (1999: 226) note, researchers rarely write fieldnotes with an audience beyond themselves in mind. The difficulties associated with using other people's fieldnotes highlights the amount of data we store in our heads rather than on paper when making written records of our observations – even when aiming to be as detailed as possible.

Another potential difficulty involves the problem of theoretical frame clashes. The theories researchers subscribe to directly shape what they focus on in their observations. If observation fieldnotes are written by someone committed to, say, sociological theories concerning the relationship between students and the socialization effects of formal schooling, a person committed to cultural psychology theories of social practice may find that the fieldnote records are not sufficient for a study that calls for analysing students' activity, interaction and meaning-making because the original study focused mostly on recording social exchanges between the students and the teacher and did not include sufficient details about classroom activity.

For further reading in this area we suggest:

- Ember, C. and Ember, M. (1998) Cross-cultural research, in H. Bernard (ed.) *Handbook of Methods in Cultural Anthropology*, pp. 647–90. Walnut Creek, CA: Altamira Press.
- Schensul, S., Schensul, J. and LeCompte, M. (1999) *Essential Ethnographic Methods: Observations, Interviews, and Questionnaires* (*Ethnographer's Toolkit*, Vol. 2). Walnut Creek, CA: Altamira Press.

Extant photographs and videos as observation data

Photographs and similar media that have not been produced by the teacher researcher can serve as an important source of observation data. These data are often referred to as *secondary observation data*, and generally take one of two forms:

- extant images available in the public domain; and
- images generated by research participants themselves.

Neither requires the researcher to be physically present at the time of image production. Including secondary observation data in a study helps to maximize data collection in an efficient manner. This is particularly useful to teacher researchers who generally conduct their research projects on their own and operate within restricted time frames. Photos and videos produced by others are rich data sources. They generally provide more detailed data than do other people's fieldnotes alone, because much of the setting for the events and activities captured on camera remains intact.

Videos of classroom lessons, school life etc., readily lend themselves to diverse worthwhile research questions and theoretical interpretations. The Hathaway Project at Deakin University in Australia has developed a multimedia case study CD-ROM for professional development and research purposes (Walker and Lewis 1998). This archives data collected about one school (Hathaway Primary) over a number of years, in a range of formats and from a range of contexts. Data include newspaper clippings, interview transcripts, video clips, audio tracks, fieldnotes, pages from the principal's meeting and events diary, copies of accident register pages, photographs (some taken by students, others showing aerial shots of the school site), school survey results, three-dimensional building plans and layouts (including 360-degree scans of areas developed using virtual reality programming protocols), artefacts such as meeting agendas, curriculum documents, student work, school newsletters and so on. The resource was not intentionally designed to be a stand-alone research database or 'case record' (Walker and Lewis 1998: 164). It nonetheless lends itself to being used in small-scale, comparative studies.

Prosser and Schwartz (1998) show how cultural inventories provided by other people's photographs can be used to examine school administration practices. They describe one study that compared and contrasted observation evidence gathered from photographs of school administrators in their offices. In particular, informal, 'at work' photos captured important patterns of difference between wealthy and economically underserved schools. Administrators in wealthy schools were regularly shown working in spacious, well-appointed offices – often lined with books; administrators in underserved schools were shown seated at small desks that were generally piled high with paperwork of one kind or another.

Teacher researchers can use the internet to locate archives of relevant photographic records of other people's observations. Useful starting places include:

- National libraries online, such as:
  - www.nla.gov.au/libraries/resource/image.html
  - www.natlib.govt.nz/en/digital/index.html
  - www.nls.uk/digitallibrary/index.html
  - www.llgc.org.uk/drych/drych_s003.htm
  - www.nlc-bnc.ca/history/index-e.html;
- The internet archive – www.archive.org;
- UNESCO Archives Portal – www.unesco.org/webworld/portal_archives/;
- University of California, Berkeley's Architecture Visual Resources Library – shanana.berkeley.edu/spiro/.

For further reading in this area we suggest:

- Grosvenor, I., Lawn, M. and Rousmaniere, K. (eds) (1999) *Silences and Images: The Social History of the Classroom*. New York: Peter Lang.
- Prosser, J. (ed.) (1998) *Image-Based Research: A Sourcebook for Qualitative Researchers*. London: Falmer.

Task

Collect newspaper images from a local paper over a one-week period. Examine these images as though you are a stranger to the area, and respond to the following questions:

- What can be inferred about your community from these images?

- What is not shown? What does this tell you?

Considerations relevant to using other people's images as observation data

When using other people's images it is important for teacher researchers to know:

- Who took them, in order to judge the likely veracity or 'representativeness' of the images. For example, a classroom photograph taken by a visiting newspaper journalist may have been carefully staged, while photographs taken by a school secretary during a school-based event are likely to be more 'authentic'.
- Under what conditions the visual record was made. For example, were teachers or students coerced into posing for the photograph? Were subjects in the video aware they were being filmed? Has permission been obtained from people depicted in the visual record for their image to be used for research or other public purposes?
- The reason the visual record was created. For example, for commercial or reporting purposes, for historical/archival purposes, for personal interest purposes?
- What kind of relationship existed between the photographer and what or who was photographed or filmed (see Prosser and Schwartz 1998; Hoggart *et al.* 2002).

Some ethical issues associated with using other people's visual records particularly relevant to teacher researchers are as follows:

- Navigating permissions to use photographs and videos as research data. Loizos (2000) advises obtaining permission in writing from people before using their visual images in a research study. Where this is impossible, the teacher researcher will need to pay attention to copyright issues instead, or to 'fair use' guidelines (most university websites contain pages with information on these topics).
- When young children are gathering photographic images for a researcher, ethical issues may arise in relation to what they take pictures of that may not have been predicted beforehand when parents signed consent to participate forms (e.g. interfamilial conflict, visitors to the house; see Moss 2001).

LeAnn Putney (in conversation, 15 January 2003) identifies some ways in which other people's video data of classrooms can unintentionally mislead:

- Sound quality can be uneven or poor, requiring access also to fieldnotes in order to interpret what is being said.
- Using other people's video data removes an important interpersonal dimension from the data that is not always captured by the camera lens or in fieldnotes. For example, a group working with LeAnn Putney viewed a videotape of a lesson

containing a segment where a young boy was running around the classroom while the teacher was speaking to the class. The students viewing the tape initially labelled the child disruptive and criticized the teacher for poor classroom management skills. Close reviewing, however, showed the child was not actually distracting anyone and soon settled back into his seat and got to work. The child had a long history of clinically diagnosed hyperactivity and the teacher and students had found the only way to deal effectively with his infrequent frenzied outbursts was to disregard them.

- Camera angles directly affect what can and cannot be seen. Video cameras are often set up in a corner of a classroom and left running, thereby capturing only one angle. This often occurs when teachers are asked by researchers to record their own teaching. If only blank wall space is shown in a video, viewers might infer that all the walls are bare (and, hence, that the teacher does not value displays of student work, or is not committed to generating a visually interesting classroom work environment). Yet the walls *not* shown might be covered in student work, bright posters etc.

Such examples underscore the fallibility of image-based data and the need to remember that photographic and video records never capture a full account of 'being there'.

For further reading on this topic, try:

- Loizos, P. (2000) Video, film and photographs as research documents, in M. Bauer and G. Gaskell (eds) *Qualitative Researching with Text, Image and Sound*, pp. 93–107. London: Sage.
- Prosser, J. (ed.) (1998) *Image-Based Research: A Sourcebook for Qualitative Researchers*. London: Falmer.

CHAPTER 12

Collecting written data in qualitative teacher research

Introduction: written data as a complex category

Written data is a complex category. Some data existing in written form – like fieldnotes and interview transcripts – are best seen as observed data or spoken data from the standpoint of qualitative research. Conversely, some data existing in forms that are not written texts – like photos, television documentaries, web pages and so on – are nonetheless best treated as written data in qualitative research.

As noted in Chapter 7, written data include very diverse items, such as policy documents, official and unofficial records, documents originally generated for personal purposes and different kinds of historical documents. Written data also include written responses to survey and questionnaire forms, textbooks and other printed school resources, and contemporary media artefacts. Works of literature and art, as well as various kinds of functional texts (labels, menus, warnings etc.) and school resources are also among the kinds of texts that constitute written data.

Such texts fall into two main groups. The first, which is the larger of the two, comprises *extant texts or documents*. These include conventional printed texts like books, as well as things like photographs, television productions and web pages that *exist independently* of the study taking place. They have not been produced as a consequence of the present research. They usually predate the study, although they also include artefacts that have been created during the research period. They would, however, still have been produced had there not been a research study at all. Examples include things like essays written by students as part of their classroom work, or teacher-made resources produced during the time the study took place, but where these were not motivated or prompted by the research.

The second group includes things like written responses to open-ended questions in surveys and questionnaires, or journals that participants have kept at the behest of the researchers. These texts *have been generated by the research* and, indeed, produced as written texts by the research subjects themselves. They differ from interview transcripts in the sense that transcripts are originally produced in spoken form, and to this extent will be different in significant ways from oral interview data in terms of how they are collected and/or how they are analysed. At the same time, they differ from fieldnotes written (produced) by the researcher. Fieldnotes are records of what research participants do as seen from the perspective of the researcher. Data written by study participants, however, are records of what research participants believe and think as seen from their own 'insider' perspectives, and reflect how they think and express themselves in writing rather than in speech. The only time interview transcripts and fieldnotes can usefully be regarded as written data is when they were produced for some other piece of research separate from the current study. Even in these cases, it will often be more appropriate to treat them as spoken or observed data (see Chapters 10 and 11).

Written data, then, refer to texts and documents produced to convey information, ideas, thoughts and reflections, memories, visions, pictures, procedures, goals, intentions, aspirations, prescriptions and so on, through the medium of signs and symbols that other people can *read* (or *view*). Some such texts have been produced in *conventional forms* of direct or indirect inscription upon material surfaces of one kind or another: printed writing, typescripts, painted or drawn texts/signs/icons, photos, graffiti and the like. Written data also include texts produced in *non-conventional forms*, by electronic and other means, to be viewed on virtual or 'screen' surfaces (e.g. television documentaries, film, video, CD-ROM and DVD material, web pages). Overall, written data span an enormous range of genres and communicative and informational purposes.

There is, of course, a genuine complication here that we cannot adequately address in this context, but which must be acknowledged. It concerns the relationship and 'interface' between 'reading' and 'viewing' or, similarly, between written data and what might be called *visual* data. There is something odd about referring to a movie as written data, although not about referring to a movie script as written data. If we want to interpret the movie as a whole we need to view it and address it on all its dimensions, including the aesthetic, the moral and so on. This may take us into areas that, at a stretch, can be regarded as analysis and interpretation of written data, yet which are very different from analysing a policy document.

If, for example, we want to analyse violence in movies or computer games that are accessed widely by young people, to what extent does this involve analysis of written data? If we transcribe the script for analytic purposes, to what extent should we transcribe it as 'words alone' and to what extent should it be more like a sophisticated transcript of spoken data, including gestures? Or, to put it another way, to what extent is multimodal data involving signs and symbols adequately understood as written data, and to what extent and on what grounds must we think of it as involving more than this? Do we try to 'separate' a multimodal resource into its different modes and relate these to categories of spoken, observed and written data for analytic purposes?

In this chapter and the chapter on analysis of written data (Chapter 15) we take a conservative line which extends as far as web pages, but not to movies or computer games. At the same time, we will refer to semiotic analysis and suggest further reading, and the issue of analysing images in context is mentioned with respect to artefacts as part of observational data.

Written data: research potential and approaches

Knowing about the research 'potential' of documents helps the researcher make informed judgements about the texts needed to address their research questions effectively, and about the role of such texts in the study overall (Stewart and Kamins 1993; May 1997; McCulloch and Richardson 2000). Written data includes:

- the potential to inform present and future decisions concerning education in general, pedagogy within a specific subject area or across subject areas, professional development for teachers, policy development, curriculum development and so on;
- the potential to provide a 'reading' or an account of a particular policy or curriculum development, a practice, a social event or other phenomenon that impacts education in some way (e.g. school accountability, standardized tests, curriculum resources, new syllabi);
- the potential to provide contextual and historical insights on an issue, event, problem or practice relevant to education: written data 'tell us about the aspirations and intentions of the period to which they refer and describe places and social relationships at a time when we may not have been born, or were simply not present' (May 1997: 157–8);
- the potential to enable the teacher researcher to (re)construct an account of a past event or practice (e.g. the literacy programme in place in the Gulugaba state school during the 1940s).

Table 12.1 summarizes some of the points at which and ways in which written data might feature in teacher research.

Primary, secondary and tertiary source documents as written data in qualitative research

Written data can be categorized in several ways important for qualitative researchers. One involves distinguishing between primary, secondary and tertiary source texts.

Primary sources are statements that have been produced or collected by actual witnesses to events and processes, or the 'originators' of particular thoughts and sequences of thoughts. These include minutes of meetings, records of transactions

Table 12.1 Some examples of written data

Method	Purpose and tools	Kinds of data collected	Used in
Locating written historical records	Within the field of education, this approach is concerned with (re)constructing past events in theorized ways in order to better understand current events as they impact on education. Examples include Graff's (1979) study of literacy and life opportunities in three nineteenth-century Canadian cities to provide a perspective on popular claims about the significance of literacy; investigating the history of secondary technical schools in England and Wales from the 1940s to the 1960s in order to better understand why they were largely unsuccessful (McCulloch 1989); etc.	Primary source documents, such as: letters, diaries and journals, public records, school attendance records, population and census records, first-person accounts, policy documents such as government White Papers and school management policies etc., newspaper reports, government reports, school development plans and proposals	Historical research or historiography, biographies, policy analysis studies
Locating policy documents	Focuses on analysing policy documents (at a range of administrative levels, usually spanning federal through to school and classroom contexts) in order to better understand or to critique administrative procedures, processes and outcomes, policy-driven education interventions and reform processes or effective policy development and implementation processes	Policy documents, including government White Papers, federal-level management and curriculum policy documents, state-level education department management and curriculum policy documents, school management and curriculum policy documents etc.	Policy analysis studies, case study, ethnography
Generating open-ended written survey data	Emphasis on gathering a range of written responses to set items from a range of people. Method includes	Large sets of data can be generated by surveys. Useful for identifying trends or	Action research, case study

Method	Purpose and tools	Kinds of data collected	Used in
	pre-printed questions or statements to respond to in writing. Questions are open-ended; that is, how, what, when, why questions and 'tell me' requests with space on the question sheet (the questionnaire) or on separate blank pages for written responses	preferences across a large number of people. Data are usually collected in categories (e.g. personal data, social practices) and in field research words instead of numbers are used to summarize the data	
Participant journals	A deliberate data collection method. Participants are asked to write these journals in order to record their personal insights into and reflections on an event, practice, concept, phenomenon	Data are often highly personal and written from an 'insider' perspective. Data can provide important insights for the teacher researcher by means of providing an alternative position on an event, process, programme etc.	Case study, action research, ethnography, narrative inquiry
Collecting websites and other digital data	There can be any number of research purposes for collecting websites and other digital data. In general, once digital texts are sampled and selected, they are collected and stored in some re-visitable form (e.g. saved to a computer hard drive or burned onto a CD-ROM or DVD). This is especially necessary where digitally mediated written conversations and websites are concerned, due to their impermanent nature. Internet use can be mapped by means of tracking software that keeps a record of websites visited.	Data include video and computer games, virtual world dialogues, instant message exchanges, mobile phone text messaging exchanges, weblogs and so on. Data can be used to study the practices of online communities or the emergence of new literacies, to critique the representation of race, class and/or gender, to analyse the semiotic choices made in presenting messages and so on	Case study, ethnography, sociolinguistic studies, multimodal analysis studies, discourse analysis studies

Method	Purpose and tools	Kinds of data collected	Used in
Collecting images and filmic data	The role played by images and filmic data in research can include documenting the representation of race, class and gender in popular culture over a specified time period, or across cultures of production; identifying core social values within a given culture, group or time period; discursive studies of government-promoted ideologies etc.	Data include photos, documentaries, training films, image-based advertisements, television news shows	Ethnographies, case study, narrative inquiry, discourse analysis studies, semiotic studies

compiled by participants, inventories assembled by employees, a theorist's original statement of his or her ideas, a research report written by the investigators, journals, logs, diaries and the like. Primary sources are important because they are produced 'as close to the action' as possible.

Secondary sources include texts written about things the author has not directly witnessed and was not a part of. They also include accounts of a theorist's ideas written by another person, a summary of research findings written by someone not involved in the original research and based on their reading of the research report and the like. Basil Bernstein's original accounts of 'the pedagogic device' are primary source documents e.g., Bernstein 1990. Subsequent authors' accounts of what Bernstein says about 'the pedagogic device' are secondary sources. So are accounts of events and processes written by people who did not experience them in person, but which are based on what they have been told by direct observers.

Tertiary sources are references that help us to locate documentary sources. Examples include bibliographies, databases, books of abstracts, indexes, archive catalogues and so on (May 1997: 161).

No document is infallible with respect to 'truth' and 'objectivity'. Primary source accounts are always filtered through some perspective or point of view: what one person 'sees' and reports can vary significantly from what another person 'sees' and reports. It is even more important to be *especially careful* when using secondary sources – whether these are accounts of other people's written records of events and processes or accounts of other people's thoughts and ideas. Interpretations of other people's accounts and records add extra layers of subjectivity to the issues or phenomena researchers want to 'get at'. We recommend going to primary sources as much as possible. Of course, as researchers we always (and inescapably) put our own interpretations on other people's texts – including primary sources. Nonetheless, we reduce the scope for subjectivity and interpretation that can lead to distortion and invention when we appeal to primary sources.

Furthermore, when we are working with textual data obtained from documents we need to remember that our research purposes may differ in important ways from the purposes for which these documents were originally written. We must take this into account when collecting written data (Hedrick *et al.* 1993: 70). This includes doing our best not to take written texts out of context. For example, it would be inappropriate to use a note scribbled in a hurry by a parent to their child as evidence that she or he is an untidy writer, or unable to develop thoughts in depth and so on. While this is an extreme example it nonetheless indicates the kind of principle to be observed when using written data as evidence. It is important to take account of the context and purposes associated with the texts we use as written data and to do our best to ensure that we are using them fairly and appropriately.

Criteria for evaluating documents as written data

When using documents as written data we need to ensure as far as possible that they constitute good-quality data – just as with spoken and observed data. We mentioned some of the issues involved here in our earlier discussion of general principles to guide data collection in Chapter 9. Using poor-quality data in research is analogous to using bad ingredients when cooking or poor materials (knotted or rotten timber, rusty steel) when building. No matter how good our research design and data analysis is, poor-quality data can only lead to poor-quality results that should not be taken seriously as *research* results. We will return briefly at the end of this book to the themes of validity and trustworthiness as criteria of good-quality data (see Chapter 16).

A number of general criteria are widely recognized among social scientists as helpful for the purposes of assessing the quality and utility of documentary and records-based (written) data (Hedrick *et al.* 1993; May 1997). These criteria include:

- Are the records or documents complete?
- Are the documents genuine or authentic copies of the original(s)?
- Are the documents dated and can they be placed on a time scale?
- Why were the data originally collected or generated?
- Are the authors of the documents believable/credible?
- What relevance does this text have in relation to the research question(s) posed for this study?
- Are the documents primary, secondary or tertiary sources? What effects will this have on the credibility of the study?
- Did the database from which the document was derived serve some hidden but deliberate political purpose that could induce systematic distortions into the study?
- What procedures were used to deal with missing information in the text (in the event that there was some)?
- Do the computerized records or documents (where they are being used) bear a close resemblance to the original records or documents?
- Are some data periodically updated or purged from the (computer) file?

- How were the original texts collected and filed, by whom and for what purposes?

Different purposes and uses for written data in qualitative research

It is worth recalling here that written sources function in two very important but different ways as data within educational research. It is helpful to remember that when we talk about data we are referring to units of information, or potential information, that we can use to help us address a research question.

Often we think of data as the information we collect after we have already established the foundations, framework, design and methodology for our project and are collecting data 'in the field'. This, however, is only half the picture. It is necessary also to regard as data – that is, as units of information or potential information relevant to a purpose – those texts we use in order to *conceptualize* our research project. To recapitulate, 'to conceptualize' a research project involves several tasks including:

- to identify clearly the research problem;
- to formulate our research purposes and questions;
- to decide on the best theoretical perspective from which to tackle the question;
- to formulate the key concepts or constructs around which we will organize the study;
- to decide on the approaches, tools and techniques we will use for collecting and analysing data;
- to decide on the kind of theories and components of theories we will use when interpreting the results that emerge from our data analysis.

Hence, we can distinguish two broad purposes and uses for texts as written *data* within qualitative research as follows:

- For informing, contextualizing, conceptualizing, theorizing and designing the research project. This pertains to those texts we use as data during the phases of reviewing relevant literature, and drawing on this to develop our conceptual and theoretical frameworks so as to produce the research design and methodology for the project.
- For generating the empirical data set from which we will ultimately derive our study results and findings. This is the data we collect 'in the field'.

Researchers are engaged in collecting written data when they search for and review relevant literature in order to inform and frame their projects *to the same extent* as when they generate, search for, locate, retrieve and assemble printed documents, web pages, photographs, records and so on in the field.

We have already dealt with data collection for the first of these purposes in Chapter 5 (see pp. 85–93). In this chapter we will focus on the tasks and processes involved in generating written data for the empirical data set in qualitative research investigations.

Task

Read through the following three research aims and suggested forms of potentially useful written data. Eliminate those that appear to be least appropriate for each set.

1   This study is a historical account of the education work of Paulo Freire, a Brazilian theorist and educator whose work spans the 1960s to the 1990s. Written data will include: open-ended written survey responses; letters written by Freire; letters written to and kept by Freire; copies of the literacy teaching resources produced by Freire and his colleagues; websites about Freirean pedagogy; photographs of Freire.

2   This investigation focuses on analysing the representation of gender in mobile phone advertising. Written data will include: mobile phone advertisements found in magazines and newspapers; local council policies on mobile phone networks; mobile phone advertisements on television; copies of monthly mobile phone bills from males and females; studies analysing male and female mobile phone conversations; films that include heavy use of mobile phones.

3   This study aims at documenting the representation of indigenous groups in commercially-produced primary school social studies resources. Written data will include: primary school social studies textbooks and teacher guides; television documentaries on different indigenous groups; social studies wall charts that document different indigenous groups; newspaper articles; open-ended written survey responses; letters written by nineteenth-century anthropologists researching in indigenous communities; websites produced by indigenous groups that aim at dispelling myths and stereotypes about the group.

For further reading in this area we suggest:

- Bell, J. (1999) *Doing Your Research Project: A Guide for First-Time Researchers in Education and Social Science*, 3rd edn. Buckingham: Open University Press.
- Hoggart, K., Lees, L. and Davies, A. (2002) *Researching Human Geography*. London: Arnold.
- Jones, S. (ed.) (1999) *Doing Internet Research: Critical Issues and Methods for Examining the Net*. Thousand Oaks, CA: Sage.
- Prosser, J. (ed.) (1998) *Image-Based Research: A Sourcebook for Qualitative Researchers*. London: Falmer.

Generating written data for the empirical data set in a qualitative research project

We will consider five types of situation in which qualitative researchers need to locate or generate written data as part of their empirical data sets. While the examples we provide cannot possibly exhaust the topic of collecting written data in qualitative research, they are nonetheless sufficiently diverse to represent typical situations in which researchers using qualitative approaches find themselves. The precise kinds or genres of documents required for obtaining the written data that are needed may differ from the types we mention here. The procedures and principles involved will, however, parallel the cases we outline in the remainder of this chapter.

Most of the written data qualitative researchers require will come from *extant* (already existing) texts. Accordingly, our discussion will deal mainly with locating extant texts. As noted earlier, however, qualitative researchers will often want to augment spoken and observed data with written responses from participants. We will begin by discussing written data collection by means of participant journals and then consider different situations involving extant texts.

Generating written data using participant journals

Participant journals are documents created by study participants at the behest of the researcher. As such, they are research products and not synonymous with the reflective journals students complete as part of their weekly classroom routine. Participant journals collect data written from the point of view of the participant, and can offer helpful insights into his or her thoughts, can signal changes over time in thinking or self-perceived mastery of something, can collect teachers' anecdotal evaluations of an intervention study in which they are participating, can act as a log of what worked and didn't work in an intervention study from the teacher's point of view as well as from the students' points of view, can document reasoning processes or the participant's feelings about an issue or phenomenon, and so on, in relation to the topic, event, practices or phenomena being studied (Clandinen and Connelly 1998, 2000). In education research, participant journals are rarely used as self-contained data sets, but are most often used in conjunction with other data collection methods (e.g. observation and fieldnotes, interviews) (Corti 2001).

There is no set format for participant journals. Some researchers simply supply study participants with notebooks and ask them to write down whatever comes to mind about a topic or event. Others choose to structure participants' reflective or anecdotal writing more explicitly by providing participants with a short list of questions to respond to, or relevant headings written across a series of empty columns. In terms of the actual journal, it can take the form of a notebook, or can comprise loose leaves within a ring binder, or can be a computer file and so on. For example, Margaret Gearon and Maria Gindidis (1998) chose to use participant journals as the primary data collection tool in their study of the ways in which teachers navigate both learning and teaching a second language simultaneously. As part of their justification for using journals in their study, they argue that journals serve two purposes:

1   Events and ideas are recorded for the purposes of later reflection.
2   The process of writing itself helps trigger insights about teaching.

Gearon and Gindidis settled on four categories of response for journal entries: personal reflection, critical reflection, classroom practice and a list of 'special topics' from which teachers participating in their study could choose to write about. These topics included prompts like the following (Gearon and Gindidis 1998: 1):

- Comment on traps you fell into when trying to use the target language in your teaching and learning in your classrooms.
- In what ways do you think your approach to teaching and learning a second language is changing? How is this course impacting on this?

The researchers also included the aims of their study in the guidelines for completing the journal entries that they gave to participating teachers.

A key characteristic of participant journals is that they should not become burdensome to produce. (In some cases, we have equipped younger children or students who struggle with standard English literacy with audio-recorders and tapes instead of notebooks with which to record their journals. These recordings are later transcribed for analysis. This is, of course, another example of how the line between 'spoken' data and 'written' data is often blurred.) It is also important when asking students to maintain participant journals not to expect them to do so for an extended period of time, to emphasize to all concerned that the journal runs secondary to schoolwork, homework and other commitments, and that the journal should not to be completed under duress or become an alienating chore. In short, participant journals should always be voluntary.

The timing of entries also needs to be considered carefully. Gearon and Gindidis (1998) report how they had to modify their original plan regarding the frequency of participants' journal entries. They initially asked participating teachers to complete a journal entry each week at the close of a professional development class on language teaching. However, participants claimed they did not have enough to write about each week and were simply repeating the content of the previous entry; the researchers decided that making journal entries once a month would still be sufficient for their study purposes while at the same time making the entries easier and more interesting for the teachers to complete.

One unavoidable limitation of participant journals is that they have been produced at the request of the researcher, and the researcher therefore cannot claim journal data as necessarily representing a participant's 'true' feelings and reflections. Gearon and Gindidis included participant journals as part of the assessment for a professional development course, while at the same time using these journals as research data. This raises significant ethical issues concerning the extent to which keeping the journals was voluntary. It also raises questions concerning the validity of data collected when assessment grades are involved. The danger is that participants in most cases are likely to write only those things they think the researchers are looking for.

In addition, the researcher also needs to keep in mind that participant journals are produced within a particular time frame and under specific conditions, and will not necessarily be generalizable to other times and contexts within a participant's everyday life. Nevertheless, participant journal entries can be useful points of reference for formulating interview questions, for guiding observations and for checking factual information.

> **Task**
>
> Take the case of Jacques (see p. 306), or some other research study with which you are familiar that could justifiably include participant journals as part of its data collection kit, and draft a set of guidelines that will help participants keep a journal for research purposes. Then answer the following questions:
>
> - What relationship should there be between the research question and the format decided on (e.g. guided, non-guided) for participant journals in a given study?
>
> - Do you think it is important to include guidelines for completing journal entries with participant journals? Why/Why not?
>
> - Should the guidelines include a reminder that the journal is not a diary and that text written in the journal may be made public in study reports and publications? Why/Why not?
>
> - How explicit should guidelines be? Why? When do guidelines become too explicit and interfere with the quality of data collected?

For further reading in this area see:

- Delamont, S. (2001) *Fieldwork in Educational Settings: Methods, Pitfalls and Perspectives*, 2nd edn. London: Routledge.
- Glesne, C. (1999) *Becoming Qualitative Researchers: An Introduction*, 2nd edn. Boston, MA: Addison-Wesley.
- Janisek, V. (1999) A journal about journal writing as a qualitative research technique: history, issues and reflections, *Qualitative Inquiry*, 5(4): 505–24.

Locating extant documents as (primary) sources of written data for qualitative research projects by searching archives

In many qualitative studies within education it is necessary to collect data that is located in archives of public records, personal writings, stock inventories and so on. This material may be old – as in the case of qualitative studies involving significant historical components – or relatively current. Some of this material will exist as physical archives of original documents in public libraries, national libraries, government departments, school administration offices and so on. Some will exist in private collections or in the collections of foundations and trusts. Increasingly, electronic copies are being made of archival material and are available online.

Locating relevant material may involve going to very different sources and drawing on different kinds of expertise. For example, if a researcher is conducting a qualitative case study and evaluation of how new technologies have been introduced into the learning programmes of a particular school or set of schools, it may be very important to know what resources were purchased, at what times and in what sequences. This might only involve five years' worth of records. Such data will probably be available in the school purchasing records – since schools are usually required to be able to account for their purchases. In this case, the relevant expert to contact with regard to accessing these documents could be the school or regional secretary or administration officer. This is not the kind of information that is likely to be obtainable from a librarian or a webmaster. A good researcher will realize that a research question concerning the introduction of new technologies must necessarily take account of the equipment involved. They will also be interested in such things as the relative expenditures made on hardware, software, teacher training in the use of new technologies and teacher professional development on pedagogical implementations of new technologies. Hence, they will need to locate relevant records and hunt down the people who can make them available. This will involve a very different kind of searching from that which uses keywords and catalogues. It will be more like searching through human networks: the researcher asks a teacher who directs them to the principal for permission to access the records; the principal leads the researcher to the secretary; the secretary locates the relevant files and photocopies them. It may also be relevant to obtain, at the same time, copies of the minutes of school committee meetings where decisions were made about what to purchase and why to purchase certain things rather than others.

At almost the opposite extreme is the example of Graff's (1979) study of literacy in the nineteenth-century city described in Chapter 7. To collect his data Graff had to locate public records (then more than 100 years old) in offices of municipal authorities in the three towns he studied. He sought assistance from his academic colleagues and tutors, and made the necessary contacts among municipal authorities, librarians, archival experts and so on. A key point to note here, however, is what Graff already had in his mind before he went looking for this written data. He had a very sophisticated research design that included ways of controlling variables. This helped him to decide what kinds of records he needed, and enabled him to avoid collecting unnecessary or irrelevant material.

Lying between these extremes is a study conducted within a Nicaraguan municipality that involved investigating women's literacy gains from the 1980 Nicaraguan Literacy Crusade ten years later (Sandiford *et al.* 1994; Lankshear *et al.* 1995). This was part of a larger study intended to investigate relationships between female literacy and children's health. The funding level dictated a study within a single area with maximum 'typicality' for the country as a whole and minimal complications that would impact on budget and on the quality of data. The Department of Masaya was eventually chosen (population 207,000). Masaya was reasonably close to the capital city, yet had an urban-rural mix that matched the average for the country as a whole – as required by the study design. It also had a reported female illiteracy rate prior to the Crusade that was substantial (48 per cent). It was close to the estimated true level at the time, and that would make it relatively simple to obtain the three cohorts: women who had become literate in school; women who had become literate in the Crusade; and women who had never become literate. Masaya had also had one of the more active and successful ongoing adult education programmes during the 1980s.

The study used different kinds of written data. These ranged from policy documents to historical records of the literacy campaign. This latter aspect was similar in many ways to the historical data used by Graff (albeit much more recent), but it served a very different purpose. The main purpose of the historical written record in the Nicaraguan study was to lead (physically) to identifying women participants who could then be surveyed (to provide 'fresh' written data) and interviewed (to provide rich spoken data for the qualitative component of the study).

The researchers first consulted the graduation register from the Crusade, available through the Ministry of Education, and searched the sections relating to the municipalities in Masaya. They also consulted the official report of the campaign and the Ministry of Education census conducted during 1989–90 when the study began. The census provided a useful baseline for tracking potential participants. In addition, the campaign records and the census (augmented by field-based inquiries) helped the researchers to identify and locate adult education promoters and coordinators who had been involved in the original Crusade and the ongoing adult basic education programme that had run until the mid-1980s. These educators had written records of participants, resources, results and outcomes of their work. The researchers scrutinized these data, finding further valuable leads to potential study participants. In the end they were able to identify and locate more than 400 women within the study area who, with a high level of confidence, could be said to have become literate through the 1980 campaign and follow-up programme. Of these, more than half agreed to participate in the project, providing a strong and sound research population (see Sandiford *et al.* 1994).

It is now possible to locate for many countries and regions (though by no means all) archives of online primary records and documents relevant to a range of qualitative research purposes. Some of those we have located (for the UK, Australia and the Pacific) are as follows:

- National Archives of Australia (www.naa.gov.au).
- John Oxley Library Internet History Collections (Australia) (www.slq.qld.gov.au/jol/collections/).
- The Public Records Office Catalogue Online (United Kingdom) (www.pro.gov.uk/catalogues/procat.htm).
- Internet Library of Early Journals: A Digital Library of 18th and 19th Century Journals and Magazines (www.bodley.ox.ac.uk/ilej/).
- Repositories of Primary Sources: Asia and the Pacific (www.uidaho.edu/special-collections/asia.html).

As with most of the examples we have provided, these sites were found using google.com and similar search engines using more or less intuitive key words and natural language phrases, such as 'online archives public records England', 'archives Australia' and 'life history archives'. It is important to note that online searches can provide valuable information about archival sources that are not available online but, rather, through libraries or special collections. Websites will usually provide contact addresses and email information the researcher can use for obtaining further assistance.

Locating non-conventional text types as written data for qualitative studies

Many qualitative research projects in education involve collecting written data in the form of non-conventional texts. Some obvious examples include qualitative studies of children interacting with CD-ROM story books (e.g. Smith 2001, 2002) or of young (and not so young) people playing video-games (Gee 2003). In order to study such interactions and activities it is necessary to select and describe the particular resources that will be used in the project. These will be texts or artefacts that the researcher believes will most effectively realize their research purposes. Cynthia Smith (2001) used several CD-ROM stories in her investigation of a young boy's patterns of engagement with CD-ROM and other story book media including traditional children's picture story books and child-generated story books. She was interested in seeing if the child's patterns of interactions with these different kinds of texts differed from one another. The CD-ROM story books she used were chosen in accordance with such criteria as having different levels of interactivity, their relationship to the sorts of things the boy was interested in and would spend time with and so on.

Another example of studies involving non-conventional written data can be found in work done by Colin Symes in Australia using photographs of school vestibules. Symes (1999) was interested in the ways semiotic analysis could be used to investigate how a school organizes and creates its vestibule to construct or promote a particular kind of image, sense of mission and overall school culture. He drew on a number of extant photographs of vestibules as well as generating new data in the form of photographs he took himself. These photos became texts which could then be subjected to semiotic and relevant forms of discourse analysis to generate accounts of the constitutive role of vestibules in creating a particular school culture, and to evaluate the success or otherwise of such constitutive efforts by schools. In this case, data collection was a matter of identifying schools that had vestibules and that Symes thought would be interesting as objects of study. To generate his study population he employed categories and dimensions such as 'public/government schools', 'private/independent schools', 'urban schools', 'rural schools', 'suburban schools', 'schools serving different socioeconomic status groups', 'single-sex schools' and 'mixed-sex schools', and used these to help guide his purposive selection of school vestibules to study.

Some of our own recent work (Lankshear and Knobel 2002, 2003) has used interlinked websites and web pages as written data for qualitative research purposes. We are interested in government initiatives promoting the internet as a resource for learning in schools. The most ambitious example developed to date is the British government's National Grid for Learning (www.ngfl.gov.uk). We explored, over many hours, the diverse resources available on the National Grid for Learning to get an overall sense of its scope and quality. We then selected typical web pages for close analysis using methods drawn from semiotic analysis, critical discourse analysis, sociolinguistic analysis and so on. Data collection was conducted on two levels. The first involved searching for large-scale government online learning initiatives. There are many of these. Existing literature and our own Google-based searches quickly identified the Grid as the most ambitious initiative yet undertaken in the English-speaking world. The second level was more refined. It involved drawing a kind of study sample of sites from the countless thousands of web pages linked to the Grid. These specific searches were guided by our immediate purposes, such as locating pages and sites relevant to the theme of early childhood literacy education. This meant we looked only for sites relevant to literacy education involving children up to the age of 8 years, which narrowed the search considerably. Sites subsequently chosen for analysis reflected our own interest in sociocultural theories of literacy, as did the kinds of analysis to which we subjected the 'written data' in the form of the websites and web pages selected.

Locating (extant) participant texts as written data in qualitative educational research

Qualitative educational research projects often use extant texts that have been produced by students as regular parts of their schoolwork, but are then used as part of a study's database to explore aspects of educational theory and practice. For example, student essays may be collected as part of an empirical data set concerned with academic writing in schools and universities. Students' examination papers and their essays might be sampled in order to compare their effectiveness and utility as a means of assessing student learning. A reasonably common kind of study in English-speaking countries has involved collecting samples of students' writing – from school as well as out of school settings – in order to analyse patterns of gendered identity formation and to understand how the social construction of gender is mediated by writing practices.

In this vein Pam Gilbert with Kate Rowe (1989) analysed a text written by a group of boys. The text was found by one of the researchers when she visited her daughter's classroom, where the text had been displayed on a wall alongside other examples of students' writing. The researchers used forms of feminist discourse analysis to identify types of violence and gender positioning in the text. This analysis became the basis for developing a theoretically and politically informed critique of genre-based and whole-language approaches to literacy education that fail to take account of content and ideology operating in children's texts.

It is important to note in this case that a single text constituted the database for an entire study within a larger research agenda. This raises a key point in relation to data collection within qualitative research: that in qualitative research the inquiry aims to achieve *depth* in the study of a social phenomenon. Consequently, in many cases the depth and sophistication of analysis is more important than the amount of data collected. It is always important to have sufficient data for one's research purposes, but it is often the case that these purposes can be met by a very small data set to which is applied strong theory and which is analysed in depth and by using powerful forms of data analysis. For example, if a researcher intends to use written texts as part or all of the empirical data set for discourse analysis it may be necessary to collect only a small number of texts, but to pay careful attention to the texts that are selected. These will be texts that appear likely to speak to wide and rich facets of a discourse. Learning how to identify such texts is often a major task. It is not mastered quickly, and is often best approached by looking carefully at how expert researchers select written texts for discourse, sociolinguistic and similar forms of analysis.

Task

1 Provide a description of 'extant participant texts'.

2 Locate a research study where extant participant texts form an important part of the empirical data set.

3 Identify the grounds on which and criteria by which the researchers chose the extant participant texts they used. If these are not stated explicitly, try to deduce from the research report the grounds on which decisions for written data collection were made.

4 If other kinds of data (written or otherwise) besides extant participant texts were collected, identify what these are.

5 Describe the particular role played by extant participant texts within the data set (e.g. is it a major role, a supporting or an augmenting role; how do extant participant texts complement other forms of written data that were collected?).

6 Identify and describe the approach to data analysis applied to the extant participant texts.

7 Comment on whether this analytic approach seems to you to be better suited to smaller or larger amounts of extant participant data. What are your reasons?

Repeat this activity for the other kinds of written data addressed in this chapter.

Locating non-participant texts as written data in qualitative educational research

Qualitative research projects that investigate schools and school systems implementing curriculum change or educational reform policies, or study aspects of classroom learning and the like, require researchers to collect a range of relevant extant documents that will provide written data for the empirical data set. Such documents include legislation texts, policy documents, curriculum documents, textbooks and other resources that have not actually been produced by people directly involved in the context being studied. A typical example is where a qualitative researcher investigates how school textbooks play a role in the process of constituting students as ideological subjects.

A short text titled 'Columbus' Voyages' (SEP 1994, our translation) provides a typical example.

Columbus' Voyages

On his first voyage Columbus left Puerto de Palos on August 3rd 1492 and, after travelling for two months, arrived on October 12th at an American island, the island of Guanahaní, which he called San Salvador.

Christopher Columbus made three more voyages in which he reached lands in the Caribbean Sea, Central America, and what today is Venezuela, but he never thought that he had reached a new continent.

The New World

After Christopher Columbus many Europeans ventured to cross the Atlantic Ocean.

Another Italian sailor, Américo Vespucio, was the one who discovered that the lands Columbus had reached were a continent.

Hence the new continent was given the name America, in memory of that Italian explorer.

Those Who Travelled to the New World

Many men left from Spain to settle the newly discovered islands. These men were priests, who sought to convert the indigenous peoples to Christianity and to teach them the Spanish alphabet.

Many poor peasants whose lands were not sufficient to sustain them also travelled to the American world, along with many others who were without work or who were being pursued by justice.

How They Lived in the New World

The Spaniards who arrived on the islands proclaimed them colonies, because they came to found dependencies for the Spanish crown.

The Spanish rulers named a government in the new lands.

The colonists exploited the mines and lands of the new possessions, using the labour of indigenous people and bringing African slaves to America.

This text can be investigated as an example of a representation of social groups coming into contact. In countries where indigenous peoples and their lands were colonized by outsiders there have often been subsequent struggles over how the colonization process and the groups involved have been portrayed and how they ought to be portrayed. The ways young people come to understand this aspect of their history and how it relates to their own identities and those of members of different cultural groups has become an important focus for research. Within this focus the roles played by texts in helping to shape young people's understandings – especially texts students encounter as formal or official curriculum content at school – has emerged as a specific research interest (see Fairclough 1992, 1995; van Leeuwen and Selander 1995; Kress 1998).

Studies in this area take diverse forms. Some focus more narrowly on textual representations of social groups coming into contact under colonization. Others take a wider perspective and address this theme as a specific case of how textbooks can function ideologically. Within such inquiries researchers might select entire books for analysis. Alternatively, they might select particular themes from a range of books or, perhaps, from a single book. In other cases the data set might comprise a combination of entire books, selected passages, particular themes and so on. As with developing questionnaire items, decisions about which specific texts to collect, how many and from which subject areas need to be made in the light of the following:

- the research questions and research purposes;
- the role to be played (major or supporting) of this written data in the study;
- the time and other resources one has available;
- the form or forms of data analysis to be employed;
- the theoretical perspective that is informing the study and, in particular, one's approach to data analysis and interpretation of findings.

Table 12.2 indicates the kind of conditions under which a text like 'Columbus' Journeys' might be selected as a unit of written data for the empirical data set of a qualitative research project (see also Chapter 15).

Table 12.2 Schema of a study using 'Columbus' Voyages' as a unit of written data

Research purpose	Research question	Data	Analytic tool or technique	Supporting theory
To investigate how written texts work ideologically with respect to understanding colonization	In what ways are different social groups in Latin America's history represented in primary-school textbooks?	Texts taken from an official school history or social studies curriculum source	Identification of the material processes (verbs) associated with the different social groups represented in each text	Systemic functional linguistics

Task

1   Make a copy of Table 12.2 using the same five headings but with blank cells beneath.

2   Conceive a qualitative research project that requires collecting some written data from extant documents. This can be data from archives, non-conventional data, participant texts, non-participant texts or any combination of these.

3   On the basis of your idea, fill in the blank cells of the table. If you wish, you could replicate the descriptions we have provided in order to get started, but it is better eventually to develop ideas of your own.

4   Make a note of the general criteria we have mentioned in this chapter for deciding how much and what kinds of written data to collect for the empirical data set of a qualitative research project.

5   Add to this list any other criteria you think are important, based on your reading about qualitative research.

6   Using all the information from Steps 1–5 above, locate two or more pieces of written data that would be appropriate for the research study you have envisaged.

7   Provide a written description of the reasons why you regard these pieces of written data as appropriate.

CHAPTER 13

Analysing spoken data in qualitative teacher research

Introduction

This chapter describes some approaches to analysing spoken data – oral language recorded by the researcher – for a range of research purposes.

Preparing and organizing spoken data for analysis

Before data can be analysed it needs to be suitably prepared and organized. Preparing spoken data for analysis usually involves turning it into written text (transcripts). 'Data analysis' is the process of *organizing these pieces of information*, *systematically identifying their key features* or relationships (themes, concepts, beliefs etc.) and *interpreting them*. The process of systematically identifying significant features in data is always informed by theory and is directly related to one's research question. It involves applying *categories* developed from a particular theory, using *concepts* identified as important by one's literature review or applying a particular *method* of analysis to the data set in order to respond to a research question. This process is one of interpreting data, and of moving data around in order to make sense of it. Interpretation processes generally answer questions such as: 'What's going on here?'; 'What does it all mean?'; and 'What is to be made of it all?' (Schwandt 1997: 4).

Organizing one's data refers to the process of preparing data in ways that enable the researcher to readily retrieve specific 'pieces' from the overall data set. Organizing data involves such things as numbering each line in a transcribed interview, numbering the pages in a fieldnote book, colour-coding data collected from different sites (e.g. different classrooms or schools), converting handwritten fieldnotes into digital documents (where the search function in a word-processing program can be used to retrieve pieces of information) and so on. Organizing data can also mean beginning to identify broad patterns within the various data collected, which facilitates the researcher's actual data analysis.

Typically, spoken data that has been audio- or video-recorded is converted into a written text called a 'transcript'. Transcripts are visual representations of verbal interactions. In preparing spoken data for analysis, the 'shape' and 'form' of the talk is maintained in the written text. In other words, the spoken language is not written as prose, but as dialogue. For example:

Example 1

Bob: How did you find out about this project?

Mavis: Oh well, it was through Ludmila and Michael, because I worked with Michael and Ludmila on other projects, and bless them, they must have thought that I would have been able to fit in here or something.

Bob: What do you think so far?

Mavis: I think its great and I love the kids. They're so smart.

In this interview excerpt the question and answer nature of the exchange between Bob and Mavis is very clear. This is the 'shape' this part of the interview took, so the transcript has been organized in a way that captures this interaction pattern.

Example 2

N3.001	*Michele*:	Okay Nicholas, now the first thing I actually want to ask you about today is in relation to your book review, did you **write** that straight onto the computer, or did you do it in pen first? Did you do a rough draft?
N3.002	*Nicholas*:	No I always uhm put it on the computer first normally so...
		[and then-
N3.003	*Michele*:	[Straight onto the computer?
N3.004	*Nicholas*:	Just straight on the computer.
N3.005	*Michele*:	Oh yeah.
N3.006	*Nicholas*:	So then I can change it '(<u>round</u>) =
N3.007	*Michele*:	Oh right.

N3.008 *Nicholas*: = and and change the words so it makes it really easier. I hate, hate writing it down 'cause then you can't change it a:nd uhm y'know it makes it a lot harder.

This example shows how researchers can begin to organize data for easy retrieval during the analysis phase. Each utterance or spoken interaction is numbered, and each number is prefixed with, in this case, 'N3', indicating that this is the transcript of the third interview with Nicholas. There are no hard and fast rules for this kind of management work. The researcher in this example devised the 'N1, N2, N3' code herself. She chose to number *utterances* rather than lines, although lines are often the appropriate unit to number. Three placeholders were used because there are more than 100 turns in this transcript, but less than 1000. The only rule needed for organizing data is for researchers to use management codes and colours that make sense to them and that they can remember easily.

This transcript represents the participants' talk (Michele and Nicholas) *verbatim*; that is, in as much detail as possible. Much more is transcribed than just the *content* of the interview at the level of words. This transcript captures repetitions, feedback sounds and statements (e.g. oh yeah, oh right), hesitations (e.g. uh, uhm), talk that overlaps (marked by the square bracket), drawn-out words (e.g. a:nd), upward inflections at the end of a word where the context is not a question (e.g. round), emphases (in bold), speech that breaks off in mid-sentence or that remains incomplete in some way (marked by a short dash) and interruptions (indicated by the equals sign at the end of one utterance and the start of another by the same speaker), in order to make available for analysis as much of the content and texture of the original interviews as possible.

Verbatim transcripts of this kind are used in ethnomethodology, conversation analysis and discourse analysis. They usually follow transcribing conventions that have been specially created for the theoretical and pragmatic needs of the research in question. In the second example above, theory from sociolinguistics has guided the production of the transcript. Each hesitation, self-correction and interruption 'told' the researcher something significant in relation to answering her research question.

Whether or not verbatim transcripts are appropriate for a particular study depends on the purpose of the study, the time the researcher has to complete it and how the transcripts will be analysed. In a study whose research question is 'How do the adults participating in this basic education programme define being literate?', it is highly unlikely that finely-detailed verbatim transcripts will be needed. On the other hand, verbatim transcripts will be necessary if one's question is 'In what ways do girls and boys establish who can say what and when during classroom group work?'

Transcripts are not neutral representations of what was said and how it was said. A transcript is a *representation* of the researcher's views, mindsets and theoretical orientation (Honan *et al.* 2000). The researcher makes decisions about what will be written down from the audio recording, how it will be written down and what will be edited out. This is evident in Examples 3 and 4 below. They are the exact same spoken language excerpt from a narrative told by a Grade 1 African American girl, but the way in which Leona's speech is *realized* or presented in each transcript is very different.

Example 3

Leona's puppy

L: L:a:st / la:st / yesterday / when / uh // m' my fa:ther / in the mórning / and he / there was a hó:ok / on top of the stairway / and my father was pickin' me up / and I got stuck on the hook / up there / an' I hadn't had breakfast / he wouldn't take me down until I finished a:ll my (break-fast) / 'cause I didn't like oatmeal either // And then my puppy ca:me / he was aslee:p, and he was- he was / he tried to get up / and he ripped my pa:nts / and he dropped the oatmeal all over hi:m / and my father came / and he said did you eat all the oatmeal / he said where's the bo:wl // He said I think the do- / I said / I think the dog . . . took it // well / I think I'll have make another can //

     (Adapted from Sarah Michaels' work in Gee *et al.* 1992: 241)

Example 4

Leona's puppy story

Part I: Introduction

  1A: Setting

   Stanza 1

        1   last yesterday in the morning

        2   there was a hook on the top of the stairway

        3   an' my father was pickin' me up

        4   an' I got stuck on the hook up there

   Stanza 2

        5   an' I hadn't had breakfast

        6   he wouldn't take me down

        7   until I finished all my breakfast

        8   'cause I didn't like oatmeal either

  1B: Catalyst

   Stanza 3

        9   an' then my puppy came

       10   he was asleep

       11   he tried to get up

> 12 an' he ripped my pants
>
> 13 an' he dropped the oatmeal all over him
>
> Stanza 4
>
> 14 an' my father came
>
> 15 an' he said, 'Did you eat all the oatmeal?'
>
> 16 he said 'Where's the bowl?'
>
> 17 I said 'I think the dog took it'
>
> 18 'Well I think I'll have t'make another bowl'
>
> (From James Paul Gee's work in Gee *et al*. 1992: 244–5)

In Example 3, Sarah Michaels was interested in tracing Leona's intonation, hesitations, speech 'repairs' and the like, in order to better understand the ways in which Leona was constructing a meaningful text for herself and for her audience. In Example 4, James Paul Gee is less interested than Michaels in false starts and repairs and more interested in the way Leona has used clauses in her talk. He has taken these clauses and smoothed them out into an 'ideal realization' of her text (Gee *et al*. 1992: 244), throwing into high relief patterns of structure and meaning in Leona's narrative. Both representations are equally valid, equally useful and readily justified by means of the theories and analytic approaches framing each approach.

There is a large literature on the non-neutrality of transcripts. For example:

- Baker, C. (1997) Transcription and representation in literacy research, in J. Flood, S. Brice Heath and D. Lapp (eds) *Handbook of Research on Teaching Literacy Through the Communicative and Visual Arts*, pp. 110–20. New York: Simon & Schuster.
- Green, J., Franquíz, M. and Dixon, C. (1997) The myth of the objective transcript: transcribing as a situated act, *TESOL Quarterly*, 31(1): 172–6.

For more on organizing spoken data, see:

- Emerson, R., Fretz, R. and Shaw, L. (1995) *Writing Ethnographic Fieldnotes*. Chicago: University of Chicago Press.
- Marshall, C. and Rossman, G. (1999) *Designing Qualitative Research*, 3rd edn. Thousand Oaks, CA: Sage.
- Stouthamer-Loeber, M. and van Kammen, W. (1995) *Data Collection and Management: A Practical Guide*. Thousand Oaks, CA: Sage.

Categorical analysis as an approach to analysing spoken data

Categorical analysis involves the systematic organization of data into groupings that are alike, similar or homogeneous (Rose and Sullivan 1996: 232). An analysis of young people's computer use might generate the following categories: in-school use, home use, use in clubs, use in other people's homes, internet café use and so on. An analysis of computer availability within a series of schools might generate different kinds of categories, such as disrepair, mistrust, teacher constraints and access issues.

Qualitative categorical analysis differs markedly from quantitative categorical analysis (and quantitative coding procedures). Quantitative categorical analysis involves 'applying a preestablished set of categories to the data according to explicit, unambiguous rules . . . [T]he primary goal [is] to generate frequency counts of the items in each category' (Maxwell 1996: 78). Although qualitative research can also make use of pre-existing category labels, it is generally directed at producing descriptive rather than 'count' categories.

While other researchers often use 'categorical analysis' and 'coding' as equivalent terms, we use 'categorical analysis' to refer to the process of developing and applying codes to data. Categorical analysis is an iterative process. It aims in the first instance to identify semantic and other kinds of relationships between data items, and to then identify logical relationships among categories of items in order to refine the number of categories to be used in writing up the study. This process may begin long before any data is collected.

A researcher investigating adolescents' computer use might begin the study with three categories of use already in mind: 'in-school', 'at home' and 'in internet cafés'. During the data analysis phase, however, the researcher might discover that these original categories help explain only part of what the young people interviewed said about their computer use. Much of the informants' data about computer use does not fit into the three original categories and, in fact, suggests additional important categories. The researcher decides it is necessary to build a taxonomy of categories. This distinguishes between 'location' and 'purpose' and between 'landlocked desktop computers' and 'wireless mobile computing devices'. It also includes additional sub-categories like 'at friends' or relations' homes', 'for pleasure', 'for school', 'to follow sport', 'to be a fan', 'to network and socialize with friends' and so on.

'Coding data' refers simply to the process of applying codes to collected information that 'flag' or remind the researcher about which data belongs in which categories. These codes get refined as more and more data are coded. To facilitate the consistency of analysis, each code used in a study requires an explicit definition or a set of criteria to guide its application.

One straightforward approach to categorical analysis involves developing codes that directly match with preset categories – the category label itself becomes the code. For example, in one of our studies we provided careful definitions of three preset categories: 'In-school computer use', 'At home computer use' and 'computer use in internet cafés'. We then went through all our data and used colours to code all the places where data corresponded to our definitions of these categories. All data pertaining to 'In-school computer use' were coded yellow, all references to 'At home computer use' were coded blue and 'Computer use in internet cafés' was coded green. Entire paragraphs, sentences and parts of sentences were coded using this system. Once this was done we produced Table 13.1 based on the coded data.

Initially, a lot of transcribed interview data in this example remained that were not

Table 13.1   Colour coding as a technique used in categorical analysis

Computer use in school (yellow)	Computer use at home (blue)	Computer use in internet cafés (green)
'At school we mainly use the computer to play maths and spelling games'	'Usually every afternoon I meet with my friends in the Yahoo chat space'	'We don't have a computer at home but I still "chat" online with other kids in Latin America 'cause I use the computers at an internet café near us'
'The other day the teacher had trouble with the computer and my friend and I had to reinstall the mouse for him'	'I like using the instant messenger function on my computer while I'm doing my homework to keep in touch with my friend from school'	'The first time I used a computer outside school was in an internet café'
	'I got a new game for my computer yesterday – it's totally cool'	

colour coded. The categories appropriate for them did not yet exist. We then revisited and scrutinized the data, finding the uncoded data suggested additional categories. These new (initially tentative) categories were then added to the three pre-existing categories and each assigned a colour. The researchers then began using these colours to code the rest of the data and allocate them to their appropriate categories.

The following examples explore categorical analysis in greater detail.

Example 1: using coding to develop and refine categories

Amanda Coffey and Paul Atkinson (1996) used categorical analysis to address the research question: 'What makes a "good" doctoral thesis in anthropology?' They collected data by interviewing anthropology professors throughout Britain. Rather than using preconceived or pre-existing categories, they decided to let the categories 'grow out of' or 'emerge from' the data. They transcribed a set of interviews and read them repeatedly, until groups of similar data that appeared significant for their research question began to appear. They then began labelling these groups of data by writing 'code labels' next to significant items (see also Strauss and Corbin 1990). In this labelling process they paid close attention to the 'categories of expression' that the people they interviewed actually used (Coffey and Atkinson 1996: 40). One of their coded transcripts is presented in Table 13.2, with the data appearing in the left-hand column and the initial code labels in the right-hand column (ibid: 41–2).

This initial step in Coffey and Atkinson's coding process yielded preliminary categories that emerged from the *words* used by interviewees. Coffey and Atkinson then began to systematically group or categorize these initial categories, which often required them to devise their own labels for these new 'superordinate' categories.

Table 13.2 A coded data transcript

Data	Code label
Odette Parry: What sorts of skills do you think it imparts, the actual process of doing a PhD?	Skills from PhD
Dr Throstle: It's a very big question. Again I think in anthropology you learn a whole lot of things that you don't normally learn in a PhD, which is partly to do with fieldwork. That trains you to carry on on your own both academically and personally, it's a social skills training of a very exciting kind...	Fieldwork Normal PhD Academic independence Personal independence Social skills Exacting
I think one of the peculiarities of anthropology is that unlike most other disciplines, certainly in the social sciences, you're dealing – unlike history for example – you don't start from one body of documentation and convert it into another kind of body of documentation...	Peculiarity Disciplines Social science History People Lives Conversation Academic text
Which is why it takes such a long time and why it's so difficult, because these two things are miles and miles apart. And it's very common, I think, for graduate students when they come back from the field to react against what they're doing, to feel that what they're writing is somehow a betrayal of or it falls far short of the relationships they had when they were in the field. Writing a rather dull piece of academic work somehow feels like a betrayal...	Time Difficult Difference Return from field Writing Relationships in the field Dull Academic work Betrayal
I think one of the problems of fieldwork, if you're away for a long time – and most anthropologists are – you lose touch to some extent with your academic and your home culture, and then you have to get back into it, and it's often a slow process when you come back.	Fieldwork Time Absence Academic culture Home culture Return

Source: Coffey and Atkinson 1996: 40

This is evident in relation to the first question and response sequence in the interview. When the researchers looked more closely at Dr Throstle's reply they found her response was saying 'there is something distinctive about anthropology as a discipline that makes it different from other disciplines' (1996: 42). Accordingly, Coffey and Atkinson (1996: 43–4) developed a superordinate category they called 'distinctiveness of anthropology'. They subsequently used this new category to look for other pieces of data where respondents said what they thought was 'special and distinctive about this subject [anthropology]':

> *Odette Parry:* What sorts of skills do you think it
>   imparts, the actual process of doing a PhD?
> *Dr Throstle:* It's a very big question. Again I think   Distinctiveness of anthropology
>   in anthropology you learn a whole lot of
>   things that you don't normally learn in a PhD,
>   which is partly to do with fieldwork. That
>   trains you to carry on on your own both
>   academically and personally, it's a social skills
>   training of a very exciting kind..

Coffey and Atkinson repeated this process to find many other superordinate categories across their interview transcripts. These categories helped them to structure subsequent interviews with anthropology professors to obtain more information relevant to their research question. Superordinate category labels also act as categories for analysing the entire data set. They make it possible to subsume data from 'lower order' or smaller, more concrete categories within larger, higher order, more abstract categories, which in turn makes the data more manageable and easier to interpret.

At the same time, Coffey and Atkinson remind researchers that it is important to retain useful preliminary and/or lower order categories from initial analyses because it is possible for information to get 'lost' or 'altered' in the transition between initial and superordinate categories. To be sure that original information is not lost or changed in ways that can be avoided, it is important to be able to check category item allocations and meanings of data at the superordinate level with earlier allocations of data within lower order categories. This calls for carefully kept, systematic records of the analysis process and outcomes.

Task

- Why didn't Coffey and Atkinson make specialized *verbatim* transcripts of their interviews, such as those shown on pages 267 and 268?

- Why do you think it was important to Coffey and Atkinson to use their respondents' own 'categories of expression' during the phase of developing the initial categories? What other approach could they have used for coding the interview data the first time in order to develop their initial categories?

- Exactly what were the 'codes' used by Coffey and Atkinson? (i.e. what form did they take? In what way are they 'codes'?)

- What kind of research problem were Coffey and Atkinson addressing in their study (e.g. existential, theoretical, practical)? How do you know?

Example 2: categorical analysis in relation to the overall research design

This example draws on some of our own research into new technologies in classrooms (Lankshear and Knobel 1997a). Our research question asked: 'What are some of the complexities educators identify that pertain to concerns about issues of equitable education in the electronic age?'

To help develop initial codes for analysing the data, we generated more specific *sub-questions* implied by the main research question. For example:

- What do teachers in this study identify as 'complexitities' when using new technologies in class?
- How do teachers in this study conceive relationships between new technologies and equitable education?
- For schools involved in this study, what appears to be the relationship between new technologies and equitable education at the level of policy?
- What role does professional development play at present in relation to using new technologies in classrooms? And in relation to using new technologies to address equity issues?
- What uses of new technologies at school do these teachers report?

Data collection and analysis approaches for the study were conceived as shown in Table 13.3.

Table 13.3 Approaches to data collection and analysis

Data to collect	Data analysis approach and resources
Interview data pertaining to teachers' articulations of the difficulties, opportunities, obstacles, pathways and so on they are facing with regard to addressing equity issues in their classrooms where access to effective uses of new technologies is concerned	Categorical analysis: Coffey and Atkinson 1996; Mason 1996; Bogdan and Biklen 1997
Interviews with students. Data will be presented as edited interview transcripts	Pattern matching analysis of observed data and artefacts
Observations of classroom practice and free-time computer use in the school	Linguistic analysis of policy documents
Collection of technology-related policy documents.	

To begin a categorical analysis of spoken data we developed some initial codes for information we expected to find in the data (based on our reading of relevant literature). These included:

- appropriate professional development (lack of, through to abundance of);
- teacher engagement in new technology use (lack of, through to abundance of);
- policy related issues or events;
- relationship between new technologies and social inequities (weak potential for addressing inequities, through to strong potential).

We converted these to shorthand codes as follows:

- PROFDEL (+ or −);
- TR-ENGAG (+ or −);
- POL;
- TECHEQUAL (+ or −).

The following initial coding of an excerpt from an interview with one teacher, Daniel, illustrates our process of categorical analysis.

D2.001	*Daniel*:	My experience of working in technology in schools has been a lot of disappointments in terms of maybe being idealistic about where we hope to get with kids and what sort of work we can get from them and that sort of thing.	Disappointment in what's done at school
D2.002	*Michele*:	So you find the kids don't engage with it, or-	PROFDEL(−)
D2.003	*Daniel*:	I think it's more a lack of training in teachers. You know, I think it's the lack of vision in the-from us, you know. The kids will go anywhere you take them, and technologically they're better-Like I find the kids coming into the [computer] lab and, while there's not much in there at the moment to do, they go straight to work. They don't need any instructions, whereas I take teachers in there and they're not [comfortable with the computers or with what's going on in the room]. But a lot of teachers don't want to engage in the whole thing.	Kids are more technologically adept than teachers TR-ENGAG(−)
D2.004	*Colin*:	What do you mean, 'they don't want to engage'?	
D2.005	*Daniel*:	Well, they just take no (interest). I don't know what it is. It's just that, I find in English teaching anyway, I don't know if it's- I've worked on joint projects with maths and science teachers and with social science teachers and things like that, but basically the people I've worked with, and I've been in this school over six years and I've been the technology coordinator there for all that time, so I've been in virtually every classroom with every teacher who's been through the place.	TR-ENGAG(−)

D2.006	*Michele*:	Yes.		
D2.007	*Daniel*:	The number of teachers who grabbed technology in my area and went on with it is probably 1 in 10, or something. We wrote into the teaching programme, I did this myself years ago with the Head of Department [in the school], that every kid had to do four or five weeks a year using technology of some sort. So we had laptop computers and things like that which we used to use. The teachers did it because it was part of the teaching programme, not because the kids were turned on by it all, or whatever.	POL	
D2.008	*Colin*:	Were the kids turned on at all?		
D2.009	*Daniel*:	Yeah, I think so. Well, the laptop thing- we've just gone into having a computer lab now. We've got some 486s networked to the library, and so on. What I found with the laptops were- we were using technology at school that was five years out of date compared to what the kids had at home. You know, we're using these little monitors, little screens like these (holds up fingers in small rectangle shape), black and white screens, and the kids at home have got- Is that a Toshiba? (pointing to Colin's laptop computer on the desk).	Out-dated technology issues	
D2.010	*Colin*:	(Nods).		

Our initial codes were useful, but certainly not exhaustive. To progress the analysis we used phrases we thought captured what was worth preserving from the initial coding and that marked out potentially viable new categories. To help keep track of our coded data we developed an organizing structure, as shown in Table 13.4. This structure drew on some of the sub-questions implied by the main research question for category headings to analyse data referring to the teachers' points of view. For other categories, we drew directly on key statements made by teachers in their interviews. Using Daniel's interviews as an illustration, our initial categorizing work is shown in Table 13.5.

Table 13.4 Organizing structure for categorical analysis of interview data

From the teachers' points of view				
Professional development	*Teacher engagement in new technology use in classrooms*	*Student adeptness*	*Relationship between new technologies and social equity*	*Reported quality of experiences with new technologies in school*

Table 13.5 Initial categorizing work based on the research question(s)

From the teachers' points of view				
Professional development	*Teacher engagement in new technology use in classrooms*	*Student adeptness*	*Relationship between new technologies and social equity*	*Reported quality of experiences with new technologies in school*
D2.003 *Daniel:* I think it's more a lack of training in teachers. You know, I think it's the lack of vision in the- from us, you know	D2.003 *Daniel:* But a lot of teachers don't want to engage in the whole thing D2.004 *Colin:* What do you mean, 'they don't want to engage'? D2.005 *Daniel:* Well, they just take no (interest) D2.007 *Daniel:* The number of teachers who grabbed technology in my area and went on with it is probably 1 in 10, or something … The teachers did it because it was part of the teaching programme, not because the kids were turned on by it all, or whatever	D2.003 *Daniel:* The kids will go anywhere you take them, and technologically they're better- Like I find the kids coming into the [computer] lab and, while there's not much in there at the moment to do, they go straight to work. They don't need any instructions		D2.001 *Daniel:* My experience of working in technology in schools has been a lot of disappointments in terms of maybe being idealistic about where we hope to get with kids and what sort of work we can get from them and that sort of thing

Subsequent analyses involved inventing codes for new emerging categories and remaining alert for further unanticipated categories. Even at the early stage of analysis illustrated here, the process was already suggesting that addressing social equity issues in classrooms might not be a priority for teachers in low-income schools (this indeed proved to be a more general pattern).

Task

- In the transcript excerpt on page 276, what does 'D2' mean?

- What does 'D2.007 Daniel' mean?

- Suggest possible justifications for each piece of data organized beneath each category in Table 13.5 (e.g. how might the researcher have decided to put 'D2.007 Daniel' into the category concerning teacher engagement?).

- Are any superordinate categories visible as yet in this preliminary analysis? What does your response suggest?

As researchers work through their transcripts categorizing pieces of data that stand out or seem especially relevant to their research question(s) it may become apparent that some presumptions, ideas or predictions underlying the problem that generated the study in the first place are questionable or unwarranted. Consider, for example, our unmet expectation that teachers would make direct links between new technologies in schools and the possibilities for addressing social inequities. Daniel was very politically and socially aware, but had nothing to say throughout his interviews that could reasonably be interpreted as applying to this category. An empty column like this one can alert the researcher to issues and potential problems. In this case we were alerted to the possibility that the idea of pursuing more equitable education by introducing new technologies to classroom learning might be so much 'pie in the sky'. Our interview transcripts suggested that the challenges teachers were facing with respect to computing access and proficiency deflected attention away from equity needs and responses.

As is obvious from this example, the researcher's initial categories may not tell the 'whole story'. Additional categories will often be required to analyse thoroughly the data that have been collected. Categories that needed to be added to our analysis of the excerpt from our interview with Daniel included: 'student adeptness with new technologies'; 'quality of technology available at school'; 'reported quality of experiences with new technologies in school'; and 'control and censorship of new technology use'. It is possible that 'funding issues' and 'quality of equipment available at school' could and should be collapsed into a superordinate category. Existing categories might need to be refined. For example, the category 'professional development' might better be subdivided into smaller categories like 'availability', 'timeliness' and 'needs-based'. This is an instance of what Coffey and Atkinson (1996) mean by letting the categories 'grow out of' or emerge from the data.

Furthermore, a given piece of data can often be allocated to more than one category. The data we collect via interviewing are always complex and never neat and easy to extract. If one finds that too many pieces of data (e.g. more than 20 per cent) are being allocated to multiple categories, this may mean that the existing category labels are too general or broad to be of real analytic use. They will need to be made more exact so that the analysis of the interview data elicits useful information that enables the researcher to respond effectively to the research question(s) driving the study.

Categorical analysis is not confined to *spoken data* alone, but can also be used with written and observed data. It is, however, an especially useful approach for beginning researchers to use when analysing spoken data.

For further reading in this area, we suggest:

- Coffey, A. and Atkinson, P. (1996) *Making Sense of Qualitative Data Analysis: Complementary Strategies*. Thousand Oaks, CA: Sage.
- Lampert, M. and Ervin-Tripp, S. (1993) Structured coding for the study of language and social interaction, in J. Edwards and M. Lampert (eds) *Talking Data: Transcription and Coding in Discourse Research*, pp. 169–206. Hillsdale, NJ: Lawrence Erlbaum.

Finally, researchers sometimes advise using specialized computer software to identify and sort categories when conducting categorical analysis of interview data. They have often had much previous experience of coding and categorizing data, understand how the process works and are able to use the software to do more efficiently the kinds of things they would otherwise have to do manually. This is a very different situation from inexperienced researchers, who may think that this software can make important decisions for them *that it cannot*. This is because such software is a tool and *not* a researcher. Code-and-retrieve software programs like NUDi*ST, HyperRESEARCH and the like have limitations we need to be aware of. These include the following:

- the software program will not *interpret* categories;
- categories need to be carefully considered prior to and following computer-based code-and-retrieve analysis;
- the software may not accommodate 'empty' categories such as the one we discussed earlier.

Sociolinguistic analysis

Sociolinguistic approaches to analysing spoken data focus on language as it is used in social interactions. When we analyse data sociolinguistically we identify elements of language use that indicate each speaker's social and cultural understandings and practices. We also identify things that get done in the world through language use, how they get done and with what consequences for which people, by looking at how language operates as a social practice within particular contexts that are 'captured' in and through spoken data. Analytic tools and techniques developed from sociolinguistics are many and diverse. They draw on several fields of sociolinguistics, including speech-act theory, interactional sociolinguistics, conversation analysis or ethnomethodology, systemic functional linguistics etc.

In this section we provide two examples where researchers have used forms of sociolinguistic analysis we believe are especially applicable in teacher research to analyse spoken data.

Example 1: analysing 'I-statements' to understand personal identity constitution

Sociolinguistic analysis can be as straightforward as analysing a particular class of statements made in an interview. In a study of teenagers, identity and literacy, James Gee and colleagues (reported in Gee 1999, 2000) analysed interviewees' 'I-statements'. These are statements that include use of the first person pronoun, 'I' in a conversation or discussion. The researchers focused on I-statements because 'where people choose to speak as an *I* is consequential for how they are here and now fashioning themselves in and through language' (Gee 2000: 415).

Using semi-structured interviews, Gee collected spoken data from six US teenagers: three from upper middle-class homes and three from working-class homes. Gee first identified all instances of I-statements occurring in the interviews and then subdivided them into groups according to the following categories (Gee 2000: 415):

- cognitive statements about thinking and knowing (e.g. 'I think ...', 'I know ...');
- affect/desire statements about desiring and liking (e.g. 'I want ...', 'I like ...');
- state and action statements about states or actions of the speaker (e.g. 'I am mature', 'I hit him back', 'I paid the bill');
- ability and constraint statements about being able or having to do things (e.g. 'I can't say anything to them', 'I have to do my paper round');
- achievement statements about activities, desires or efforts that relate to mainstream achievement or distinction (e.g. 'I challenge myself', 'I want to go to MIT or Harvard').

These categories partly grew directly out of what the young people said. They were also, however, informed directly by sociolinguistic theories that assign a range of particular functions to groups of 'process words' or verbs (e.g. mental processes include verbs like think, know, believe).

Gee employed an uncomplicated research design. This involved collecting interview data from teenagers from different social class backgrounds and analysing it using five categories of I-statements. This deceptively simple design generated information that yielded very interesting findings.

The findings centred on differences in language use between the upper middle-class students and the working-class students who participated in the study. Gee found that in terms of I-statements, the upper middle-class students used I-statements most in relation to cognitive and achievement items, whereas the working-class students' I-statements tended to emphasize affect and desires, abilities and constraints, and states and actions. Gee (2000: 416) summarizes his findings as shown in Table 13.6.

Gee interpreted these findings to mean that the upper middle-class students used language that drew directly on their 'lifeworld' and experiences of having parents who are professionals, and understanding school discourses and public sphere institutions at a reflective, 'meta' level. This world enabled them to 'distance themselves from the social, cultural and political inequalities of our new time and to hold a firm belief in their own essential merit and worth, despite a very ready acknowledgement of their privileged circumstances' (Gee 2000: 419). Gee described these teenagers as being well

Table 13.6 Gee's findings

	Working-class			Upper middle-class		
	Sandra	Jeremy	Maria	Emily	Ted	Karin
Category A						
Affect/desire	32	21	28	8	12	13
Ability and constraint	7	7	7	1	4	2
State and action	39	49	40	24	18	7
Subtotal	78	77	75	33	34	22
Category B						
Cognitive	22	23	23	54	50	65
Achievement	0	0.5	2	13	22	13
Subtotal	22	23.5	25	67	72	78

on their way to becoming 'shape-shifting portfolio people' – people who are able to work collaboratively and interactively, for longer hours and with less supervision, on a series of often unconnected projects, and who can 'continuously design and redesign their work processes, functions, and relationships' (Gee 2000: 414). These shape-shifting attributes are integral to becoming a high echelon worker in the new capitalist workplace.

By contrast, the working-class students in the study seemed to emphasize 'dialogic interaction' – social interactions and their position within it – with little or no direct reference to school discourses and the effects of public sphere institutions on their lives. Gee points out that, ironically, despite this kind of dialogic interaction being promoted in many school reform movements, the students who appear most to display such qualities are working-class students who 'face a future without a stable working class' (p. 419).

Task

- Why do you think Gee decided to use 6 students in his study (rather than, say, 2 or 10 or 35)?

- Gee uses numbers to summarize his data, yet his study is without a doubt a qualitative one. How could this be? What does this suggest for our understandings of the features of qualitative research?

- Gee interprets his data analyses by means of reference to 'new capitalism' theory (see Gee *et al.* 1996). What other theories might have used to interpret his findings and why? Which theories would be unsuitable to use in helping to interpret this data?

- Why is I-statement analysis best suited to spoken data and not, say, fieldnotes?

> **Task**
>
> Complete the following matrix by entering into the empty columns what you think may have been Gee's research purpose(s) and research question(s). You may want to provide a number of alternative possibilities based on the information in the other columns and the description of Gee's research project provided above and in his article (Gee 2000).
>
> | Research purpose | Research question | Data to collect | Data analysis approach and (possible) sources |
> |---|---|---|---|
> | | | Interviews with three working-class and three upper middle-class teenagers | Transcribe interviews and analyse the I-statements |

For further reading in this area we recommend:

- Gee, J. (1999) *An Introduction to Discourse Analysis: Theory and Method*. New York: Routledge.
- Hatch, E. (1992) *Discourse and Language Education*. Cambridge: Cambridge University Press.
- Schiffrin, D. (1994) *Approaches to Discourse*. Cambridge, MA: Blackwell.

Example 2: using a systemic functional linguistics approach to data analysis to investigate the role of oral narratives in mother-daughter relations in a low socioeconomic status neighbourhood

During recent years numerous qualitative researchers have shown great interest in various forms of *oral narratives* as a means for understanding people's worldviews, values, beliefs, practices, rituals, likes and dislikes, life experiences and so on. According to Deborah Schiffrin, '[t]he ability of narrative to verbalize and situate experience as text (both locally and globally) provides a resource for the display of self and identity' (1996: 167).

Our example concerns the role of oral narratives in mother-daughter relations within an economically disadvantaged area of an Australian metropolitan city. The research question is: 'What role do oral narratives play in eight mother-daughter relationships within a long-term economically disadvantaged area of Brisbane?'

Study participants were eight mother-daughter dyads identified via word-of-mouth suggestions. We use anecdotes from one mother-daughter dyad here to illustrate analytic approaches at different levels of complexity based on systemic functional linguistics.

These anecdotes were collected using semi-structured interviews in the home of a 12-year-old girl (Hannah) in an area of Brisbane that for decades has been officially designated 'socioeconomically disadvantaged'. Hannah's parents had bought a house in the area almost 20 years previously. Julia (Hannah's mother) felt they had been duped by the estate agent, who had convinced them to accept a government grant to buy the house without telling them about the suburb's reputation and its official status as an 'underprivileged' zone. At the time of the study, Hannah's father's salary was at a level higher than that of approximately 85 per cent of Australian wage and salary earners.

The data revealed *anecdotes* as a key narrative strategy used by Julia to explain why she felt she did not 'belong' in the residential area in which they lived. Hence, anecdotes are the unit of analysis. Within systemic functional linguistics, an 'anecdote' is defined as a short account of an interesting or instructive event, often with a humorous twist or end to it. Structurally, anecdotes follow a general pattern:

Opening statement or comment

- Who?
- Where?
- When? (optional)
- Subject matter or topic of the anecdote.

Event(s)
- What happened, usually in chronological sequence.

Punchline or 'moral'
- The speaker's reason(s) for telling this anecdote (e.g. to entertain, to instruct, to explain).

Evaluation (optional)
- A personal comment (e.g. 'I would hate that to happen to me', 'So, in the end, he was really stupid for getting out of the car').

In this excerpt from the interview data the anecdotes have been given in italics.

H4.529	*Julia:*	*I don't belong here. I don't fit into this area, sort of thing. I don't ... sort of ... I don't really sort of (fit the type) ((soft laugh)). Y'know, like I went down to the shops the other day and bought this outfit ... on a whim ((laughs)). Well, other people around here don't do that sort of thing. Like, y'know they're sort of ... scratching for money.*
H4.530	*Michele:*	Mmm.
H4.531	*Julia:*	Like it's been so easy to talk to you because you're interested in old china, and old furniture, and old houses, and it's just easy to talk to you. You know, you just don't **strike** that up at school. The other ladies don't, have that interest. Y'know, they just don't.
H4.548	*Michele:*	What would their interest be, then?
H4.549	*Julia:*	Mostly it's ... they will talk about other people, which, is

just something I just refuse to do, and just don't like doing that. Yeah, no, it passes just the general comment. It sort of goes into the ... cattiness and ...

H4.550 *Michele:* Oh ri:ght. So you don't have any close female friends around?

H4.551 *Julia:* *(2.0) No, I don't. Didn't really ma- oh, one lady up at school I'm fairly friendly with but ... they're just a different class, you see. No other way to say it. They're very rough talking and mean. I mean you're really careful with these people. These people actually- I mean like, this one woman's husband's brother has been in jail and he actually beats people up because they irritate him.*

Analysing anecdotes
Basic approach
A useful and straightforward approach to analysing the structure of the anecdotes told by Julia involves turning the general structural elements of anecdotes into questions:

Opening statement or comment

- Who is involved in this anecdote? What relationship do they have with the speaker?
- In what ways does the opening statement or comment frame what follows?

Event(s)
- What happened?
- Where did the event etc. take place?
- When did the event or phenomenon take place?
- What do these events *mean* for the speaker, or appear to mean?

Punchline or 'moral'
- What seems to be the speaker's reason(s) for telling this anecdote (e.g. to entertain, to instruct, to explain)?

Evaluation (optional)
- What judgement does the speaker make in relation to the punchline of the anecdote? What bearing does this have on the opening statement?

Using a double-column layout, the researcher can then line up the data beside the structural features of the anecdotes, and respond to analytic questions relating to each key structural feature (see Table 13.7).

More complex approach
Structural analysis can be made as complex as the researcher considers appropriate in accordance with the research purpose, aim and time frame. The following example presents a considerably more complex narrative structure analysis guide than the previous one.

Table 13.7 Generic structure analysis of an oral anecdote

Anecdote 1	*Structural analysis tools*
(1) I don't belong here. I don't fit into this area, sort of thing. I don't … sort of … I don't really sort of (fit the type) ((soft laugh))	**Opening statement or comment** • *Who is involved in this anecdote?* The narrator's opening statement clearly signals the self-referentiality of this anecdote • *In what ways does the opening statement or comment frame what follows?* The opening lines set up a kind of argument in the anecdote – which is carried over into a later anecdote – that Julia does not belong in this area because she is not like the 'other' people here
(2) Y'know, like I went down to the shops the other day and bought this outfit (3) … on a whim ((laughs))	**Event(s)** • *What happened?* Julia went shopping and bought a new outfit to wear • *Where is this taking place?* In the area in which Julia currently lives • *When?* The other day (i.e. fairly recently) • *What do these events mean for the speaker or appear to mean?* This was impulse shopping – Julia tells how she acted on a whim – that didn't have to be carefully budgeted for, or perhaps not even thought about very carefully (Julia's pause before saying 'on a whim' signals to the listener that this piece of information is important)
(4) Well, other people around here don't do that sort of thing. Like, y'know they're sort of … scratching for money	**Punchline or 'moral'** • *The speaker's reason(s) for telling this anecdote?* Julia's purpose appears to be twofold: first, she clearly signals to the listener that she is not 'scratching for money' because she is able to purchase clothes on a whim (and implies that she can do this whenever she likes); and second, that because she is not scratching for money and able to buy things on a whim, then she is *not like the other people in her area* **Evaluation (optional)** • *What judgement does the speaker make in relation to the punchline of the anecdote? What bearing does this have on the opening statement?* Julia makes no explicit evaluation of people who 'scratch for money'. Instead, her evaluation is actually her opening statement: 'I don't belong here'. By placing this evaluative comment first, Julia emphasizes her sense of difference from others living in the area, and alerts the listener to how the anecdote needs to be interpreted (i.e. Julia is not like them)

Cultural context

- What appears to be the purpose of or reason for this oral narrative? How do I know?

- In what ways does the speaker seem to achieve or not achieve his or her apparent, or enacted, purpose? What is the evidence for my judgement?

- What effect does the specific text type (e.g. narrative, recount, anecdote) seem to have on the telling and receiving of the story? How do I know?

Social context

- What is the subject matter of this oral narrative? What relationship does it have to the conversation or interview in which it is embedded? Does this subject matter appear in other oral narratives by the same narrator, and if so, what does this tell me? (Does it appear in other narratives by different tellers?)

- What does the narrative 'say' about the relationship between the speaker and the listener(s)? What effect does this have on the story and its reception? What is my evidence?

- What does the narrative tell me about the social roles and relationships in the teller's life, as seen from the narrator's perspective (e.g. the role of women in disadvantaged areas, the role of being a mother in a particular family, the role of being a child in a particular family)? How does this compare across the same narrator's oral narratives?

- In what ways might this narrative encode explanations about everyday life for the narrator?

Textual features

Generic structure

- Does the text type of the narrative have a conventional generic structure (e.g. orientation, conflict, resolution, coda/evaluation of stories, the orientation, events, and coda of recounts)? If not, why not? What does this tell me?

- Does the writer use the various stages effectively and appropriately?

Cohesion

- In what ways does the narrator make the story *cohere*? In other words, what use does the narrator make of contextualizing cues (e.g. 'we were living in Southerden Street then', or 'It happened on the corner near the supermarket'); temporal cohesive ties such as 'and then', 'after that' or 'before you were born'; and relational cohesive ties such as 'you remember how/when/him' or 'she was married to my brother at the time' statements.

Grammar

- What effect do repeated grammatical structures have on the story (e.g. embedded clauses will make the story much more complex than simple clause structures)? Are these repeated in other narratives by this same teller?

- What does the dominant grammatical order (i.e. syntax) or sentence order within an oral narrative tell me, if anything (i.e. studying syntax – the order of words in a sentence – can help identify cultural differences in language use; see Gee *et al.* 1992)?

- What effects do tense, pronouns, prepositions and so forth have in terms of carrying the speaker's purpose in and for the narrative (think about Gee's analysis of I-statements described earlier in this section)?

Vocabulary

- What effect do the narrator's language choices have in relation to the speaker's subject matter and purpose (e.g. how does she describe the area in which she lives? What processes or verbs does she use in relation to herself, her daughter(s)? What use does she make of content words? etc.)?

Task

Use the structural analysis guide above to analyse the first anecdote told by Julia.

- What do you notice? What did the analysis guide above enable you to do and 'see' that our analysis in Table 13.7 did not?

- When would you elect to use each? (What kind of research purpose would it need to be? What kind of research question? What kind of timeline?)

- Would it be possible to use *both* analysis guides in the same study? Why/why not?

Comparative analysis

The analysis becomes usefully more complex still when Hannah's anecdotes and other narratives are analysed and compared with her mother's. The following excerpt is from a transcript of an interview recorded ten days before the data was collected from which Julia's anecdotes were taken. The 'anecdote' is unconventional because it is a 'wish' rather than something that has actually occurred. It nonetheless has a conventional anecdote structure.

| H2.119 | *Michele:* | Right. Uh-huh, what if you had three wishes just for yourself? |
| H2.120 | *Hannah:* | U:hmm … u:hmm … that my scho:ol- that all my friends and all the people in my class and friends and stuff, that- and that my school was like in out in the country- we lived |

out in the <u>country</u>. So we're like based out in the country, and I still have all my friends and the <u>teachers</u>. 'Cause I'd like to live out there. I don't like living here.

H2.121 *Michele:*   Why- How come you

                [do-

H2.122 *Hannah:*   [Oh I like- **I like** living here but, I like the country better.

An incomplete analysis of Hannah's anecdote is shown in Table 13.8.

Table 13.8   An incomplete analysis of Hannah's anecdote

Anecdote	*Structural analysis tools*
(1) [I wish] that my scho:ol- that all my friends and all the people in my class and friends and stuff, that- and that my school was like in out in the country- we lived out in the <u>country</u>	**Opening statement or comment** • *Who is involved in this anecdote?* Hannah, all her friends, her teachers, all the people in her class at school • *In what ways does the opening statement or comment frame what follows?*
(2) So we're like based out in the country, and I still have all my friends and the <u>teachers</u>	**Event(s)** • *What happened?* • What do these events mean for the speaker or appear to mean?
(3) 'Cause I'd like to live out there. I don't like living here	**Punchline or 'moral'** • The speaker's reason(s) for telling this anecdote?
(4) Oh I like- **I like** living here but, I like the country better	**Evaluation (optional)** • *What judgement does the speaker make in relation to the punchline of the anecdote?* • *What bearing does this have on the opening statement?*

Task

Complete the analysis of Hannah's anecdote begun in Table 13.8.

Hannah's data, like Julia's, was rich in anecdotes. She said she liked nothing more than listening to her mother and aunts swapping tales about growing up in northern New South Wales. In interviews when both were present Hannah would ask her mother to recount particular events she obviously knew by heart, but whose recounting was still rich in meaning and significance for her. For example, Hannah begged Julia to 'tell the story about the thistles and the cart and the electric fence'. Julia told the tale, with elaborations and asides from Hannah.

Analysis of these and other anecdotes collected from Hannah and Julia support an interpretation of the data that suggests Hannah understands how her mother feels that their present location within a traditionally socioeconomically disadvantaged area is a mistake: that they are middle-class people living in a lower-class area. Hannah's anecdotes suggest also that she is aware that her mother does not like living where they do. Their present situation is one of not belonging in the area, and the past – particularly living in the country – is a happier, less complex and altogether more enjoyable life. For Hannah, this may be an uneasy apprenticeship. It suggests she is torn between loyalty to her mother and her mother's feelings of alienation, and her own life experiences in the area in which she clearly likes her school and many of the people in it.

There are, obviously, numerous ways in which the data collected from Hannah and her mother might be analysed and interpreted (see Knobel 1999; Honan *et al.* 2000). It is clear, however, that systemic functional linguistics provides the researcher with a set of useful tools and techniques for analysing spoken data in ways that enable comparisons across narratives collected from one or more persons. Many researchers, of course, regard comparison as a primary element of rigorous qualitative investigation (see Athanases and Heath 1995).

For suggested further reading in this area we suggest:

- Gee, J., Michaels, S. and O'Connor, M. (1992) Discourse analysis, in M. LeCompte, W. Millroy and J. Preissle (eds) *The Handbook of Qualitative Research in Education*, pp. 227–91. San Diego, CA: Academic Press.
- Lieblich, A., Tuval-Mashiach, R. and Zilber, T. (1998) *Narrative Research: Reading, Analysis, and Interpretation.* Thousand Oaks, CA: Sage.

Discourse analysis

While discourse analysis is a branch of sociolinguistics it differs from other sociolinguistic approaches to analysing spoken data (like conversation analysis and interactional sociolinguistics) in two important ways:

1 In discourse analysis the data analysis usually focuses first on the *purpose* and *meaning* of the overall text or transcript prior to employing more 'micro' forms of analysis of the kinds traditionally used in sociolinguistics, or even linguistics proper. In this way, discourse analysis focuses on *discourse* – meaningful stretches of language – in relation to social, cultural and cognitive processes and outcomes (Gee *et al.* 1992: 228).

2 Discourse analysis deliberately draws attention to complex relationships in language use, social systems and social structures or institutions. Hence discourse analysis can provide insights into operations of power, interests, coercion, identity constitution, ideology and so on at a *political level* in ways that may not be possible within other forms of sociolinguistic analysis.

Hence, we treat discourse analysis separately here.

In this section we briefly describe two variants of discourse analysis employed in some of the work done by James Gee and Gunther Kress respectively. The work of both, however, involves very much more than the minimal elements we focus on here.

James Gee's approach to discourse analysis as D/discourse analysis

Much of Gee's discourse analysis work builds on his celebrated distinction between *Discourse* and *discourse*. Discourse (large 'D') refers to ways of being in the world. Discourses involve particular ways of talking, acting, thinking, believing, dressing, reading, writing, gesturing, moving and so on. We talk, act, think etc. differently when we are 'in' different Discourses. When a woman is *being a mother* (acting out of or responding to the world from within the mother Discourse), she will speak, dress, act etc. more or less differently from when she is *being an executive* (or the wife of an executive), *a neighbour, a feminist, a lover* etc.

We all 'belong to' multiple Discourses, although any two people will tend to belong to different combinations of Discourses and, often, to different versions of Discourses. For example, to be a teenager (in the teenager Discourse) in the USA will involve a different *way of being* to some extent from being a teenager in Toowoomba, Australia. Being a Mexican will take a very different form for a lawyer living in Polanco (a wealthy suburb in Mexico City) than for a farm labourer living in rural Tabasco.

The particular Discourses we belong to as individuals shape our identities and create *social positions* (or perspectives) from which we are 'called' or 'invited' to speak, act, dress, think, read, write, move, gesture and so on. Many of the Discourses we belong to are those we have been recruited to without being aware of it, and which we have not chosen to 'join'. In some cases it may be very difficult, if not impossible, to participate effectively in a particular Discourse if it does not cohere well with the other Discourses we belong to and are proficient in.

Gee distinguishes between primary and secondary Discourses. A person's primary Discourse is what they are socialized into within their face-to-face kinship group (e.g. their family). Our primary Discourse shapes our initial ways of speaking, habitual ways of acting, views, values, beliefs, experiences and our 'first' social identity (Gee 1991: 7, 1992: 108). Secondary Discourses socialize people outside of their immediate family groups, within institutions and other forms of social groupings and social practice. Secondary Discourses require communication with non-intimates, and expect members to act in ways that are strongly conventionalized.

When Gee talks about discourse with a small 'd' he means stretches or pieces of language that make sense. The key point here is that these stretches of language do not make sense *in their own right*, but only through their location within a Discourse. A stretch of language that makes sense in one Discourse may make no sense within another Discourse, or may make a different sense within a different Discourse. To speak or write in the manner of one Discourse could even get us into a lot of trouble, or make us the subject of scorn or rejection, if spoken (or written) in the context of a different Discourse.

Gee has a particular view (indeed, a theory) about how people *make sense* (realize meanings and purposes successfully) through their discourse (stretches of language) within Discourses. Making sense involves using what he calls a 'referential system', a 'contextualization system' and an 'ideological system' (Gee 1988: 36) (see Table 13.9).

Table 13.9 Components of discourse systems

Referential system	This is concerned with literal meaning:
	What do I want to say? What information do I want to convey? How do I want my language to hook up to the world?
Contextualization system	This is concerned with social relations:
	How do I want what I have to say contextualized; that is, how do I want it placed in the context of what has already been said, in the context of what I take the relationships between myself and my hearer(s) to be and in the context of what I take us all to mutually share in the way of knowledge and beliefs?
Ideological system	This is concerned with values, beliefs and worldview:
	What deeper themes, images and ideas do I want to communicate about myself, my social group or the world; that is, what 'worldview' or 'ideology' do I want to express?

Against this background we can illustrate Gee's approach to discourse analysis using two transcripts made from recordings of two women participating in a course designed to prepare them for employment. One task in the course was to practise doing job interviews and to try and perform a successful interview. Participants were being asked to participate in the Discourse of being a job seeker, or a potential employee, and to engage in the specific aspect of being a job seeker that involves 'doing a job interview'.

Note that in the following transcripts the forward slashes ('/') are *prosody marks*, indicating where the speaker paused or how they 'phrased' their talk.

Transcript 1

Q: Have you had any previous job experience that would demonstrate that you've shown initiative or been able to work independently?

1　Well / ... yes when I / ... OK / ... there's this Walgreen's Agency/
2　I worked as a microfilm operator / OK /
3　And it was a snowstorm /
4　Ok / and it was usually six people / workin' in a group /
5　Uhum / and only me and this other girl showed up /
6　and we had quite a lot of work to do /
7　and so the man / he asked us could we / you know / do we / ... do we thinks we could finish this work /
8　so me 'n' this girl / you know / we finished it all /

Transcript 2

Q: One more question was that ah, this kind of work frequently involves using your own initiative and showing sort of the ability to make independent judgements. Do you have any ... can you tell me about any previous experience which you think directly shows ... demonstrates that you have these qualities?

1 Why / ... well / as far as being capable of handling an office /
2 say if I'm left own /
3 I feel very capable /
4 I had a situation where one of my employers that I've been /
5 ah previously worked for /
6 had to go on / a.. / a trip for say / ah three weeks and /
7 he was / ... I was left alone to .. / handle the office and run it /
8 And at that time / ah I didn't really have what you would say / a lot of experiences /
9 But I had enough experience to / .. deal with any situations that came up while he was gone /
10 and those that I couldn't / handle at the time /
11 if there was someone who had more experience than myself /
12 I asked questions / to find out / what procedure I would use /
13 If something came up / and I didn't know / who to really go to /
14 I would jot it down / or write it down / on a piece of paper /
15 so that I wouldn't forget that.../
16 if anyone that / was more qualified than myself /
17 I could ask them about it /
18 and how I would go about solving it /
19 So I feel I'm capable of handling just about any situation /
20 whether it's on my own / or under supervision

Analysing the D/discourse

The first step involved in this discourse analysis is to show in the transcript where the person is conveying information (referential system), establishing a context and communicating themes, values, ideas etc. (ideological system). This can be done by any kind of coding system, such as the following:

word = referential system

<u>word</u> = contextualization system

1 Why / ... well / as far as being capable of handling an office /
2 say <u>if I'm left (on my) own</u> /
3 **I feel very capable /**
4 <u>I had a situation where one of my employers that I've been</u> /
5 <u>ah previously worked for</u> /

6   had to go on / a.. / a trip for say / ah three weeks and /
7   he was / ... I was left alone to .. / handle the office and run it /

Once the transcripts have been prepared the analysis can begin.

Task

Using the coding system shown above:

1   Identify the speaker's referential devices and strategies in the second transcript above. The questions listed for the referential system in Table 13.9 will help here.

2   Identify the contextualization devices and strategies in the second transcript.

•   How might you use these two dimensions of analysis in your own research?

Analysing Transcript 1
Gee focuses on the extent to which the speaker in the first interview transcript conveys information and context in 'hidden' rather than explicit ways. With respect to the *referential system*, the speaker explicitly conveys that there was a snowstorm and that she usually worked in a group of six people. However, what she does not make explicit, but which is very important for the success of the interview, is that despite the snowstorm she still went to work (whereas most of the others did not). Moreover, along with just one other woman she was actually able to complete the work of six people in one day. And it seems that the two of them did this without any supervision whatsoever.

In terms of the *contextualizing system*, this speaker provides explicit contextual information in line 1 (a Walgreen's Agency). But the remaining contextual information is described only in terms of pronouns ('the man', 'we', 'this girl', 'me'). This would presume that the interviewer knew the people the woman was referring to. In many (if not most) interview situations, however, this presumption would not be appropriate. As with her use of the referential system, the important sense to be made would fail. Yet, as Gee's analysis of the discourse suggests, the first speaker has actually done in her work experience the kind of thing the interview question was looking for. But she may have failed to communicate this effectively given the kinds of expectations operating in the secondary Discourse context of the job interview.

In terms of Discourse, Gee's analysis suggests the first speaker may have drawn more on her understandings and experiences from her primary Discourse than on understandings from the relevant secondary Discourse. For example, her extensive use of pronouns to contextualize her account belongs to face-to-face communications between familiars. Similarly, the way she mentions the second woman emphasizes collaboration rather than promoting herself. However, job interviews often expect individuals to promote themselves and to make themselves look the best. Therefore, the first speaker may be a 'victim' of drawing on the wrong Discourse at the wrong time, and of having the 'wrong' kind of Discourse experiences to succeed in the discursive context of interviewing for work.

Analysing Transcript 2

Looking at the seven lines of coded interview transcript presented on page 293–4 we can see the second speaker selected 'referential and contextualization devices and strategies that are conventionally used, valued and rewarded in such tasks' (Gee 1988: 35). She informs the interviewer explicitly that she feels very capable and was left for three weeks to handle the office on her own. This quality of explicitness is maintained throughout the interview at the level of conveying information. The same is true for her use of contextualizing devices. The context is always very explicit and clear: 'if I'm left [on my] own'; and so on.

When Gee uses the *ideological system* to analyse the second transcript, however, he finds something potentially problematic with this interview. The speaker appears to contradict herself:

> She claims in line 9 to have enough experience to 'deal with any situations that came up' while the boss was gone. She then immediately, in line 10, mitigates this statement by mentioning 'those [situations] I couldn't handle.' She goes on to mention people with more expertise than her (thus taking the focus off her own expertise) and mentions asking them what procedure she should follow for problems she couldn't handle. . . . After [an] extended discussion focusing on what she doesn't know, rather than on what she does know, she concludes in lines 19–20 that she feels 'capable of handling just about any situations whether on my own or under supervision'.
>
> (Gee 1988: 36)

Gee interprets this as suggesting that the speaker regards being 'left alone on the job as just another form of supervision, in this case supervision by other people's greater knowledge and expertise' (1988: 36). Without judging the interview response as 'good' or 'bad', Gee notes it 'conflicts with an ideology that many mainstream job sites represent, an ideology of individualism, autonomy, and self-assertion' (1988: 36). Moreover, in terms of the interviewer's original question, and despite her superior control of the referential and contextualizing systems, the second speaker does not provide evidence that she has the qualities the question is looking for. To this extent, the second interviewee's answer could be judged less satisfactory than that of the first.

This approach to discourse analysis can perform work that many other forms of analysis cannot. Gee notes that these transcripts were initially published and commented on by two other authors. Both identified the second transcript as a successful job interview response and the first as unsuccessful. They particularly noted that the first speaker uses 'Black English', which is often unacceptable in job interviews. ('Black English' is an identifiable form of English spoken by many African-Americans who come from low socioeconomic groups: see Gee 1998: 336.) While this is largely true, Gee's analysis can show that the first interviewee has substantive experience the second interviewee lacks. His analysis can also locate contradictions in the second interview. Despite this, the second person would probably be more likely to win a job on the basis of her interview than the first. She would get the job despite *not* having the experience the question calls for, whereas the first person might not get a job despite *having* the relevant experience. This shows how Discourses are political. Having access to the 'right' Discourses – which enable us to speak the 'right' discourses – creates advantage over others who do not (yet may have the right kinds of experiences and qualities for success were they given the opportunity). D/discourse analysis is able to reveal how the world operates at a political level to advantage some and disadvantage others, and to show how this is *arbitrary*. This kind of discourse analysis has been used by numerous researchers to track how school Discourses confer advantage on members of some Discourse communities and systematically disadvantage learners from other Discourse communities (see e.g. Michaels 1981, 1986; Heath 1983; Gee 1996: Chs 5 and 6).

Three questions from Gunther Kress for locating 'systematically organized ways of talking'

Kress's view of discourse is similar in important respects to Gee's. Kress observes that people who speak the same general language (e.g. Spanish or English) may nonetheless speak quite differently from one another. The differences between Black and Standard English evident in the interview transcripts above are a case in point. Similarly, in a large school we are likely to find administrators speaking quite differently to classroom teachers within the school setting. Such differences, however, do not exist simply at the level of words (lexicon), or even at the levels of syntax and phonology (Kress 1985: 5). They extend to *what* people can say, *how* they can view the world, the *kinds* of things they can talk (or write) about, the *orientation* they can take toward these things and so on.

To understand what kinds of difference exist empirically between language users, why these differences exist and what their significance is, says Kress, we need to begin from the idea that speakers (and listeners, readers, writers, viewers etc.) are not isolated individuals. Rather, they are *social agents* located within varying 'networks of social relations' and in particular places within the social structure. We must look at differences in language use and between language users not simply in *linguistic* terms but from a perspective that is at once both linguistic and social (Kress 1985: 6). From this perspective we find that language users who speak (and write) similarly to each other 'share membership' in particular social institutions and networks. Thus they share in certain common practices, values, meanings, demands, permissions and prohibitions (Kress 1985: 6).

Kress claims that social institutions and social groupings and networks have to a greater or lesser extent their own 'specific meanings and values' (although there will often be some overlap). In addition, they each articulate these values and meanings in *systematic ways*: they have organized their language and developed systematic ways for communicating, transmitting, regulating and governing the values and meanings that operate within the particular institution or grouping. Kress calls these 'systematically-organized modes' of talking (including reading and writing) *discourses*:

> Discourses are systematically-organised sets of statements which give expression to the meanings and values of an institution [in a very broad sense of institution].

Beyond that, they define, describe and delimit what it is possible to say and not possible to say (and by extension what it is possible to do and not to do) with respect to the area of concern of that institution, whether marginally or centrally. A discourse provides a set of possible statements about a given area, and organises and gives structure to the manner in which a particular topic, object, process is to be talked about. In that it provides descriptions, rules, permissions and prohibitions of social and individual actions.

(Kress 1985: 6–7)

Hence, people who share membership within a network or institution built around an ideal of sustainable development (e.g. particular kinds of environmentalists) will talk about 'resources' and 'resource management', 'the future', 'being responsible' etc. differently from economic entrepreneurs, executives of logging or mining companies, loggers and miners. They will not only *talk* differently about such things, but also *see* them differently and *live* them differently. Some things mining company executives *see* will very likely be 'invisible' to sustainable development environmentalists and vice versa. A thought that one group thinks may, literally, be unthinkable to the other.

Membership in particular discourses shapes what one can do, be, think, value and so on, and plays a powerful role in constituting who and what we are (and are not). At the same time that discourses enable us to be someone (or other) and something (or other), they close other possibilities off from us. Moreover, they do this in ways that naturalize their particular orientation toward and perspective on social life. They make their meanings and values seem *natural and inevitable* to their recruits, when they are really *socially constructed and contingent*. By making their values and meanings seem natural, however, discourses make if difficult (if not virtually impossible) for their members to contemplate trying to get 'outside' of them and consider other ways of doing and being.

When we analyse discourse from this kind of perspective we try to understand what discourse(s) a person is 'coming from' when they talk or write about something. We ask: 'What discourse is *informing* and *defining* what they say about this aspect of the world? How is this likely to shape what they understand and do (and do not understand and not do) in the world? How can we, as researchers, actually *identify* what discourse (or discourses) is operating within a given segment of spoken data? How, in other words, can we *detect* the operation of particular discourses in spoken data?'

As Kress shows, this can be quite straightforward yet very powerful as a means for interpreting, understanding and explaining certain social phenomena. Kress provides three questions to be used conjointly as a tool for identifying which discourse is operating in a segment of spoken data. This tool was initially developed for analysing *written* texts, but is easily applicable to analysing spoken texts (see Table 13.10).

To make the process even easier we can add a question to be used in preparing the transcripts for analysis: namely, 'What is the topic being spoken about in this segment of data?' When we read the data, then, we locate and code the topic(s) being spoken about: for example, by using a colour to locate the places in the data where a particular topic is introduced or emphasized.

Table 13.10 Data analysis tool for analysing discourses in written and spoken data

Critical discourse analysis of written texts	*Critical discourse analysis of spoken texts*
Why is this topic being written about?	Why is this topic being spoken about?
How is this topic being written about?	How is this topic being spoken about?
What other ways of writing about this topic are there?	What other ways of speaking about this topic are there?

When that is done we can further identify (by using colours, letter codes or whatever kind of code we choose) the pieces of data relevant to considering *why* the topic is spoken about and *how* it is being spoken about.

To identify what *other* ways there are of speaking about the topic – which helps with specifying the discourse that is operating in the data, by revealing what it is *not* – we need knowledge of other discourses (or other varieties of the same discourse) pertaining to that topic. Here we may be able to appeal to our own available knowledge and experience. Alternatively, we may have to seek information about other possible ways of speaking about the topic.

Example 1
In the following transcript (Richards cited in Hatch 1992: 99) the context is a class in a school where the teacher (T) and students (S1, S2 etc.) are discussing a topic:

T: Marriage and divorce. ((writes divorce on the board))

S1:   And so when you divorce you don't need a lawyer.

S2:   In this case yes you do.

S1:   It's very expensive.

S3:   (   ) come late in the United States you can ah easy divorce you don't.

T: Mm?

S3:   Quickly.

T: It used to be a very complicated LON::G process. Ah now there are some places that offer divorces very cheap and very fast.

S2:   How about Reno Las Vegas?

T: Huh

S2:   How about Reno in Las Vegas?

S1:   Yes I think in Las Vegas you can

S3:   (   ) quickly you

T: Then that's one of the places you can get a quickie.

The teacher indicates that the lesson theme is marriage and divorce. Yet only divorce is discussed in this data segment. It seems likely that the topic is being discussed as part of the school curriculum. The first comment from S1 contains a clue that the topic may be being discussed in relation to legal aspects, since there is reference to needing a lawyer. Thereafter, however, the topic is discussed from the standpoint of getting quick and easy divorces. This may indicate the operation of a 'permissive' or 'liberal' discourse that sees divorce as perfectly acceptable, and that may even expect it to be the norm. From this perspective, it might be seen as more humane to be able to end the marriage quickly, rather than having a long process that can intensify pain and acrimony.

Other ways of discussing the topic might treat marriage as sacrosanct, as a union that has been blessed by God and undertaken in God's presence. From this perspective it would be wrong for divorce to be too quickly and easily available since it might encourage people to take marriage less seriously and see any marriage relationship as expendable.

Alternatively, the data could be read in terms of the topic being discussed from the standpoint of a fast, 'here and now' view of the world, in which 'good' means 'immediate' and 'efficient' and 'easy'. This might be some kind of 'services-oriented' discourse, in which getting a divorce is nothing more than obtaining a service, and as such it should be fast, 'on demand' and as straightforward as possible.

Task

Return to the transcript excerpt from the interview with Daniel (pp. 276–7). Analyse the excerpt using Kress' three discourse analysis questions. Then address these questions:

- What, if anything, do Kress' three questions help you to 'see' that your first reading of the transcript did not?

- What discourses do you see operating in Daniel's talk?

- What do Kress' three questions help you to 'see' that categorical analysis may not have? What does this suggest about categorical analysis? What does this suggest about discourse analysis as practised by Kress?

For further reading in this area we suggest:

- Fairclough, N. (1989) *Language and Social Power*. London: Longman.
- Fairclough, N. (1995) *Critical Discourse Analysis*. London: Longman.
- Gee, J. (1999) *An Introduction to Discourse Analysis: Theory and Method*. New York: Routledge.
- Kress, G. (1985) *Linguistic Processes in Sociocultural Practice*. Geelong: Deakin University Press.
- Kress, G. (1996) Representational resources and the production of subjectivity:

questions of the theoretical development of critical discourse analysis in a multi-cultural society, in R. Caldas-Coulthard and M. Coulthard (eds) *Texts and Practices: Readings in Critical Discourse Analysis*, pp. 15–31. London: Routledge.

CHAPTER 14

Analysing observed data in qualitative teacher research

Introduction

This chapter describes some important elements of preparing and organizing observed data for the purposes of analysis. It then discusses three widely used approaches to analysing observed data. These are pattern matching, open coding and domain, taxonomic and componential analysis respectively.

Preparing and organizing observed data for analysis

Even short-term observations (e.g. one classroom lesson, one afternoon in a student's home) can generate large amounts of observation data. It is important that the researcher can organize and file data in ways that make it manageable and easily retrieved for purposes of analysis, comparison, or for writing up as examples that support a claim or interpretation. LeCompte and Schensul (1999: 37) refer to this preparation period as 'housekeeping': a systematic 'tidying up' of data. 'Tidying up' typically involves developing some kind of orderly filing system.

Researchers can organize their fieldnotes in various ways. They can be filed according to the basic unit of analysis. In a multiple case study, for example, this might be a particular person or persons. Alternatively, fieldnotes might be organized according to the dates the data were collected, or according to some theme or topic being investigated and so on. LeCompte and Schensul point out that, 'the kinds of files maintained for a project depend on the research questions asked and the purposes of the research'. They list a number of types of files that researchers can use for organizing their data (1999: 38):

- *Chronological files*: all materials generated on any given day are kept together.
- *Genre files*: these files maintain specific kinds of data or specific text types: log, maps, photographs, diaries, artefacts, story transcripts, descriptive notes, journals, meeting minutes, separately.
- *Cast-of-character files*: these maintain separate files for everything said, done, or relevant to each significant person, group of people, or programme in a study.
- *Event or activity files*: the researcher maintains separate files for key events and activities, or categories of events and activities.
- *Topical files*: the researcher arranges data by category – for example, data pertaining to a category of disease, type of meeting, specific class, theme, type of behaviour or any other topic of interest.
- *Quantitative data files*: these contain survey, network, elicitation and other numerical data.

Task

Devise a research question for each organization type in LeCompte and Schensul's list above. For example, a cast-of-character filing system would be needed for the question: 'During a two-week period, what language, social purposes and practices do four adolescents living in South Amboy, New Jersey, enact in their everyday lives?'

Our own qualitative research mainly uses case study designs. Accordingly, we usually organize our data case by case. For example, in a recent project (see Bigum *et al.* 2000; Rowan *et al.* 2002), the research team focused on one small group of students, teachers and other invited adults in each of four different schools. Data were organized in four different storage folders: one folder for each site, with fieldnotes and other documents (*post facto* notes, artefacts, tapes etc.) ordered chronologically within each file. Similarly, when we studied the uses of new technologies in four school sites as part of a larger nationwide study involving several other researchers, we organized our data in separate storage folders on a site-by-site basis (Lankshear *et al.* 1997). While we prefer to use large ring-binder folders, other researchers prefer hanging files and filing boxes or cabinets, large, colour-coded envelopes and so on (see e.g. Stouthamer-Loeber and van Kammen 1995).

The process of systematically organizing and preparing data for analysis requires much more than simply filing it in storage folders, however. While our immediate focus is on *observed data*, this is a good point for looking at data management tasks more generally. We will use an in-depth study of the in-school and out of school language and literacy practices of four adolescents (Knobel 1997, 1999) as the illustrative example. There were five main forms of observed data in the study:

- observations written into sturdy, spiral-bound notebooks;
- observations written from memory directly into computer files (one word-processed file for each student for a total of four word-processed files, with each file organized from the earliest to the latest date of observations);
- collected artefacts (including photocopied and hand-drawn copies of wall charts from the classroom, copies of textbooks, copies of student work, lists of books in the classroom and at home, copies of school report cards);
- student-kept journals in which they wrote about literacy events that had some sort of personal significance to them;
- interviews (each student was interviewed three times, and their respective teachers were interviewed twice), and a range of audio-taped lessons and group-work sessions.

The fieldnote books were chosen as the primary reference system for organizing data systematically. Each spiral-bound book was labelled with the first letter of the name of the student (the case) to whom it corresponded. For example, all books pertaining to Jacques were labelled 'J'. Each book was given a number to indicate which book it was chronologically. Thus, the first book for Jacques was numbered '1', the second '2' and so on. (The researcher's name and contact details were included on the inside cover of each book in case any got lost.) Each page was numbered. These procedures meant that any piece of data taken from the fieldnote books for purposes of analysis could be given an identifying retrieval code. This allowed immediate and rapid location of the detailed notes pertaining to a given 'retrieval tag' during the analysis process. For example, in the following excerpt from a fieldnote book, the tag 'J1:7' means the data were taken from the first book of fieldnotes focusing on Jacques, page 7 (which happened to be during a maths lesson):

> Ms B. asks what 'ha' [hectare] means. Jacques raises his hand, and she calls on someone else. Ms B. tells them to cut out a 1cm square. Jacques checks with me that that's one square on the grid paper he'd been given.

These retrieval tags were included with each piece of data throughout successive draft 'write-ups' until the final report was produced and edited. Such data management strategies make it easy for teacher researchers to extract pieces of data from fieldnotes, with the option of returning easily to the notes to check the context of a piece of data or to verify what came next or what had come before.

The same kinds of organizational codes were also assigned to artefacts and audio-tapes and inserted at appropriate points within the fieldnotes. Thus, the fieldnote excerpt J1:7 also has 'T1, 10/11' marked beside it with a red pen in the fieldnote book. This indicates that this lesson was recorded on the first audiotape made during the study of Jacques on 10 November. This section in the fieldnotes also has 'A10' written beside it, indicating that the tenth artefact collected during the course of this case study corresponds to this lesson. As a result, particular 'pieces' of spoken and written data could be accessed rapidly and in relation to other associated forms of data during analysis. This procedure reminds the researcher that they have an audiotape of a particular observed event for which they have written fieldnotes, and/or that they have an artefact from the lesson showing what the students were working on.

Task

- In what other ways from those described above might data be organized so that the different types can be cross-referenced?

- What are the benefits of having a system of data organization? Do you think there could be any disadvantages associated with systematic organization of observed (and other) data?

- How do you think a researcher might store and organize all of the tapes recorded during a case study?

- How might a researcher cross-reference from hand-written fieldnotes in books to *post facto* notes on computer file?

For further reading in this area try:

- Emerson, R., Fretz, R. and Shaw, L. (1995) *Writing Ethnographic Fieldnotes*. Chicago: University of Chicago Press.
- LeCompte, M. and Schensul, J. (1999) *Analyzing and Interpreting Ethnographic Data (Ethnographer's Toolkit*, Vol. 5). Walnut Creek, CA: Altamira Press.
- Miles, M. and Huberman, A. M. (1994) *Qualitative Data Analysis: An Expanded Sourcebook*, 2nd edn. Thousand Oaks, CA: Sage.
- Stouthamer-Loeber, M. and van Kammen, W. (1995) *Data Collection and Management: A Practical Guide*. Thousand Oaks, CA: Sage.

In the remainder of this chapter we describe three key approaches to analysing observed data.

Pattern matching

Pattern matching (or pattern analysis or pattern recognition) is the process of identifying patterns discernible across pieces of information. Within this general conception of pattern matching two main variants can be distinguished.

Robert Yin (1994: 106), talks about a 'pattern matching logic'. He defines this as a process of comparing 'an empirically based pattern with a predicted one (or several alternative predictions)'. For Yin, pattern matching involves more than *finding* significant patterns – repeated instances of an action, problem, event and the like – within the data set. It involves the researcher testing his or her theorized *predictions* that certain patterns would appear in the data.

For example, the literature on psycholinguistic approaches to reading suggests that poor readers (unlike good readers) will not make use of a broad range of reading strategies. Such strategies include using syntax understandings and word analysis skills, predicting what kind of text it is going to be, predicting what word is likely to come next and so on. A researcher investigating a group of children who struggle with literacy might use this literature to predict more or less the precise patterns of reading difficulties these children will have. Pattern matching, in Yin's sense, would involve locating patterns in the data and seeing how they compare to the researcher's informed prior predictions.

The patterns predicted for a study are directly influenced by the theory used to frame that study. In the previous example, psycholinguistic theories of reading shaped what the researcher looked for in terms of patterns of reading difficulty. In the following example, for a quite different context, the predicted patterns are shaped by organizational theory:

> In the *pattern-matching* strategy, an empirically based pattern is compared with a predicted pattern or several alternative predicted patterns. For instance, suppose a newspaper is about to institute a new management tool: a regular series of meetings between top management and reporters, excluding editors. Based on organizational theory, a researcher might predict certain outcomes – namely, more stress between editors and reporters, increased productivity, weakened supervisory links and so on. If analysis of the case study data indicates that these results did in fact occur, some conclusions about the management change can be made. If the predicted pattern did not match the actual one, the initial study propositions would have to be questioned.
>
> (original emphasis Wimmer and Dominick 1994: 156)

Pattern matching logic can be used in studies designed to test or critique claims and interpretations made by others. For example, it is widely believed that much literacy failure at school is due to parents not caring about and supporting reading and writing at home. A researcher could collect data about children's and parents' literacy practices at home. If the predicted pattern (i.e. parents not caring about literacy) does not appear in the data to the extent predicted, the study could be used to partially critique interpretations made in previous studies.

David Fetterman takes a different stance from Yin on identifying patterns as a data analysis method. He emphasizes the process of patterns emerging from the data itself. Identifying patterns in this sense does not require the researcher to 'test' patterns reported in the literature against patterns in the data. In Fetterman's account of the pattern-finding process the researcher begins with a 'mass of undifferentiated ideas and behavior, and then collects pieces of information, comparing, contrasting, and sorting gross categories and minutiae until a discernible pattern of behavior becomes visible' (1989: 92).

Yin's and Fetterman's approaches to pattern matching are equally legitimate. Fetterman's approach may be more manageable for beginning researchers, however. Whichever approach is taken, researchers need to have read through their fieldnotes many times and be very familiar with them before they will be able to 'see' or identify patterns in the data. One way of making patterns more 'obvious' or 'visible' is to ask reflective questions while reading through the data. For example:

- What's going on here?
- Who is doing what?
- Have I seen this particular event or action before? Is it significant (and why or why not)?
- What things are happening or being done more than once? What does this mean or suggest?

Pattern matching (like other analytic approaches) includes using 'both creative and critical faculties in making carefully considered judgments about what is really significant and meaningful in the data' (Patton 2002: 467). There are no simple 'hard and fast' rules for responding to these questions. Identifying patterns in data requires researchers to draw on prior reading, previous research and classroom experiences, and their common sense in ways that make the process of justifying identified patterns relatively obvious and straightforward.

The following excerpt is from fieldnotes about Jacques (see Chapter 11) during class time.

(1:50pm). Ms B. asks class who hasn't brought a book for art lesson. Jacques raises his hand. Ms B. shifts students so that children with books are sitting together.

Ms B. tells non-art children to do some work on their social studies project, or to copy down their homework. Jacques takes out his homework book.

He is watching the teacher help Emily get started with her art project. He tells me he forgot his book (needed for the art project).

Jacques gives some help to Jason with gluing the corners of Jason's book. Jason asks Jacques if that's enough glue, and Jacques tells him to put more glue near the spine of the book. Jacques shifts the glue pot so that Jason can put his brush in the glue.

Jacques writes:

Homework

- Project
- News article
- Bring a hard covered book (the teacher had 'Bring a book' on the black-board)
- Write a list of everything you know about Area – $\triangle$, , $\bigcirc$ (at least ten things)

Jacques asks Ms B. how much longer until they go to concert practice. Ms B. tells him they should've gone an hour ago – he looks at me and tells me he won't start his homework then. Jacques holds Emily's paper for her.

(2:10) Someone complains about the heat, and Ms B. explains that it's hot every summer in Queensland. Jacques calls out, 'Get an airconditioner!'

Emily shows me a project book with glued-in newspaper clippings inside it. She tells me that they have to collect seven clippings by the end of the term. Jacques looks wide-eyed and I ask him how many he has collected. Jacques laughs and draws '0' in the air with his finger. He tells me he was going to start last week, but will probably get to it next week (he laughs).

Ms B. comes to the desk and helps Emily and Jason. Jacques tells her that he can't think of things about area. Ms B. reminds him of his maths lesson (earlier that day) and Jason reminds him about the formulas they covered in that lesson.

(2:20pm) Jacques comments on the smoke outside the classroom and a police car that has driven into the school parking lot. He looks over at Emily's work and asks for clues about area and his homework. Jason tells him some formulas. Jacques works on his homework, making changes as Jason and Emily make suggestions.

Jacques takes out his social studies book and tells me more about the newspaper articles he has to collect. He tells me he has got his mum 'fixed up' to look for some clippings today.

Ms B. asks Jacques if he has started his newspaper clipping assignment. He nods, then sits with all of his books closed.

(2:37) Ms B. tells the non-art people to take out their handwriting books. Some boys take their desk trays out and start to tidy them. Jacques tidies his desk tray as well. Ms B. tells the class they have to do page 31 in their handwriting books, and then tidy their desks, then they can go and play outside. Jacques puts his desk tray back and takes out his handwriting book.

> *Jacques*: Hey uhm, Miss B. What page is it?
>
> *Ms B.*: Thirty-one.
>
> *Jacques*: Just thirty-one, is it?
>
> *Jacques*: I haven't heard any fire engines.

He leans over and pats Emily on the arm and tells her, 'It's all right.' She tells him she hates it when he does that. He says he does it so that she'll get angry.

(2:53pm) A mother arrives to take her daughter home from school. The bushfire is now near their house in McDowell (a city suburb). Jacques makes 'doo-Doo-doo-Doo-doo' music.

Jacques writes in his handwriting book.

Some children have put their chairs up on their desks and are outside. Emily, Anne and Jason have left. In fact, most of the children are gone now. Jacques writes in his handwriting book. He finishes and walks into the middle of the room, holding his open book in both hands, and calling: 'Miss B! Miss B!' He comes back to me and says, 'I can go.' (J1: 19–29)

One pattern evident in this fieldnote excerpt involves Jacques' tactics for avoiding actually *doing* any work. Data that support (or 'construct') this pattern include:

- Jacques didn't bring a hard-covered book so can't participate in the art lesson.
- Jacques spends time watching the teacher help others.
- Jacques helps Jason to glue the corners of Jason's book.
- Jacques checks with the teacher when concert practice is due to start and decides not to begin doing his homework.
- Jacques spends time chatting with classmates about work he *should* be doing or should have done.
- Jacques arranges with his mother ('fixes her up') that she will collect newspaper clippings for him, instead of him doing it himself.

As Fetterman suggests, pattern matching is similar in many respects to categorical analysis (see Chapter 13) or open coding (see below), or content analysis (see Patton 2002). In each case researchers generate broad categories or classes of data out of individual pieces of data that appear similar in relevant respects. The fact is that all analysis involves some kind of categorization, by its very nature. Pattern matching, however, differs from categorical analysis, open coding and content analysis in an important way: pattern matching analysis works from the general to the particular, whereas categorical analysis and open coding work from the particular to the general. Pattern matching first requires broad sweeps through the data, and a process of 'testing out' or comparing and contrasting data to see if there are enough examples of a particular kind to claim a pattern is there. (At the same time, the researcher pays attention to items of data that do not fit the pattern under construction. These variations or exceptions help the researcher to more clearly define each pattern and to distinguish between patterns.) We can see this in the example of Jacques. There is a sense in which 'checking out with the teacher what time concert practice is scheduled for' is a quite different kind of act (in and of itself) from 'helping Jason glue the corners of his book'. But when taken together in the large context that can be discerned from initial broad sweeps through the data, and in conjunction with other 'pieces' of observed behaviour, they start to emerge as part of a large pattern of schoolwork avoidance behaviour.

Categorical analysis, on the other hand, begins with labelling pieces of data – usually small pieces as demonstrated in the example provided by Coffey and Atkinson in Chapter 13. It then evolves into a process of 'collapsing' similar categories into each other so that only a few manageable categories remain. Open coding is similar in this respect to categorical analysis.

For organizing and managing pattern analysis, Fetterman suggests constructing matrices as tools for comparing and contrasting pieces of data (Fetterman 1989: 96). Pattern matching analysis of fieldnotes concerning Jacques could be organized as shown in Table 14.1.

Table 14.1 Example of pattern matching analysis of fieldnotes

	Tactics for avoiding school work	*Being a 'joker'*
During class	Jacques didn't bring a hard-covered book so can't participate in the art lesson Jacques checks with the teacher when concert practice is due to start and decides not to begin doing his homework	Someone complains about the heat, and Ms B. explains that it's hot every summer in Queensland. Jacques calls out, 'Get an airconditioner!' A mother arrives to take her daughter home from school. The bushfire is now near their house in McDowell. Jacques makes 'doo-Doo-doo-Doo-doo' music.
During school breaks (morning tea, lunchtime)		
At home	Jacques arranges with his mother ('fixes her up') that she will collect newspaper clippings for him, instead of him doing it himself.	

The types of patterns researchers focus on include:

- *Daily patterns and activity patterns* (e.g. classroom timetables, school timetables, the patterns visible in each maths lesson in a class, play patterns during school breaks).
- *Action patterns* (such as in our example of Jacques; rituals and routines, games).
- *Discursive patterns* (the interaction between institutions and people, such as the effects of a new rule on students and teachers).
- *Relational patterns* (e.g. which child appears to be most disliked in the class and why, which teacher is most complained about and why, the relationship between a teacher and her class).
- *Belief patterns.*

The patterns identified in a data set by one researcher may, of course, be quite different from those identified by others, or even from what the same researcher might identify working from the basis of a different theoretical framework. The only recognized criteria for pattern matching are that a particular pattern identified by a researcher be recognizable by other people who read the data (or who read evidence provided for the pattern in the research report), and that this pattern can adequately be supported by evidence.

For further reading in this area we suggest:

- Fetterman, D. (1998) *Ethnography: Step by Step*, 2nd edn. Newbury Park, CA: Sage.

- Miles, M. and Huberman, A.M. (1994) *Qualitative Data Analysis: An Expanded Sourcebook*, 2nd edn. Thousand Oaks, CA: Sage.
- Patton, M. (2002) *Qualitative Research and Evaluation Methods*, 3rd edn. Thousand Oaks, CA: Sage.
- Yin, R. (1994) *Case Study Research: Design and Methods*, 2nd edn. Thousand Oaks, CA: Sage.

Open coding

Open coding is most closely associated with the grounded theory approach to qualitative research (e.g. Strauss and Corbin 1990), but is widely used in other qualitative research approaches. Anselm Strauss and Juliet Corbin (1990: 62) describe open coding as a process of:

1 'Breaking down' data into discrete parts.
2 Examining these parts closely and comparing them for similarities and differences.
3 Asking questions about the phenomena that are suggested by this comparing and contrasting work.

The process of breaking data down involves selecting an observation, a sentence or a paragraph from fieldnotes, taking it apart and giving a name to each discrete incident, idea or event. This name 'stands for or represents a phenomenon' (Strauss and Corbin 1990: 63). Each item is compared with others, and similar items (events, phenomena etc.) are assigned the same label. The aim of open coding is to develop conceptual categories and subcategories that help describe and explain phenomena observed during a field-based research study.

Strauss and Corbin suggest at least two different kinds of question to ask of the data (1990: 63):

- What is this?
- What does it represent [or mean]?

Other researchers have developed alternative or complementary lists of analytic questions to ask during the open coding process. Mertens (1998: 352) advises asking 'basic questions such as: Who? When? Where? What? How? How much? And Why?' Pidgeon and Henwood (cited in Potter 1998: 120) suggest asking 'What categories or labels do I need in order to account for what is of importance to me in this paragraph?' Charmaz (cited in Potter 1998: 120) offers the following series of open coding guide questions:

- What is going on?
- What are the people doing?
- What is the person saying?
- What do these actions and statements take for granted?
- How do structure and context serve to support, maintain, impede or change these actions and statements?

Other researchers prefer to employ reflective questions that help researchers keep one eye firmly fixed on their research question, aim and purpose. Emerson *et al.* (1995: 146) list the following questions:

- What are people doing? What are they trying to accomplish?
- How, exactly, do they do this? What specific means and/or strategies do they use?
- How do members talk about, characterize, and understand what is going on?
- What assumptions are they making?
- What do I see going on here? What did I learn from these [field]notes?
- Why did I include them?

Open coding generally follows three sequential steps:

1　Applying conceptual codes to the data.
2　Grouping sets of like codes into conceptual categories.
3　Identifying the properties of each category and locating each instance of a phenomenon belonging to this category along a continuum (i.e. 'dimensionalizing' the data).

Applying conceptual codes to data

Strauss and Corbin (1990: 64), first introduced in Chapter 2, page 38, provide an extended example of how open coding works in analysing observed data. The words in bold type in the extract that follows are the *initial labels* (what they call 'conceptual codes') Strauss and Corbin have given to the phenomena they observed.

Suppose you are in a fairly expensive restaurant. The restaurant is built on three levels. On the first level is a bar, on the second a small dining area, and on the third, the main dining area and the kitchen. The kitchen is open so that you can see what is going on. . . . While waiting for your dinner, you notice a lady in red. She appears to be just standing there in the kitchen, but your common sense tells you that a restaurant wouldn't pay a lady in red just to stand there, especially in a busy kitchen. . . .

You notice that she is intently looking around the kitchen area, **a work site**, focusing here and then there, taking a mental note of what is going on. *You ask yourself, what is she doing here? Then you label it* **watching**. Watching what? **Kitchen work**.

Next, someone comes up and asks her a question. She answers. This act is different from watching, so you code it as **information passing**.

She seems to notice everything. *You call this* **attentiveness**.

Our lady in red walks up to someone and tells him something. Since this incident also involves information that is passed on, *you also label it*, **information passing**.

Although standing in the midst of all this activity, she doesn't seem to disrupt it. To describe this phenomenon, you use the term **unintrusiveness**.

She turns and walks quickly and quietly, **efficiency**, into the dining area, and proceeds to **watch** the activity here also.

She seems to be keeping track of everyone and everything, **monitoring**. But monitoring what? Being an astute observer you notice that she is monitoring the quality of the service, how the waiter interacts with and responds to the customer; the **timing of service**, how much transpires between seating a customer, their ordering, the delivery of food; and **customer response and satisfaction** with the service.

A waiter comes with an order for a large party, she moves in to help him, **providing assistance**.

The woman looks like she knows what she is doing and is competent at it, **experienced**.

She walks over to a wall near the kitchen and looks at what appears to be a schedule, **information gathering**.

When open coding observed data, researchers are concerned with understanding the data conceptually rather than simply descriptively. In the example above, all of the words in bold text are concepts rather than mere descriptive labels. They aim to get at 'deeper-than-surface-level properties and qualities' of the things being observed: properties that will ultimately do work in explaining relationships between bits of the world from the perspective employed by the researcher. The conceptual codes in bold tell us something about *how* the researcher is 'seeing' what they are observing, and *where* they are coming from. A different researcher coming from a different 'space' will conceptualize differently the surface features of what a 'look' would reveal to practically anybody who 'looked' at a scene.

Task

Try to imagine the fictitious scene observed by Strauss and Corbin, and try to imagine another (different) observer looking at the same scene (but coming from another conceptual 'space'). Then:

1 Rename some or all of Strauss and Corbin' phenomena (i.e. insert different codes in bold).

2 Provide a basis for your renamings (e.g. suppose the researcher was a nutritional expert, an academic working in public health, a journalist, a restaurant reviewer, a management consultant). What effects do different social roles have on the concepts developed to describe what is happening?

In Strauss and Corbin's coding of the restaurant scene, their conceptual codes address the kinds of things that are of interest to qualitative researchers. Matthew Miles and Michael Huberman (1994: 58) suggest coding for four main kinds of things that are of interest to social researchers. They call these 'conditions', 'interactions among actors', 'strategies and tactics' and 'consequences'. They also report a list produced by Bogdan and Biklen (1997):

1 *Setting/context:* general information on surroundings that allows you to put the study in a larger context.
2 *Definition of the situation:* how people understand, define, or (appear to) perceive the setting or topics on which the study bears.
3 *Perspectives:* ways of thinking about their setting shared by informants (study participants) ('how things are done here').
4 *Ways of thinking about people and objects:* understandings of each other, or outsiders, of objects in their world (more detailed than above).
5 *Process:* sequence of events, flow, transitions and turning points, changes over time.
6 *Activities:* regularly occurring kinds of behaviour.
7 *Events:* specific activities, especially ones occurring infrequently.
8 *Strategies:* ways of accomplishing things: people's tactics, methods, techniques for meeting their needs.
9 *Relationships and social structure:* unofficially defined patterns such as cliques, coalitions, romances, friendships, enemies.
10 *Methods:* problems, joys, dilemmas of the research process – often in relation to comments by observers.

Such lists are guides to the kind of 'things' in the data researchers should be trying to code conceptually. Such guides are never anything more than that. Not all elements of every guide will be found within a study. Some may have only a small role in the study. The purpose of such guides is to provide researchers with starting points from which to launch their analyses via open coding.

After analysing at least some of the collected data, the researcher generally develops acronyms or shorthand versions of their codes (Strauss and Corbin 1990; Miles and Huberman 1994; Patton 2002). These shorthand codes can then be used to more quickly analyse remaining data. For example, in our example of the lady in red from Strauss and Corbin, 'watching' could become WATCH, 'kitchen work' could become KITWORK and 'information passing' could become INFOPASS. Again, these shorthand codes are invented by the researcher, with the only real criteria for development being that the codes are easily remembered and are not too long or complex. These shorthand codes and their long versions or explanations are generally listed on a sheet of paper or written into a book. Researchers can use these lists to remind themselves of the codes they are using, or to check whether they need to add new codes to their lists.

Once they have decided on their codes, researchers should also make notes of decisions made during the coding process (e.g. why this particular piece of data was coded as WATCH and not as INFOPASS). It is also a good idea to make notes about categories that seem to be emerging, comments about the codes used, about categories and data in relation to the literature read prior to implementing the study and so on, during the coding process. These kinds of notes become invaluable when writing up the study.

Strauss and Corbin emphasize the need to attach *conceptual* labels to data, rather than descriptive ones. As they point out, 'it is not unusual for beginning researchers to summarize rather than *conceptualize* data. That is, they merely repeat briefly the gist of the phrase or sentences, but still in a descriptive way' (1990: 64–5). For example, instead of 'information gathering' the beginning researcher might write something like 'reads the schedule' or 'talks to the waiter' or 'asks the waiter a question'. Analysing data by means of phrases like these tends to result in cumbersome analysis and makes it very difficult to categorize similar pieces of data.

Developing categories in open coding approaches

Once researchers begin attaching conceptual coding labels to data, general groups of similar concepts typically emerge. Initially, these will often be provisional and will change as more data is analysed. In developing categories from the codes the researcher aims to bring large amounts of data under the umbrella of 'higher-order organizers' that can be kept to manageable numbers. Searching out the relationships between these higher-order organizers will ultimately enable the researcher to describe, explain and interpret the scene.

To continue with the same example, Strauss and Corbin start to ask 'who, what, which, where, why and how' questions of what they have previously coded. For instance, why is she monitoring these various things? When she is monitoring is she concerned with the same things as when she is watching what is going on in the kitchen? How do the personal quality codes (like 'experienced' and 'attentiveness' and 'unintrusiveness') relate to the monitoring? Proceeding in this way is precisely what it is like to develop categories within open coding. Strauss and Corbin suggest that after a while the researcher might categorize a lot of the codes under the more general idea (a category label) of **work** the woman is doing in order to **assess and maintain the flow of work**. The researcher can then gather all the conceptual codes referring to 'the work bits' under the category or general label of **types of work for assessing and maintaining work flow**.

This, however, will not serve for the conceptual codes like 'attentiveness' and 'experienced'. These relate to qualities the woman displays in doing her work, rather than the work itself. They belong to a different category – perhaps the category of qualities associated with being good at that kind of work (if the observer has the impression that she is doing well whatever it is she is doing). Strauss and Corbin suggest a category of **conditions for being good** (at that kind of work). This in turn forces the issue of what the woman's work *is* that she is good at. Who or what *is* she? They decide on the idea that she is a **work orchestrator** (1990: 66–7).

This categorizing process has yielded a higher level category under which all the initial conceptual codes can be accommodated: **food orchestrator**. And this category has two subcategories: **Types of work for assessing and maintaining work flow** and **Conditions for being a good food orchestrator**.

Conceptual category labels can be 'invented'. This is what Strauss and Corbin have done in the example above. Alternatively, labels can come directly from the theory and/or literature informing the study, or else they can grow directly out of something a person says or from a label already in existence (see Coffey and Atkinson 1996). The process of 'formalizing' or deciding upon a category involves identifying its chief attributes or properties.

Properties and dimensions

Analysis is a process of breaking things down into smaller parts in order to understand these parts in their own right and their relationship to other parts. Once we have done this we are able to reassemble them in the form of an account that shows an understanding of what we have been investigating and that explains important aspects of it, or otherwise provides insights and understanding that permit appropriate actions or responses.

By identifying *properties* of categories (and the components of categories) and the dimensions of these properties, researchers reach the 'finest' level of analysing their observed data by means of open coding. Properties are 'attributes or characteristics of a phenomenon' (Strauss and Corbin 1990: 70). Systematically identifying properties and 'dimensionalizing' them are important processes because they form the basis for identifying or developing relationships among categories (and subcategories) and contribute directly to building theory, advancing explanations and producing interpretations that can support recommendations, suggestions for resolving problems and so on.

In the case of Strauss and Corbin's example, the researcher will move from the main category identified (food orchestrator) to finer and finer points of analysis. This means moving first to the subcategories and then to the individual elements or components of these. So, to analyse in detail the category 'food orchestrator' we might start with the subcategory 'types of work involved in assessing and maintaining work flow'. This subcategory breaks down the main category. But it can in turn be broken down further into the various types of work – watching, monitoring and so on. Each of these types can be analysed in terms of their properties.

An activity like watching can be assigned such properties as 'frequency', 'extent' and 'intensity' (Strauss and Corbin 1990: 71) (see Table 14.2). 'Watching' is something a 'food orchestrator' will do 'more or less of' (frequency). She or he will do more or less of it over a wider or narrower range of facets (extent). And in doing it she or he will do so with more or less 'effort' (intensity) and for a longer or shorter time (duration). These properties will be gauged in relation to particular incidents (or recorded instances) of the types of work being enacted. In order to plot these in detail Strauss and Corbin assign dimensions to each property, which can be applied to concrete incidents and show how properties and dimensions can be developed as a matrix to become an analytic tool (1990: 72). Once all the data have been coded, the researcher needs to repeat the process, checking codes, revising them, renaming some until clear-cut categories and concepts emerge from the analysis.

The process can be illustrated by reference to the observations of Jacques. The successive passes through the data that suggest work avoidance as a pattern might equally be arrived at through open coding of the data. One way of categorizing Jacques might be as a 'schoolwork avoider'. This might yield a subcategory containing types of

Table 14.2 Dimensions of the conceptual category 'watching'

Type within subcategory	Properties	Dimensional range (applied to each incident)
Watching	Frequency	often – – – – – – – – – never
	Extent	more – – – – – – – – less
	Intensity	high – – – – – – – – low
	Duration	long – – – – – – – – short

work avoiding strategies. These would include things like 'helping', 'enlisting' (getting others to do his work for him), 'diverting' (as when he redirects attention away from the work at hand by asking a question about concert practice), 'forgetting' (leaving a book at home that he will need that day) and so on (see Table 14.3).

Table 14.3 Examples of dimensionalized categories in open coding approaches to data analysis

Types of work avoiding strategies	Properties	Dimensional range (applied to each incident)
Helping	Frequency	Often, but varies. More in 'hands-on' lessons like art and physical education
	Range	Mainly with one or two students, also teacher
	Extent	Across a broad range of actions (filling glue pots, fetching stapler, gluing ends of cover)
	Duration	Several minutes is common
Enlisting	Frequency	
	Range	Others in work group, mother
	Extent	Quite wide – from specific aspects of a task to entire task
Diverting	Frequency	
	Extent	
	Duration	

For further reading in this area we suggest:

- Emerson, R., Fretz, R. and Shaw, L. (1995) *Writing Ethnographic Fieldnotes.* Chicago: University of Chicago Press.
- LeCompte, M. and Schensul, J. (1999) *Analyzing and Interpreting Ethnographic Data (Ethnographer's Toolkit,* Vol. 5). Walnut Creek, CA: Altamira Press.
- Miles, M. and Huberman, A.M. (1994) *Qualitative Data Analysis: An Expanded Sourcebook,* 2nd edn. Thousand Oaks, CA: Sage.
- Strauss, A. and Corbin, J. (1990) *Basics of Qualitative Research: Grounded Theory Procedures and Techniques.* Newbury Park, CA: Sage.

Domain and taxonomic analysis

Domain analysis

Qualitative researchers often want to identify the cultural meanings of practices they are studying. A powerful yet relatively straightforward technique that can be used here is what James Spradley (1980) calls *domain analysis*. This is a process in which data about social situations obtained by observation and means of data collection are analysed to identify domains of cultural meaning. This approach emerged from anthropology and is based on the assumption that people 'classify the world around them into domains' (Borgatti 1999: 15). This in turn informs and shapes the way we interact with the world and with each other.

Spradley defines a social situation as a 'stream of behavior (activities) carried out by people (actors) in a particular location (place)' (1980: 86). A line of people getting onto a bus, or a group of people crossing a street intersection, or several women and children talking while they sit on seats in a waiting room, are everyday examples of social situations. So is a group of students reading at their desks, or sitting together in a part of the playground, or gathered together around a computer.

Consider a researcher observing a classroom. Several students are gathered around the teacher at the front of the room. Most of the students are reading and writing at their desks, individually or in pairs and small groups. In one corner of the classroom, at a small cluster of tables, a boy appears to be folding pieces of paper and occasionally using the stapler. A lot of the time he seems to be doing little or nothing. The part of the room where he is working looks like a self-contained space, physically separate and different in appearance from the other spaces in the room. The researcher might record in their fieldnotes that between 9.30 a.m. and 11.30 p.m. this boy spent time, largely on his own, in this area of the room. They might also include various descriptions that are entered against specific points in time. For example, they might record the time in the margin (e.g. 10.23 a.m.) and write something like: 'Jacques takes one of the folded pieces of paper and very slowly and carefully staples in two places down one side'. They might also record the size of the folded piece of paper and sketch a diagram of the physical space and the materials visible there.

These fieldnotes describe some aspects of a social situation. But on their own they say nothing about what that social situation *means* in cultural terms: either at the level of the meaning of the physical space or at the level of the boy's activity. If it subsequently looks as though this could be a significant social situation in terms of the study purposes and research question, the researcher will need to analyse it. In this event they may decide to use domain analysis. The purpose of a domain analysis is to move systematically from observations of a social situation to identifying a cultural scene and some of its apparent or shared cultural meanings.

A cultural domain can be defined as 'a set of items, all of which a group of people define as belonging to the same type' (Borgatti 1999: 116). This set of items comprises a 'category of cultural meaning' and usually includes smaller categories within it (Spradley 1980: 88). Spradley conceptualizes cultural domains and the process of identifying them in fieldnotes by reference to a concrete method of analysis that involves three elements. He calls these 'the cover term', 'the included terms' and the 'semantic relationship' respectively.

The *cover term* is the name given to the cultural domain. It is the name of a category that includes smaller categories. The *included terms* are the smaller categories that are included in the cultural domain, whose cover term covers them. The *semantic relationship* links the included terms and the cover term. 'Semantic', of course, refers to meaning, and the role of domain analysis is to reveal domains of cultural meaning. There are various kinds of semantic relationships, some of which we will identify shortly.

Meanwhile, a simple example of the kind of thing domain analysis might reveal is as follows. Let us imagine that as a result of applying domain analysis to fieldnotes of extended observations of learning activities in a classroom (using the semantic relationship 'is a kind of'), the researcher arrives at a cultural domain of pedagogical approaches employed in this classroom. Within the larger category of 'pedagogical approach' one of the smaller subsumed categories is 'small-group work'. The example is presented visually in Figure 14.1.

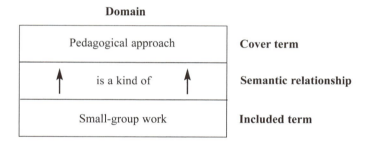

Figure 14.1   A visual representation of cultural domain building (Spradley 1980: 88)

Domain analysis involves identifying regularities in our data that we can organize as categories of cultural meaning by finding semantic relationships between elements of social situations. Making domain analyses is relatively easy once we know what they are and what their research role and significance is. We can begin a domain analysis from various points. For example, we can begin from the 'cover term' end, by searching our data to see of we can find names or terms or concepts that we have used over and over again in recording our observations. This repeated use of terms might be a clue to patterns or regularities that can reveal cultural domains. If we find such repetitions occurring over entire segments of data we might decide that some of these are suggesting possible cover terms. We can then begin to look for patterns of included terms and semantic relationships associated with these recurring terms or concepts.

Alternatively, we can begin from the semantic relationships, which is the approach Spradley recommends. For example, we can read our video-recorded observations (in conjunction with fieldnote and spoken data) looking for instances of things that are kinds or types of other things, or parts of other things. In fact, there are many different semantic relationships, of which 'being a kind of' is only one. Spradley provides a very helpful list of semantic relationships (see Table 14.4). When we have such a list and understand the kind of work its components can be made to do in data analysis, we can apply them to our descriptions of social situations to try and discover patterns of cultural meaning. Spradley notes those semantic relationships that he has found especially useful as a starting point for analysing cultural domains in a range of research projects. He provides technical names for the relationships and describes their form (see Table 14.4).

Table 14.4 List of semantic relationships (Spradley 1980: 93)

Relationship	Form
1 Strict inclusion	X is a kind of Y
2 Spatial	X is a place in Y, or X is a part of Y
3 Cause-effect	X is a result of Y
4 Rationale	X is a reason for doing Y
5 Location for action	X is a place for doing Y
6 Function	X is used for Y
7 Means-end	X is a way to do Y
8 Sequence	X is a step (stage) in Y
9 Attribution	X is an attribution (characteristic) of Y

Spradley explains that when working with domain analysis it is useful to prepare specially-designed worksheets, and to use them as we read our data by filling them in as we go. Domain analysis worksheets are sheets of paper (or a spreadsheet on a computer) that have spaces for the cover term, for a particular semantic relationship and for the included term. Such a worksheet could look like that shown in Figure 14.2. In order to identify included terms associated with particular cover terms, we can use what Spradley calls 'structural questions about cover terms', which include asking who, what, when and where questions. For example, 'What are all the different kinds of pedagogical approaches that might be recognizable as such within a classroom?'

We can begin undertaking a domain analysis of observed data by selecting one semantic relationship and, after preparing domain analysis worksheets, settling on some fieldnotes for analysis. We then search the fieldnotes for data that seem to indicate a semantic relationship and for possible cover terms and/or included terms that suggest how a domain of meaning might be presented.

When one semantic relationship seems to be exhausted we can move on to others, building up a list of all the domains that are identified in the course of the analysis. Later, of course, we will have to select from the overall list of identified domains those we think are most important, useful or relevant in the light of our research question. During the data analysis phase however, domain analysis can be done in an extensive way in order to obtain an overall sense of regularities and 'shape' within the social situations observed, and of some of the cultural meanings that play out in those social situations.

1 Semantic relationship: Strict inclusion
2 Form: X (is a kind of) Y
3 Example: small-group work (is a kind of) pedagogical approach

Included terms	Semantic relationship	Cover term
Small group work		
	is a kind of	Pedagogical approach
_____		
_____		_____

Included terms	Semantic relationship	Cover term
	is a kind of	
_____		
_____		_____
_____		
_____		
_____		

Figure 14.2 Domain analysis worksheet

After some time going through fieldnotes a researcher might find the cultural domain of 'pedagogical approaches' building up, and a new cultural domain of 'learning software' emerging (see Figure 14.3).

An example of using domain analysis: Jacques' ways to avoid reading and writing in class
Fieldnotes made during classroom observations of Jacques were used to produce a domain analysis along the following lines.

Social situation. For two hours on each of two consecutive days Jacques could be seen at or near a table in one corner of the classroom, working with scissors, a stapler and paper. By the end of the second occasion he had produced several tiny 'books' measuring approximately 6 × 5cm, each containing several pages. Several of these booklets were collected, copied and filed as research artefacts. Observations over the two days were recorded as fieldnotes in the notebook dedicated to Jacques.

Relevant data. When analysing observational data using domain analysis, researchers usually employ other kinds of data besides fieldnotes – especially interview

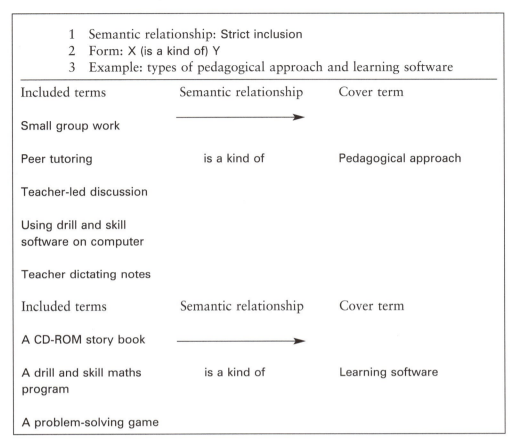

1 Semantic relationship: Strict inclusion
2 Form: X (is a kind of) Y
3 Example: types of pedagogical approach and learning software

Included terms	Semantic relationship	Cover term
Small group work		
Peer tutoring	is a kind of	Pedagogical approach
Teacher-led discussion		
Using drill and skill software on computer		
Teacher dictating notes		

Included terms	Semantic relationship	Cover term
A CD-ROM story book		
A drill and skill maths program	is a kind of	Learning software
A problem-solving game		

Figure 14.3 Building a domain analysis worksheet (adapted from Spradley 1980: 94)

data and artefacts that seem relevant to identifying a cultural domain. In the case of this example with Jacques, the researcher (Michele) had access to several forms of data. In terms of Spradley's list of semantic relations, the overall data set supported multiple potential options for identifying a domain. The data contained information that the desk area had been set up as a 'Writers' Centre'. This was a designated space for students to formally 'publish' narratives they had finished writing in preparation for assessment. Such information would, for example, support a domain built on the semantic relation of location for action ('X is a place for Y'): 'The Writers Centre is a place for formally producing final copies of written work'. This, however, was only *part* of the data that could be used in efforts to move from the social situation in question to the meanings of the cultural scene playing out in that social situation.

Making the domain analysis. In this particular case, only after a large and varied body of data from diverse observations, interviews and artefacts had been considered was it possible to identify the domain that seemed most useful for constructing the cultural meanings being enacted within this social situation. Deciding on the domain drew heavily on observational fieldnotes similar to the following segments from extracts that had also been used with pattern matching as an analytic procedure. It is common to use multiple analytic approaches and, in many cases, triangulating analyses from similar yet distinct analytic approaches lends greater confidence to our results.

(1) Jacques goes and gets more glue for Emily and Jason (who are still working on their art projects), then takes the bottle over to another boy who'd asked for some.

Jacques: Anyone else want some glue?

He stands talking to two boys, then returns to his seat.

(2) Class has started and Jacques is pushing an overhead projector on a trolley around the classroom. The wheels on the trolley are squeaking terribly and Jacques seems to be taking his time in positioning the trolley 'just so'. Ms B. tells him to leave it right where it is, but Jacques tells her it needs to go closer and begins shifting the trolley yet again and Ms B. tells him to leave it where it is.

(3) Ms B. tells the class to take out their worksheets on China from the seminar on China the previous Friday. Jacques sits without moving for a little while, then spends some time looking through the contents of his desk until he finds the worksheet. Other children in the class complain about having to do the worksheet. Jacques talks with Emily and Anne. He appears to be copying the answers from Emily's page. Emily moves her worksheet away from Jacques and covers it up with her hand. Jacques tells Ms B. he doesn't understand the worksheet. Ms B. doesn't respond. Jacques asks a boy near him if he can borrow the boy's worksheet. The boy shakes his head, and Jacques responds:

Jacques: C'mon, man ((pulls a sad face with his bottom lip pushed out as far as it will go, then laughs)).

(4) ((Maths lesson, Jacques and his good friend, Sean, have been teamed up with Kylie by Ms B. for some group work)) Jacques and Sean don't say anything to Kylie, and she avoids looking at them – she looks around the room and doesn't say anything.

Jacques: Hey Kylie, c'mon. Start doing the work.

Ms B. brings them over some solid shapes ((e.g., a pyramid, a cube)).

Ms B.: Here's a hard one for you ((handing them a cone))

Jacques: Oh, here you go Kylie ((hurriedly passing the shape to her))

In addition to such observation fieldnotes, interview data were also relevant to understanding the kinds of social situations described in the fieldnotes. Some interview data contained interesting information with regard to Jacques' activity in the Writers' Centre. An interview with Jacques' teacher revealed that he had throughout the school year written a series of very short stories of about 10–15 words in each of the 'books' he had produced during timetabled narrative writing periods. Other interview data provided by Jacques' teacher, as well as by Jacques' mother and by Jacques himself, indicated that Jacques greatly disliked reading and writing at school. It also revealed that he had been seen by his current and previous teachers as having problems with literacy, and that he was extremely anxious about school and afraid of being regarded as a 'dumbo'. In fact, he would sometimes become ill as a result of the level of this anxiety.

On the basis of many segments of data it was finally decided that the means-end semantic relationship ('X is a way to do Y') best captured the cultural meaning of this and other similar or related social situations in the classroom in which Jacques was involved. In the domain analysis, 'Spending time in the Writers' Centre' becomes an *included term* falling under the *cover term* 'Avoiding literacy work'. The cultural domain became 'Ways to avoid literacy work in class'. Other included terms within this cultural domain are:

- 'helping others with small tasks' (e.g. helping Jason glue his book);
- 'forgetting to bring things needed for the lesson';
- 'drawing attention to things going on elsewhere';
- 'claiming not to have heard instructions for tasks';
- 'passing on tasks to others'.

Task

Complete the following worksheet to capture the domain analysis we have just described with regard to social situations involving Jacques. (Note that the example *began* with the social situation of Jacques in the Writers' Centre, but then continued by providing excerpts from fieldnotes from several other social situations. Collectively, these and similar segments of data give rise to the cultural domain we identified above.) Drawing on all the data excerpts about Jacques in the classroom presented in this chapter, see if you can produce a different domain analysis. Think of possible alternatives for the *semantic relationship*, the *cover term* and the *included terms* (e.g. focus on the teacher, Ms B., instead of Jacques, or focus on Jacques' use of humour).

    1   Semantic relationship:

    2   Form:

    3   Example:

Included terms	Semantic relationship	Cover term
_____	⟶	_____
_____		
_____		

Before leaving domain analysis a final comment is in order. Readers will have noticed how we have reached virtually the same analytical outcome with respect to Jacques' practices in the classroom using domain analysis as can be reached using pattern matching. In fact, the more we explore data analysis in our careers as researchers, the more we will find that discrete forms of analysis seem to have important things in common and will often produce similar results from the same data. We have already encountered one instance of similarity in the section on open coding, where we found numerous points in common between open coding and categorical analysis. Such similarities are not really surprising. The point is that all forms of analysis look for patterns and regularities (as well as discrepancies and anomalies) in data. They all involve systematic procedures. Not surprisingly, similarities and apparent overlaps will emerge.

In the cases of domain analysis and pattern matching there are important differences in scope and aim. Domain analysis is a specialized technique for identifying cultural meanings, and the patterns (regularities, groupings under categories etc.) that emerge are built around networks of semantic relationships. In pattern matching, however, the patterns may be of any kind (not necessarily cultural in nature). Pattern matching tends to generate broad brush-stroke kinds of analysis. We can use pattern matching in analysis of texts, spoken data and observed data, irrespective of our theoretical framework or study focus. In the case of Jacques, pattern matching has been used to analyse social situations in ways that can lead to descriptions of cultural meaning. But pattern matching has many uses beyond this type, whereas domain analysis does not. Within studies concerned with cultural meaning one might equally well use pattern matching or domain analysis. Some researchers might favour domain analysis because it offers greater structure, data summary power and focus than pattern matching.

Taxonomic analysis

Taxonomic analysis focuses on included terms within a cultural domain, and looks for relationships among the included terms. This provides more detailed information about how a cultural domain is organized. Cultural domains are in many ways systems of items that are related in particular ways (Borgatti 1999: 117). Once the researcher is aware of how a cultural domain is organized, it is possible to make this component of the overall meaning of a cultural scene *explicit*.

Spradley (1980) offers a useful heuristic perspective on the relationship between taxonomic analysis and research that seeks to identify cultural meanings. As an angle on what is involved in actively *doing* taxonomic analysis, Spradley describes what it is like for 'insiders' to unconsciously employ the kinds of taxonomies researchers have to construct in order to identify cultural meanings (the 'insider' acquires these categories as part of their *enculturation*). Spradley's example is of a person who goes to a shop to buy a particular news magazine. In this case, the magazine is not visible because it has been tucked away behind a different magazine. But the person knows to look for it there (and finds it): they have gone to that part of the magazine display that contains news magazines, after looking past the sports magazines, hobby magazines, house and garden magazines, books, comics and, even, newspapers.

As an 'outsider', the researcher is trying to uncover and make explicit some 'code' of cultural meanings that insiders 'automatically' employ, even though they may not be aware of this and, in fact, may not be able to articulate it. Domain analysis begins this process by trying to identify single components or elements of the code of cultural meanings. Taxonomic analysis carries the process one step further in terms of detail, by looking for relationships and components, or included terms, of a cultural domain.

Trying to describe and understand a cultural scene – to explicate the meanings realized and enacted within social situations – involves trying to discover what the meaningful *parts* are, and laying them out in order to understand the relationships between them. Once they have identified the parts of 'the code of cultural meaning', the qualitative researcher can then begin to reassemble the parts in the form of an interpretation which is presented as a description, but as a description which can to a large extent be explained in various ways.

Spradley (1980: 116–19) suggests a series of steps for conducting a taxonomic analysis:

1   Begin by selecting a cultural domain that contains plenty of information. The more included terms there are that are already apparent at the beginning of the taxonomic analysis process the easier it is to make the analysis.
2   Identify similarities among items and use them to create subcategories. This will make the taxonomic analysis more manageable and convey more structured or organized information at a glance (which in turn will make subsequent analysis easier and will allow for better quality description of the cultural scene).
3   Look for further included terms. This is a means of *expanding* the detail available in our observations. It allows us to find more in our data by getting us to attend more closely to detail.
4   Look for larger domains that can subsume smaller ones as subsets. This is a further way of making the analysis more informative and more powerful and refined. For example, our initial domain analysis of what students do in the classroom might reveal a cultural domain we call 'wasting time in class'. This would contain many examples of 'ways to waste time', 'places for wasting time', 'kinds of time wasting' and so on. We might also initially identify a further domain comprising ways of 'maximizing time spent off task' (e.g. where students find ways of diverting activity away from what they are supposed to be doing by asking the teacher lots of questions, deliberately creating digressions or raising irrelevant issues). We might subsequently decide that a better way of understanding what is going on is to collapse these two domains into a more encompassing domain like 'resistance to doing schoolwork'.
5   Create a preliminary taxonomy. This involves laying out the taxonomic analysis of a domain or multiple domains in some kind of visual form that conveys the

relationships between cover terms, included terms and multiple domains economically and usefully. These can take the form of tables with several rows and columns, or flow charts of lines and arrows, tree diagrams etc.

6 Check out the preliminary analysis by making further focused observations. One advantage of beginning analysis during the data collection phase is that it gives the researcher a chance to fill gaps and check preliminary categories and patterns. This might involve checking to see if there are more included terms that can be added to a domain (have any been missed?), or simply verifying that some of the additional categories generated on the basis of the data are actually apparent in the site.

7 Complete the taxonomy. This means bringing the process to closure and moving on to generate descriptions, interpretations and explanations by relating taxonomic and other forms of analysis to the research question and research purposes.

The result of a good taxonomic analysis is that it helps us to understand how a number of cultural domains are related to each other or, as Spradley says, how a number of cultural domains are *organized*.

Example of a taxonomic analysis
If we consider the cultural domain of 'ways of avoiding literacy work (work involving reading and writing) in class' in relation to Jacques, a preliminary taxonomic analysis, based on what we have described, might look like Figure 14.4. This is a taxonomic analysis of a single domain. In the section on pattern matching we included some brief fieldnote entries related to the pattern of Jacques being a joker (see Table 14.1). If, for argument's sake, a cultural domain was constructed for 'ways of being a joker', it could be developed as a taxonomy with the same broad shape as Figure 14.4. The middle 'column' might comprise different distinguishable 'types' of jokes, such as 'witty retorts' ('get an air conditioner'), 'clowning about', 'playing tricks on classmates' and so on. The right-hand column would contain specific examples of each kind of joking activity.

There might be a third and a fourth domain as well (their possible details need not concern us here). Let us imagine that multiple domains have been constructed around observations of Jacques in contexts involving literacy practices for school learning purposes. To interpret *all* the data about Jacques related to a research question that asks what kinds of literacy practices do four adolescents enact within school and out of school settings, it might be decided to collapse these multiple domains into 'ways of trying to avoid being seen as a dumbo'. This might be decided on the grounds that there are other clusters of domains that are equally rich and important – such as ones concerned with 'being a worker' and 'being a Jehovah's Witness' (Knobel 1999, 2001). The overall interpretation of Jacques' literacy practices might be distorted by treating 'ways of avoiding school literacy work' and 'ways of being a joker' as separate domains of cultural meaning associated with his language and literacy enactments. Clear and economical taxonomic analyses make it possible to lay out the richness and complexity of a case at a glance. This enables the researcher to preserve this richness in the research report while maximizing the economy and efficiency of the frame of

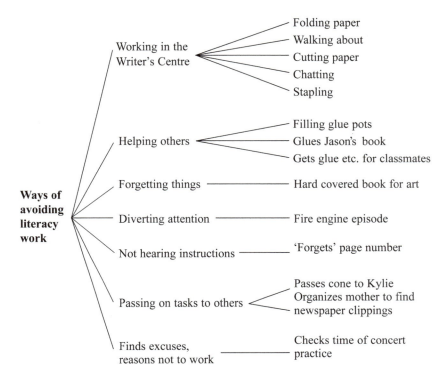

Figure 14.4 Preliminary taxonomic analysis

interpretation. It is also an invaluable analytic 'tool' for generating in the first place components that will eventually contribute to the overall study results and interpretation.

Task

Conduct a literature search to identify one or more examples of taxonomic analysis being employed in educational research.

- How does the researcher's procedure compare with the one we have described here based on the work of Spradley?

- If there are differences, what are the pros and cons of the respective approaches?

- What other analytic approaches, if any, has the author used in their study? How are these related to the taxonomic analysis?

- Do you think the study could have been better conducted using some other kind of analysis? If so, what kind? What are your reasons for this judgement?

For further reading in this area we suggest:

- Borgatti, S. (1999) Elicitation techniques for cultural domain analysis, in J. Schensul, M. LeCompte, B. Nastasi and S. Borgatti (eds) *Enhanced Ethnographic Methods: Audiovisual Techniques, Focused Group Interviews, and Elicitation Techniques*, pp. 115–51 (*Ethnographer's Toolkit*, Vol. 3). Walnut Creek, CA: Altamira Press.
- Fetterman, D. (1998) *Ethnography: Step by Step*, 2nd edn. Newbury Park, CA: Sage.
- Spradley, J. (1980) *Participant Observation*. New York: Holt, Rinehart & Winston.

CHAPTER 15

Analysing written data in qualitative teacher research

Introduction

The particular tools and approaches to data analysis presented in Chapters 13 and 14 are not, of course, necessarily confined to analysing the types of data addressed in their respective chapters. For example, we discuss pattern matching in relation to *observed* data (Chapter 14), yet it is equally applicable to spoken and written data. The same holds for open coding, categorical analysis and content analysis. Theme analysis and various kinds of discourse and linguistic analysis can likewise be applied to multiple kinds of data. On the other hand, some techniques like conversation analysis, domain analysis, event analysis and semiotic analysis (among others) *are* confined to particular kinds of data.

This chapter focuses on qualitative content analysis, linguistics-based text analysis approaches to analysing written texts, and semiotic analysis. These, obviously, are not the only approaches available for analysing the kinds of texts we count here as written data. Other approaches include constant comparative methods, discourse analysis methods, various kinds of philosophical analysis and hermeneutic methods. The three approaches addressed in this chapter are, however, among the most commonly used and useful in teacher research. Moreover, the qualitative content analysis and linguistics-based text analysis options are not confined to analysing written texts. They can be used, particularly, with interview transcripts and fieldnotes.

Organizing documents and documentary evidence for analysis

Written data can comprise a part or the whole of the data set for a study. Case studies, ethnographies, action research methodologies and other field-based approaches to research typically use written data to enhance the depth and breadth of information collected by via observation and interview. On the other hand, in many sociolinguistic and discourse studies, historical studies, policy analyses and theoretical studies, extant documents are the *sole* data collected for analysis. In both cases some kind of systematic method for locating, organizing and readily retrieving documents for analytic purposes is required.

Matthew Miles and A. Michael Huberman suggest creating 'document summary forms' for keeping track of a document's origins, its significance within the study, the content of the document and so on (Miles and Huberman 1994: 54). These document summary forms also enable the researcher to retrieve documents rapidly from files when they are needed. Figure 15.1 is a sample document summary form suggested by Miles and Huberman (1994: 55).

Completing these forms will always be idiosyncratic. Some researchers will write summary information in one colour and comments on the document in another (in Figure 15.1 the comments are between double parentheses). The 'IPA programme' in the document summary must be familiar to the researchers, since they have not needed to explain it for future reference.

The only 'rules' regarding document summary forms are that they must be:

- useful – having appropriate summary categories (relative to the research question, aim and purpose) that capture key data elements needed for the study;
- manageable – not too many categories to fill in, portable, with a key to abbreviations etc.

This kind of form-keeping is particularly useful for summarizing and keeping track of documents the researcher cannot keep. For example, very few historical studies include texts that are or become the private property of the researcher. Institutional or privately funded archives are usually the source of the letters, codices, books, treatises, artworks, policies, decrees etc. comprising the researcher's data set. For such texts the researcher needs to keep records of where each is, how it can be accessed for reading (when, where and by whom), who to contact for accessing it and the lead time required, relevant details about the information contained in the text for the research question etc.

Document summary forms are also useful for managing documents that the researcher is able to keep (or buy copies of, or photocopy etc.). As with artefacts (see Chapter 14), the researcher needs to decide whether documents will be grouped and filed according to:

- cases or people;
- origins;
- date written or published;

Document Summary Form: Illustration

DOCUMENT FORM   **Site:** Carson

                                                        Document: 2

Name or description of document: **Date received or picked up:** Feb. 13

The Buffalo (weekly sheet)

Event or contact, if any, with which the document is associated:

Paul's explanation of the administration team's functioning   **Date:** Feb. 13

Significance or importance of the document:

Gives schedule for all events in the district for the week. Enables coordination, knits two schools together

Brief summary of contents:

Schedule of everything from freshman girls' basketball to 'Secret Pals Week' in the elementary school

Also includes 'Did you know' items on the IPA programme (apparently integrating the IPA news)

And a description of how administration team works: who is on the team, what regular meetings deal with, gives working philosophy (e.g. 'we establish personal goals and monitor progress' ... 'We coordinate effort, K-12, and all programmes' ... 'We agree on staff selection'). Concluding comment: 'It is our system of personal management'

Also alludes to the 26 OPERATIONAL GUIDELINES (Document 16)

((I'll guess that the administration explanation does not appear every week – need to check this))

IF DOCUMENT IS CENTRAL OR CRUCIAL TO A PARTICULAR CONTACT

(e.g. a meeting agenda, newspaper clipping discussed in an interview), make a copy and include with write-up, otherwise, put in document file

---

Figure 15.1 Document summary form

- date collected;
- type (e.g. written document, artwork).

Document summary forms not only remind the researcher of the content of each document, but also where each document is stored, which always makes for easy and rapid retrieval.

For further reading in this area try:

- May, T. (1997) *Social Research: Issues, Methods and Process*, 2nd edn. Buckingham: Open University Press.
- McCulloch, G. and Richardson, W. (2000) *Historical Research in Educational Settings*. Buckingham: Open University Press.
- Miles, M. and Huberman, A.M. (1994) *Qualitative Data Analysis: An Expanded Sourcebook*, 2nd edn. Thousand Oaks, CA: Sage.

Qualitative content analysis

Content analysis is 'a research method that uses a set of procedures to make valid inferences from text' (Weber 1985: 9). According to Robert Weber, these inferences are usually concerned with the author or 'sender' or the text (and message in the text), the text or message itself and the readers or audience of the message or text. For example, a researcher might apply content analysis to a carefully selected set of comics from a range of countries in order to analyse the amount and degree of violence they contain. The researcher might find that comics produced in country X are at least twice as violent as comics produced in any other country in the study. On the basis of careful argument, extensive reading of research and the content analysis, the researcher might infer that comic producers in country X believe their readers prefer violent comics much more than do comic producers in country Y or Z. The researcher has studied the violence in selected comics in order to use these 'cultural artefacts' (the comics as texts) to 'unlock' and understand social views and ideologies encoded in them. Content analysis can also be used to identify 'pertinent features such as comprehensiveness of coverage or the intentions, biases, prejudices, and oversights of authors, publishers, as well as all other persons responsible for the content of materials' (Palmquist 1999: 1).

The emphasis on 'making inferences' within content analysis does not imply that any inference is necessarily acceptable:

> There are strict limitations on the inferences a researcher can make with content analysis. For example, inferences about motivation or intent can not normally be made, nor can the researcher infer what the effect of seeing such content would be on a viewer. Content analysis is only analysis of what is in the text. A researcher cannot use it to prove that newspapers intended, for example, to mislead the public, or that a certain style of journalism has a particular effect on public attitudes. The most common inferences in content analysis make use of concepts like unconscious bias or unintended consequences, and these are not the same as saying intentional bias or intended effect.
>
> (O'Connor 2001: 1)

> **Task**
>
> - What distinction is being made in the quote from O'Connor's work above?
>
> - What significance does it have for researchers using content analysis?
>
> - Why are there 'strict limitations on the inferences a researcher can make with content analysis'? Where do these limitations originate? Who imposes them?

Within qualitative research, then, content analysis is concerned with the kinds of messages texts send, and with what social norms and ideologies these messages encode. A key assumption underpinning content analysis is that frequent use of particular words, or a particular form of wording, and the use of a certain vocabulary – or discourse – carries information about worldviews, ideologies and social contexts at the time the text was produced (see Bauer 2000). Content analysis is used to analyse *texts*. 'Texts', however, are not confined to conventional printed matter. Content analysis can be used to analyse:

- policy documents;
- written responses on qualitative surveys;
- newspaper reports;
- textbooks and other text-based school resources;
- institutional texts (e.g. teachers' guides, handbooks);
- traditional fine art pieces through to popular art forms;
- popular song lyrics or poems;
- movies, television shows and television advertisements;
- differences in narrative forms;
- internet websites etc.

Traditionally, content analysis has been employed within quantitative research, focusing on word or phrase counts, and has assumed that words have fixed and single, unambiguous meanings. Although qualitative content analysis can include word counts, it rejects a 'one word/one meaning' relationship and, instead, focuses on one or more of the following elements.

Manifest and latent meanings. Manifest meaning refers to the surface meaning, themes and main ideas of the text as primary content (Mayring 2000: 2). *Latent meaning* refers to present or potential meaning that is not immediately apparent. For example, the manifest meaning of the line from a play script, 'Brrr, I'm cold' signifies that the speaker feels cold. On the other hand, the latent or implied meaning of this sentence could vary greatly, depending on who says it and within what context. For example: 'Would you close that window please', or even 'You don't care about me at all because if you did you would not have let me get cold', and so on.

Meaning-in-use or semantics. For example, the word 'critical' can signify something important, or a crisis-point, or an issue, or negative feedback etc., depending on how it is used and in what context.

Syntax. How something is said, written or presented (see Bauer 2000: 134).

Metaphors. The words we use to describe things (i.e. a representation or system of codes of cultural functions) (see Jackson 1998).

Synonyms and words sharing similar connotations in addition to each word's literal meaning. Content analysis is often an attractive option for analysing written data because it is well suited to dealing with large amounts of data and for comparing a number of texts, either of the same type or across a period of time. It 'reduces the complexity of a collection of texts' by distilling key features into a short summary or description (Bauer 2000: 132), and can help researchers construct 'indicators of worldviews, values, attitudes, opinions, prejudices and stereotypes, and compare these across communities' (Bauer 2000: 134). In addition, content analysis is often more rigorous than the impressionistic analyses that sometimes emerge from pattern matching (Weber 1990; Jackson 1998; Palmquist 1999).

At the same time, however, content analysis approaches have some well-recognized limitations. There is a risk of over-reduction and oversimplification of data and findings, because content analysis is concerned with classifying words, terms and meanings into fewer words, terms and meanings. Hence, it is possible to leave out or overlook important details. Moreover, problems often arise concerning the ambiguity of words and meanings. At a more substantial level of concern, there is a risk when using content analysis of downplaying the theory that informs the study. This occurs where researchers focus on redescribing or summarizing the data by means of their content analysis, instead of interpreting their findings by means of a clearly articulated theoretical position. Merely redescribing data does not contribute new knowledge to the field. It is also possible to over-extend inferences drawn from the analysis so that the link between the data and the inferences made from it becomes tenuous and difficult to sustain. Finally, it is common to find content analysts disregarding the purposes of the text, such as why it was produced, by whom and for what audience. Such details are important since they help the researcher decide how to 'read' the text (Bauer 2000).

Approaches to qualitative content analysis

Although content analysts themselves admit that defining 'content analysis' and describing approaches to it is a difficult task, we can identify three large 'families' of approaches. These are 'word count analysis', 'content categories analysis' and 'definitional content analysis'.

Word-count analysis

This approach – seemingly quantitative on the surface – tallies the appearances of words (or images, or music etc.) in a text, but does not apply statistical formulations to these tallies. Instead, counts are usually presented as percentages, and these are interpreted using pre-formulated research hypotheses.

Content categories analysis

Content categories 'may consist of one, several, or many words. Words, phrases, or other units of text classified in the same category are presumed to have similar meanings' (Jackson 1998: 1). Categories are constructed logically, according to shared characteristics of items. Basic units of analysis tend to be single words or very short phrases. Each category is carefully and thoroughly defined so that analysis remains consistent across the text or texts.

Definitional content analysis
The unit of analysis remains at the word level, but the researcher is also interested in reading the text on either side of the focus word or phrase. This is (a) to understand the meaning of the focus word or phrase in each instance, and (b) to understand the context of each instance of the word or phrase being sought. We demonstrate this approach on page 337.

These approaches to qualitative content analysis are typically used *deductively*. The researcher begins with concepts, words, meanings or key elements they want to analyse within the document (Patton 2002). In her study of adolescents' language and literacy practices within school and non-school settings, Michele analysed how 'social purpose' was construed in the Queensland English syllabus for Grades 1 to 10. The primary unit of analysis was the phrase 'social purpose' and its variants (e.g. 'social purposes', 'socially purposeful'). Each instance of this basic unit of analysis was located and scrutinized. Comparisons were drawn between each instance of the term

Table 15.1 Definitional content analysis: an example

Research problem	Research question	Research aim	Data to be collected	Data analysis approach	Guiding sources
A teacher researcher has been reading a number of 'acceptable use' policies associated with computer use at schools within the local region. The teacher is wanting to maximize the usefulness and effectiveness of computer use within her school, and is curious about how new technology use is defined and described in a range of school-produced documents	What assumptions are made about new technology use in a range of school-generated policies?	To compare local policies on technology use in schools with effective approaches to new technology use as reported in relevant research	Official technology use policies developed by schools (these policies are often available on the internet, or are published as part of the school prospectus or handbook)	Qualitative content analysis, with an emphasis on definitional analysis	Bauer 2000 Jackson 1998 Patton 2002 Bigum *et al.* 2000 Cuban 2001 Lankshear *et al.* 1997

'social purpose' within the syllabus document and the formal definition of 'social purpose' provided within systemic functional linguistics (a key theory informing the syllabus). This analysis indicated that in the syllabus statement social purposes were presented as fixed, singular, and tied directly and primarily to texts. This contrasted with what had been expected prior to undertaking the analysis: namely, that social purposes would be construed as complex, 'in process' and genuinely *social*.

On occasion, however, researchers may prefer to work *inductively* – searching through the text, word by word, phrase by phrase, or paragraph by paragraph to distil important ideas and themes contained therein. Key content emerges during the process of reading through a text numerous times. For example, a researcher might make repeated readings through the diary entries of a male teacher made during the 1950s while working in a one-teacher school in rural Australia. This can throw up key words and phrases – like words concerning emotional health, access to resources, classroom management – that then become linchpins in the researcher's content analysis of the diary.

An example of content analysis

In this section we demonstrate 'definitional content analysis'. The research context is summarized in Table 15.1 on page 335.

Qualitative content analysis usually involves six steps:

1 Organize the text for analysis and determine unit(s) of analysis – in this case, our first unit of analysis is the word 'student', followed by 'teacher' – and hypotheses concerning these units of analysis if they are included in the study. In the current study, we are interested in comparing how policies in our data set define what 'counts' as acceptable student use and teacher use where new technologies are concerned. Because the policies concern *use* specifically, selecting 'use' as a unit of analysis is too broad to be all that helpful.
2 Read through the texts to be analysed a number of times, marking each and all instances of the specific unit of analysis in the texts.
3 Decide whether contextual or other latent-meaning related items also need to be coded.
4 Develop lists, categories or other organization schemes (e.g. hierarchies, location or concept maps) and allocate the units of analysis accordingly.
5 Revisit texts and check to see what has been inadvertently 'missed out' or over-looked (e.g. oblique references to new technology use not identified during steps 1 to 3). The researcher may also 'test' out hypotheses at this stage, using the categories developed from the initial analysis along with expected or hypothesized categories from the literature, to see what is present and not present in the text.
6 Interpret results in the light of the theories framing the study.

The following example uses two excerpts from a school's 'acceptable use' (of computers) policy. This policy is a public document that can be downloaded from the internet; however, we have decided to remove specific identifiers from within the excerpts that follow.

Step 1

The text is organized for content analysis by numbering each line to assist subsequent data retrieval.

Step 2

All instances of the word 'student', including pronouns that clearly refer to students and oblique references (e.g. 'graduates', 'users'), are identified using bold.

Step 3

All related and important contextual and latent meaning, or implied information, is indicated by the use of italics. (Each numbered entry below corresponds to one single line in the original document.)

(1) In a free and democratic society, access to information is a fundamental right of citizenship.

(2) Electronic information resources offer multiple opportunities of educational value. [The school] supports

(3) *access by* **students** and staff *to rich information resources* and encourages staff and **students** *to*

(4) *develop the information research skills necessary to analyse and evaluate such resources.* [school] Net

(5) is provided for **students** and staff *to collaborate, produce, publish, conduct research*, and *to*

(6) *communicate with others on a local, national, and international level.* In return, **every [school] user** is

(7) expected to *use these resources for educational purposes only, to act in a responsible, ethical, and*

(8) *legal manner; and to conform to network etiquette that includes being polite, using appropriate*

(9) *language, and respecting privacy.*

(10) The availability of the School network and computers will shift the way **students** *share*

(11) *ideas, transmit information, and contact others.* As **students** are connected to the global community,

(12) **their** *use of new tools and systems bring new responsibilities and opportunities.* This policy covers

(13) the use of technology and equipment that may be used by **students** to *access off campus resources*

(14) *including but not limited to the Internet, commercial information, electronic mail, bulletin board*

(15) *systems, and sites accessed through video conferencing technology.* To *ensure the proper and*

(16) *appropriate use* of computers and the network available at [this] High School, **students** who use

(17) them *must conform to the following rules and regulations. By signing this form*, **you** *agree* to all of

(18) the rules and regulations. Failure to comply with these rules may result in the loss of all computer

(19) and network use privileges.

(20) **Section 1, General Use Policies**

(21) 1 **Students** *may use* computers and network outlets (drops) in lab settings or designated areas

(22) on campus, but classes have a priority over students using computers or drops for personal

(23) use. You may be asked to move from a computer or a drop in the event that a class needs to

(24) use it.

(25) 2 **Students** *may not use* computers or network drops in classrooms, departments, or teacher

(26) workrooms without the expressed permission of the teachers in whose rooms these computers

(27) or drops are located.

(28) 3 **Students** using the internet at school *must only* visit appropriate internet sites (sites with no

(29) explicit scenes, sites with no pirate software, etc.).

(30) 4 To prevent viruses and other dangerous programs from spreading around campus, **students**

(31) *are not permitted* to install or execute any unauthorized programs, regardless of how the

(32) programs were acquired or the intent of the user.

(33) 5 As federal law prohibits the downloading, possession, or use of any unlicensed software,

(34) violators will be held accountable and legal proceedings may be initiated.

(35) 6 To protect the safety of **all students**, *no* online chat of any sort *will be allowed* on campus.

(36) This includes, but is not limited to, IRC, AOL, Java-based chat (Yahoo Chat, Infoseek Chat,

(37) Lycos Chat, etc.) and ICQ.

(38) 7 **Students** *using* school equipment for email purposes *may only* send, receive, or display

(39) appropriate messages and attachments (no threats, obscene language, etc.).

(40) 8 Personal computer peripherals are prohibited on campus.

(41) 9 Irvine High School assumes no responsibility for the deletion of and/or failure to store private

(42) files. Irvine High School has a limit on the amount of network space you may use; you may

(43) not attempt to bypass this limit.

(44) 10 **Students** *are prohibited* from using school equipment for business or profit purposes.

(45) 11 **Students** *are prohibited* from intentionally wasting computer time and network resources.

(46) 12 **Students** *are prohibited* from revealing their home address or phone number or that of another

(47) person.

(48) 13 **Students** *are prohibited* from falsifying permission, authorization, or identification documents.

(49) 14 **Students** *may not* plagiarize any material obtained from the internet. All sources used for

(50) academic work must be done so with proper citation.

Task

- To what extent do you accept our initial analysis presented in the text above? What are the reasons for your judgement?

- Why have we included the phrase, 'every [school] user', in our content analysis (see line 6)?

- There are at least three lines with ambiguous references to students (lines 18–19, 34, 42). Where are they ambiguous? Why have we chosen not to code them as pertaining directly to our key word, 'students'? What does this suggest about content analysis and the decisions researchers need to make? Would it be wrong to include these three ambiguous references in our analysis? Why/why not?

- What does this tell you about content analysis?

Step 4

This involves organizing or grouping the bold and italicized elements in a helpful way. How best to do this is for the researcher to decide. As noted above, however, the approach needs to be logical and relate directly to the research question and the purposes that shape the study. We have chosen a table format.

Taking the first instance of 'student' in our text (line 3, third word), we see it is tied directly to 'access'. This becomes our first entry:

Content item	Definition
Student (use of new technologies)	Requires access to information

Other relevant (contextual) matter highlighted in italics – most of line 4, all of line 2, and half of line 3 – also pertain to 'requires access to information'. This is added to the growing analytic table as follows:

Content item	Contextual information
Student (use of new technologies)	Requires access to information, which includes: rich information resources developing necessary information research skills for analysing and evaluating information collaborating, producing, publishing and conducting research communicating with others on a local, national and international level

Further uses of the word 'student' and new contextual information are added to the analytic table in the same manner. Categories of content now begin to emerge from the data:

Content item	Definition
Student (use of new technologies)	Requires access to information and networks, which include: rich information resources developing necessary information research skills for analysing and evaluating information collaborating, producing, publishing and conducting research communicating with others on a local, national and international level sharing ideas (from line 11) transmitting information (from line 11) contacting others (from line 11) new tools and equipment (from line 12) internet commercial information email bulletin board systems sites accessed through video-conferencing technology
Student (use and administration expectations)	School administration expects that students use new technologies for educational purposes only, including: acting in a responsible manner acting in an ethical manner acting in a legal manner conforming to network etiquette (including: being polite, using appropriate language, respecting privacy) (taking on) new responsibilities and opportunities (from line 12) conforming to rules and regulations (from line 17)

This process is continued until we reach the end of the excerpts.

Step 5
We repeat Step 4 until no more categories and additions appear.

Step 6
The analytic procedure we have demonstrated has only begun to open the analysis up. It needs to be developed and refined much more before we are in a position to address the question concerning what assumptions are made about new technology uses in policies generated at the school level. In fact, the opening two content items emerging in the analysis appear to be in tension. One is associated with the view that the school provides access to new technologies that will open up new ways of collaborating and working with others. The other indicates the administration's expectations regarding student responsibilities and duties associated with using new technologies. It is possible that even at this early stage of the analysis we are getting clues that part of the interpretation might be concerned with the presence of tensions, if not contradictions, in assumptions about new technology use within school policies. (And it must be remembered that the analysis here pertains to just two excerpts from a single school.) Certainly, if the theory we were using in the study as a whole were one that saw policies as *political* and, to that extent, as sites of potential tension and struggle, then our interpretation might well fasten onto the kind of tension our content analysis is suggesting at this early stage.

Task

- Complete the qualitative content analysis of the policy text. You may need to add new categories (e.g. students and *un*acceptable use).

- What do you notice? To what extent is there a possible tension here between the purpose of this document and the way in which student use of new technology is characterized or presented?

- We have emphasized throughout this book that specific analytic methods are not necessarily confined to only one type of data. Re-analyse the above excerpt using domain analysis (see Chapter 10). For example, the semantic relationship, 'X is an element of acceptable technology use', or 'X is a characteristic of "unacceptable" technology use', could be used to generate the domain.

- What do you notice?

- What does this tell you about data analysis in general?

- What does this tell you about what approach to data analysis you select for any given study?

For further reading in this area we suggest:

- Bauer, M. (2000) Classical content analysis, in M. Bauer and G. Gaskell (eds) *Qualitative Researching with Text, Image and Sound*, pp. 131–51. London: Sage.
- Bernard, R. (2000) *Social Research Methods: Qualitative and Quantitative Approaches*. Thousand Oaks, CA: Sage.
- Patton, M. (2002) *Qualitative Research and Evaluation Methods*, 3rd edn. Thousand Oaks, CA: Sage.

Linguistics-based text analysis

Linguistics-based text analysis of written data involves identifying regularities, patterns and other tendencies that stand out in the *language features* of texts – for example, in terms of lexis, grammar, syntax and so on. In this section we will consider two types of approach to analysing extant texts. We refer to these as *critical* and *non-critical* approaches to linguistics-based text analysis respectively.

Critical linguistics-based text analysis

Teacher researchers have interests in diverse kinds of written data for diverse purposes. Equally, they have access to different kinds of analytic approaches to use on written data. Some of these, like the approach used by Gee (1999), can be used to identify ideological characteristics of educationally significant texts. Critical linguistics-based analysis is such an approach. Teacher researchers can investigate the ideological 'workings' of written data by asking the following kinds of questions and developing analytic techniques to address them (adapted from Kress 1985; Wallace 1992; Lankshear 1997; Knobel 1998):

- What is the subject matter or topic of this text?
- Why might the author have written this text?
- Who is the intended audience? How do I know?
- What kind of person would find this text unproblematic in terms of their values, beliefs, worldviews etc.?
- What worldview and values does the author hold or appear to hold? How do I know?
- What knowledge does the reader need to bring to this text in order to understand it?
- Who would feel 'left out' in this text, but should logically be included? Is this exclusion a problem? Are there important 'gaps' or 'silences', or over-generalizations in this text? For example, are different groups talked about as though they constitute one homogeneous group?
- Does the author write about a group without including *their* perspectives, values, beliefs in relation to the things or events being reported?
- Who would find that the claims made in this text clash with their own values, beliefs or experiences?

Example: textual representations of colonization

The following example shows how elementary analytic tools can be used to address such questions and how educationally significant texts work ideologically at the level of word choices. It draws on the short text titled 'Columbus' Voyages' presented near the end of Chapter 12. This text was produced by Mexico's Department of Public Education for use in upper primary-school social studies lessons (SEP 1994). It contains an introduction addressed to parents and teachers. This identifies weaknesses in history teaching and states that the new textbook aims to provide teachers with a high-quality resource for use in history lessons.

Those Who Travelled to the New World

Many men left from Spain to settle the newly discovered islands. These men were priests, who sought to convert the indigenous peoples to Christianity and to teach them the Spanish alphabet.

Many poor peasants whose lands were not sufficient to sustain them also travelled to the American world, along with many others who were without work or who were being pursued by justice.

How They Lived in the New World

The Spaniards who arrived on the islands proclaimed them colonies, because they came to found dependencies for the Spanish crown.

The Spanish rulers named a government in the new lands.

The colonists exploited the mines and lands of the new possessions, *using* the labour of indigenous people and bringing African slaves to America.

Elementary forms of word analysis can be used to identify the social groups referred to in this text, locate key words associated with these groups and examine ideologies and worldviews constructed and promoted by the author's word choices.

Those who 'travel' in the text are exclusively Europeans: priests, poverty-stricken peasants and political refugees. African slaves were 'brought', rather than travelled, to the 'New World'. This inscribes the slaves' status as goods and chattels (rather than people). The second subtitle in our excerpt prepares readers for information about how those who travelled to the New World *lived*. The text, however, focuses entirely on acts associated with the colonizers and their resources. The use of 'New World' in this text reinforces an orientation towards Mexican history that is resolutely Eurocentric.

We can also examine how the respective social groups are represented in terms of the qualities and features attributed to them. This can be done by coding key nouns (or *actors*) and their associated verbs (or *processes*), and inserting the words into columns in a table. In the text below the actors have been identified in bold and the processes in italic. In theoretical terms this analytic approach might be seen as drawing on concepts from systemic functional linguistics (see Halliday 1985; Kress and van Leeuwen 1996).

Those Who Travelled to the New World

Many **men** *left* from Spain to settle the newly discovered islands. **These men** *were* **priests,** who *sought to convert* the **indigenous peoples** to Christianity and to *teach* them the Spanish alphabet.

Many poor **peasants** whose lands were not sufficient to sustain them also *travelled* to the American world, along with many **others** who *were* without work or who *were being pursued* by justice.

How They Lived in the New World

The **Spaniards** who *arrived* on the islands *proclaimed* them colonies, because they *came to found dependencies* for the Spanish crown.

The **Spanish rulers** *named* a government in the new lands.

The **colonists** *exploited* the mines and lands of their new possessions, *using* the labour of **indigenous people** and *bringing* **African slaves** to America.

The results of identifying the processes associated with the actors can be tabulated as shown in Table 15.2. Even this elementary and incomplete tabulation of the identity attributes of the groups reveals many ideological characteristics of the text when we relate the words back to our orienting questions. We can see at a glance who is 'active' in this text and who is not. 'Indigenous people' and 'African slaves' are practically rendered invisible by comparison with priests, Spanish colonists and peasants. Important social differences between the various European groups are elided by casting all groups as more or less equally active in colonizing 'the New World'. Yet these groups had very different experiences. Many wealthy Spaniards were given rich farm land by the Spanish sovereign, whereas Spanish peasants had to eke out a living as labourers or farm on marginal land. The apparent passivity of indigenous peoples intimated by the text distorts history. Many accounts by individuals from indigenous and Spanish groups alike show that Mexico's indigenous peoples were far from passive toward colonization. Similarly, the only gender reference is to males ('many men'). Historical evidence shows that women played an active and often pivotal role in colonization. They also, of course, endured subservient and repressed roles within daily life. In the text, however, they are simply invisible. The most readers can assume from the text is that women's experiences of colonization was the same as men's.

Table 15.2 Sample tabulation of actors and processes in 'Columbus' Voyages'

Many men/priests	Poor peasants/those without work/those being persecuted	Spaniards	Spanish rulers	Colonists	Indigenous people	African slaves
• left	• travelled	• arrived	• named	• exploited		
• were	• were	• proclaimed		• bringing		
• sought (to convert)	• were being pursued	• came				
• (to) teach						

Ironically, for a text intended to enhance teaching and learning about history, the 'ideal readers' of this text – those for whom the text reads without friction or tension – will include teachers who are most 'at home' with traditional Eurocentric representations of Mexican history. It is likely that teachers who are themselves indigenous and/or are cognizant of and sensitive to non-European accounts of the colonization of Latin America, and/or are politicized women, would be troubled about using this text in their history lessons.

Task

Obtain a social studies or history school textbook and apply the kind of analysis we have modelled in this section. Then answer the following questions:

- What did your structured analysis tell or 'show' you that you hadn't noticed on your first reading of the text you analysed?

- What purposes might be served by a critical discourse analysis of school textbooks?

- What other texts might lend themselves readily to critical discourse analysis? How do you know?

- What might critical discourse analysis tell you that social semiotic analysis might not? When might you use critical discourse analysis and not social semiotic analysis?

Non-'critical' linguistics-based text analysis

Use of linguistics-based analysis for *evaluative* purposes other than identifying how texts work ideologically is quite common within teacher research. This section describes two options for what we call non-critical linguistics-based analysis of educationally significant texts.

Consider, for example, a researcher investigating the suitability of particular texts for reading instruction with a class of third grade students reading at a measured 8-year-old reading level. The researcher might find it useful to analyse the linguistic features of the selected texts to compare them against criteria and norms associated with an 8-year-old reading level. Such measures as *lexical density* and *readability* can be used for this purpose.

Analysing by lexical density measurement

'Lexical density' refers to the proportion of *content words* in a text. This indicates the grammatical complexity of the text. Content words are usually nouns, verbs and adverbs, carrying concrete and observable information. They can be distinguished from *function words* which 'are often determiners (e.g., the, a, this, those), pronouns (e.g., he, whom, you, what, which), prepositions (e.g., in, after, on, above, beside), conjunctions (e.g., because, therefore, though, if, when), [and] adverbs of time and place (now, next, soon, here, there)' (Lê 1997: 1). The higher the lexical density, the more complex a text will be, because of the greater amount of information contained within its phrases and clauses. Lexical density is measured by counting the number of content words in each phrase and clause of a given text. Lê offers the following examples of lexical density analysis (content words are in italics):

Low lexical density

- You may *want* to *go* there every *week*. (3)
- It *is* not *logical* to *think* in that *way*. (4)

High lexical density

- *Schools teach various subjects ranging* from *maths* to *languages*. (7)
- *History tells horrific stories* about *human civilization*. (6)
- *Kids want food, drink*, and *love* from *kind teachers*. (7)

Formal, planned texts like business letters, policy documents and textbooks usually have high lexical density, while spontaneous (usually) spoken texts generally have low lexical density (Halliday 1985).

Task

- Find examples of sentences that have a high lexical density. In what kinds of texts do they most often appear?

- Find a text you would normally give to an 8-year-old and determine its lexical density.

- How might you use lexical density to answer the question, 'Are the selected texts suitable for students reading at an 8-year-old level?'

For further reading in this area see:

- Martin, J. (1992) *English Text: System and Structure*. Philadelphia, PA: John Benjamins Publishing Company.

Analysing by readability measures
Measuring 'readability' refers to gauging how difficult a text is, and assigning a 'reading age' or school grade level to it. Tests of readability are usually applied to 100-word samples from the text. The researcher counts the number of complete sentences and the number of words with three or more syllables. Some tests apply mathematical equations to the resulting raw counts, others use graphs to determine a text's reading 'level'. Popular readability tests include the Flesch Readability Test, Fogg's Readability Test and Fry's Readability Graph. We use Fogg's test of readability here. It focuses on sentences and syllables to gauge readability, as follows:

1 Take a sample of 100 words from the selected text.
2 Count the number of complete sentences in the 100-word sample.
3 Count the number of words in each complete sentence.
4 Divide the number of words by the number of sentences to arrive at an average sentence length for the sample.
5 Count the number of words with three or more syllables. This number automatically becomes the percentage of long or potentially difficult words in the sample (e.g. 25/100 words have three or more syllables). For Fogg's test a syllable is a vowel sound: 'coconut' is three syllables; 'dessert' is two. 'Non-words' (numbers, symbols, dates and acronyms) count as one syllable.
6 Add the average word length for sentences in the sample (e.g. 10) to the percentage

of words having three or more syllables (e.g. 25) (10 + 25 = 35). The sum of these two figures gives the overall readability score for the selected text.

The lower the readability score, the more 'readable' or 'comprehensible' the text is assumed to be. Tabloid newspapers are considered generally to have a Fogg readability index of around 25, and broadsheet newspapers are in the vicinity of 40.

Task

1 Apply Fogg's Readability Test to a 100-word passage taken from a book (preferably one likely to be read by school students).

- What role does linguistic knowledge play in this test of readability?

- What role might a readability test play in a research study?

2 Using the same 100-word sample, analyse the lexical density of ten randomly selected phrases and clauses in this text.

- Compare and comment on the results achieved by testing the readability of the text and determining its lexical density.

- How might you go about presenting or summarizing the findings from each method?

- What implications does this exercise have for analysing written texts?

For further reading try:

- Online automated algorithms for judging the readability of webpages: www.juicystudio.com/fog/; www.eplaybooks.com/schools/readtest.htm.
- Clariana, R. and Bond, C. (1993) Using readability formulas to establish the grade level difficulty of software, *Journal of Computing in Childhood Education*, 4(3): 255–61.

Semiotic analysis

Semiotics is the systematic study of *signs* and *sign systems* (e.g. linguistic, visual, musical and procedural systems), their meaning, the ways in which signs convey meaning, and sign-making (Kress and van Leeuwen 1996; Seel 1999). Semiotics is especially useful for analysing image-based information. Some theorists believe we are moving increasingly toward image-driven communication forms (Hodge and Kress 1988; Kress 1998; Lemke 1998), making semiotics an important approach to data analysis in education research.

Classical semiotics builds on three key concepts: 'sign', 'signifier' and 'signified'. Each sign has a representational element (signifier) where something 'stands in' for something else, and a meaning element (signified) invoked by the representational element. As a signifier the Nike swoosh represents both the Nike company and the image Nike has built to accompany its product.

Whereas semiotics has traditionally focused on signs, many researchers have recently become interested in the sign-making processes occurring in people's everyday lives, and regard these processes – rather than signs *per se* – as central to the semiotic study of meaning systems (see Kress and van Leeuwen 1996). Such processes occur when someone constructs – through language, image, text, gestures, sound or other representations of objects or ideas – a sign arising from 'the cultural, social and psychological history of the sign-maker, and … focused by the specific context in which the sign is produced' (Kress and van Leeuwen 1996: 6). The study of signs and sign-making helps us understand more about how societies and the people within them function. Societies are 'composed of groups with varying, and often contradictory, interests'. Thus 'the messages produced by individuals will reflect the differences, incongruities and clashes which characterize social life' (Kress and van Leeuwen 1996: 18).

Kress and van Leeuwen distinguish three broad schools of semiotic thought and practice: the 'Prague School' (1930s – early 40s); the 'Paris School' (1960s and 70s) and 'Social Semiotics' (1970s – ongoing). We will focus here on some aspects of social semiotics.

Social semiotic analysis

Michael Halliday's systemic functional linguistics (e.g. Halliday 1985) is a key element in the social semiotic theory of communication (see e.g. Hodge and Kress 1988; Kress and van Leeuwen 1996; Kress and Jewitt 2003). Social semiotics draws directly on three *meta*functions developed originally by Halliday.

Ideational metafunction
This deals with the representation of experiences and things and the connections between them, which involves the sign-maker in making choices about how to represent objects, interactions, relations between things and/or experiences, processes etc. The ideational metafunction answers the question: 'What is this about?'

Interpersonal metafunction
This deals with representing social relations between the producer of a sign and the receiver (or reproducer) of the sign. Any semiotic system (e.g. image-based, language-based) 'must be able to project a particular social relation between the producer, the viewer and the object represented' (Kress and van Leeuwen 1996: 41). The interpersonal metafunction answers the questions: 'Who is this text or sign produced for, and by whom?' and 'What is the implied relation between them, and how do we know?'

Textual metafunction
This deals with texts defined as 'complexes of signs which cohere both internally and [externally] with the context for which they were produced' (Kress and van Leeuwen

1996: 41). For example, different compositional arrangements (or 'layout') enable the 'realization' or production and reception of different textual meanings. Placing a block of text on the left and an image on the right of a page draws the (left to right) reader's attention first to the text and then to the image, which makes the text most salient in terms of attention and importance. Placing the image on the left and the block of text on the right draws attention first to the image, then to the text, making the image most salient. The textual metafunction answers the question, 'What are the effects of the representational choices made in order to produce this text or sign?'

Table 15.3 A template for guiding social semiotic analysis

Social semiotic metafunction	Layout	Typographical features	Length or size of items	Ratio between text and images	Colour
Ideational metafunction What is this about?					
Interpersonal metafunction Who is this text or sign produced for, and by whom? What is the implied relation between them, and how do we know?'					
Textual metafunction What are the effects of the representational choices made in order to produce this text or sign?					

These three metafunctions also provide a useful frame for organizing and presenting data analyses (see Table 15.3).

Kress (1996, 1998) offers a helpful example of social semiotic analysis in action. He presents the front page of the German broadsheet newspaper *Frankfurter Allgemeine*, and the front page of the English tabloid the *Sun*. The *Frankfurter Allgemeine* has the newspaper's banner at the top. The page is completely covered in densely-spaced blocks of small-type text. By contrast, the *Sun*'s tabloid-sized front page is almost entirely taken up with one headline and then three pictures (only one relevant to the headline). The headline is much larger than the banner. Kress makes use of the three metafunctions to guide his analysis, and across each metafunction he focuses on the representational effects of layout, typographical features, the length or size of items and the ratio between text and images. For Kress, these features capture the 'world-view' and reading expectations of each newspaper's producers and readers.

Kress suggests that the typographical and layout features on the front page of the *Frankfurter Allgemeine* are a sign that its producers want to provide readers with as much information (the ideational metafunction) as possible, and believe readers will take the time and effort to concentrate on each article in its entirety: 'The length of the items suggests that this is a reader who would not wish to be "short changed", who wishes to have a serious treatment of an issue' (Kress 1998: 25). The typography (font types, sizes and format) differentiates varying types of newspaper articles like news reporting, regular columns and feature articles (the textual metafunction). The specific types of font used impact directly on the relationship between the producers of this newspaper and its readers. The banner is set in a gothic font. Kress says this suggests an 'old' newspaper, which has been reporting the news for a long time and is, therefore, to be trusted and relied upon (the interpersonal metafunction). Kress reads the typographical features on this page as emphasizing rationality. Kress advises his own readers that the features he has selected for analysis should not be regarded as simply the formal aspects of a newspaper's front page. Rather, the *Frankfurter Allgemeine* speaks to, and is read by, 'a particular kind of reader' (Kress 1998: 25). This reader is comfortable with the features on the front page and throughout the newspaper, even though reading it requires extended concentration and application. Kress' interpretation of his analysis is that the paper and its readers share a common political objective: to promote and maintain conservatism.

The *Sun*'s front page uses very different representational resources. It appears to emphasize display rather than information. Very little text appears on the front page (ideational metafunction). This is signalled by the huge headline fonts and the large photographs (textual metafunction). The front page is printed in colour (whereas the *Frankfurter Allgemeine* is entirely in black ink). Kress suggests that these semiotic differences signal different readerships between the two papers (interpersonal metafunction). The *Sun*'s organization of the representational resources suggests a reader 'who does not have the time, the skill, the concentration or willingness to read in a focused fashion. This is a reader who just wants to get her or his perceptions immediately, directly. Information must be presented in a pleasurable fashion ... hence particularly the colour' (Kress 1998: 25–6).

In his discussion and interpretation, Kress (1998: 27) focuses in particular on the effects of the representational choices made and resources drawn on by the producers of each newspaper:

> It seems to me that radically different resources are employed in the two cases; radically different transformative potentials made available; radically different subjectivities produced. If the *Frankfurter Allgemeine* feels friendly to its habituated reader, then we must assume that the *Sun* feels at least equally friendly to its readers also. But these are very different kinds of friends; if you can tell someone's character by the friends they have, then we have here fundamentally different social subjects.

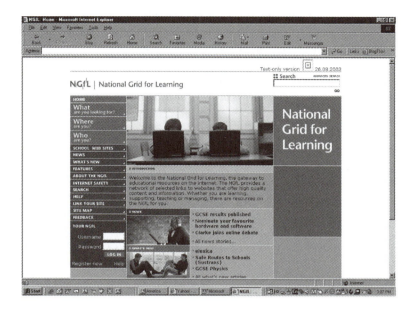

Figure 15.2 Part of the National Grid for Learning web page (www.ngfl.gov.uk)

Analysing a website

Kress' three metafunctions and his four specific analytic tools (layout, typography, the ratio of text to images and colour) can be used to undertake social semiotic analysis of internet web pages. Figure 15.2 shows the front page of the National Grid for Learning website overseen by the British Educational Communications and Technology Agency. This is the 'start' page for the UK government's education and community internet initiative, widely known as the Grid (see Lankshear and Knobel 2003).

Ideational metafunction
Layout
A bar of mostly blank space runs across the top of the web page. The remainder of the page is divided into three columns set within a blank, white border. Each column comprises stacked rectangular shapes. The overall message is one of order, signalling that viewers are likely to find well-organized and useful information on this page. The first column divides into three main parts. These act as a menu or site guide. The first part has a place of prominence according to English-language reading conventions (i.e. the top left-hand corner of the page is the most salient point on a page or screen). This offers possible routes for accessing information (prompting viewers to respond to questions such as 'What?', 'Who?' and 'Where?'). The second offers a more detailed menu of categories of information and resources accessible via the website. The third section offers viewers the opportunity to register for updates to the website.

The second column divides into three sections. The first consists of a photograph. The second presents a welcome message and brief explanation of the website. The third offers three categories of hyperlinks: 'news', 'what's new' and 'features'. These hyperlinks are updated regularly.

The third column is subdivided into three. This balances it with the first column, although only the first section in this final column contains any text.

Typographical resources

The font styles and sizes reinforce the no-nonsense message sent by the carefully constrained layout. The font is sans-serif and appears to be Verdana. This font is used by some popular commercially oriented websites like Amazon.com. It is a 'clean', easy to read font that looks very professional yet not too formal. The font formatting is minimal, using only four font size differences, bold and words written all in capitals. This makes for a clean-looking, very easy to read text. Words in bold tend to be key words in menus or hyperlinks and generally act as titles. Words written in capitals tend to be single-word labels for hyperlinks to specific key areas within the website. The largest font size is reserved for the name of the website given at the top of the third column. The next largest font size is used for the route options into the website that appear in the top section of the first column. The smallest font size is used for the welcome message that appears more or less in the middle of the page. The effect of the font sizes is to draw viewers' attention to the top left and right corners of the page where respectively the principal menu buttons for content are located and the name of the Grid is given. Viewers' attention is thus drawn to easily-accessed navigational paths through the site, while at the same time the name of the Grid is emphasized, which is important, given the relative 'newness' of the initiative.

There is little written text on this page. Blocks of colour and coloured photographs account for most of its bulk. Most of what written text there is consists of labels for hyperlinks rather than extended passages of text. The relative absence of text and the significantly high proportion of hyperlinks to other web pages and websites underscore the role of this particular site. It is to act as an online stepping-off place into the UK's national communications network for schools and communities.

If you look at this site on a computer, you will see that the colours are a mix of bright and semi-pastel. Key items are highlighted with a rich red background. Other main options – like the more detailed hyperlink menu in the first column and the log-in function – are also given strong background colours. Apart from those in the images, the colours are all solid, further reinforcing the 'dependable', 'no-nonsense' message sent by the layout, fonts and text-image ratio. The use of strong, solid colours also sends a message of freshness and 'modern-ness'. This helps reassure viewers that the information available via the website is likely to be up-to-date and reliable.

Taken together the layout, the typographical features of the text, the length of items, the ratio between text and images and the colours all send a clear message to viewers. They are dealing with a rational, systematic, up-to-date and reliable site that will enable access to a wealth of information and resources by means of multiple routes.

Interpersonal metafunction

The website's URL tells us this page was produced for/by the UK government. The language, images and layout used in constructing the page suggest it is intended for use by 'everyday people'. The 'blocky' style suggests an assumption that users will want a fuss-free approach, and will appreciate minimal text and maximum access paths to information and resources. The overall layout appears to be aimed at adults. There are no cute icons of the type usually present on web pages designed explicitly for younger users. Locating the main menu items in a highly salient position on the page suggests the designers wanted to make this site as easy to navigate as possible. The tiny white arrows in the bottom right-hand corner of each menu or navigational button support this analysis. They act as visual cues to the nature of each button or hyperlink (a signal to 'click here'). There is also a strong hint that the designers had 'newbies' – people with little or no previous internet experience – in mind when they designed this page. Dedicating the most salient position on the page to providing structured routes into the site's content is an unusual design strategy: compare this with, say, eBay's website (www.ebay.com).

The decision to use a sans-serif font makes for a less formal text than books or pamphlets, which tend to be printed in serif fonts. A less formal font may make for a less intimidating website – particularly for newbies. Furthermore, the minimal amount of text and large number of hyperlinks suggests the designers assumed that the 'ideal' users of this page would not want to spend much time wading through copious amounts of text.

The 'tenor' (or 'tone') overall is professional, inviting and supportive, but not overly warm or friendly. Interestingly, many of the websites recommended by the Grid are clearly intended for use by primary and secondary school students (Goodson *et al.* 2002). Hence, the front page to the Grid site sends a message that its designers expect adults to be involved actively in their children's internet use.

Textual metafunction

Textual metafunction analysis examines

- the effects of (or messages sent by) the genre features of the text
- cohesion within the text and between the text and its ostensive purpose (e.g., cohesive ties, intertextuality), and
- grammar (e.g., syntax, tense, pronouns, prepositions).

The designers of this web page apparently assumed that viewers would find general categories most useful for finding the information they want. Users can refine these categories by following a sequence of hyperlinked pages until they arrive at the information or resources they seek or expect. Use of the personal pronouns 'you' and 'your', and addressing the viewer directly (e.g. 'Welcome to the National Grid for Learning'), establishes a personal and immediate relationship between page and viewer. The use of written questions to help guide navigation emphasizes the intention that the website be helpful and useful. The questions used are straightforward and easy to answer (i.e. 'What are you looking for? Who are you? Where are you?'). The question sequence is likewise indicative. It suggests the designers assumed that in the first instance people would be motivated to use this website by a desire to find information about or resources to assist with formal education. For example, the designers assume viewers will know what the acronym 'GCSE' means, and that they will be interested in news about National Astronomy Week, safe routes to school and other people's lists of favourite websites etc.

One way to make textual selection more explicit is to ask: 'How else, or in what other ways, could this page have been designed and the information in it represented?' For example, replacing the sans-serif font title in the top right-hand corner with, say, a gothic font would convey a completely different image of the Grid website.

Task

Compare and explain the effects of the following changes on the messages sent by the National Grid for Learning web page.

1   Changing all the colours to primary colours.

2   Changing the current sans-serif font to a serif font.

3   Doing away with the white background surrounding the body of the page.

4   Replacing the colour photographs with black and white images.

5   Removing the images altogether.

6   Replacing the three-column layout with a linear layout (where instead of columns, the hyperlinks simply follow on one from the other in a top-to-bottom line).

- Why are school websites judged to be salient enough to be a dedicated hyperlink from this page?

- What role does the textual metafunction play in semiotic research?

- What evidence might you need to draw on to support textual metafunction analysis?

- In what ways is social semiotic analysis different to, say, sociolinguistic analysis (see Chapter 13) or content analysis?

On the basis of this preliminary analysis we conclude that the front page for the Grid (a non-commercial page) is aimed mostly at adults rather than students, and provides multiple supports for navigating the website intended to be useful particularly for newcomers to the internet. The overall message sent is one that expects adults to be involved directly in young children's and school students' internet use.

Task

Using the following or similar texts, conduct a social semiotic analysis containing a comparative dimension. Remember to focus on the (a) ideational metafunction, (b) the interpersonal metafunction and (c) the textual metafunction of each web page.

- www.whitehouse.gov

- www.fed.gov.au

- www.ebay.com

- www.amazon.com

- www.stanford.edu/~davidf/

- www.coatepec.net

Finally, for further reading in this area, try:

- Bauer, M. and Gaskell, G. (eds) (2000) *Qualitative Researching with Text, Image and Sound*. London: Sage.
- Chandler, D. (2002) *Semiotics: The Basics*. London: Routledge.
- Kevelson, R. (ed.) (1998) *Hi-Fives: A Trip to Semiotics*. New York: Peter Lang.
- Kress, G. and van Leeuwen, T. (1996) *Reading Images: The Grammar of Visual Design*. London: Routledge.
- Van Leeuwen, T. and Selander, S. (1995) Picturing 'our' heritage in the pedagogic text: layout and illustrations in an Australian and a Swedish history textbook, *Journal of Curriculum Studies*, 27: 501–22.

PART 4

Research quality and reporting

CHAPTER 16

Quality and reporting in teacher research

Introduction

Previous chapters have discussed concepts, issues, criteria, principles, methods and procedures involved in teachers designing and implementing research related to their work and professional identities. Some important issues and questions about the conduct of teacher research remain, however. In this final chapter we take up two key areas:

- How can we judge the quality of a research study? What makes a good study *good*? How do we decide which research studies to take seriously and to accept?
- How can we report our research well? What counts as good research reporting?

Quality in research

For much of the twentieth century, educational researchers provided one kind of answer to the question about quality in research. This answer was developed within a quantitative perspective on educational research which, of course, has been the dominant educational research paradigm since the nineteenth century. The hegemony of quantitative conceptions of quality was extended to the emerging paradigm of qualitative research during the mid-twentieth century. In recent decades, however, a different kind of answer has been emerging within qualitative research as this research orientation has become better defined and more prominent. It is helpful to understand the traditional approach to quality in (quantitative) research in order to appreciate what is meant by the still-emerging approach within qualitative research. In the next section we briefly outline the traditional view. The following sections will then deal with the relatively new approach that has emerged over the past 30 years. This is the approach we find most useful in doing our own work and assessing the work of other qualitative researchers.

There is one final preliminary point to make, which concerns the position of document-based research with respect to quality. Document-based research, as we have already established (see Chapters 5, 7 and 12), is a tricky category because it can take many different forms. Moreover, a large part of document-based research has often been regarded as 'scholarship' rather than research and thought to operate under different rules, standards and criteria from research understood as a process of collecting 'fresh' empirical data (hence, the category of 'research and scholarship' which often appears in academic reporting pro formas).

Our approach is to treat document-based inquiry as research, but to see it as a complex case. For example, much philosophical research might be seen as having one key criterion so far as quality is concerned: namely, rigour and elegance of argumentation. Good-quality philosophical research is ensured by applying competently the kinds of 'skills' described in the latter part of Chapter 5. There we considered the skills of identifying and assessing claims, analysing and clarifying concepts, developing helpful distinctions and categories, and evaluating arguments in relation to the quality of data. These skills, however, apply to the quality of philosophical and similar forms of research as a whole. From this standpoint, good-quality philosophical research is research that identifies and assesses key claims *well*, at the level of reading the relevant literature (collecting data), and at the level of writing (analysing the data, identifying results, drawing conclusions and stating one's position). It is research that handles key concepts competently, at the level both of scrutinizing other people's accounts of concepts and of advancing one's own. It is research that generates clear and useful distinctions, taxonomies and categories in order to lay out different positions clearly, to pinpoint the differences between them and to argue one's case about which is the position one favours and why. And it is research that observes the integrity of logic in following and developing arguments according to where good reasoning leads. While there are other 'skills' and different 'versions' of such skills to the ones we identify in Chapter 5, we would argue that the ones we have described constitute a legitimate ideal of quality in philosophical and similar forms of research.

At the same time, as we saw in the case of Harvey Graff's (1979) study (see Chapter 7), the quality of document-based research sometimes draws on criteria and standards associated with quantitative inquiry. To undermine the status of literacy as an efficacious independent variable, Graff had to design a study in which variables could be controlled in the manner of a quantitative experimental design. This committed his study to standards of classical 'internal validity' and, probably, to the demands of 'external reliability' as well.

'Quality' as 'validity' and 'reliability'

In the past, the quality of a research study has been judged according to its demonstrated (internal and external) *validity* and (internal and external) *reliability*. These concepts were based on an assumption that by doing research it was possible to arrive at – or, at least, to get close to – a 'true' or 'correct' account of 'how things are' in the world. Traditional concepts of validity and reliability were based on the idea that physical and social worlds exist in a given way and that through the rigorous and expert application of research procedures we could come to know these worlds more or less as they are. This view of research quality was developed within quantitative inquiry and is usually associated with a 'positivistic' approach to research.

Validity

From this perspective, as discussed in Chapter 8, *internal validity* involves employing a sound and rigorous research design and methodology, using data collection and analysis techniques expertly to obtain accurate findings, and advancing correct interpretations of the study results. Hence, internal validity concerns those features and qualities within a study that enable it to get close to 'truth' or 'maximum likelihood' because it is well organized and faithfully conducted. By contrast, a study's *external validity* refers to the extent to which its findings can be generalized to entire populations or all cases. For example, a study of 400 6-year-old children's learning processes will be seen as having external validity if it is believed its findings can be generalized to all 6-year-old children within the population with which the study is concerned. There are many other more specific forms of validity recognized within quantitative and qualitative research, such as content validity, face validity, construct validity, predictive validity and so on (for a useful account see Cohen *et al.* 2000: Ch. 5). They all have a similar concept at heart – the idea of employing procedures so that some aspect of the research (like an instrument, a result or a finding) gets as close as it can to its target or to realizing its purpose.

Louis Cohen, Lawrence Manion and Keith Morrison (2000: 115–17) present an excellent summary statement of ways to enhance validity from the present perspective across quantitative and qualitative studies at each of the key points in a project. At the research design stage researchers should ensure they have enough time to do the project well and that their methodology is appropriate for the study question and purposes. They must take care with their sampling designs, ensuring that the sample is the right size and the right kind for the study purposes. They must also be clear about the kind of data they need and that they identify the most appropriate instruments to use for collecting that data. In the data collection phase itself it is important to try to minimize the Hawthorne effect (e.g. people trying harder or behaving differently because they know they are part of a study), to take steps to get high return rates of questionnaires, and to match control and experimental groups fairly. It is also important to use data collection instruments carefully and consistently and to triangulate data in appropriate ways. During data analysis researchers can enhance validity by coding data carefully, being aware of the 'halo effect' (e.g. assigning greater significance to some responses over others because of feelings of affinity toward certain participants or hoped-for data or outcomes), avoiding selective use of data and so on. At the reporting stage key procedures include making sure that the claims one makes do not outstrip the data available for supporting them, and that the study has indeed addressed the research purposes and, in particular, the research question.

Reliability

Reliability can be understood in terms of consistency, stability (or lack of variation) and 'replication'. The general ideal of reliability is that if the same thing is done again under the same (or equivalent) conditions with the same (or equivalent) subjects it will produce the same result. To ensure a study's *internal reliability* it is important to do such things as collect one's data the same way with Person A as with Person Z and to ensure that an interview question means the same thing to Person A as it does to Person Z and so on. If the research is being done by a team, then the internal reliability of the study means ensuring that each team member collects data the same way, analyses the data the same way and interprets results of data analysis in the same way. *External reliability* is evaluated according to the extent to which it is possible for other researchers to replicate the study in the same or in similar settings. In other words, if a research study is externally reliable, 'a researcher using the same methods, conditions, and so forth, should obtain the same results as those found in a prior study' (Wiersma 1999: 6–7).

Reliability can be pursued by ensuring that the instruments one uses are themselves reliable, and that an appropriate time between testing and retesting is chosen so that differences in scores can reasonably be assumed to result from interventions rather than extraneous factors. If one is using a pre-test/post-test design, reliability can be enhanced by using equivalent forms of tests known to produce similar results when other things are equal at the 'pre' and 'post' points respectively. Within qualitative studies this kind of reliability might be approximated (if the researcher wants to) by numerous procedures. These include taking care to interview different participants consistently and trying to organize one's observation techniques to increase the chances that how and what one observes on a particular occasion is close to how and what one would observe on another occasion. Checking one's observations and interpretations against those made by another person coming from a similar theoretical perspective and with similar purposes in mind is another reliability enhancing procedure.

Challenges to the traditional approach to assessing the quality of research

During the past three decades qualitative researchers have increasingly challenged the general concepts and assumptions underlying traditional validity and reliability measures. Most radically, they are questioning the claim that there is some fixed reality or truth that can be 'discovered' by means of investigation and measurement (see e.g.

Lincoln and Guba 1985; Lather 1991; Glesne and Peshkin 1992; LeCompte and Preissle 1993; Carspecken 1996). More specifically, they are arguing that strict concerns for replicability and consistency of methods, conditions and outcomes in establishing the reliability of a study's findings often generate problems many qualitative researchers are keen to avoid. Such concerns, it is alleged, ignore subtleties and contradictions in the data, tend to construct simplified readings of the complex phenomena under study and usually overlook the *effects of the researcher* on data and interpretations.

Qualitative researchers who have argued for a new approach to assessing the quality of research nonetheless believe that some form of verification of claims and data interpretations in qualitative research is required. Moreover, they suggest that the process of showing that a qualitative research study is sound and of 'good quality' may actually be more difficult and rigorous than established processes that use traditional validity and reliability checks. Conceptions of what counts as demonstrating that one has produced a sound research study are still being developed and refined within qualitative research. Already, however, the alternative perspective on research quality that is emerging within qualitative research has generated at least two broad categories of criteria that researchers can use to evaluate the quality of their studies. These are known as 'communicative validity' and 'trustworthiness'. We discuss each in turn below.

Quality as 'communicative validity'

Communicative validity is concerned with judging the quality of the research *process* – including interpretations and claims made in the final study report (Lather 1991; Carspecken 1996). The ideal of communicative validity is to present readers with carefully argued interpretations and claims, and adequate evidence to support them. It is not interested in making claims about the replicability of a study or the generalizability of its findings and interpretations. Communicative validity is well suited to research that does not aim to control variables, and that does not assume that there is a single, fixed and universal reality to be 'discovered' through research.

Communicative validity emerges from the interaction between readers and the reported research. Claims that a qualitative research study is 'valid' are based more on the soundness of the argument 'communicated' in the research report and the evidence used to support these claims, than on the essential 'truth' of statements (see Carspecken 1996: 55). To achieve communicative validity researchers must ensure that readers can judge their arguments to be coherent, logical and substantiated. Communicative validity is achieved when readers think 'yes, of course' in response to interpretations and claims made about data and in relation to the research question driving the study. Phil Carspecken (1996: 55) speaks of this new form of validity as a 'communicative interaction' and a consensus between readers and the report produced by the researcher. Joe Kincheloe (2003) prefers the term 'anticipatory accommodation' to explain how people judge the validity of claims made in a qualitative study by means of comparing and contrasting the study with their 'knowledge of a variety of comparable contexts'. Steinar Kvale (1994) sees communicative validity in terms of a dialogue between the researcher and participants, between the research report and the reader, and between various readers and discussants.

Various research-related strategies contribute directly to the communicative validity of any research report. We discuss three here:

- cross-examining multiple sources of data or evidence;
- participant checks;
- outsider audits.

These strategies overlap, providing researchers with a range of complementary insights into data analysis and interpretation. Further strategies include strip analysis, using negative cases, peer debriefing and focus group discussions (see Lincoln and Guba 1985; LeCompte and Preissle 1993; Carspecken 1996; Fetterman 1998).

The three strategies discussed here are widely used in qualitative research. Collectively, they provide an *audit trail* for verifying claims. Lincoln and Guba (1985: 319) discuss audit trails in terms of inviting experts not involved in the study itself to evaluate each phase of the study by scrutinizing raw data records, data reduction and analysis products, interpretations of analyses and the quality of the final report. An audit trail can also refer to the evidence and explanations provided in a research report that enable readers themselves to 'audit' or evaluate how researchers interpreted the results of their analyses and reached particular conclusions.

Multiple sources of evidence

Making use of multiple sources of evidence to support a claim strengthens the 'believability' of the claim and increases the likelihood of obtaining 'yes, of course' responses from readers. To support an interpretation that a student (Layla) spent much of her time in class trying to be 'invisible', the researcher could present excerpts of data from multiple sources when writing the research report. These multiple sources could include classroom observations, data gathered during interviews with Layla's teacher and with Layla herself, as well as data from observations of Layla outside the classroom, conversations with Layla's mother and so on. Multiple sources of data can also be used to explain complex phenomena, because 'the more we examine our data from different viewpoints, the more we may reveal – or construct – their complexity' (Coffey and Atkinson 1996: 14).

Use of multiple sources of data is similar to, but not synonymous with, traditional strategies of triangulation. In traditional triangulation researchers are interested in aggregating data 'to produce a fully rounded, more authentic, portrayal of the social world' (Coffey and Atkinson 1996: 14). Traditional triangulation can, however, become highly reductive since it is concerned with convergence: with arriving at a single, tidy interpretation to explain the 'truth' about a phenomenon.

The kind of non-traditional triangulation we personally prefer is different. It aims to maximize the range of data sources drawn on in the course of a study in order to identify points of divergence and contradictions as well as of convergence. Besides locating convergences it aims to identify counter patterns of evidence that force us to re-examine interpretations. It also identifies evidence enabling the researcher to include a selection of possible interpretations of the phenomenon under study, or to include a diverse range of participant perspectives in the final report (see Lather 1991; Fetterman 1998).

Participant checks

Participant checks (sometimes called 'member checks') involve interactions between the researcher, the interpreted data and key participants in the research study. They seek to verify researcher constructions or representations of what happened, who was involved and so on. In most cases researchers send to key participants draft copies of the entire report, or sections of the report pertaining to them, and ask them to read and respond to this material. The researcher asks participants to 'check' whether they have been characterized or described in a reasonable way by the researcher. They are also asked to check if what they are reported as having said and meant is compatible with what they remember saying and meaning, and whether the way events are reported agrees with how they remember these events happening.

Some researchers only send transcripts of interviews to participants to have them check and verify that what they said and meant is represented appropriately in the transcript. We personally prefer to send drafted reports to participants so that they can read about themselves and their lives within the context of the study and our interpretations as a whole.

Joe Kincheloe and Peter McLaren explicitly link participant checks with representation issues within the research report. They claim researchers should be concerned particularly with the 'credibility of portrayals of constructed realities' (1994: 151). They argue that all research constructs 'the way things are' and that researchers need to pay attention to and reflect upon the language used to describe people, places, events and the like, along with ideologies encoded into text through these language choices.

For more on 'representation' in research reports see:

- Boon, J. (1982) *Other Tribes, Other Scribes*. Cambridge: Cambridge University Press.
- Clifford, J. and Marcus, G. (1986) *Writing Culture: The Poetics and Politics of Ethnography*. Berkeley, CA: University of California Press.
- Fuchs, M. (1993) The reversal of the ethnographic perspective: attempts at objectifying one's own cultural horizon. Dumont, Foucault, Bourdieu? *Thesis Eleven*, 34: 104–25.
- Manganaro, M. (1990) Textual play, power, and cultural critique: an orientation to modernist anthropology, in M. Manganaro (ed.) *Modernist Anthropology: From Fieldwork to Text*, pp. 3–47. Princeton, NJ: Princeton University Press.
- Rabinow, P. (1977) *Reflections on Fieldwork in Morocco*. Berkeley, CA: University of California Press.

- Taussig, M. (1987) *Shamanism, Colonialism, and the Wild Man*. Chicago: University of Chicago Press.

One last note needs to be made at this point. Participant feedback sometimes generates additional validity issues. What people say they do, or think they did or said, does not necessarily match what they did or what they actually said. The researcher may then be faced with what to do with additional information generated by the participant checks that cannot be verified or that does not appear anywhere in the data collected by the researcher. Generally, participant checks are rarely sufficient on their own for assuring communicative validity.

Outsider audits

Asking other researchers to read and evaluate drafts of one's research report is another useful strategy for maximizing the communicative validity of a study. The researcher's colleagues and others with knowledge of the research area conduct these 'outsider audits', notably at conferences (Glesne and Peshkin 1992: 147). When interested outsiders closely question the assumptions and interpretations within a study, their comments can highlight for the researcher some of his or her previously unexamined beliefs and presuppositions.

Verifying and validating the quality of a study, however, is not limited to meeting communicative validity criteria alone. It also requires the researcher to pay attention to trustworthiness.

Quality as 'trustworthiness'

Trustworthiness is concerned with the 'believability' of a study, and the degree to which a reader has faith in the study's *worth*. In this sense trustworthiness depends on researchers clearly demonstrating they have collected data that are sufficient for their research needs (determined in large part by the research questions they have asked). Trustworthiness also requires that the study be coherent. This means that the overall logic of the research question(s), theoretical framing, and data collection and analysis designs is explicit, justified and appropriate. Generating trustworthiness in a research report, then, requires investigators to meet two key criteria: sufficiency and coherence.

Sufficiency

'Sufficiency' refers to the amount of data collected for a study and the quality of evidence provided to support interpretations. Generally, enough data have been collected when information begins to be repeated to the point of redundancy (Fetterman 1998) and you are no longer collecting any new information. Sufficiency also refers to having enough evidence to support claims and interpretations made in relation to the data and research question.

Assessing data quality is a little more subjective. It typically involves evaluating the interpretive possibilities the data make 'available' to the researcher (and the degree to which these interpretations are reliable and address the research questions). Data that enable only limited interpretations or clichéd interpretations are not good-quality data. For example, suppose our research question is, 'What are some of the ways in which six high-achieving males in primary school construct their in-school identities?' If the data set we collect about a student allows us to say *only* that 'X is always a good student' in response to the research question, then the data set is severely limited and hence, of low quality relative to our research question.

A key to collecting data 'of sufficiency' is to construct a sound and coherent research design (Knobel and Lankshear 1999; Cohen *et al.* 2000). Other things being equal, having a well-formed and manageable research question, a worthwhile research problem and aim, and a clear plan of what needs to be done will enhance our chances of collecting data that let us address our research question in a full and satisfying manner. Moreover, making the research design, data collection design and data analysis design explicit in a research report enables readers to evaluate what was done, how it was done and what was found. While a researcher can *claim* the trustworthiness of a study, ultimately only the readers of the study's report can *verify* it.

Coherence

One way to make explicit the overall coherence of the methodology and designs of a study is to provide detailed accounts of research decisions and reasons behind these decisions (i.e. justification). This can be done in a separate section or chapter of the report, or woven into the main argument. The challenge can be approached from two complementary angles. In the following example the researcher believes a case study design is the best option for tackling the research question. The rationale argues first that an ethnographic design (an apparently plausible option) is not viable for the present study.

> The constraints of the present study militate against full-blown ethnographic fieldwork. These constraints include official time frames for completing doctoral study at my university, and the unavailability of any local long term ethnographic research programs into which I could have hooked this study.
>
> (Knobel 1997: 117)

The second step is to advance the positive case in favour of case study being a viable option:

> A multiple case study design can accommodate ethnographic methods of data collection and thus affords scope for the kind of detailed investigations and data required to meet my present needs. This design decision is supported by case study practitioners themselves. For example, Robert Yin points out that 'the distinctive need for case studies arises out of a desire to understand complex social phenomena'.
>
> (Knobel 1999: 117)

Another way of making the overall coherence of the methodology and designs of an investigation explicit is to use a matrix or table like Table 16.1 to summarize the design and methodology of a study.

Table 16.1 Demonstrating the study's coherence and credibility

Research purpose	Research question	Data collection design	Data to be collected	Data analysis design	Informing sources

Discussing this kind of matrix within the research report demonstrates to readers that the researcher has a good grasp of what it means to conduct rigorous research, and has applied this understanding to developing a coherent project. Alternatively, the researcher can construct this kind of 'coherence check' matrix as a separate text apart from the report, and use it to develop arguments about 'appropriateness' by explicating the 'match' between the research question, the research methodology and the data collection and analysis designs. In this latter case, while the matrix does not appear in the report, it has served to help the researcher to make the research process coherent *and* explicit.

Task

We have spoken about credibility being one aspect of the believability of a research study.

1   In your own words, describe the difference between 'sufficiency' and 'credibility'.

2   Explain the relationship between 'trustworthiness' and 'communicative validity'.

Justifying one's research methodology and design decisions is another way to strengthen the credibility of a study. One of the easiest ways to justify decisions is to cite previous research and up-to-date methodological literature in support of a claim about the usefulness of a design or methodological decision. In the following passage the researcher justifies a decision *not* to aim at external validity by citing a number of authoritative sources on the matter:

Increasingly, however, researchers working with sociocultural theories do not claim 'typicality' for their case study findings. Instead, such researchers aim for transportable findings and ideas, rather than at attaining a fixed, transcendental truth or a limiting kind of relativity. Thus, researchers who aim for transportable research findings and so forth recognize that the reader of a case study report brings personal experiences and understandings to bear on interpretations and findings (see, for example, Merriam 1988, Zeller 1995).

> David Bloome, Dorothy Sheridan and Brian Street (1993: 18) neatly capture the main difference in approaches when they distinguish between constructing *typical* cases that are intended to be generalized to all cases everywhere, and *telling* cases that are used to investigate theoretical propositions and social relationships through specific cases and from a particular theoretical stance. It is the latter – that is, telling cases – in which I am most interested at present.
>
> (Knobel 1997: 121)

A study's credibility is enhanced when all three sets of strategies – explicitness, appropriateness and justification – are used within the report.

The trustworthiness of a study is *cumulative*. It is built up over the course of conducting and reporting the study. To collect sufficient data or evidence within a study to support claims and interpretations made in relation to these data, researchers need to ensure the study is thoroughly and carefully planned from the beginning. Sufficiency is also enhanced when multiple data collection tools and techniques are employed so that the data collected are rich in overlapping details. By locating a study within a supporting network of theoretically and/or methodologically similar studies that readers have previously judged to be trustworthy, a researcher can enhance its coherence and credibility. Credibility is also strengthened by making explicit the logical and coherent links between a study's research purpose, its research questions, its research aim, its data collection design, the data that need to be collected and the data analysis design set.

Quality as defensible interpretation

When researchers have completed analysing the data their projects are almost finished. *Almost.* They still have to complete the task of *interpreting the analysis* in the light of their research purposes and frameworks, validity checks of analyses, relevant theoretical and research literature, ideas and comments of peers and so on. The completed data analysis on its own is *not* an answer to the research question or a response to the original problem. A comparison can be seen here with an industrial chemist completing the chemical analysis for developing a pain relief formula. The analysis does not constitute the finished product. It still has to be 'interpreted' into a tablet or capsule of a particular strength, suitable for a particular age range, level of pain and so on.

Harry Wolcott (2001: 33) explains how interpretation, unlike analysis, is derived not from 'rigorous, agreed-upon, carefully specified procedures, but from our efforts at sensemaking, a human activity that includes intuition, past experience, emotion – personal attributes of human researchers that can be argued endlessly but neither proved or disproved to the satisfaction of all'. Of course, the sense made of the data has to be justified and clearly relevant to the data analysis. Interpretations cannot be invented by the researcher, but are a kind of imposed order that involves offering sound explanations of what took place in the data, drawing conclusions and extrapolating from the data to relevant contexts and practices, making inferences, accounting for data that does not 'fit' an analysed pattern or category, accounting for other irregularities, considering alternative or rival interpretations and selecting the 'best' in the light of the research purpose and questions of a study. Michael Patton (2002: 480) identifies three common forms data interpretation can generally take:

- making the obvious obvious;
- making the obvious dubious;
- making the hidden obvious.

The first form focuses on confirming what is already known about a practice or event. The second calls a taken-for-granted position or social phenomenon into question and generally includes evidence-based critiques of extant practices and assumptions. The third draws attention to previously unconsidered relationships, events, practices and the like that impact directly on education or the population being studied. While interpretations are not confined to these three foci, they provide a useful interpretive focus for beginning researchers.

Interpretations of one's data analysis can never be fully complete or exhaustive because they will always be sensemaking accounts made from a particular standpoint and not some other possible and equally valid standpoint. There is insufficient space here for us to deal with the issue of interpreting outcomes of data analysis in the depth and detail that it deserves (see instead Wolcott 2001). We can, however, briefly indicate how important and delicate the matter of interpreting data analysis is by referring to the analysis of Jacques' 'ways of avoiding literacy work in class' (see Chapter 14).

The preliminary taxonomic analysis offered in Chapter 14 (see p. 327) suggested that Jacques employed at least seven ways to avoid undertaking work involving literacy in the classroom. The domain analysis generated a cultural domain called 'ways of avoiding work'. The preliminary taxonomic analysis further refined this by providing and organizing a diverse range of *ways* to avoid literacy work, and various *instances* of these ways. But this comprises nothing more than an analytic description of Jacques' behaviour. How are we to understand this description and, perhaps, try to explain it? This is where interpretation is required in addition to analysis.

What sense should be made of all these forms of avoidance behaviour? Numerous options are available for interpreting the data analysis pertaining to ways of avoiding literacy work. For example, there is a large and well-established research and theoretical literature about student resistance to school and classroom-based learning (e.g. Willis 1977; Giroux 1983). In addition, there is a psychological literature about motivation that could prompt an interpretation that Jacques was not motivated to learn and, therefore, was engaging in avoidance behaviour (e.g. McKenna and Kear 1990; Gambrell *et al.* 1996). Jacques' avoidance practices were initially interpreted as forms of resistance. This interpretation cohered well with other aspects of the data such as the fact that Jacques identified himself personally very closely with the culture of work. He described himself as being 'a working man' not a 'pencil man', and he stated his wish to leave school as soon as possible and start working. This was consistent with an interpretation that Jacques was an example of a student who did not value school learning. He wanted to join the adult world, was not happy at school and, consequently, actively resisted being there.

This is a plausible interpretation, and quite reasonable. It could be supported by existing literature and by a strong corpus of theory and research. And it certainly coheres with other data in the study, and with the analysis of that data. This preliminary interpretation was presented to Jacques' mother as a written statement. She read it and tactfully but firmly responded that she did not agree. She said that Jacques was extremely *anxious* about school. He did not want to be seen as a 'dumbo' or a 'dud' (Jacques' own words that he used to describe someone who is not smart, who is unsuccessful, a *'failure'*). Jacques did *not* reject school and was *not* resisting learning. Rather, he was trying to prevent what he himself recognized as his learning difficulties becoming too apparent to his peers. He was trying to protect his dignity and self-esteem as much as he could by minimizing the opportunities for others to see that he could not 'do it' and was, therefore, a dumbo.

This is a very different interpretation from 'resistance'. Yet the data analysis in terms of 'ways of avoiding literacy work in class' is compatible with both interpretations – as well as with others. Ultimately, Jacques' mother's assessment of the initial interpretation proved decisive, illustrating the value of checking the validity of one's interpretations by seeking feedback from the participants in the study whenever it is possible and appropriate.

Such examples remind researchers of the dangers of over-relying on conventional linear, cause-and-effect reasoning when making interpretations. The aim of qualitative research is to make events, phenomena, programmes, people and the like as usefully complex as possible in order to better understand in contextualized ways the who, what, when, why and how of what was studied. Interpreting the results of data analysis is risky. Very often multiple interpretations of our data are possible. Indeed, this is probably the normal situation. It is very common for alternative interpretations to seem equally plausible. The good researcher will always be alert to the importance and the hazards of interpretation, and will look to every possible resource to find the decisive factor or clue that seems to favour one interpretation over all the others.

Even then, however, there is no guarantee that the interpretation we finally decide upon is the 'right' one. This, of course, is a hazard in all social science research. Ultimately, there are no guarantees of the veracity of our interpretations. They are, precisely, *interpretations* of social and cultural phenomena and of social and cultural beings. Although it is impossible to arrive at a single 'true' interpretation in any research we can strive to practise research as rigorously and honestly as possible. This is all we can reasonably ask of researchers.

Reporting research

The ideas already addressed with respect to ensuring quality in our research have major implications for how we report it. When we report our study we must take care to do so in ways that communicate to readers that the study is coherent, the interpretations are warranted, the data are sufficient for addressing the research question, the representations of people, processes and other phenomena are fair and so on.

There are, however, further important issues about research reporting that have to do with decisions concerning what *medium* and *mode* of reporting to use on particular occasions and/or for particular audiences.

For many *educational* researchers the primary, if not the sole, *medium* of reporting will be a final report geared to academic audiences. This may take the form of a research thesis, a final research report to one's university or funding foundation, scholarly papers in refereed journals, research monographs and the like. *Teacher* researchers, however, will often be less concerned with this reporting medium (although in some cases it will be a requirement) than with other options. Reporting their research will often take the form of presentations to colleagues, professional development participants, parents and other members of their school's community, education administrators and professional association conference delegates. Hence, in place of the formal academic research report, monograph, chapter or article, a teacher researcher's medium of reporting may be a professional or community newsletter, a departmental bulletin or magazine, a professional development CD or video, or a slideshow-assisted seminar presentation.

At the same time, teacher researchers will face decisions about what constitutes a suitable *mode* for reporting on a particular occasion and for a particular audience. The mode includes such options as using vignettes or scenarios, narrating or 'storying' the research, making a 'documentary' about the research or even 'performing' the research as some kind of play or conversation. Other modes are poster displays, a series of web pages, a simulation, a manual, a collage and so on. Teacher researchers often like to use metaphors, anecdotes, analogies and similar devices to present their work. Such options are often entertained on the basis that formal prose or the constraints of the printed page are not seen as appropriate for a particular audience or occasion or, perhaps, for the subject matter of the research. It is important to recognize that reporting research is not all of a piece and that it is important to select a medium and mode of reporting that is appropriate for a particular audience.

When one is reporting research one will not always be reporting *all* of it. In some contexts it will be appropriate to report the study as a whole; in others it will be more appropriate to report a specific aspect. The choice of medium and/or mode of reporting may vary according to how much of the original research is to be reported, to whom and in what kind of setting.

We believe there is a key criterion to be considered when teacher researchers are making decisions about how to report their research on particular occasions: when we report research we must ensure that we are indeed reporting *research*. Whatever the occasion, audience or aspects of our work that we are reporting may be, we need to ensure that our presentation reveals the 'researchness' of our work. Hence, the medium and the mode that we choose *must* be capable of allowing us to do more than simply describe 'bits' of our work. They must also permit us to be able to communicate what it is about these 'bits' that distinguish them as aspects of *research* work.

So, for example, if a teacher researcher is reporting some of their work to a community group they will be keen to pitch the presentation at a level and in a 'register' that engages and informs the audience. At the same time, part of their task of informing the audience about the study as research will involve showing how the information being conveyed is more than just a 'story' or an account of 'something that was observed', or a portrait of a classroom event that was 'interesting' or 'noteworthy'. The objective will be to show how the aspect in question is related to a significant educational problem or issue, and to a question that was framed to address this issue. It will be to convey something about how this particular facet of the study contributes to enhancing our understanding the issue/problem/question to which it is related.

This does not require speaking to this audience as one might to a specialist research audience or to one's colleagues. The key is to get the 'pitch' right for the audience. But one must *not* abdicate one's responsibility to report research – if that is what one is claiming to be doing. Any audience a teacher researcher is likely to be reporting research to is capable of grasping the 'logic' and significance of some facet of a research project, if it is presented clearly. When researchers are clear about their own work as research it is not difficult to work out how to present it to lay audiences in ways that communicate important features of the 'researchness' of their topic or theme. Once more, the kind of 'logic' we have carried throughout this book comes into play here. Careful summations of our work using the kinds of matrices we have presented throughout can help us get the clarity we need for communicating our research *as research* to lay audiences.

Of course, if one wants just to present some interesting bits of information to an audience, give an illustrated talk or spin anecdotes about things that may have occurred in the context of a project, that is another matter. In such instances, however, one should not portray what one is doing as 'reporting research'. Within teacher research specifically and academic educational research more generally, a great deal of 'research reporting' (including, unfortunately, some of our own!) is, in fact, no such thing.

This returns us to the point we began from: our six generic features of research. When researchers report their research – be this in written, oral or multimodal form – they are 'delivering' a *version* of what we have identified as the sixth generic feature of research. This is a statement or artefact that reflects and enacts the other five features. It also says something about what we conclude from our research and about what implications it may have for our work. A full report will do all of this and at length. A report on some specific aspect or aspects will do certain parts of this, and more briefly. But no matter how specific or small the part is that a particular act of reporting does, the audience should come away having learned something about:

- How the study was *designed* to address a research *question*.
- How and why the data drawn on in the present report were *collected* and what

makes these data *pertinent* to the question.
- How and why these data were *analysed* the way they have been.
- What *ideas* and *perspectives* have guided us in handling the aspects being dealt with in the current reporting activity or artefact.
- How we have *interpreted* the results from the analysis that are the subject of the present report and why we have *confidence* that this interpretation is worth taking seriously.

We believe that teacher researchers who realize this ideal exemplify one of the key hallmarks of being an educational professional. They are also a thorn in the side of governments and administrations whose policies would short-change the ideal of a democratic education worthy of that name. Our hope is that this book will contribute something worthwhile towards building a 'crowd of thorns'. If ever the cause of democratic education needed such a crowd it needs it now.

Bibliography

Addison, J. and McGee, S. (eds) (1999) *Feminist Empirical Research: Emerging Perspectives on Qualitative and Teacher Research*. Portsmouth, NH: Heinemann.

Adler, P. and Adler, P. (1998) Observational techniques, in N. Denzin and Y. Lincoln (eds) *Collecting and Interpreting Qualitative Materials*, pp. 79–109. Thousand Oaks, CA: Sage.

Afferbach, P. and Johnston, P. (1984) On the use of verbal reports in reading research, *Journal of Reading Behavior*, 16(4): 307–22.

Aidman, A. and Reese, D. (1996) *Pocahontas*: problematizing the pro-social. Paper presented to the Annual Meeting of the International Communications Association, Chicago, IL, 23–7 May.

Akinnaso, F. and Ajirotutu, C. (1982) Performance and ethnic style in job interviews, in J. Gumperz (ed.) *Language and Social Identity*, pp. 119–44. Cambridge: Cambridge University Press.

Anderson, N. (1994) No, Belinda set everything up . . . *QUICK*, 54: 8–11.

Anderson, N. (1996) *When Technology and Equity Become Partners*. Brisbane: Department of Education, Queensland.

Anderson, N. (1999) Inclusion: can teachers and technology meet the challenge? Unpublished PhD Thesis, Queensland University of Technology.

Anderson, N. (forthcoming) *Equity and Learning Technologies in Literacy Education*. New York: Peter Lang.

Angeles, P. (ed.) (1992) *The HarperCollins Dictionary of Philosophy*, 2nd edn. New York: HarperCollins.

Apple, M. (1979) *Ideology and Curriculum*. New York: Routledge.

Apple, M. (1996) *Cultural Politics and Education*. New York: Teachers College Press.

Aries, P. (1965) *Centuries of Childhood: A Social History of Family Life*. New York: Random House.

Athanases, S. and Heath, S. (1995) Ethnography in the study of the teaching and learning of English, *Research in the Teaching of English*, 29(3): 263–87.

Atkinson, P. and Hammersley, M. (1998) Ethnography and participant observation, in N. Denzin and Y. Lincoln (eds) *Strategies of Qualitative Inquiry*, pp. 110–36. Thousand Oaks, CA: Sage.

Aubrey, C., David, T., Godfrey, R. and Thompson, L. (2000) *Early Childhood Educational Research: Issues in Methodology and Ethics*. London: Routledge.

Austin, J. (1962) *How To Do Things With Words*. Oxford: Oxford University Press.

Baker, C. (1997) Transcription and representation in literacy research, in J. Flood, S. Heath and D. Lapp (eds) *Handbook of Research on Teaching Literacy Through the Communicative and Visual Arts*, pp. 110–20. New York: Simon & Schuster.

Baker, C. and Freebody, P. (1989) *Children's First Schoolbooks: Introductions to the Culture of Literacy*. London: Basil Blackwell.

Barton, D. (1997) Family literacy programs and home literacy practices, in D. Taylor (ed.) *Many Families, Many Literacies*, pp. 101–9. Portsmouth, NH: Heinemann.

Bauer, M. (2000) Classical content analysis, in M. Bauer and G. Gaskell (eds) *Qualitative Researching with Text, Image and Sound*, pp. 131–51. London: Sage.

Bauer, M. and Gaskell, G. (eds) (2000) *Qualitative Researching with Text, Image and Sound*. London: Sage.

Bell, J. (1999) *Doing Your Research Project: A Guide for First-Time Researchers in Education and Social Science*. Buckingham: Open University Press.

Bereiter, C. (2002) *Education and the Mind in the Knowledge Age*. Mahwah, NJ: Lawrence Erlbaum.

Berg, L. and Mansvelt, J. (2000) Writing in, speaking out: communicating qualitative research findings, in I. Hay (ed.) *Qualitative Research Methods in Human Geography*, pp. 161–82. London: Oxford University Press.

Bernard, R. (2000) *Social Research Methods: Qualitative and Quantitative Approaches*. Thousand Oaks, CA: Sage.

Bernstein, B. (1973a) *Class, Codes and Control*, Vol. 1. London: Routledge & Kegan Paul.

Bernstein, B. (1973b) *Class, Codes and Control*, Vol. 2. London: Routledge & Kegan Paul.

Bernstein, B. (1990) *The Structuring of Pedagogic Discourse (Class Codes and Control*, Vol. 4). London: Routledge.

Bernstein B. (1996) *Pedagogy, Symbolic Control and Identity: Theory Research Critique*. London: Taylor and Francis.

Berthoff, A. (1987) The teacher as researcher, in D. Goswami and P. Stillman (eds) *Reclaiming the Classroom: Teacher Research as an Agency for Change*, pp. 28–39. Portsmouth, NH: Boynton/Cook-Heinemann. The original paper was presented in 1979 at the Annual Conference of the Association of English Teachers in San Diego.

Bigum, C., Knobel, M., Lankshear, C., Rowan, L. and Doneman, M. (2000) *Confronting Disadvantage in Literacy Education: New Technologies, Classroom Pedagogy, and Networks of Practice*. Canberra, ACT: Language Australia.

Bissex, G. (1987) What is teacher research? in G. Bissex and R. Bullock (eds) *Seeing For Ourselves: Case-Study Research by Teachers of Writing*, pp. 4–5. Portsmouth, NH: Heinemann Educational Books.

Bogdan, R. and Biklen, S. (1997) *Qualitative Research for Education: An Introduction to Theory and Methods*, 3rd edn. Boston, MA: Allyn & Bacon.

Boon, J. (1982) *Other Tribes, Other Scribes*. Cambridge: Cambridge University Press.

Borgatti, S. (1999) Elicitation techniques for cultural domain analysis, in J. Schensul, M. LeCompte, B. Nastasi and S. Borgatti (eds) (1999) *Enhanced Ethnographic Methods: Audiovisual Techniques, Focused Group Interviews, and Elicitation Techniques (Ethnographer's Toolkit*, Vol. 3), pp. 115–51. Walnut Creek, CA: Altamira Press.

Bottorff, J. (1994) Using videotaped recordings in qualitative research, in J. Morse (ed.) *Critical Issues in Qualitative Research Methods*, pp. 242–61. Thousand Oaks, CA: Sage.

Branch, J. (2000) The trouble with think alouds: generating data using concurrent verbal protocols, in A. Kublik (ed.) *CAIS 2000: Dimensions of a Global Information Science* (Proceedings of the 28th Annual Conference). Alberta: Canadian Association for Information Science. www.slis.ualberta.ca/cais2000/branch.htm (accessed 13 October 2002).

Britzman, D. (1998) *Lost Subjects, Contested Objects: Toward a Psychoanalytic Inquiry of Learning.* Albany, NY: State University of New York Press.

Britzman, D. and Dippo, D. (2003) Admitting 'a perhaps': Maxine Greene and the project of critical theory, in M. Peters, C. Lankshear and M. Olsen (eds) *Critical Theory and the Human Condition: Founders and Praxis.* New York: Peter Lang.

Brodkey, L. (1996) *Writing Permitted in Designated Areas Only.* Minneapolis, MI: University of Minnesota Press.

Burnett, C. and Myers, J. (2002) 'Beyond the frame': exploring children's literacy practices, *Reading: Literacy and Language*, 36(2): 56–62.

Busfield, W. (1999) Puberty survey anger, *The Australian*, 30 June.

Caldas-Coulthard, R. and Coulthard, M. (eds) (1996) *Texts and Practices: Readings in Critical Discourse Analysis.* London: Routledge.

California Learning Interchange (2003) www.gse.uci.edu/cli/index.html (accessed 8 January 2003).

Capra, F. (1996) *The Web of Life: A New Scientific Understanding of Living Systems.* New York: Anchor Books.

Carspecken, P. (1996) *Critical Ethnography in Educational Research: A Theoretical and Practical Guide.* New York: Routledge.

Castells, M. (1996) *The Rise of the Network Society.* Oxford: Blackwell.

Castells, M. (1997) *The Power of Identity.* Oxford: Blackwell.

Castells, M. (2000) *End of Millennium*, 2nd edn. Oxford: Blackwell.

Castells, M. (2001) *The Internet Galaxy: Reflections on the Internet, Business and Society.* Oxford: Blackwell.

Cattin, P. and Subhash, C.J. (1979) Content analysis of children's commercials, in N. Beckwith (ed.) *Educators' Conference Proceedings*, pp. 639–44. Chicago: American Marketing Association.

Cazden, C. (1988) *Classroom Discourse: The Language of Teaching and Learning.* Portsmouth, NH: Heinemann.

Cazden, C. (2001) *Classroom Discourse: The Language of Teaching and Learning*, 2nd edn. Portsmouth, NH: Heinemann.

Chandler, D. (2002) *Semiotics: The Basics.* London: Routledge.

Clandinin, J. and Connelly, F. (1998) Personal experience methods, in N. Denzin and Y. Lincoln (eds) *Collecting and Interpreting Qualitative Materials*, pp. 150–78. Thousand Oaks, CA: Sage.

Clandinin, J. and Connelly, F. (2000) *Narrative Inquiry: Experience and Story in Qualitative Research.* San Francisco, CA: Jossey-Bass.

Clariana, R. and Bond, C. (1993) Using readability formulas to establish the grade level difficulty of software, *Journal of Computing in Childhood Education*, 4(3): 255–61.

Clifford, J. and Marcus, G. (eds) (1986) *Writing Culture: The Poetics and Politics of Ethnography*. Berkeley, CA: University of California Press.

Cochran-Smith, M. and Lytle, S. (1993) *Inside/Outside: Teacher Research and Knowledge*. New York: Teachers College Press.

Coffey, A. (1996) The power of accounts: authority and authorship in ethnography, *Qualitative Studies in Education*, 9(1): 61–74.

Coffey, A. and Atkinson, P. (1996) *Making Sense of Qualitative Data Analysis: Complementary Strategies*. Thousand Oaks, CA: Sage.

Cohen, L., Manion, L. and Morrison, K. (2000) *Research Methods in Education*, 5th edn. London: RoutledgeFalmer.

Cole, J. (2003) What motivates students to read? Four literacy personalities, *The Reading Teacher*, 56(4): 326–36.

Cole, M. (1996) *Cultural Psychology: A Once and Future Discipline*. Cambridge, MA: Harvard University Press.

Coles, G. (200) *Misreading Reading: The Bad Science that Hurts Children*. Portsmouth, NH: Heinemann.

Comber, B. (2000) What really counts in early literacy lessons, *Language Arts*, 78(1): 39–49.

Cook-Gumperz, J. (1981) Persuasive talk: the social organization of children's talk, in J. Green and C. Wallat (eds) *Ethnography and Language in Educational Settings*, 25–50. Norwood, NJ: Ablex.

Cook-Gumperz, J. (1993) Dilemmas of identity: oral and written literacies in the making of a basic writing student, *Anthropology and Education Quarterly*, 24(4): 336–56.

Cook-Gumperz, J. (ed.) (1986) *The Social Construction of Literacy*. Cambridge, MA: Cambridge University Press.

Cooper, H. (1998) *Synthesizing Research: A Guide for Literature Reviews*. Thousand Oaks, CA: Sage.

Cope, B. and Kalanztis, M. (eds) (1993) *The Powers of Literacy: A Genre Approach to Teaching Writing*. London: Falmer.

Corti, L. (2001) Using diaries in social research, *Social Research Update, 2*. www.soc.surrey.ac.uk/sru/SRU2.html (accessed 24 May, 2003).

Creswell, J. (1994) *Research Design: Qualitative, Quantitative, and Mixed Method Approaches*. Thousand Oaks, CA: Sage.

Creswell, J. (2001) *Educational Research: Planning, Conducting, and Evaluating Quantitative and Qualitative Research*. Upper Saddle River, NJ: Prentice Hall.

Creswell, J. (2002) *Research Design: Qualitative, Quantitative, and Mixed Method Approaches*, 2nd edn. Newbury Park, CA: Sage.

Cuban, L. (2001) *Oversold and Underused: Computers in Classrooms*. Boston, MA: Harvard University Press.

Cushman, E. (1998) *The Struggle and the Tools: Oral and Literate Strategies in an Inner City Community*. Albany, NY: State University of New York Press.

Davidson, C. (in preparation) Classroom interaction and talk in writing time in primary classrooms. Brisbane: University of Queensland PhD thesis project.

Davidson, L. (2002) Digital recording advice for research interviews, davidson.cba.hawaii.edu/digitalrecording.html (accessed 12 October 2002).

Delamont, S (1992) *Fieldwork in Educational Settings: Methods, Pitfalls and Perspectives.* London: Falmer Press.

Delamont, S. (2001) *Fieldwork in Educational Settings: Methods, Pitfalls and Perspectives*, 2nd edn. London: Routledge.

Denscombe, M. (1998) *The Good Research Guide for Small-Scale Social Research Projects.* Buckingham: Open University Press.

Denzin, N. (1997) The practices and politics of interpretation, in N. Denzin and Y. Lincoln (eds) *Collecting and Interpreting Qualitative Materials*, pp. 313–46. Thousand Oaks, CA: Sage.

DEQ (Department of Education, Queensland) (1994) *English in Years 1 to 10 Queensland Syllabus Materials: English Syllabus for Years 1 to 10.* Brisbane: Department of Education.

Dunn, K. (2000) Interviewing, in I. Hay (ed.) *Qualitative Research Methods in Human Geography*, pp. 50–82. Melbourne: Oxford University Press.

Ember, C. and Ember, M. (1998) Cross-cultural research, in H. Bernard (ed.) *Handbook of Methods in Cultural Anthropology*, pp. 647–90. Walnut Creek, CA: Altamira Press.

Emerson, R., Fretz, R. and Shaw, L. (1995) *Writing Ethnographic Fieldnotes.* Chicago: University of Chicago Press.

Ennis, R. (1969) *Ordinary Logic.* Englewood Cliffs, NJ: Prentice Hall.

Ericsson, K. (1988) Concurrent verbal reports on text comprehension: a review. *Text*, 8(4): 295–325.

Ewing, M. *et al.* (1998) The hard work of remembering: memory work as narrative research, in J. Addison, J. and S. McGee (eds) *Feminist Empirical Research: Emerging Perspectives on Qualitative and Teacher Research*, pp. 112–26. Portsmouth, NH: Heinemann.

Fairclough, N. (1989) *Language and Power.* London: Longman.

Fairclough, N. (1992) *Discourse and Social Change.* Oxford: Polity Press.

Fairclough, N. (1995) *Critical Discourse Analysis.* London: Longman.

Fetterman, D. (1989) *Ethnography: Step by Step.* Thousand Oaks, CA: Sage.

Fetterman, D. (1998) *Ethnography: Step by Step*, 2nd edn. Newbury Park, CA: Sage.

Fieser, J. (2001) *The Internet Encyclopedia of Philosophy.* www.utm.edu/research/iep/e/ethics.htm (accessed 21 Jan. 2001).

Finders, M. (1997) *Just Girls: Hidden Literacies and Life in Junior High.* New York: Teachers College Press.

Fink, A. and Kosecoff, J. (1998) *How To Conduct Surveys: A Step-by-Step Guide.* Thousand Oaks, CA: Sage.

Fiske, J. (1994) *Media Matters.* Minneapolis, MI: University of Minnesota Press.

Fitz-Gibbon, C. and Morris, L. (1987) *How to Analyze Data.* Newbury Park, CA: Sage.

Flick, U. (1998) *An Introduction to Qualitative Research.* Thousand Oaks, CA: Sage.

Fishman, S. and McCarthy, L. (2000) *Unplayed Tapes: A Personal History of Collaborative Teacher Research.* New York: Teachers College Press.

Flynt, E. and Cooter, R. (2001) *Reading Inventory for the Classroom.* Upper Saddle River, NJ: Prentice Hall.

Fontana, A. and Frey, J. (1998) Interviewing: the art of science, in N. Denzin and Y. Lincoln (eds) *Collecting and Interpreting Qualitative Materials*, pp. 47–78. Thousand Oaks, CA: Sage.

Forero, M. (2001) Effect of classroom use of the web on the self-efficacy of minority students in at-risk learning situations. Unpublished doctoral dissertation, Stanford University, School of Education, Palo Alto.

Fraenkel, J. and Wallen, N. (1996) *How to Design and Evaluate Research in Education*, 3rd edn. New York: McGraw-Hill.

Frankfort-Nachmias, C. and Nachmias, D. (1992) *Research Methods in the Social Sciences*. London: Edward Arnold.

Freebody, P. (1992) A socio-cultural approach: resourcing four roles as a literacy learner, in A. Watson and A. Badenhop (eds) *Prevention of Reading Failure*, pp. 48–60. Sydney: Ashton Scholastic.

Freebody, P., Ludwig, C. and Gunn, S. (1996) *Everyday Literacies In and Out of School in Low Socioeconomic Status Urban Communities*, Vol. 2. Canberra: Department of Employment, Education and Training.

Freire, P. (1972) *Pedagogy of the Oppressed*. Harmondsworth: Penguin.

Freire, P. (1974) *Education for Critical Consciousness*. London: Sheed & Ward.

Fuchs, M. (1993) The reversal of the ethnographic perspective: attempts at objectifying one's own cultural horizon. Dumont, Foucault, Bourdieu? *Thesis Eleven*, 34: 104–25.

Gage, N. (1994) The scientific status of research on teaching, *Educational Theory*, 44(4): 371–83.

Gambrell. L., Palmer, B., Codling, R. and Mazzoni, S. (1996) Assessing motivation to read, *The Reading Teacher*, 49(7): 518–33.

Garfinkel, H. (1972) Remarks on ethnomethodology, in J. Gumperz and D. Hymes (eds) *Directions in Sociolinguistics: The Ethnography of Communication*, pp. 301–24. New York: Holt, Rinehart & Winston.

Gearon, M. and Gindidis, M. (1998) Research related to teachers' strategies for the simultaneous learning and teaching of a second language. Paper presented to the Australian Association for Research in Education. November. www.aare.edu.au/98pap/gea98162.htm (accessed 1 December 2003).

Gee, J. (1988) Discourse systems and aspirin bottles: on literacy, *Journal of Education*, 170(1).

Gee, J. (1991) What is literacy? in C. Mitchell and K. Weiler (eds) *Rewriting Literacy: Culture and the Discourse of Other*, pp. 3–12. New York: Bergin & Garvey.

Gee, J. (1992) *The Social Mind: Language, Ideology, and Social Practice*. New York: Bergin & Garvey.

Gee, J. (1993) Critical literacy/socially perceptive literacy: a study of language in action, *Australian Journal of Language and Literacy*, 16(4): 333–355.

Gee, J. (1996) *Social Linguistics and Literacies: Ideology in Discourses*, 2nd edn. London: Falmer Press.

Gee, J. (1998) *Introduction to Human Language: Fundamental Concepts in Linguistics*. New York: Pearson.

Gee, J. (1999) *An Introduction to Discourse Analysis: Theory and Method*. New York: Routledge.

Gee, J. (2000) Teenagers in new times: a new literacy studies perspective, *Journal of Adolescent and Adult Literacy*, 43(5): 412–20.

Gee, J. (2002) Millennials and Bobos, Blue's Clues and Sesame Street: a story for our times, in D. Alvermann (ed.) *Adolescents and Literacies in a Digital World*, pp. 51–67. New York: Peter Lang.

Gee, J. (2003) *What Video Games Have to Teach Us About Learning and Literacy*. New York: Palgrave.

Gee, J., Michaels, S. and O'Connor, M. (1992) Discourse analysis, in M. LeCompte, W. Millroy and J. Preissle (eds) *The Handbook of Qualitative Research in Education*, pp. 227–91. San Diego, CA: Academic Press.

Gee, J.P., Hull, G. and Lankshear, C. (1996) *The New Work Order: Behind the Language of the New Capitalism*. Sydney: Allen & Unwin.

Geertz, C. (1973) *The Interpretation of Cultures*. New York: Basic Books.

Gerot, L. and Wignell, P. (1994) *Making Sense of Functional Grammar*. Cammeray, NSW: Antipodean Educational Enterprises.

Gerstl-Pepin, C. and Gunzenhauser, M. (2002) Collaborative team ethnography and the paradoxes of interpretation, *Qualitative Studies in Education*, 15(2): 137–54.

Gilbert, P. and Rowe, K. (1989) *Gender, Literacy and the Classroom*. Melbourne: Australian Reading Association.

Giroux, H. (1983) *Theory and Resistance in Education: A Pedagogy for the Opposition*. South Hadley, MA: Bergin & Garvey.

Glaze, J. (2002) Ph.D. study and the use of a reflective diary: a dialogue with self, *Reflective Practice*, 3(2): 153–66.

Glesne, C. (1999) *Becoming Qualitative Researchers: An Introduction*, 2nd edn. Boston, MA: Addison-Wesley.

Glesne, C. and Peshkin, A. (1992) *Becoming Qualitative Researchers: An Introduction*. White Plains, NY: Longman.

Goffman, E. (1967) *Interaction Ritual*. New York: Anchor Books.

Goodson, I. (1994) *Studying Curriculum*. New York: Teachers College Press.

Goodson, I., Knobel, M., Lankshear, C. and Mangan, M. (2002) *Social Spaces/Cyber Spaces: Culture Clash in Computerized Classrooms*. New York: Palgrave Press.

Graff, H. (1979) *The Literacy Myth: Literacy and Social Structure in the Nineteenth Century City*. New York: Academic Press.

Green, B. and Bigum, C. (1993) Aliens in the classroom, *Australian Journal of Education*, 37: 119–41.

Green, J. and Meyer, L. (1991) The embeddedness of reading in classroom life: reading as a situated process, in C. Baker and A. Luke (eds) *Towards a Critical Sociology of Reading Pedagogy*, pp. 141–60. Philadelphia, PA: John Benjamins.

Green, J. and Wallat, C. (eds) (1981) *Ethnography and Language in Educational Settings*. Norwood, NJ: Ablex.

Greene, M. (1978) *Landscapes of Learning*. New York: Teachers College Press.

Greene, M. (1995a) Choosing a past, inventing a future, in W. Ayers (ed.) *To Become a Teacher: Making a Difference in Children's Lives*, pp. 65–77. New York: Teachers College Press.

Greene, M. (1995b) *Releasing the Imagination: Essays on Education, the Arts, and Social Change*. San Francisco, CA: Jossey-Bass.

Gregory, E. (2001) Sisters and brothers as language and literacy teachers: synergy between siblings playing and working together, *Journal of Early Childhood Literacy*, 1(3): 301–22.

Grejda, G. and Hannafin, M. (1992) Effects of word processing on sixth graders' holistic writing and revisions, *Journal of Educational Research*, 85(3): 144–9.

Griffiths, M. (1997) '*Content analysis of children's commercials': Philippe Cattin and Subhash C. Jain (A Review)*. www.aber.ac.uk/media/Sections/textan01.html (accessed 25 May 2001).

Grosvenor, I., Lawn, M. and Rousmaniere, K. (eds) (1999) *Silences and Images: The Social History of the Classroom*. New York: Peter Lang.

Guba, E. and Lincoln, Y. (1988) Naturalistic and rationalistic enquiry, in J. Keeves (ed.) *Educational Research, Methodology, and Measurement: An International Handbook*, pp. 81–5. Oxford: Pergamon Press.

Gumperz, J. (1982a) *Language and Social Identity*. Cambridge, MA: Cambridge University Press.

Gumperz, J. (1982b) Fact and inference in courtroom testimony, in J. Gumperz (ed.) *Language and Social Identity*, pp. 163–94. Cambridge, MA: Cambridge University Press.

Gumperz, J. (1986) Interactional sociolinguistics in the study of schooling, in J. Cook-Gumperz (ed.) *The Social Construction of Literacy*, pp. 45–68. Cambridge, MA: Cambridge University Press.

Gumperz, J. and Hymes, D. (eds) (1972) *Directions in Sociolinguistics: The Ethnography of Communication*. Oxford: Basil Blackwell.

Gutierrez, K. (1993) How talk, context, and script shape contexts for learning: a cross-case comparison of journal sharing, *Linguistics and Education*, 5(3/4): 335–65.

Hak, T. (2003) *Qualitative Methods for Improving the Quality of Survey Data*. London: Sage.

Halasa, K. (1998) *Annotated Bibliography: Ethics in Educational Research*. www.aare.edu.au/ethics/aareethc.htm. Accessed 22 November 2003.

Halliday, M. (1985) *An Introduction to Functional Grammar*. London: Edward Arnold.

Hamilton, M. (2000) Expanding the new literacy studies: using photographs to explore literacy as a social practice, in D. Barton, M. Hamilton and R. Ivanic (eds) *Situated Literacies*, pp. 16–34. London: Routledge.

Harper, D. (1998) On the authority of the image: visual methods at the crossroads, in N. Denzin and Y. Lincoln (eds) *Collecting and Interpreting Qualitative Materials*, pp. 130–49. Thousand Oaks, CA: Sage.

Harris, K. (1979) *Education and Knowledge*. London: Routledge.

Hatch, E. (1992) *Discourse and Language Education*. Cambridge, MA: Cambridge University Press.

Hay, I. (2000) Glossary, in I. Hay (ed.) *Qualitative Research Methods in Human Geography*, pp. 183–98. Melbourne: Oxford University Press.

Heath, S. (1983) *Ways With Words: Language, Life and Work in Community and Classrooms*. Cambridge, MA: Cambridge University Press.

Hedrick, T., Bickman, L. and Rog, D. (1993) *Applied Research Design: A Practical Guide*. Newbury Park, CA: Sage.

Heyl, B. (2001) Ethnographic interview, in P. Atkinson, A. Coffey, S. Delamont and L. Lofland (eds) *Handbook of Ethnography*, pp. 369–83. London: Sage.

Hicks, D. (2002) *Reading Lives: Working-Class Children and Literacy Learning*. New York: Teachers College Press.

Hilts, P. (1995) Conference is unable to agree on ethical limits of research, *New York Times*, 15 January.

Hine, C. (2000) *Virtual Ethnography*. London: Sage.

Hitchcock, G. and Hughes, D. (1995) *Research and the Teacher: A Qualitative Introduction to School-Based Research*, 2nd edn. London: Routledge.

Hodas, S. (1993) Technology refusal and the organizational culture of schools, *Education Policy Analysis Archives*, 1(10): 1–19.

Hodder, I. (1998) The interpretation of documents and material culture, in N. Denzin and Y. Lincoln (eds) *Collecting and Interpreting Qualitative Materials*, pp. 110–29. Thousand Oaks, CA: Sage.

Hodge, R. and Kress, G. (1988) *Social Semiotics*. Ithaca, NY: Cornell University Press.

Hoggart, K., Lees, L. and Davies, A. (2002) *Researching Human Geography*. London: Arnold.

Honan, E., Knobel, M., Davies, B. and Baker, C. (2000) Producing possible Hannahs: theory and the subject of research, *Qualitative Inquiry*, 6(1): 9–32.

hooks, b. (1994) *Teaching to Transgress*. New York: Routledge.

Hopkins, D. (1993) *A Teacher's Guide to Classroom Research*, 2nd edn. Buckingham: Open University Press.

Hospers, J. (1996) *An Introduction to Philosophical Analysis*, 4th edn. Englewood Cliffs, NJ: Prentice Hall.

Hull, G. and Schultz, K. (2002) Negotiating the boundaries between school and non-school literacies, in G. Hull and K. Schultz (eds) *School's Out! Bridging Out-of-School Literacies with Classroom Practice*, pp. 1–10. New York: Teachers College Press.

Hymes, D. (1972) Toward ethnographies of communication, in P. Giglioli (ed.) *Language and Social Context*, pp. 21–44. Harmondsworth: Penguin.

Hymes, D. (1996) *Ethnography, Linguistics, Narrative Inequality: Toward an Understanding of Voice*. London: Taylor & Francis.

In-Time (2003) In-Time video lessons. www.intime.uni.edu/video.html (accessed 8 January 2003).

Jackson, J. (1998) Explore the strengths and weaknesses of classical content analysis: content analysis and objectivity, language and metaphor. www.spinworks.demon.co.uk/pub/content2.htm (accessed 25 May 2001).

Janisek, V. (1999) A journal about journal writing as a qualitative research technique: history, issues and reflections, *Qualitative Inquiry*, 5(4): 505–24.

Johnson, A. and Sackett, R. (1998) Direct systematic observation of behavior, in H. Bernard (ed.) *Handbook of Methods in Cultural Anthropology*, 301–33. Walnut Creek, CA: Altamira Press.

Jones, K. (2001) Becoming just another alphanumeric code: farmers' encounters with the literacy and discourse practices of agricultural bureaucracy at the livestock auction, in D. Barton, M. Hamilton and R. Ivanič (eds) *Situated Literacies: Reading and Writing in Context*, pp. 70–90. London: Routledge.

Jones, S. (ed.) (1999) *Doing Internet Research: Critical Issues and Methods for Examining the Net*. Thousand Oaks, CA: Sage.

Kantor, R., Green, J., Bradley, M. and Lin, L. (1992) The construction of schooled discourse repertoires: an interactional sociolinguistic perspective on learning to talk in preschool, *Linguistics and Education*, 4(2): 131–72.

Keating, E. (1999) The ethnography of communication, in P. Atkinson, A. Coffey, S. Delamont and L. Lofland (eds) *Handbook of Ethnography*, pp. 285–301. London: Sage.

Kelman, H.C. (1967) Human use of human subjects: the problem of deception in social psychological experiments, *Psychological Bulletin*, 67, 1–11.

Kempe, A. (1993) No single meaning: empowering students to construct socially critical readings of the text, *Australian Journal of Language and Literacy*, 16(4): 307–22.

Kenner, C. (2000) Biliteracy in a monolingual school system? English and Gujarati in South London, *Language, Culture and Curriculum*, 13(1): 13–30.

Kevelson, R. (ed.) (1998) *Hi-Fives: A Trip to Semiotics*. New York: Peter Lang.

Kincheloe, J. (2003) *Teachers as Researchers: Qualitative Inquiry as a Path to Empowerment*, 2nd edn. New York: Falmer.

Kincheloe, J. and McLaren, P. (1994) Rethinking critical theory and qualitative research, in N. Denzin and Y. Lincoln (eds) *Handbook of Qualitative Research*, pp. 139–57. Thousand Oaks, CA: Sage.

Kincheloe, J. and McLaren, P. (2000) Rethinking critical theory and qualitative research, in N. Denzin and Y. Lincoln (eds) *Handbook of Qualitative Research*, 2nd edn. Thousand Oaks, CA: Sage.

Kincheloe, J. and Steinberg, S. (1997) *Changing Multiculturalism*. Buckingham: Open University Press.

Knobel, M. (1993) Simon says see what I say: reader response and the teacher as meaning-maker, *Australian Journal of Language and Literacy*, 16(4): 295–306.

Knobel, M. (1997) Language and social practices in four adolescents' everyday lives. Unpublished doctoral thesis, Faculty of Education, Queensland University of Technology, Brisbane.

Knobel, M. (1998) Critical literacies in teacher education, in M. Knobel and A. Healy (eds) *Critical Literacies in the Primary Classroom*, pp. 89–111. Newtown, NSW: Primary English Teaching Association.

Knobel, M. (1999) *Everyday Literacies: Students, Discourse and Social Practice*. New York: Peter Lang.

Knobel, M. (2001) 'I'm not a pencil man': how one student challenges our notions of literacy 'failure' in school, *Journal of Adolescent and Adult Literacy*, 44(5): 404–19.

Knobel, M. (2003) Rants, ratings and representations: issues of validity, reliability and ethics in researching online social practices, *Education, Communication and Information*, 3(2): 187–210.

Knobel, M. and Lankshear, C. (1999) *Ways of Knowing: Researching Literacy*. Newtown, NSW: Primary English Teaching Association.

Knobel, M. and Lankshear, C. (2001) *Maneras de Ver: El Análisis de Datos en Investigación Cualitativa*. Morelia: Instituto Michoacano de Ciencias de la Educación.

Kraft, N. (2001) Certification of teachers – a critical analysis of standards in teacher education programs, in J. Kincheloe and D. Weil (eds) *Standards and Schooling in the United States: An Encyclopedia*. Santa Barbara, CA: ABC-Clio.

Krashen, S. (2002). Another urban legend, *Rethinking Schools* 16(4). www.rethinkingschools.org/archives/16_04/Urb164.htm.

Kress, G. (1985) *Linguistic Processes in Sociocultural Practice*. Geelong, VIC: Deakin University Press.

Kress, G. (1996) Representational resources and the production of subjectivity: questions of the theoretical development of Critical Discourse Analysis in a multicultural society, in R. Caldas-Coulthard and M. Coulthard (eds) *Texts and Practices: Readings in Critical Discourse Analysis*, pp. 15–31. London: Routledge.

Kress, G. (1998) Visual and verbal modes of representation in electronically mediated communication: the potentials of new forms of text, in I. Snyder (ed.) *Page to Screen: Taking Literacy into the Electronic Era*, pp. 53–79. Sydney: Allen & Unwin.

Kress, G. (2002) *Literacy in the New Media Age*. London: Routledge.

Kress, G. and Jewitt, C. (eds) (2003) *Multimodal Literacy*. New York: Peter Lang.

Kress, G. and van Leeuwen, T. (1996) *Reading Images: The Grammar of Visual Design*. London: Routledge.

Kucan, L. and Beck, I. (1997) Thinking aloud and reading comprehension research: inquiry, instruction, and social interaction, *Review of Educational Research*, 67(3): 271–99.

Kulick, D. and Stroud, C. (1993) Conceptions and uses of literacy in a Papua New Guinean village, in B. Street (ed.) *Cross-cultural Approaches to Literacy*, pp. 31–61. Cambridge: Cambridge University Press.

Kunkel, D., Smith, S., Suding, P. and Beily, E. (2002) *Coverage in Context: How Thoroughly the News Media Report Five Key Children's Issues – A Study Commissioned by the Casey Journalism Center on Children and Families*. College Park, MD: University of Maryland.

Kvale, S. (1994) Validation as communication and action: on the social construction of validity. Paper presented at the Annual Meeting of the American Education Research Association. New Orleans, 4–8 April.

Lampert, M. and Ervin-Tripp, S. (1993) Structured coding for the study of language and social interaction, in J. Edwards and M. Lampert (eds) *Talking Data: Transcription and Coding in Discourse Research*, pp. 169–206. Hillsdale, NJ: Lawrence Erlbaum.

Lancy, D. (2001) *Studying Children and Schools: Qualitative Research Traditions*. Prospect Heights, IL: Waveland Press.

Lankshear, C. (1997) *Changing Literacies*. Buckingham: Open University Press.

Lankshear, C. (1998) Meanings of 'literacy' in educational reform discourse, *Educational Theory*, 48(3): 351–72.

Lankshear, C. and Knobel, M. (1997a) Different worlds? Technology-mediated classroom learning and students' social practices with new technologies in home and community settings, in C. Lankshear *Changing Literacies*, pp. 164–87. Buckingham: Open University Press.

Lankshear, C. and Knobel, M. (1997b) *Abbotsdale*. www.geocities.com/c.lankshear/abbotsdale. html (accessed 9 September 2003).

Lankshear, C. and Knobel, M. (1997c) *The Moral Consequences of what we Construct Through Qualitative Research*. www.geocities.com/c.lankshear/moral.html (accessed 9 September 2003).

Lankshear, C. and Knobel, M. (2000) *El Estudio Crítico-Social del Lenguaje y la Alfabetización*. Morelia: IMCED.

Lankshear, C. and Knobel, M. (2002) Young children and the National Grid for Learning, *Journal of Early Childhood Literacy*, 2(2): 167–94.

Lankshear, C. and Knobel, M. (2003) *New Literacies: Changing Knowledge and Classroom Learning*. Buckingham: Open University Press.

Lankshear, C. and Snyder, I. (2000) *Teachers and Technoliteracy*. Sydney: Allen & Unwin.

Lankshear, C., Sandiford, P., Montenegro, M.M., Sanchez, G., Coldham, C. and Cassel, J. (1995) Twelve years on: women's literacy in a Nicaraguan municipality, *International Journal of Lifelong Education*, 14(2): 162–71.

Lankshear, C., Bigum, C., Durrant, C., Green, B., Honan, E., Morgan, W., Murray, J., Snyder, I. and Wild, M. (1997) *Digital Rhetorics: Literacies and Technologies in Education – Current Practices and Future Directions*. Canberra: Department of Employment, Education, Training and Youth Affairs.

Lather, P. (1991) *Getting Smart: Feminist Research and Pedagogy With/in the Postmodern*. New York: Routledge.

Lather, P. (1993) Fertile obsession: validity after poststructuralism, *The Sociological Quarterly*, 34(4): 673–93.

Latour, B. (1993) *We Have Never Been Modern*. Cambridge, MA: Harvard University Press.

Lê, T. (1997) *Modules*. Launceston: University of Tasmania, Australia. www.educ.utas.edu.au/ users/tle/Courseware/GENRE/Unit.html # Up (accessed 26 May 2001).

Leander, K. and McKim, K. (2003) Tracing the everyday 'sitings' of adolescents on the internet: a strategic adaptation of ethnography across online and offline spaces, *Education, Communication and Information*, 3(2): 211–40.

LeCompte, M. and Preissle, J. (1993) *Ethnography and Qualitative Design in Educational Research*, 2nd edn. San Diego, CA: Academic Press.

LeCompte, M. and Schensul, J. (1999) *Analyzing and Interpreting Ethnographic Data (Ethnographer's Toolkit*, Vol. 5). Walnut Creek, CA: Altamira Press.

LeCompte, M., Schensul, J., Weeks, M. and Singer, M. (1999) *Researcher Roles and Research Partnerships (Ethnographer's Toolkit*, Vol. 4). Walnut Creek, CA: Altamira Press.

Lemke, J. (1995) *Textual Politics: Discourse and Social Dynamics*. London: Taylor & Francis.

Lemke, J. (1998) Metamedia literacy: transforming meanings and media, in D. Reinking, L. Labbo, M. McKenna and R. Kiefer (eds) *Handbook of Literacy and Technology: Transformations in a Post-Typographic World*, pp. 283–301. Hillsdale, NJ: Erlbaum.

Levine, A. (1996) America's reading crisis: why the whole language approach to teaching reading has failed millions of students, *Parents*, 16: 63–5, 68.

Lieblich, A., Tuval-Mashiach, R. and Zilber, T. (1998) *Narrative Research: Reading, Analysis, and Interpretation*. Thousand Oaks, CA: Sage.

Lincoln, Y. and Guba, E. (1985) *Naturalistic Inquiry*. Beverley Hills, CA: Sage.

Loizos, P. (2000) Video, film and photographs as research documents, in M. Bauer and G. Gaskell (eds) *Qualitative Researching with Text, Image and Sound*, pp. 93–107. London: Sage.

Luke, A. and Freebody, P. (1997) Shaping the social practices of reading, in S. Muspratt, A. Luke and P. Freebody (eds) *Constructing Critical Literacies: Teaching and Learning Textual Practice*, pp. 185–225. Sydney: Allen & Unwin.

Lyon, G.R. (1997) *Report on Learning Disabilities Research: From Testimony of G. Reid Lyon on Children's Literacy*. Washington, DC: Committee on Education and the Workforce, U.S. House of Representatives.

Madison, G. (1988) *The Hermeneutics of Postmodernity: Figures and Themes*. Bloomington, IN: Indiana University Press.

Manganaro, M. (1990) Textual play, power, and cultural critique: an orientation to modernist anthropology, in M. Manganaro (ed.) *Modernist Anthropology: From Fieldwork to Text*, pp. 3–47. Princeton, NJ: Princeton University Press.

Manitoba Education and Training (n.d.) *Let's Get Started: An Initial Assessment Pack for Adult Literacy Programs*. Winnipeg, MAN: Manitoba Education and Training.

Marquart, J.M. (1990) A pattern-matching approach to link program theory and evaluation data, *New Directions for Program Evaluation*, 47: 93–107.

Marshall, C. and Rossman, G. (1999) *Designing Qualitative Research*, 3rd edn. Thousand Oaks, CA: Sage.

Martin, J. (1992) *English Text: System and Structure*. Philadelphia, PA: John Benjamins Publishing Company.

Martin, J., Matthiessen, C. and Painter, C. (1997) *Working with Functional Grammar*. London: Edward Arnold.

Marzano, R. and Kendall, J. (1997) *The Fall and Rise of Standards-Based Education: A National Association of School Boards of Education (NASBE) Issues in Brief*. Aurora, CO: Mid-Continent Research for Education and Learning.

Mason, J. (1996) *Qualitative Researching*. London: Sage.

Maxwell, J. (1996) *Qualitative Research Design: An Interpretative Approach*. Thousand Oaks, CA: Sage.

May, R. and Patillo-McCoy, M. (2000) Do you see what I see? Examining a collaborative ethnography, *Qualitative Inquiry*, 6(1): 65–87.

May, T. (1997) *Social Research: Issues, Methods and Process*, 2nd edn. Buckingham: Open University Press.

Mayol, P. (1998) Part 1: Living, in M. de Certeau, L. Giard and P. Mayol, *The Practice of Everyday Life Vol 2 : Living and Cooking*. Minneapolis, MN: University of Minnesota Press.

Mayring, P. (2000) Qualitative content analysis, *Forum: Qualitative Social Research*, 1(2). www.qualitative-research.net/fqs-texte/2-00/2-00mayring-e.htm (accessed 21 May 2001).

McCulloch, G. (1989) *The Secondary Technical School: A Usable Past?* London: Falmer Press.

McCulloch, G. and Richardson, W. (2000) *Historical Research in Educational Settings*. Buckingham: Open University Press.

McGuinness, D. (1997) *Why Our Children Can't Read and What We Can Do About It: A Scientific Revolution in Reading*. New York: The Free Press.

McKenna, M. and Kear, D. (1990) Measuring attitude toward reading: a new tool for teachers, *The Reading Teacher*, May: 626–37.

McLaren, P. (1986) *Schooling as a Ritual Performance*. London: Routledge.

McLaren, P. (1995) *Critical Pedagogy and Predatory Culture*. New York: Routledge.

McLaren, P. (1997) *Revolutionary Multiculturalism: Pedagogies of Dissent for the New Millennium*. Boulder, CO: Westview Press.

McQuillan, J. (1998) *The Literacy Crisis: False Claims, Real Solutions*. Portsmouth, NH: Heinemann.

McWilliam, E. (1995) *In Broken Images: Feminist Tales for a Different Teacher Education*. New York: Teachers College Press.

Mead, M. (1928) *Coming of Age in Samoa: A Psychological Study of Primitive Youth for Western Culture*. New York: William Morrow.

Merriam, S. (1998) *Qualitative Research and Case Study Applications in Education*. San Francisco, CA: Jossey-Bass.

Mertens, D. (1998) *Research Methods in Education and Psychology: Integrating Diversity with Quantitative and Qualitative Approaches*. Thousand Oaks, CA: Sage.

Michaels, S. (1981) 'Sharing time': children's narrative styles and differential access to literacy, *Language in Society*, 10(3): 423–42.

Michaels, S. (1986) Narrative presentations: an oral preparation for literacy with first graders, in J. Cook-Gumperz (ed.) *The Social Construction of Literacy*, pp. 94–116. Cambridge: Cambridge University Press.

Miles, M. and Huberman, A.M. (1994) *Qualitative Data Analysis: An Expanded Sourcebook*, 2nd edn. Thousand Oaks, CA: Sage.

Millard, E. (1997) *Differently Literate: Boys, Girls and the Schooling of Literacy*. London: Falmer Press.

Minium, E., King, B. and Bear, G. (1993) *Statistical Reasoning in Psychology and Education*. New York: Wiley.

Moje, E. (2000) 'To be part of the story': the literacy practices of gangsta adolescents, *Teachers College Record*, 102(3): 651–90.

Moss, G. (2001) Seeing with the camera: analysing children's photographs of literacy in the home, *Journal of Research in Reading*, 24(3): 279–92.

Murray Research Center (2003) *Data Archive*. www.radcliffe.edu/murray/data (accessed 10 January 2003).

Myhill, D. (2002) *Developing Learning Through Talk*. Exeter: University of Exeter. www.ex.ac.uk/~damyhill/talk/index.htm (accessed 25 January 2003).

National Center for Education Statistics (NCES) (1994) *Data Compendium for the NAEP 1992 Reading Assessment of the Nation and the States*. Washington, DC: US Department of Education.

Norris, N. (1998) Curriculum valuation revisited, *Cambridge Journal of Education*, 28(2): 207–19.

O'Connor, T. (2001) *Qualitative Research Methods.* faculty.ncwc.edu/TOConnor/308/308lect09.htm (accessed 25 May 2001). Currently located at: faculty.ncwc.edu/jchristensen/POL/308/308lect09.htm (accessed 28 January 2004).

Ozga, J. (2000) *Policy Research in Educational Settings: Contested Terrain.* Buckingham: Open University Press.

Pahl, K. (2002) Ephemera, mess and miscellaneous piles: texts and practices in families, *Journal of Early Childhood Literacy*, 2(2): 195–220.

Palmquist, M. (2003) Differences between experimental and quasi-experimental research. Unpublished manuscript. writing.colostate.edu/references/research/experiment/pop3e.cfm (accessed 12 September 2003).

Palmquist, R. (1999) *Introduction to Research in Library and Information Science: Content Analysis.* www.gslis.utexas.edu/~palmquis/courses/content.html (accessed 25 May 2001).

Papert, S. (1993) *The Children's Machine: Rethinking School in the Age of the Computer.* New York: Basic Books.

Patton, M. (2002) *Qualitative Research and Evaluation Methods*, 3rd edn. Thousand Oaks, CA: Sage.

Pikulski, J. (1994) Preventing reading failure: a review of five effective programs, *The Reading Teacher*, 48(1): 30–39.

Plummer, K. (2001) Life stories in ethnographic research, in P. Atkinson, A. Coffey, S. Delamont and L. Lofland (eds) *Handbook of Ethnography*, pp. 395–406. London: Sage.

Popkewitz, T. (1993) *A Political Sociology of Educational Reform: Power/Knowledge in Teaching, Teacher Education, and Research.* New York: Teachers College Press.

Potter, J. (1998) Qualitative and discourse analysis, in A. Bellack and M. Hersen (eds) *Comprehensive Clinical Psychology*, Vol. 3, pp. 117–44. Oxford: Pergamon Press.

Pritchard, D. (ed.) (1994) *American Heritage Dictionary.* New York: Dell Publishing.

Prosser, J. (ed.) (1998) *Image-Based Research: A Sourcebook for Qualitative Researchers.* London: Falmer.

Prosser, J. and Schwartz, D. (1998) Photographs within the sociological research process, in J. Prosser (ed.) *Image-Based Research: A Sourcebook for Qualitative Researchers*, pp. 115–30. London: Falmer.

Psathas, G. and Anderson, T. (1990) The 'practices' of transcription in conversation, *Semiotica*, 78(1/2): 75–99.

Putney, L. (1996) You are it: meaning making as a collective and historical process, *The Australian Journal of Language and Literacy*, 19(2): 129–43.

Rabinow, P. (1977) *Reflections on Fieldwork in Morocco.* Berkeley, CA: University of California Press.

Reese, L. and Gallimore, R. (2000) Immigrant Latinos' cultural model of literacy development: an evolving perspective on home-school discontinuities, *American Journal of Education*, 108(2): 103–34.

Reich, R. (1992) *The Work of Nations.* New York: Vintage Books.

Reid, J., Kamler, B., Simpson, A. and Maclean, R. (1996) 'Do you see what I see?' Reading a different classroom scene, *International Journal of Qualitative Studies in Education*, 9(1): 87–108.

Rosas, R., Nussbaum, M., Cumsille, P., Marianov, V., Correa, M., Flores, P., Grau, V., Lagos, F., López, X., López, V., Rodríguez, P. and Salinas, M. (2003) Beyond Nintendo: design and assessment of educational video games for first and second grade students, *Computers and Education*, 40(1): 71–94.

Rose, D. (2000) Analysis of moving images, in M. Bauer and G. Gaskell (eds) *Qualitative Researching with Text, Image and Sound*, pp. 246–62. London: Sage.

Rose, D. and Sullivan, O. (1996) *Introducing Data Analysis for Social Scientists*, 2nd edn. Buckingham: Open University Press.

Rossman, G. and Rallis, S. (1998) *Learning in the Field: An Introduction to Qualitative Research*. Thousand Oaks, CA: Sage.

Rowan, L., Knobel, M., Bigum, C. and Lankshear, C. (2002) *Boys, Literacies and Schooling: The Dangerous Territories of Gender Based Literacy Reform*. Buckingham: Open University Press.

Ryan, T. (2001) The role of leadership within an action research study of secondary science assessment praxes, *International Electronic Journal for Leadership in Learning*, 5(8).

Salkie, R. (1995) *Text and Discourse Analysis*. London: Routledge.

Sandiford, P., Lankshear, C., Montenegro, M.M., Sanchez, G., Coldham, C. and Cassel, J. (1994) The Nicaraguan literacy crusade: how lasting were its effects? *Development in Practice*, 4(1): 5–17.

Sarroub, L. (2002) In-betweenness: religion and conflicting visions of literacy, *Reading Research Quarterly*, 37(2): 130–49.

Schensul, S., Schensul, J. and LeCompte, M. (1999) *Essential Ethnographic Methods: Observations, Interviews, and Questionnaires (Ethnographer's Toolkit*, Vol. 2). Walnut Creek, CA: Altamira Press.

Schiffrin, D. (1994) *Approaches to Discourse*. Cambridge, MA: Blackwell.

Schiffrin, D. (1996) Narrative as self-portrait: sociolinguistic constructions of identity, *Language in Society*, 25: 167–203.

Schratz, M. and Walker, R. (1995) *Research is Social Change: New Opportunities for Qualitative Research*. London: Routledge.

Schwandt, T. (1997) *Qualitative Inquiry: A Dictionary of Terms*. Thousand Oaks, CA: Sage.

Searle, J. (1969) *Speech Acts: An Essay in the Philosophy of Language*. Cambridge: Cambridge University Press.

Searle, J. (1971) What is a speech act? in J. Searle (ed.) *The Philosophy of Language*, pp. 39–53. Oxford: Oxford University Press.

Seel, N. (1999) Educational semiotics: school learning reconsidered, *Journal of Structural Learning and Intelligent Systems*, 14(1): 11–28.

SEP (Secretariat de Educación Publica) (1994) *Los Descrubrimientos de Cristóbal: Historias sobre una Historia*. México, DF: Secretariat de Educación Publica.

Silverman, D. (1985) *Qualitative Methodology and Sociology: Describing the Social World*. Aldershot: Gower.

Simon, R. and Dippo, D. (1986) On critical ethnographic work, *Anthropology and Education Quarterly*, 17(4): 195–202.

Smith, C. (2001) Click and turn the page: an exploration of multiple storybook literacy, *Reading Research Quarterly*, 36(2): 152–83.

Smith, C. (2002) Click on me: an example of how a toddler used technology in play, *Journal of Early Childhood Literacy*, 2(1): 5–20.

Smith, J.C. (2001) *Research Guide: Human Relations Area File*. www.bu.edu/library/guides/hrafhome.html (accessed 8 January 2003).

Spear-Swerling, L. (n.d.) Straw men and very misleading reading: a review of misreading reading, *Learning Disabilities Online*. www.ldonline.org/ld_store/reviews/swerling_coles.html.

Spradley, J. (1980) *Participant Observation*. Fort Worth, TX: Holt, Rhinehart & Winston.

Spradley, J. (1997) *The Ethnographic Interview*. Belmont, CA: International Thomson Publishing.

Stark, R., Roberts, L. and Corbett, M. (2002) *Contemporary Social Research Methods Using MicroCase*. Florence, KY: Wadsworth.

Steinberg, S. and Kincheloe, J. (eds) (1997) *Kinderculture: The Corporate Construction of Childhood*. Boulder, CO: Westview Press.

Stenhouse, L. (1975) *An Introduction to Curriculum Research and Development*. London: Heinemann.

Stenhouse, L. (1985) The case study tradition and how case studies apply to practice, in J. Rudduck and D. Hopkins (eds) *Research as a Basis for Teaching: Readings from the Work of Lawrence Stenhouse*. London: Heinemann.

Stewart, D. and Kamins, M. (1993) *Secondary Research: Information Sources and Methods* 2nd edn. Thousand Oaks, CA: Sage.

Stewart, J. (1996) The blackboard bungle: California's failed reading experiment, *LA Weekly*, 18(14): 22–9.

Stouthamer-Loeber, M. and van Kammen, W. (1995) *Data Collection and Management: A Practical Guide*. Thousand Oaks, CA: Sage.

Strauss, A. and Corbin, J. (1990) *Basics of Qualitative Research: Grounded Theory Procedures and Techniques*. Newbury Park, CA: Sage.

Street, B. (1984) *Literacy in Theory and Practice*. Cambridge: Cambridge University Press.

Street, B. (2001) *Literacy and Development: Ethnographic Perspectives*. London: Routledge.

Symes, C. (1999) First impressions: the semiotics of school vestibules, in C. Symes and D. Meadmore (eds) *The Extra-Ordinary School*, pp. 15–40. New York: Peter Lang.

Tancock, S. (1997) Catie: A case study of one first grader's reading status, *Reading Research and Instruction*, 36(2): 89–110.

Tannen, D. (1984) *Conversational Style: Analyzing Talk Among Friends*. Norwood, NJ: Ablex.

Tannen, D. (1994) *Gender and Discourse*. Oxford: Oxford University Press.

Tashakkori, A. and Teddlie, C. (1998) *Mixed Methodology: Combining Qualitative and Quantitative Approaches*. Newbury Park, CA: Sage.

Tashakkori, A. and Teddlie, C. (eds) (2002) *Handbook of Mixed Methods in Social and Behavioral Research*. Thousand Oaks, CA: Sage.

Taussig, M. (1987) *Shamanism, Colonialism, and the Wild Man*. Chicago: University of Chicago Press.

Taylor, T. and Cameron, D. (1997) *Analysing Conversation: Rules and Units in the Structure of Talk*. Oxford: Pergamon Press.

Tett, L. (2000) Excluded voices: Class, culture, and family literacy in Scotland, *Journal of Adolescent and Adult Literacy*, 44(2): 122–8.

Thorndike, E.L. (1918) The nature, purposes, and general methods of measurements of educational products, in G.M. Whipple (ed.) *National Society for the Study of Educational Products: Seventeenth Yearbook*, pp. 16–24. Bloomington, IL: Public School Publishing.

Thorne, S. (2003) Artifacts and cultures-of-use in intercultural communication, *Language Learning and Technology*, 7(2): 38–67.

Trochim, W. (1985) Pattern matching, validity, and conceptualization in program evaluation, *Evaluation Review*, 9: 575–604.

Van Leeuwen, T. and Selander, S. (1995) Picturing 'our' heritage in the pedagogic text: layout and illustrations in an Australian and a Swedish history textbook, *Journal of Curriculum Studies*, 27: 501–22.

Vogt, W.P. (1999) *Dictionary of Statistics and Methodology: A Non-Technical Guide for the Social Sciences*, 2nd edn. Newbury Park, CA: Sage.

Volk, D. and de Acosta, M. (2001) 'Many differing ladders, many ways to climb …': literacy events in the bilingual classroom, homes, and community of three Puerto Rican kindergartners, *Journal of Early Childhood Literacy*, 1(2): 193–223.

Wadsworth (2003) *MicroCase Data Archive*. www.microcase.com (accessed 8 January 2003).

Walford, G. (2001) *Doing Qualitative Educational Research: A Personal Guide to the Research Process*. London: Continuum.

Walker, R. and Lewis, R. (1998) Media convergence and social research: the Hathaway Project, in G. Prosser (ed.) *Image-Based Research: A Sourcebook for Qualitative Researchers*, pp. 162–75. London: Falmer.

Wallace, C. (1992) *Reading*. Oxford: Oxford University Press.

Weber, R. (1985) *Basic Content Analysis*. Thousand Oaks, CA: Sage.

Weber, R. (1990) *Basic Content Analysis*. Thousand Oaks, CA: Sage.

Wentling, R.M. and Palma-Rivas, N. (1997) *Current Status and Future Trends of Diversity Initiatives in the Workplace: Diversity Experts' Perspective*. Berkeley, CA: National Center for Research in Vocational Education, University of California.

Westgate, D. and Edwards, A. (1994) *Investigating Classroom Talk*, 2nd edn. London: Routledge.

Wiersma, W. (1999) *Research Methods in Education: An Introduction*, 7th edn. Boston: Allyn & Bacon.

Wignell, P. (1998) A woman's place: a discussion of the place of linguistic analysis in critical literacy in the upper primary school, in M. Knobel and A. Healy (eds) *Critical Literacies in the Primary Classroom*, pp. 41–52. Newtown, NSW: Primary English Teaching Association.

Williams, A. and Gregory, E. (2001) Siblings bridging literacies in multilingual contexts, *Journal of Research in Reading*, 24(3): 248–65.

Willis, P. (1977) *Learning to Labour*. Farnborough, UK: Saxon House.

Wimmer, R. and Dominick, J. (1994) *Mass Media Research: An Introduction*. 4th edn. Belmont, CA: Wadsworth.

Wolcott, H. (2001) *Writing Up Qualitative Research*, 2nd edn. Thousand Oaks, CA: Sage.

Yin, R. (1994) *Case Study Research: Design and Methods*, 2nd edn. Thousand Oaks, CA: Sage.

Name index

Subject index